THE SOUL OF THE EYE

by the same author

Six Great Painters
Painting in Eighteenth-Century Venice
From Giotto to Cézanne
Dürer
The Later Italian Paintings in the Collection of Her Majesty the Queen
Rococo to Revolution
Early Renaissance
Fifty Works of English Literature We Could Do Without (co-author)
Painting at Court
The Life and Death of Mozart
High Renaissance
Art and Architecture in Eighteenth-Century France (co-author)
The Case of Walter Pater
Giambattista Tiepolo

Fiction

Tempting Fate
An Affair on the Appian Way
Men at Work

THE SOUL OF THE EYE

An Anthology of Painters and Painting

Edited by

MICHAEL LEVEY

COLLINS
8 Grafton Street, London W1

William Collins Sons & Co. Ltd
London · Glasgow · Sydney · Auckland
Toronto · Johannesburg

First published 1990

BRITISH LIBRARY CATALOGUING IN PUBLICATION DATA

The soul of the eye: an anthology of painters and painting.
1. Visual arts, history
I. Levey, Michael *1927–*
709

ISBN 0-00-217824-9

Photoset in Linotron Sabon by
Rowland Phototypesetting Ltd
Bury St Edmunds, Suffolk
Printed and bound in Great Britain by
William Collins Sons & Co. Ltd, Glasgow

To

MRS GRACE L. GINNIS

with warm appreciation and gratitude

CONTENTS

INTRODUCTION

I HAVE NEVER FORGOTTEN the first picture I ever consciously saw. I was about five years old when I became aware of it, hanging big and black-framed in the small dining-room of my parents' small house. Without understanding why, I found it fascinating. It made me eager to look at more pictures, and then more and more, until the activity became a large part of a lifetime. And as I grew up I realized that it had probably been, in aesthetic terms, a 'bad' picture – for which I happen to be extremely grateful.

The period was the early 1930s. Ours was a typically modern, modest home where no one claimed much visual taste. Yet we had what we called pictures on the walls – coloured reproductions, framed and glazed – where most of our neighbours had none. Ours would, however, have driven to drink the great critic of the day, Roger Fry. They were not even respectable reproductions of famous old masters (except, oddly, for Van Dyck's 'Balbi Children', of which, even more oddly, I was later to purchase the original for the National Gallery).

I never knew the painters' names, but I knew the titles, and my first picture was entitled 'A Very Gallant Gentleman'. As I sat at meal-times, I gazed at a space of blizzard more dun-coloured than white, which had blotted out everything except the shape of a tent or tents, some piled stores and possibly a sledge. All that was otherwise visible was a solitary muffled figure staggering blindly through the whirling snow. I knew he would die, I am sure, well before I learnt that he was Captain Oates, giving up his life in the hope of helping his comrades on Scott's doomed Antarctic expedition, and described by the words of the picture's title on the cairn set up approximately where he died.

Even today, when I have heard about significant form, and Cézanne, and about Cubism, and some later 'isms', I cannot manage a totally natural smile of derision in front of such pictures as that one I effortlessly recall across the years. I shall always pause before the picture which tells a story, even if I subsequently move on literally and aesthetically. I suspect I am not alone in thus pausing. More important, I think we should be careful never to mock the person, child or adult, whose eye is engaged in this way. The imagination has been stimulated, though it may be a naïve imagination and one that possibly requires a richer visual diet than is provided by two apples on a plate, however marvellously painted. At worst, here is an imagination not entirely torpid.

Looking intently is what matters most – looking, and finding in that activity (and it is an active process) excitement and pleasure which, once discovered, last as long as eyesight. Amid the many artistic snobberies of today, almost the most pernicious is that concerning reproductions, particularly those in colour. This is still the way in which most people are likely to encounter paintings for the first time. If then the image takes priority over brushwork and technique, that is no more harmful than a preliminary, not to say necessary, reading of *Emma* for its story. Much great Western art, from Duccio to Delacroix, is firmly attached to subject-matter; to ignore that is both unhistorical and silly. All of us, too, should encourage our eyes to range widely before we settle, if we do, on what is traditionally or fashionably accepted as 'good' art (the canons of which are, incidentally, far less fixed than is commonly assumed). Voracity is preferable to any tendency towards aesthetic anorexia; true taste can only come after wide experimenting at innumerable visual banquets where may be served up a jumble of things conventionally 'bad' as well as 'good'.

Among the least appreciated freedoms of the imagination in its sampling of all the arts is the freedom to dislike. The greatest critics have inclined to be partisan and violently opinionated. To the scholar may be left the actually impossible task of providing a 'balanced' account of a given art or artist. I hope there will always be room for an unbalanced account, fired by enthusiasm (whether pro or anti) which conveys a commitment to the basic cause of art.

Since the criterion when looking at pictures is essentially one of how much pleasure is given (a respectable scholastic definition already formulated by St Thomas Aquinas), it follows that there is nothing reprehensible in preferring a picture of heather in the Highlands, or of Napoleon's retreat from Moscow, to a late work by Rembrandt. It is certainly better to enjoy a pleasurable sensation when looking at either of the former than to feign one out of respect when looking at the latter. On a genuine sensation, some more sophisticated framework can – probably will – be built, which may culminate in proper appreciation of Rembrandt's late work.

I know that for myself too early exposure to nothing but images of the traditional best in European painting would have sapped my instinctive, indiscriminate visual appetite. A picture-book, pictorial imagination craved high and highly coloured drama to explode in the quiet, cream-toned constriction of our dining-room. There the loudest sound was the snap, crackle and pop of breakfast cereal inundated in milk.

'A Very Gallant Gentleman' was rarely referred to, and probably its presence somewhat disconcerted such visitors as glanced at it. Not its art but, I suspect, its underlying ethic was what had appealed to my father. In a different way, I, too, was stirred by it, regardless of the truth of the incident, but not to any thought of emulation. It did not frighten me or sadden me; nor was I concerned about whether I liked it as a painting. For me it was simply a miraculously direct way of experiencing keen and varied emotions, of a kind not encountered in my daily life – all through the medium of sight.

This anthology celebrates the pleasure of looking at pictures of many different styles and schools within Western European painting, celebrating the role of spectator almost as much perhaps as that of creator. So vast a subject could provide material for hundreds of anthologies without exhausting it. In fact, as far as I am aware, there are comparatively few such anthologies, at least in English, and certainly few where the compiler has ranged with such possibly reckless broadness as I have done.

I have conceived my task very much as making an anthology: the plucking of some flowers for pleasure rather than the assembling of a botanical text-book. It is definitely not a selection of art-historical writing; nor is it meant to provide a representative survey of the reputations, or the opinions, of every great painter (still less every great critic of painting) down the centuries. There are good books in existence which contribute to those more strictly scholarly ends. All the same, I hope I have given space for artists' voices to be heard, often in comment upon another artist. And I have made every effort to tap a vein which is particularly rich in English literature, of reference to painters and painting by poets and novelists. Those 'amateurs', practitioners sometimes of what used to be called the pencil, as well as of the pen, often bring perceptiveness and nearly always enthusiasm to what they say. A paragraph by Rilke, for example, seems to tell us more about Cézanne than tomes by learned professors of art history.

England has produced two superb writers on the visual arts, Ruskin and Pater, who were not poets or novelists but whose writings take on the fervour of poetry under the inspired stress of intense visual imagination. Their approach may be dismissed in some erudite circles, though it should be recognized that their prose is not purposelessly 'fancy' but is powered by a joy in looking which is infectious. Whole anthologies exist of Ruskin's writings, and it has been quite difficult to stop quoting him on every other page. Pater offers no comparable flow of riches, though perhaps even greater subtlety when he does finally fashion a bead of observation. I have included several passages of his, not omitting that on the 'Mona Lisa', which deserves its fame but which also deserves study for its uncannily convincing, pre-Freudian analysis of the creative process.

Once one starts to name names, however, there arise jostling and hubbub. Alberti, Baudelaire, Constable and Goethe have to be heard. Degas could be cited constantly, less for his devastating *mots* than for his sustained defence of the sheer artfulness of art. And then there is the verve and wit of Diderot. Reynolds is extraordinarily acute in unexpected ways and movingly generous in summing up Gainsborough, whose own sparkling letters complement the vitality of his work. Always quotable is Vasari, the Scheherazade of art history. And further sources are provided by patrons, collectors and dealers, and by contracts. Altogether, a vast mass of material exists. Much of it is available in English, but here and there I have taken and translated from other languages.

Heterogeneous as is the material culled for this anthology, and varied as it is meant to be in its emphases and its tone, it has, I hope, a certain unity. It celebrates painting as great and serious, as well as enjoyable, not to be held in lower esteem than literature and music (as it sometimes is): mysteriously and magically palpable in its imagery, and unparalleled among the arts in its immediacy. If somewhere in this book some phrase should prompt the reader to go out and *look*, it will have justified itself.

The principle of its arrangement is strictly alphabetical, regardless of whether an extract concerns a painter or a topic. Not only does it help the reader, I hope, in gauging the book's scope, but also I should like to think it encourages browsing by the variations and sometimes unexpected juxtapositions thus produced. I could, of course, have easily arranged much of the material under individual painters, but the effect would have lacked variety and made for a different sort of anthology. Because some painters' names are lacking among the headings – as, for example, Canaletto and Caravaggio – it should not be assumed that they are necessarily lacking from the book; and indeed the persistent reader will encounter both those painters. To someone anxious to check rapidly which painters are, or are not, included, I recommend the admirable index, expertly compiled by Mr Douglas Matthews, to whom I am warmly grateful.

To my three successive editors I am very greatly indebted. The book was commissioned by Dan Franklin, whose initial enthusiasm fired mine. Ariane Goodman gently and shrewdly guided the project at its early stage. Stuart Proffitt has been understanding, generous and intellectually stimulating to work with. I have benefited from his perceptive comments and his knowledge, and gratefully adopted many of his suggestions. It is a pleasure to acknowledge also my debt to Joy Law for her patient, scrupulous care over bibliographical and copyright matters.

For valued advice, suggestions and loan of books I am warmly grateful to Cecil Gould, Neil MacGregor, Iris Murdoch, David Rodgers and Christopher White. Particular thanks go to Denys Sutton for his steady interest and ever-helpful indications of out-of-the-way material. I should also like to thank the staff of the London Library, and indeed the Library itself for its facilities.

Finally, I must record a very special debt of gratitude to Mrs Grace L. Ginnis, who for so many years has typed so efficiently from my increasingly illegible manuscripts. Her care has extended to each resulting book, and to her I dedicate this one as a small token of deep appreciation.

London, 1989 MICHAEL LEVEY

A NOTE ON SOURCES

A detailed reference for each passage included in the anthology will be found in the Sources and Acknowledgements on page 260.

The author and publishers gratefully acknowledge the co-operation of copyright holders in granting permission to print relevant extracts. They apologise for any oversight, but every effort has been made to trace holders of copyright material.

THE SOUL OF THE EYE

You do not see *with* the lens of the eye. You see *through* that, and by means of that, but you see with the soul of the eye.

John Ruskin, *The Eagle's Nest*

ACADEMIES

The Academy [the Florentine Academy of Design] had been inaugurated in January 1563. Within a month severe discontent arose over the admission and election policy. On March 28, 1563, Borghini reported to the Duke [Cosimo I, de' Medici] that six members had openly revolted, a behaviour which he thought preposterous. Two days later the rebellious six themselves sent a complaint to Cosimo, which brought forth the following rejoinder: 'His Excellency says to carry on with the work and not with words, and not to pay heed to so much babble and humbug, because that is the way not of getting things done, but merely of spreading scandal.'

The animosity among the Academy members sprang not only from personal dislikes and jealousies but also from the controversy which had divided Italian artists ever since the question had first arisen concerning the pre-eminence of painting over sculpture or vice versa.

R. AND M. WITTKOWER, *The Divine Michelangelo: The Florentine Academy's Homage on his Death in 1564*, 1964

... The Period is now arrived when the Royal Academy has completed the 25th year from its foundation. On this occasion, impressed by motives of duty and gratitude, the members of this body presume humbly to acknowledge to their gracious Founder and Patron, the benefits derived from the institution: where rising merit has received encouragement, the Public taste been improved; and the distinction conferred on the constituent Members of this Academy has advanced the dignity of the Polite Arts, throughout your majesty's dominions.

While reviewing these important advantages resulting from your Majesty's institution, it is our most ardent desire to perpetuate this Epocha by an indellible [*sic*] record.

Thus shall we express to posterity our sentiments and veneration for a Monarch, in whose reign and under whose patronage, the Arts have flourished beyond all former example in Britain.

JOSEPH FARINGTON, *Approved address for the Royal Academy's submission to George III, December 1793 (Farington Diary, Volume I)*

'As a function,' resumed Reginald, 'the Academy is a failure.'

'You think it would be tolerable without the pictures?'

'The pictures are all right, in their way; after all, one can always *look* at them if one is bored with one's surroundings, or wants to avoid an imminent acquaintance.'

'Even that doesn't always save one. There is the inevitable female whom you met once in Devonshire, or the Matoppo Hills, or somewhere, who charges up to you with the remark that it's funny how one always meets people one knows at the Academy. Personally, I *don't* think it's funny.'

SAKI, 'Reginald on the Academy' (*Reginald*, 1904)

AGE

He is very old, but is still the best painter of them all.

ALBRECHT DÜRER, *Letter from Venice, 7 February 1506, referring to Giovanni Bellini*

Dürer was writing home to his friend Willibald Pirkheimer in Nuremburg, having already mentioned his amicable relations with Bellini. Bellini's birth-date is not established but he may well have been in his mid-seventies at the time.

Our master went with the rest of us to one of the suburbs [of Amboise] to see Messer Leonardo Vinci of Florence, an old man of more than seventy, the most outstanding painter of our day. He showed the Cardinal [Luigi of Aragon] three pictures, one of a certain Florentine woman portrayed from life at the request of the late Magnificent Giuliano de' Medici, another of the young St John the Baptist as a young man and one of the Madonna and Child set in the lap of St Anne. All three works are quite perfect, though nothing good can now be expected from his brush as he suffers from paralysis in the right hand.

ANTONIO DE BEATIS, *The Travel Journal of Antonio de Beatis, 10 October 1517*

De Beatis was the Cardinal's chaplain and kept a journal of his tour, chiefly of Northern Europe, in 1517–18. Leonardo da Vinci was sixty-four years old at the time of the visit; he had settled in France in 1516. The portrait referred to may conceivably be the 'Mona Lisa', now in the Louvre, where are the other two pictures shown to the Cardinal. Leonardo was in fact left-handed.

Portrait of Signora Sophonisba [Anguissola], done from the life in Palermo in the year 1624, on 12 July, her age being 96 years, still having her memory with her brain most alert, very courteous and although through great age she has lost her sight, she would all the same delight in putting pictures in front of her, and then by putting her nose to the picture, she was able to make out a little of it, and she took great pleasure in doing this. As I was making her portrait, she gave me many hints, such as not to take the light from too high, in case the shadows in the wrinkles of old age become too strong, and much other good advice, while she told me the events of her life from which I came to know that she was a painter from nature and very skilled and that the greatest misfortune she had was that because of her failed eyesight she was no longer able to paint, although her hand was firm without a tremor.

SIR ANTHONY VAN DYCK, *Notation on his drawing of Sophonisba Anguissola in his sketchbook*

It is a pity he was persuaded to display this depressing production at an age when there is little hope of making amends . . .

EUGÈNE DELACROIX, *Letter referring to Ingres' 'Jesus among the Doctors', 1862*

ALBRECHT ALTDORFER

'No,' said Picasso, 'I've been copying Altdorfer. It's really fine work! There's everything there – a little leaf on the ground, one cracked brick different from the others. There's a picture with a sort of little closed balcony – the closet, I call it. All the details are integrated. It's beautiful. We lost all that, later on. We've come all the way to Matisse – colour. It may be progress but it's something different.'

PABLO PICASSO, 1955

AMATEURS

now damn Gentlemen, there is not such a set of Enemies, to a real artist in the world as they are, if not kept at a proper distance. *They* think . . . that they reward your merit by their Company & notice; but I, who blow away all the chaff & by G— in their Eyes too if they dont stand clear, know that they have but one part worth looking at, and that is their Purse.

THOMAS GAINSBOROUGH, *Letter to William Jackson, 2 September 1767*

AMBITION

[Léon] Bonnat brought Degas to the Salon to look at a painting by one of his pupils, *Hunter bending his bow*. 'How well he aims, doesn't he, Degas?' 'Yes, he aims at a medal.'

AMBROISE VOLLARD, *Souvenirs d'un marchand de tableaux*, 1937

AMERICAN SCENERY

The painter of American scenery has, indeed, privileges superior to any other. All nature here is new to art. No Tivolis, Ternis, Mount Blancs . . . hackneyed and worn by daily pencils of hundreds . . .

THOMAS COLE

Cole (1801–48) arrived in America in 1818 from England. He became a leading figure in the painting of American landscape and was to say after a final visit to Europe that neither the Alps nor the Appennines dimmed in his eyes 'the beauty of our own Catskills'.

ANAMORPHOSIS

Like perspectives, which rightly gaz'd upon
Show nothing but confusion, – ey'd awry
Distinguish form.

WILLIAM SHAKESPEARE, *Richard II*, Act I, Scene 2.

At the right Honorable the Lord Gerards at Gerards Bromley, there are pictures of Henry the Great of France and his queen, both upon the same indented board, which if beheld *directly*, you only perceive a confused piece of work; but if *obliquely*, of one side you see the king's and on the other the queen's picture, which I am told (and not unlikely) were made thus.

DR ROBERT PLOT, *The Natural History of Staffordshire*, 1686

FRA ANGELICO

Her [Mary Shelley's] remarks on art, once she lets go of Rio's skirts are amazing – Fra Angelico, for instance, only painted Martyrs, Virgins, &c., she had no eyes for the divine *bon-bourgeoisie* of his pictures; the dear common folk of his crowds, those who sit and listen (spectacle at nose and bent into a comfortable heap to hear better) at the sermon of the Saint – and the children, and women, – divinely pure they all are, but fresh from the streets and market place – but she is wrong, every where . . .

ROBERT BROWNING, *Letter to Elizabeth Barrett*
11 September 1845

Shelley's widow had published her 'Rambles in Germany and Italy . . .' in 1844. Alexis-François Rio was the author of a highly influential book urging the religious qualities to be found in the 'early' masters: 'De la poésie chrétienne . . .', 1836.

Now the peculiarity and merit (as it appears to me) of Fra Angelico is, that his virgins are neither vague nor individual – even while doing nothing, they breathe of heaven in their repose – they are visible incarnations of the beauty of holiness, and yet not mere abstractions – they are most emphatically feminine – the ideal of womanhood as the chosen temple of the Trinity; they are to the Madonnas of other painters what Eve may be supposed to have been to her daughters before the Fall – their lineaments seem to include all other likenesses, to assume to each several votary the semblances he loves most to gaze upon. It was because Fra Angelico's whole life was love, diverted by his vow of celibacy from any specific object, that his imagination thus sought for and found inspiration in heaven. Next to the Madonna, I may mention the heads of Our Saviour, of the Apostles and Saints in Fra Angelico's pictures, as excelling in expression and beauty, as well as those of the elect in his representations of the Last Judgment; his delineations of the worldly, the wicked, the reprobate, are uniformly feeble and inadequate; his success or failure is always proportioned to his moral sympathy or distaste.

LORD LINDSAY, *Sketches of the History of Christian Art*, 1847

A man long trained to love the monk's visions of Fra Angelico, turns in proud and ineffable disgust from the first work of Rubens which he encounters on his return across the Alps. But is he right in his indignation? He has forgotten, that while Angelico prayed and wept in his olive shade, there was different work doing in the dank fields of Flanders.

JOHN RUSKIN, *The Stones of Venice*, Volume I, 1851

ART GALLERIES

Marvell's enchanting poem 'The Gallery' invites 'Clora' to view his soul as he has composed it 'into one Gallery', with several vividly-described pictures of her. The references in the last line of the verse quoted below are to Charles I's collection (sold by the Commonwealth), which included the pictures he had purchased from the Gonzaga collection at Mantua.

These Pictures and a thousand more,
Of Thee, my Gallery does store;
In all the Forms thou can'st invent,
Either to please me, or torment:
For thou alone to people me,
Art grown a num'rous Colony;
And a Collection choicer far
Then [*sic*] or *White-hall*'s, or *Mantua*'s were.

ANDREW MARVELL, 'The Gallery' (*Miscellaneous Poems*, 1681)

I conceive that our National Gallery should be a subject of self-congratulation to every Englishman who sees it; that every Englishman should say, in the pride of his heart, that in collecting it in so short a time his country has done what no other country could achieve.

ANTHONY TROLLOPE, 1861

The National Gallery had been founded in 1824. Trollope's touching pride in the achievement of it was largely justified, and if any single person deserves the credit it is the first Director, Sir Charles Eastlake, who was to die in office in 1865.

There is generally a disposition to be prodigal of ornaments and gilding in such buildings [picture galleries]. Without pretending that all decoration should be proscribed, yet I believe that there is less disadvantage in erring by deficiency than by excess; in fact, the pictures, etc., are the most precious objects, and it is to them that we must attract attention. Let me add, that one of the most injurious things to the effect of pictures is their accumulation – their being crammed all together; the position they then occupy, so different from that for which the painters destined them, diminishes the illusion which each would produce if it were in its proper place. Few, except the intelligent connoisseur and amateur, on seeing a picture exhibited in a gallery, experience all the effect which the artist wished to produce.

M. E. CHEVREUL, *The Laws of Contrast of Colour*

Some piquancy resides in reading today, when the British fashion in art gallery decoration and hanging tends to have reverted to Victorian standards, the views of Chevreul, a distinguished French chemist; his 'De la loi du contraste simultané des couleurs' was first published in 1839.

The Imperial Hermitage alone repays a journey to St Petersburg; and for a whole fortnight I visited almost every day the picture and sculpture galleries of this vast and rich museum, and in the end I left with the feeling I had done but inadequate justice to these valuable and exhaustless collections. I am tolerably well acquainted with the great museums in the south and west of Europe, and I was interested to find that the Hermitage does not suffer by comparison with the Vatican, the Museum of Naples, the Galleries of Florence, the Louvre in Paris, and the great Picture Gallery in Madrid. In some departments, indeed, St Petersburg has the advantage over other capitals . . . the Dutch pictures are not to be equalled save in Holland or in Dresden; the Spanish School has no competitor save in Madrid and Seville; the portraits by Vandyck, and the sketches by Rubens, are only surpassed in England and Bavaria.

J. BEAVINGTON ATKINSON, *An Art Tour to Northern Capitals of Europe*, 1873

The pictures at Hampton Court are not cared for as they should be. Dozens are misnamed – the good and the bad are muddled together many in dark rooms where one cannot see them properly and the best would be so much better seen, enjoyed, known and cared for if they were in the National Gallery (as your property) where I know they would ever remain!

. . . The Hampton Court Gallery wants fresh varnish and fresh frames for some pictures, then a great weeding out of the very valuable and beautiful pictures from the trash and the right names and dates put on the pictures because there are some awful blunders in the names and it only misleads the public, besides being a disgrace in our day where learning and science have done so much for gaining an accurate knowledge of art and artists of bygone days.

THE CROWN PRINCESS FREDERICK OF GERMANY, *Letter to Queen Victoria, 8 December 1879*

The project of founding a Gallery of Modern Art in Dublin is no longer an idea, it is now an accomplished fact. Till today Ireland was the only country in Europe that had no Gallery of Modern Art. There is not even a single accessible private collection of Modern Pictures in this country. That reproach is now removed.

The National Gallery of Ireland has a fine collection of works by the old masters, yet Sir Walter Armstrong himself says: – 'I would place the importance of a modern Gallery even before that of a National Gallery.' To those actively engaged in Art this must be so, as it is his contemporaries that teach the student most, their successes that inspire him, for their problems are akin.

SIR HUGH LANE, *Prefatory notice to the Illustrated Catalogue of the Municipal Gallery of Modern Art, Dublin*, 1908

By dint of taking one room in the Uffizzi [*sic*] and resolving to look at every picture in it without exception, I saw things I should never have seen otherwise. Including an Adam and Eve of Cranach, not specially remarked in Baedeker, and skied. In another room I discovered for myself the exceeding beauty of the small Dutch pictures.

ARNOLD BENNETT, *Journals* (Florence), 1910

You that would judge me, do not judge alone
This book or that, come to this hallowed place
Where my friends' portraits hang and look thereon;
Ireland's history in their lineaments trace;
Think where man's glory most begins and ends,
And say my glory was I had such friends.

W. B. YEATS, 'The Municipal Gallery Revisited' (*Last Poems*, 1936–1939)

FRANCIS BACON

I do feel the need to paint. I paint for the excitement which comes when the image comes across but I also hope luck will work with me in paint. I have always painted to excite myself. For me images are ways of unlocking the valves of sensation. It is when you stop fumbling around and the image crystallises or when you realize you can take it much further.

FRANCIS BACON, interview in the *Sunday Times*, 25 September 1988

BAD PICTURES

The painter generally loves pictures *qua* pictures . . . Charles Keene, sitting over one of the last little fires that warmed him in the Hammersmith Road, confided to me, with one of his immortal and comprehensive winks, 'Ye know, I *like* bad pictures. But don't tell Jimmy.' And if we like bad pictures, sometimes, we know the faults of the great pictures quite well, intimately. But we love them none the less for that, rather the more, as a man might his mistress for her freckles. But if *we* may say she is freckled, *you* mustn't, or we shall call you out.

WALTER SICKERT in *The New Age*, 1910

'Jimmy' is, of course, Whistler, a great admirer of Keene (1823–91).

FRA BARTOLOMMEO

I was especially struck with the genius of the monk Fra Bartolommeo, who was a man of the most devout, tender, and earnest spirit. There is a small picture of his here [in the Uffizi], which I discovered for myself. It is about the size of this sheet of paper, in two divisions, and represents the 'Adoration' and the 'Presentation in the Temple'. The figures are about two-thirds of a finger-length in size, but finished in the most exquisite and consummate manner, with the most brilliant colouring, the brightest decorations, and in the most genial sunshine. You can see in the picture itself, that the pious master has taken delight in painting it, and in finishing the most minute details; probably with the view of giving it away, to gratify some friend. It seems as if the painter belonged to it, and still ought to be sitting before his work, or had only this moment left it.

FELIX MENDELSSOHN (BARTHOLDY), *Letter from Florence, 25 June 1831*

BEHAVIOUR

The Lives of Painters say that Rafael Died of Dissipation. Idleness is one Thing & Dissipation Another. He who has Nothing to Dissipate Cannot Dissipate; the Weak Man may be Virtuous Enough, but will Never be an Artist.

Painters are noted for being Dissipated & Wild.

WILLIAM BLAKE, annotation to Reynolds' *Discourses.*

Ingres will live and die the servant of ladies, said he smiling.

J. A. D. INGRES, *as he helped his female guests on with their furs, 8 January 1867.*

The night was cold, and the guests were worried about the aged painter's exposure to it. He caught a chill and died on 14 January.

Poor Rossetti! a Prince among his fellows. Well do I remember with strong affection the barbaric court in which he reigned with the joyous simple ingenuous superiority as he throned it in Chelsea. The fascinating ease of the Italian, the sweet southern sunniness of temperament that ignored the vulgar haste and interested elbowing of his surroundings. What a sad comedy it all was seen now by the light of the sequel! His life, a rare example of trusting peacefulness, to the more turbulent ones, avoiding all noise and discussion of the exhibition, all vexation of . . . [*original break*]

JAMES WHISTLER, notes for possible memoirs

My dear fellow, you behave as if you had no talent.

EDGAR DEGAS to Whistler

GIOVANNI BELLINI

The most important conception in Byzantine painting depends on the worship of ikons, on the holiness of the panel . . . all artists up to Giovanni Bellini maintained the holiness of the panel . . .

Among the many pictures by Giovanni Bellini and his predecessors there are no historical subjects, and even the narratives depend on the earlier representations: there is always a saint preaching and a number of the faithful listening.

J. W. von Goethe, *Early Paintings and Recent Restorations in Venice*, 1790

The Baptism of Christ in the Church of San Lorenzo, Vicenza, by Giov. Bellini is the only Christian head of the Saviour that I have ever seen.

George Meredith, *Letter to Tom Taylor, 10 September 1866*

Samuel Butler's passion for Bellini was manifested in several ways but seldom more amusingly than when he got into conversation with two English barristers, met in a Belgian hotel, about art matters and they played Raphael 'as a safe card.'

I admitted the beauty of line in the Virgin's drapery [in Raphael's 'Sistine Madonna'] and also that the work was an effective piece of decoration, but I said it was not inspired by devotional or serious feeling of any kind and for impressiveness could not hold its own with even a very average Madonna by Giovanni Bellini.

Samuel Butler, *Notebooks*, 1887

But his rendering of emotion is not that of a dramatist, capable of realising imaginatively the whole range of human passion; nor has the event any interest for him. His pictures each render a single emotional state; and that in his earlier works is almost always some phase of the emotions of pity and love. In all his versions of the Madonna and Child the exact shade and variety of the feelings are perfectly explicit, and almost always distinct; and the richness of his invention is shown by the perfect harmony of the particular feeling expressed by the mother with the pose and expression of the Child.

In his early works, then, pathos is the dominant emotion; and even in his later ones, for all their genial serenity, there is an undercurrent of the same feeling. But the pathos which his figures express is never sickly or sentimental; rather it is, as Bellini feels it, the inevitable result of their condition as human beings; and if a single phrase might stand for what Bellini has expressed more intimately than any other artist, it must be Virgil's –

'Sunt lachrymae rerum et mentem mortalia tangunt.'

Roger Fry, *Giovanni Bellini*, 1899

BLINDNESS

Those are indeed unfortunate who, after most arduous studies to the end that they may assist others and leave a reputation behind them, are not allowed, either through sickness or death, to complete the works which they have begun. And it very often happens in cases where they have almost brought their works to completion, that they suffer from the presumption of those who endeavour to cover their own ass's hide with the honoured skin of a lion. And although Time, which is called the father of Truth, sooner or later brings the truth to light, yet they are for some time defrauded of the honour due to their labours. This was the case with Piero della Francesca of the Borgo a San Sepolcro. A consummate arithmetician, geometrician and perspectivist, the blindness which came upon him in his old age and the termination of his life, prevented him from displaying the results of his labours and the numerous books written by him, which are still preserved in his native Borgo.

GIORGIO VASARI, *'Life' of Piero della Francesca*, 1568

Oh, my dear girl, how awful it is not to be able to see clearly any more! I have had to give up drawing and painting and for years now content myself with sculpture . . . But if my eyesight continues to dim I won't even be able to model any more. What shall I do with my day then? I shall die of boredom and disgust.

EDGAR DEGAS, from Alice Michel, 'Degas et son Modèle', 1919

. . . Oh my dearest Louie, how I should like to see your Courbet with you, but my dear my sight doesn't permit me to see pictures. The sight of the left eye on which all depends is returning very slowly it is 5 months today since the operation. I see no signs of having sight enough to see in the summer.

MARY CASSATT, *Letter to Louisine Havemeyer, 22 March 1920*

BONINGTON

His name was Richard Parkes Bonington. We all loved him. I used to say to him sometimes, 'You are king in your own realm and Raphael could not have done what you do. Don't worry about other people's qualities or the proportions of their pictures, since your own are masterpieces.'

EUGÈNE DELACROIX, *Letter to Théophile Thoré*, 1861.

Thoré was writing a book on painters of all schools and asked Delacroix for details about Bonington, whom he had known well from about 1816 or 1817. Replying at length, Delacroix included this poignant recollection; Bonington had died in 1828, aged twenty-seven.

BOTTICELLI

Sandro di Botticello, most excellent painter in panel and on wall: his things have a virile air and are very well judged and fully proportioned.

An agent in Florence to Ludovico il Moro, Duke of Milan, c. 1485

I Alessandro painted this picture at the end of the year 1500[?] in the troubles of Italy in the half time after the time according to the 6th chapter of S. John in the second woe of the Apocalypse in the loosing of the devil for three and a half years then he will be chained in the 12th chapter and we shall see clearly [?] . . . as in this picture.

BOTTICELLI, *Inscription in Greek on the 'Mystic Nativity' (National Gallery, London)*

But this master so often disfigures his pictures by bad drawing and worse painting, and by such a revelling in ugliness – notably seen in his 'Venuses' in our collection [National Gallery] – as to make it a matter of wonder to me how admirers can be found for them.

W. P. FRITH, *My Autobiography and Reminiscences*, 1887

Even M. Angelo shirks sometimes, but Botticelli never; he thinks well about it before he begins, and does what's beautiful always.

SIR EDWARD BURNE-JONES, Bt., 29 October 1895

From the conversations of Burne-Jones, recorded by his studio assistant, Thomas Rooke.

BRAQUE

Here is Georges Braque. He leads an admirable life. He strains passionately toward beauty and he attains it, one could almost say, effortlessly.

His compositions have the harmony and the plenitude we were waiting for. His decorations bear witness to a taste and a culture guaranteed by his instinct.

Seeking within himself for the elements of the synthetic motifs that he depicts, he has become a creator.

He no longer owes anything to his surroundings. His mind has purposely induced the twilight of reality, and suddenly a universal rebirth is taking place plastically within him and outside him.

He expresses a beauty full of tenderness, and the mother-of-pearl of his paintings gives iridescence to our understanding.

A richly coloured lyricism of which we have too few examples fills him with harmonious enthusiasm, and St Cecilia herself plays on his musical instruments.

In his valleys, the bees of all youthfulness buzz and gather their honey, and the happiness of innocence languishes on his civilised terraces.

He is an angelic painter. Purer than other men, he does not pay heed to anything foreign to his art that would make him fall from the paradise he inhabits.

Let no one come here looking for the mysticism of the pious, the psychology of *littérateurs*, or the conclusive logic of scholars! This painter composes his paintings according to his absolute concern for complete originality, complete truth. And if he relies on human means, human methods, it is in order to ensure the reality of his lyricism. His canvases have the unity that gives them their necessity.

For the painter, the poet, and artists in general, each work becomes a new universe with its own laws. (This is what differentiates artists from other men, and especially from scientists.)

Georges Braque knows no rest, and every one of his paintings commemorates an effort that no one before him has yet attempted.

GUILLAUME APOLLINAIRE, *Preface to the Catalogue de l'Exposition Braque*, 1908

PIETER BREUGHEL THE ELDER

'I am afraid the sunset will be a failure,' she remarked presently regarding anxiously the sky. And as she spoke a bird skimmed past her with a satin quilt.

O Charity! She watched it, spellbound, soar above the trees. In some cosy cottage garden *his* gift would fall like a bolt from the blue. Only the Flemish primitives could do justice to the surprise.

How the elder Brueghel would have delighted in the scene . . . The fence, the rows of stiff hollyhocks, the invalid at her casement, the children rolling in the dust, the father busy digging, the immodest courtship in the back-yard, and the sudden appearance of the struggling bird over the low thatched roof.

What an admirable Primitive it would have made!

RONALD FIRBANK, *The Artificial Princess*, 1934

Snow scenes lent themselves particularly well to Breughel's style of painting. For a snowy background has the effect of making all dark or coloured objects seen against it appear in the form of very distinct, sharp-edged silhouettes. Breughel does in all his compositions what the snow does in nature. All the objects in his pictures (which are composed in a manner that reminds one very much of the Japanese) are paper-thin silhouettes arranged, plane after plane, like the theatrical scenery in the depth of the stage. Consequently in the painting of snow scenes, where nature starts by imitating his habitual method, he achieves an almost disquieting degree of fundamental realism. Those hunters stepping down over the brow of the hill towards the snowy valley with its frozen ponds are Jack Frost himself and his crew. The crowds who move about the white streets of Bethlehem have their being in an absolute winter, and those ferocious troopers looting and innocent-hunting in the midst of a Christmas card landscape are a part of the very army of winter, and the innocents they kill are the young green shoots of the earth.

ALDOUS HUXLEY, *Along The Road*, 1925

CARPACCIO

Memories of Carpaccio, the magnificent, the delightful – it's not for want of such visitations, but only for want of space, that I haven't said of him what I would . . . He and the Tintoret are the two great realists, and it is hard to say which is the more human, the more various. The Tintoret had the mightier temperament, but Carpaccio, who had the advantage of more newness and more responsibility, sailed nearer to perfection. Here and there he quite touches it, as in the enchanting picture, at the Academy, of St Ursula asleep in her little white bed, in her high clean room, where the angel visits her at dawn; or in the noble St Jerome in his study at S. Giorgio Schiavoni. This latter work is a pearl of sentiment, and I may add without being fantastic a ruby of colour. It unites the most masterly finish with a kind of universal largeness of feeling, and he who has it well in his memory will never hear the name of Carpaccio without a throb of almost personal affection.

HENRY JAMES, *Italian Hours*, 1909

CÉZANNE

Today I went to see his [Cézanne's] pictures again; it's remarkable what an environment they create. Without looking at a particular one, standing in the middle between the two rooms, one feels their presence drawing together into a colossal reality. As if these colours could heal one of indecision once and for all. The good conscience of these reds, these blues, their simple truthfulness, it educates you; and if you stand beneath them as acceptingly as possible, it's as if they were doing something for you. You also notice, a little more clearly each time, how necessary it was to go beyond love, too; it's natural, after all, to love each of these things as one makes it: but if one shows this, one makes it less well; one *judges* it instead of *showing* it. One ceases to be impartial; and the very best – love – stays outside the work, does not enter it, is left aside, untranslated: that's how the painting of sentiments came about (which is in no way better than the paintings of things). They'd paint: I love this here; instead of painting: here it is. In which case everyone must see for himself whether or not I loved it. This is not shown at all, and some would even insist that love has nothing to do with it. It's that thoroughly exhausted in the action of making, there is no residue. It may be that this emptying out of love in anonymous work, which produces such pure things, was never achieved as completely as in the work of this old man; his inner nature, having grown mistrustful and cross, helped him to do it.

RAINER MARIA RILKE, *Letter from Paris to his wife, 13 October 1907*

The often quoted saying of Cézanne's that he wished to make of Impressionism something durable like the art of the Museums, has been quoted too often. I know he wanted to. But he only wanted to, and tried to, while countless others before and after him not only wanted to do so, but did it, and will do it when Cézanne is only remembered as a curious and pathetic by-product of the Impressionist group, and when Cubism has gone as lightly as it has come.

WALTER SICKERT, 'Mesopotamia–Cézanne' in the *New Age*, 5 March 1914

I have a kind of block against Cézanne, because when I was a student he was the great god of the people who taught me. I've never been interested in the kind of experimentation he was conducting. I used to do it as a joke: that thing in a still-life where the tension is so great that when he painted the table behind the apple re-appearing on the other side it was at a different level. I often used to do that as a joke about Cézanne. But to me that kind of passion is rather phoney, it's a kind of bullying. I think these [Cézanne's early work] are bullying pictures.

PETER BLAKE, interview in *The Independent*, 12 July 1988

CIMA DA CONEGLIANO

'Cima's Madonnas are dull, dull, dull,' Mrs Shamefoot was saying, looking over the Monsignor's shoulder at her own reflection in the glass.

RONALD FIRBANK, *Vainglory*, 1915

CLAUDE

My Dear Sir,
I have the pleasure to inform you that the Claude [view of Delphi] has been sold to Earl Wemyss for the very handsome price of 1500 Guineas in ready Rhino. The old fellow to whom Stewart had wrote some time ago, ordered the Claude and [Van Dyck] Venus down upon condition of paying 2000

Guineas for the two if they pleased him – he was amazingly taken with the Claude and asked the lowest price, which was stated as above, and he the day following concluded the bargain . . . My own opinion is that the Claude is monstrous well sold . . . and if you can get a companion to it in his fine sparkling manner I think it would make a very desireable [*sic*] purchase and suit the Old Boy. Indeed fine Claudes of any size are always desireable purchases, and on this subject I may observe that those which are most admired at present in England are the fine pictures of his middle manner which are high finished, painted with a full pencil, and sparkling. You have seen the Evening of the [Roman] Empire in Lord Radnor's Collection, that is reckoned his finest manner. The Boulogne [*recte* Bouillon] Claudes purchased by Angerstein last year at so enormous a price are likewise in the same manner, the finest in an afternoon. The sun coming sparkling over the Sea, and the waves highly finished with yellow white and green tints – Landscape – Buildings etc. etc. I describe the style particularly as that most in vogue, at the same time such pictures fall to the lot of few, but when they can be had, large, or small, they are treasures.

WILLIAM BUCHANAN, *Letter from Edinburgh to James Irvine, 20 March 1804*

William Buchanan (1777–1864) was a shrewd Scottish art dealer and speculator, whose 'Memoirs' (1824) are a fascinating mine of information about dealing and collecting. James Irvine (1759?–1831) was a Scottish artist who often acted as his agent in Italy.

I do not wonder at you being jealous of Claude. If anything could come between our love it is him.

JOHN CONSTABLE, *Letter to his wife, 1823*

When I came in this midday, Goethe sat already at table with Court Councillor Meyer, in talk about Italy and objects of art, Goethe had put out a portfolio of Claude Lorrain, in which Meyer selected and pointed out to us that landscape, of which the newspapers announced that [Sir Robert] Peel appropriated to himself the original for £4,000. We must confess that it is a beautiful piece and that Peel has not made a bad purchase.

J. P. ECKERMANN, *Conversations with Goethe*, (14 April 1829)

Claude is the most ardent worshipper that ever was of the *genius loci*. Of his landscapes one always feels that 'some god is in this place'. Never, it is true, one of the greater gods: no mysterious and fearful Pan, no soul-stirring Bacchus, or all-embracing Demeter; scarcely, though he tried more than once deliberately to invoke them, Apollo and the Muses, but some mild local deity, the inhabitant of a rustic shrine whose presence only heightens the glamour of the scene.

ROGER FRY in the *Burlington Magazine*, 1907

COLLECTORS

In the House of Messer Michel Contarini at the Misericordia (Venice)
August 1543

. . . There is a little picture about one foot large, representing Our Lady nursing the Child, in half length, painted in colours, by Leonardo da Vinci, a very powerful and highly finished work.

There is a small portrait of Messer Alvise Contarini of M . . . , who died some years ago, and in the same picture there is the portrait of a nun of San Secondo. On the cover of these portraits is represented a landscape, and the leather case of the whole picture is adorned with gold foliage. It is a perfect work by Giacometto.

There is a small coloured replica of the life of St Christopher, which Mantegna painted in Padua at the Eremitani, by Mantegna himself, a fine little work.

. . . The above mentioned Messer Michel has many little pictures on vellum and panel which he did himself from Mantegna, Raphael, and other masters' cartoons, cleverly colouring them in Giacometto's manner.

THE ANONIMO (MARCANTONIO MICHIEL)

. . . I remember that at that time I had conceived a passion for sacred pictures of really good workmanship. And having gone one day to Milan and being a guest in the house of St Charles [Borromeo], I had a great wish to become possessor of a painting representing the Nativity of Our Lord, and when someone present with perhaps excessive boldness interposed on my behalf, I asked for the gift of it. Then the Saint told me in the most kindly way, that it was indeed a noble piece of painting and it was not a little that I demanded; but, having with his words, as it were, raised the price of the picture and after keeping me for some time in suspense, he then of his own accord made me a present of it. I later placed this same picture in our house and it was indeed a souvenir to be jealously guarded in memory of its donor, St Charles. . . .

FEDERICO BORROMEO, *Commentarius*, 1627

This picture is by Barocci and is in the Ambrosiana, Milan.

. . . A few days later I was walking in the new rooms of his [Cardinal Mazarin's] palace and was in the small gallery tapestried in wool with the story of Scipio designed by Giulio Romano, the Cardinal's finest tapestry, which had belonged to the Marshal de Saint-André, when I heard him approaching, from the sound of his slippers as he dragged them along like someone very feeble, recovering from a severe illness. I hid under the tapestry and heard him say, 'All this must be left behind!' He paused at each step, for he was very weak, and turned from side to side, and casting his eyes on whatever object attracted his attention, he said from the depth of his heart: 'All this must be left behind!', and turning round, he ended by saying 'And all that too! What trouble I have taken to acquire these things! Can I abandon them without regret? I shall never see them again where I am going.' I heard these words very clearly. They touched me perhaps more than they touched him . . . . I was unable to suppress a heavy sigh, and he heard me. 'Who is there?' he said. 'Who is there?' – 'It is I, Monseigneur, who was waiting for the moment to speak to your Eminence about a very important letter from M. de Bordeaux which I have just received.' – 'Come near, come near,' he said to me in a plaintive tone. He was naked under his camlet robe lined with miniver, and had on his nightcap. He said to me, 'Give me your hand; I am very weak, I can't do anything.' – 'Your Eminence had best sit down.' And I meant to fetch him a chair. 'No,' he said, 'no. I am glad to walk and I have something to attend to in my library.' I offered him my arm, and he leant on it. He did not want me to talk to him about business matters. 'I am not', he said, 'in a state to listen to them. Speak about them to the King and do what he tells you. I have other matters now in my head.' And reverting to his thought: 'Look, my friend, at this beautiful picture by Correggio, and then at that Venus of Titian's, and that incomparable *Deluge* by Antonio Carracci (for I know you love pictures and are very knowledgeable about them). Ah, my poor friend, all this must be left behind! Farewell, dear paintings which I have loved so much and which have cost me so much!'

LOUIS-HENRI DE LOMÉNIE, COMTE DE BRIENNE,
Mémoires, c. 1684

The five dealers [Duveen, Knoedler's, Wildenstein, Seligman, and Stevenson Scott] reconciled themselves to pooling their inventories as well as their aggressiveness. They decided to prepare a list of the Hundred Greatest Paintings in the World and offer them to [Henry] Ford; thus in one transaction they could convert America's richest man into America's richest collector. Like most other collectors, each dealer had persuaded himself that the paintings he owned were better than any owned by his rivals, and the task of selecting the hundred greatest resulted in many acrimonious debates, during which the surf of controversy rose so high that the scheme was in danger of foundering. But the gravity of the crisis and the grandeur of the objective made for compromise, and finally the hundred paintings were agreed on.

The pictures, each of which was accompanied by a scholarly text, were reproduced in three magnificent volumes; the dealers were going to present these books to Mr Ford as an invitation to the dance. Representatives of the five firms and the three magic books went, by appointment, to Dearborn. Representing Duveen Brothers, as always, was Duveen himself. The international worldlings from New York were astonished at the simplicity of Ford's style of living; compared to Duveen's house on Madison Avenue, or even some of his clients' houses, Ford's house was almost primitive. Mr Ford was unaffectedly pleased to see them and when they displayed the superbly illustrated volumes of the hundred greatest pictures, his delight was immeasurable. He jumped up and called Mrs Ford in to share his enthusiasm. 'Mother, come in and see the lovely pictures these gentlemen have brought,' he said, as Duveen later told the story. Mrs Ford came in and admired the books as much as her husband had. 'Yes, Mr Ford,' said Duveen, the spokesman for the delegation, 'we thought you would like them. These are the pictures we feel you should have.' Ford teetered on the narrow threshold between admiration and possession. 'Gentlemen,' he said, 'beautiful books like these, with beautiful coloured pictures like these, must cost an awful lot!' 'But, Mr Ford, we don't expect you to *buy* these books,' Duveen hastened to explain. 'We got them up specially for you, to show you the pictures. These books are a present to you'. Ford turned to his wife. 'Mother, did you hear that?' he said. 'These gentlemen are going to give me these beautiful books as a present. Yes, gentlemen,' he continued, 'it is extremely nice of you, but I really don't see how I can accept a beautiful, expensive present like this from strangers.' For perhaps the first time in his life, Duveen was inarticulate. Such innocence was confounding. It was a classic example of the worldling defenceless against the Man from Home. When at last he found speech, he explained that the books had been got up to interest Ford in buying the pictures whose simulacra they contained. At this revelation, Ford's amazement vanished and he became again a man of business. 'But, gentlemen,' he said, 'what would I want with the original pictures when the ones right here in these books are so beautiful?'

S. N. Behrman, *Duveen*, 1952

I also had great money difficulties to keep both [Jackson] Pollock and the gallery going, and often found myself in the position of having to sell what I called an old master. Thus, I was once forced to part with a marvelous Delaunay of 1912, called *Disks*, which I had bought from him in Grenoble, when he was a refugee from occupied Paris. This picture later turned up in the Museum of Modern Art. Its loss is one of the seven tragedies of my life as a collector.

The second was my stupidity in not availing myself of the opportunity of buying *La Terre Labourée*, by Miró, in London in 1939 for fifteen hundred dollars. Now, if it were for sale, it would be worth well over fifty thousand.

The third tragedy was selling a 1936 Kandinsky, called *Dominant Curve*, in New York during the war, because I listened to people saying it was a Fascist picture. To my great sorrow I later found it in my uncle's collection in an exhibition in Rome.

The fourth was not buying Picasso's *Pêche de Nuit à Antibes*, because I had no cash on hand, and did not have the sense to sell some capital, which my friend and financial adviser Bernard Reis told me to do when the picture was offered to me in 1950; and now that, too, is in the Museum of Modern Art.

The fifth was having to sell a Henri Laurens sculpture and a beautiful Klee water color in order to pay Nellie van Doesburg's passage to New York; and the sixth to have all but two of my last remaining Klees stolen from Art of This Century. But the worst mistake of all was giving away eighteen Pollocks. However, I comfort myself by thinking how terribly lucky I was to have been able to buy all my wonderful collection at a time when prices were still normal, before the whole picture world turned into an investment market.

PEGGY GUGGENHEIM, *Out of This Century*, 1980

COLOUR

If the artist abandons himself to his feeling, colour presently announces itself. Black no sooner inclines to blue than the eye demands yellow, which the artist instinctively modifies, and introduces partly pure in the light, partly reddened and subdued as brown, in the reflexes, thus enlivening the whole.

J. W. VON GOETHE, *Theory of Colours*, 1810

Colour is nothing if it does not accord with the subject and if it does not increase the effect of the painting through the imagination.

EUGÈNE DELACROIX, *Journal*, 2 January 1853

Hence, as I have said elsewhere, the business of a painter is to paint. If he can colour, he is a painter, though he can do nothing else; if he cannot colour, he is no painter, though he may do everything else. But it is, in fact, impossible, if he can colour, but that he should be able to do more; for a faithful study of colour will always give power over form, though the most intense study of form will give no power over colour. The man who can see all the greys, and reds, and purples in a peach, will paint the peach rightly round, and rightly altogether, but the man who has only studied its roundness, may not see its purples and greys, and if he does not, will never get it to look like a peach; so that great power over colour is always a sign of large general art-intellect. Expression of a most subtle kind can be often reached by the slight studies of caricaturists; sometimes elaborated by the toil of the dull, and sometimes by the sentiment of the feeble; but to colour well requires real talent and earnest study, and to colour perfectly is the rarest and most precious power an artist can possess.

JOHN RUSKIN, *Modern Painters*, Volume IV, 1856

Color, as the strange and magnificent expression of the inscrutable expression of eternity, is beautiful and important to me as a painter; I use it to enrich the canvas and to probe more deeply into the object. Color also decided, to a certain extent, my spiritual outlook, but it is subordinated to life and, above all, to the treatment of form. Too much emphasis on color at the expense of form and space would make a double manifestation of itself on the canvas, and this would verge on craft work. Pure colors and broken tones must be used together, because they are the complements of each other.

MAX BECKMANN, July 1938

COMPLIMENTS

Sure some propitious Planet then did Smile,
When first you were conducted to this Isle:
(Our Genius brought you here, t'inlarge our Fame)
(For your good Stars are ev'ry where the same)
Thy matchless hand, of ev'ry Region free,
Adopts our Climate; not our Climate thee

JOHN DRYDEN, 'To Sir Godfrey Kneller' (*Annual Miscellany*, 1694)

Kneller's appetite for a fulsome compliment was notorious; an amusing example is provided by an anecdote of Pope's (see here under DREAMS*).*

In you, sir, the world will expect to see accomplished what I have failed to achieve.

SIR JOSHUA REYNOLDS, to the young Thomas Lawrence, *c.*1790

When the entire court was assembled before the picture [David's 'Sacre de Napoléon'], Napoleon, his head covered, walked for more than half an hour in front of this thirty-foot-long canvas, examining every detail with the most scrupulous attention, while David and all the bystanders remained motionless and mute. The solemnity of this visit, and the extreme curiosity everyone had to know what the Emperor's verdict on the work would be, created – according to those present – a profound impression. At last, still gazing at the picture, Napoleon began to speak, saying 'It's good, very good, David. You have grasped my concept completely. *You have made me a French chevalier.* I congratulate you on transmitting to future centuries the proof of affection I wished to give her who shares with me the cares of reigning.' At that moment the Empress Josephine approached the Emperor from the right, while at his left David listened. Then, Napoleon stepped a couple of paces towards David, raised his hat and, with a slight bow, said 'David, I salute you.' 'Sire,' responded the painter, 'I accept your salutation in the name of all artists, happy to be the one whom you deign to address.'

M. E. J. DELÉCLUZE, *Louis David, son Ecole et son temps*, 1855

The tale is told that one day M. Horace Vernet went to see Peter Cornelius [active in Rome early in the nineteenth century with the German 'Nazarene' painters; later director of the Academy at Munich]. He overwhelmed him with compliments, but had to wait a long time to be repaid; for Peter Cornelius congratulated him only once during the whole interview – and that was on the quantity of champagne he was able to consume without suffering ill effects! True or false, the story has the ring of poetic truth.

CHARLES BAUDELAIRE, *The Salon of 1846*

CONTRACTS

On the 24th day of April [1453], Master Enguerrand Quarton, of the diocese of Laon, painter, resident in Avignon, made a contract and agreement with the said Dominus Jean de Montagnac – both contracting parties being present – for painting an altarpiece according to the manner, form and prescription contained and set forth article by article on a sheet of paper, which they passed to me, written in French, whose tenor follows and is such:

Here follows the list of items of the altarpiece that Messire Jean de Montagnac has commissioned from Master Enguerrand, painter, to be placed in the church of the Carthusians, Villeneuve-les-Avignon, on the altar of the Holy City.

First: There should be the form of Paradise, and in that Paradise should be the Holy Trinity, and there should not be any difference between the Father and the Son; and the Holy Ghost in the form of a dove; and Our Lady in front as it will seem best to Master Enguerrand; and the Holy Trinity will place the crown on the head of Our Lady.

Item: The vestments should be rich; those of Our Lady should be of white damask with a design made according to the judgment of said Master Enguerrand; and surrounding the Holy Trinity should be cherubim and seraphim . . . .

Item: In Paradise below should be all the estates of the world arranged by said Master Enguerrand.

Item: Below the said Paradise, there should be the heavens in which will be the sun and the moon according to the judgment of said Master Enguerrand.

Item: After the heavens, the world in which should be shown a part of the city of Rome . . . .

Item: Said altarpiece shall be made in fine oil colours and the blue should died in the flower of his studies and adhuc sua messis in herba erat ['his be fine German blue, and the gold that will be used on the frame as well as around the altarpiece should be fine gold and burnished.

Item: Said Master Enguerrand will show all his knowledge and skill in the Holy Trinity and in the blessed Virgin Mary, the other parts to be done according to the dictates of his conscience.

Item: On the back of the altarpiece will be painted a fine hanging of crimson [*cremesine*] with a fleur-de-lis design.

A promise was given, I declare, by the same Master Enguerrand to execute these things faithfully and according to the foregoing description, from the next [feast of] St Michael, for the next one continuous year, for the price of one hundred and twenty florins, each at the value of twenty-four *sous* of the currency of Avignon.

From the full contract as given in W. STECHOW,
Northern Renaissance Art, 1400–1600, 1966

And the aforementioned Master Dieric [Bouts] has contracted to make this altarpiece [the Holy Sacraments altarpiece for St Peter's, Louvain] to the best of his ability, to spare neither labour nor time, but to do his utmost to demonstrate in it the art which God has bestowed on him, in such order and truth as the Reverend Masters Jan Vaernacker and Gillis Bailluwel, Professors of Theology, shall prescribe to him with regard to the aforementioned subjects. And it is understood that said Master Dieric, after having begun work on this altarpiece, shall not contract any other work of this kind until this one has been completed. For his work said Master Dieric shall be paid and receive the sum of two hundred Rhenish guilders of twenty stivers each: to wit, twenty-five Rhenish guilders as soon as he has begun to paint this altarpiece . . . .

From the full contract of 15 March 1464, as given in W. STECHOW, *Northern Renaissance Art, 1400–1600*, 1966

Be it known and manifest to whoever sees or reads this document that, at the request of the reverend Messer Francesco di Giovanni Tesori, presently Prior of the Spedale degli Innocenti at Florence, and of Domenico di Tomaso di Curado [Ghirlandaio], painter, I, Fra Bernardo di Francesco of Florence, Jesuate Brother, have drawn up this document with my own hand as agreement contract and commission for an altar panel to go in the church of the abovesaid Spedale degli Innocenti with the agreements and stipulations stated below, namely:

That this day 23 October 1485 the said Francesco commits and entrusts to the said Domenico the painting of a panel which the said Francesco has had made and has provided; the which panel the said Domenico is to make good, that is, pay for; and he is to colour and paint the said panel all with his own hand in the manner shown in a drawing on paper with those figures and in that manner shown in it, in every particular according to what I, Fra Bernardo, think best; not departing from the manner and composition of the said drawing; and he must colour the panel at his own expense with good colours and with powdered gold on such ornaments as demand it, with any other expense incurred on the same panel, and the blue must be ultramarine of the value about four florins the ounce; and he must have made and delivered complete the said panel within thirty months from today; and he must receive as the price of the panel as here described (made at his, that is, the said Domenico's expense throughout) 115 large florins if it seems to me, the abovesaid Fra Bernardo, that it is worth it; and I can go to whoever I think best for an opinion on its value or workmanship, and if it does not seem to me worth the stated price, he shall receive as much less as I, Fra Bernardo, think right. . . .

From the contract as given in M. BAXANDALL, *Painting and Experience in Fifteenth-century Italy*, 1972

The altarpiece, of 'The Adoration of the Magi' (1488), remains in the Spedale in Florence. See also Henry James under COPIES.

COPIES

First, get executed two good copies [of M. Q. de La Tour's portrait of Voltaire], after which we will have others done. But what I should like is this: that the first copy was executed with all the copyist's *savoir faire* and skill, so that it can serve as the original for the others. After the first copy is finished, I would ask you to have it looked at and retouched by Latour. Meanwhile, you should send me my original, well framed and well packed-up, and from the first copy have a miniature done for me that can be worn on a ring.

VOLTAIRE, *Letter to his Parisian man of affairs, 12 April 1736*

Mr Floyd is a virtuoso and collector of pictures; he was almost in fits when he saw the copy of the little Correggio I gave the Duchess, and asked in a trembling voice, if the original was the same size as the copy, and if I had omitted any particular in the background? When I assured him, the size and *every speck* was as nearly the same as I could make them, he recovered himself, and said, '*Then mine is still an original, for it is some inches bigger, and has a palm tree in it.*' I never saw such symptoms of virtuosoship, I could hardly keep my countenance.

MRS DELANY, *Letter to Mrs Dewes*, 19 December 1760

The difference between a bad Artist & a Good One Is: the Bad Artist Seems to Copy a Great deal. The Good one Really Does Copy a Great deal.

WILLIAM BLAKE, annotation to Reynolds' *Discourses*

. . . I fear that, for myself, the memory of the Transfiguration, or indeed of the other Roman relics of the painter wouldn't save the Raphaels. And yet this was so far from the opinion of a patient artist whom I saw the other day copying the finest of Ghirlandaios – a beautiful Adoration of the Kings at the Hospital of the Innocenti. Here was another example of the buried art-wealth of Florence. It hangs in an obscure chapel, far aloft, behind an altar, and though now and then a stray tourist wanders in and puzzles awhile over the vaguely-glowing forms, the picture is never really seen and enjoyed. I found an aged Frenchman of modest mien perched on a little platform beneath it, behind a great hedge of altar-candlesticks, with an admirable copy all completed. The difficulties of his task had been well-nigh insuperable, and his performance seemed to me a real feat of magic. He could scarcely move or turn, and could find room for his canvas but by rolling it together and painting a small piece at a time, so that he never enjoyed a view of his *ensemble*. The original is gorgeous with colour and bewildering with decorative detail, but not a gleam of the painter's crimson was wanting, not a curl in his gold arabesques. It seemed to me that if I had copied a Ghirlandaio in such conditions I would at least maintain for my own credit that he was the first painter in the world. 'Very good of its kind,' said the weary old man with a shrug of reply for my raptures; 'but oh how far short of Raphael!' However that may be, if the reader chances to observe this consummate copy in the so commendable Museum devoted in Paris to such works, let him stop before it with a due reverence; it is one of the patient things of art. Seeing it wrought there, in its dusky nook, under such scant convenience, I found no bar in the painter's foreignness to a thrilled sense that the old art-life of Florence isn't yet extinct. It still at least works spells and almost miracles.

HENRY JAMES, *Italian Hours*, 1909

COROT

SIR ROBERT CHILTERN (*rising*): But you have not seen my Corots yet. They are in the Music-room. Corots seem to go with music, don't they? May I show them to you?

MRS CHEVELEY (*shaking her head*): I am not in a mood to-night for silver twilights, or rose-pink dawns. I want to talk business.

OSCAR WILDE, *An Ideal Husband*, Act I, 1895

The winter of 1916 marked the beginning of John's picture-collecting craze. At a sale in the Plaza Hotel he saw a Corot – 'Nymphs Bathing' – which he could not resist adding to the Cuyp 'Landscape' he had already bought from the Collection of Sir John Murray Scott. We had met George Russell, the famous Irish writer, poet, and painter, better known as 'A.E.', many times in Dublin at the home of Dr and Mrs Oliver St John Gogarty. When he came to America on a lecture tour I had a 'tea' for him at 270 Park Avenue. Many of our friends wanted to meet him. Some of the ladies, having read his works, expected to see a very poetic person instead of a heavy-set bearded man. On entering the hall where we had a 'Corot' hanging facing the door, he remarked, 'There's my dream. I dreamt last night I painted a Corot.'

LILY MCCORMACK, *I Hear You Calling Me: The Life of Count John McCormack*

CORREGGIO

. . . Correggio's little *putti* breathe, live and laugh with a grace and reality such that one is compelled to laugh and be happy with them.

ANNIBALE CARRACCI, *Letter of 1580 to Ludovico Carracci*

Unfortunately, the authenticity of the letter in which this sentence occurs is not beyond doubt.

One fact makes me begin to see myself as *a great* connoisseur. I recognize Correggio's brush before I see his name in the catalogue! But then Correggio has his own manner and all his male figures and heads resemble the Christ in the Vatican, and his women the Danaë in the Borghese Palace [*recte* Villa].

PETER ILYICH TCHAIKOVSKY, *Letter of 1880 from Rome*

THE CREED OF A DYING PAINTER

LOUIS [DUBEDAT]. (*He feebly folds his hands and utters his creed*): I believe in Michael Angelo, Velasquez, and Rembrandt; in the might of design, the mystery of color, the redemption of all things by Beauty everlasting, and the message of Art that has made these hands blessed: Amen. Amen. (*He closes his eyes and lies still*).

BERNARD SHAW, *The Doctor's Dilemma*, Act IV, 1908

CRITICS

Do not be an art critic, but paint – therein lies salvation.

PAUL CÉZANNE, *Letter to Emile Bernard*, 1904

Art critics are useless or harmful.

Futurist Manifesto, 1910

CRUELTY TO ANIMALS

The prints [of the 'Four Stages of Cruelty'] were engraved with the hope of, in some degree, correcting that barbarous treatment of animals, the very sight of which renders the streets of our metropolis so distressing to every feeling mind. If they have had this effect, and checked the progress of cruelty, I am more proud of having been the author, than I should be of having painted Raphael's Cartoons.

WILLIAM HOGARTH in *Anecdotes of William Hogarth* edited by J. B. Nichols, 1833

Rather less expected, perhaps, is the awareness of a great Victorian animal-painter, though one unwilling to act on his conscience.

There is something in the toil and trouble, the wild weather and savage scenery that makes butchers of us all. Who does not glory in the death of a fine stag? on the spot – when in truth he ought to be ashamed of the assassination . . . . Still, with all my respect for the animal's inoffensive character – my love of him *as a subject for the pencil* gets the better of such tenderness – a creature always picturesque and *never* ungraceful is too great a property to sacrifice to common feelings of humanity.

SIR EDWIN LANDSEER, *Letter to Lord Ellesmere, 1837*

THE CUBISTS

Finally, in their desire to take stock afresh of the world that surrounded them, the Cubists had effectively stripped bare many of the problems that had underlain painting and sculpture since the beginning of time. Artists, except those intent only on duplicating their subject in an illusionistic way, had always been aware of the need to reconcile their representation of it with the abstract demands of the aesthetic medium in which they were working; forms must be balanced to achieve a satisfactory composition, in painting volumes in depth must be arranged to produce also a harmonious surface pattern, and so on. The outlook of the Cubists . . . was intensely realistic, and a true appreciation of their painting depends ultimately on the spectators' ability to reconstruct or identify its subject-matter. But because they were less directly conditioned by visual appearances than any other school of painting since the Renaissance, they were able to evolve more abstract pictorial and sculptural techniques to solve the problems of recreating or reinterpreting the material world through an artistic medium. Never before had the duality between representation and abstraction been so clearly stated as it was in the Cubist paintings of Picasso, Braque and Gris, in the years immediately preceding the war. In these paintings one is aware at once of the presence of an easily identifiable subject, but the eye is simultaneously stimulated by the presence of an equally obvious underlying abstract pictorial structure with which the representational elements are fused and related.

JOHN GOLDING, *Cubism: A History and an Analysis 1907–1914* rev. edn., 1988

DALI

When I was three, I wanted to be a cook. When I was six I wanted to be Napoleon. Since then my ambition has done nothing but grow.

At the age of 29, I undertook my first American Campaign. On the day I disembarked in New York, my photograph appeared on the cover of *Time* Magazine. It showed me wearing the smallest mustache in the world. Since then the world has shrunk considerably while my mustache, like the power of my imagination, continued to grow.

SALVADOR DALI, from the preface to *Dali's Mustache*, 1954

DEALERS

Monet showed us a photograph of one of his canvases portraying his father looking at the sea; the picture is said to be in America. He sold it for 400 francs to Pratt, whose widow sold it for 40,000 to Durand-Ruel, and Monet wanted to buy it back from the dealer. He pointed out the pole with a flag on either side of the composition, and mentioned that at the time this composition was considered very daring. 'I'm very fond of flags,' he added. 'On the first national holiday on June 30th, I went out with my working equipment to the rue Montorgueil; the street was decked out with flags and the crowd was going wild. I noticed a balcony, I went up and asked permission to paint, which was granted me. Then I came down again incognito. Ah! it was a good time, a good time, although living wasn't always easy. Durand-Ruel was our guardian angel, but as his admiration for us brought him to the worst financial disaster, he was obliged to move to America. For some time there was no longer anyone to buy our canvases from us, and then I sought out Georges Petit. It wasn't easy to persuade him. His father had done us a lot of harm. People who hadn't wanted impressionists on the rue Laffitte bought them on the rue de Sèze. Competition arose between the two streets and was very profitable to us. I remember, one day, going to Arnold and Tripp with two canvases under my arm, but I wasn't admitted to the back of the shop, where the two partners and their employees examined what I had brought. They were having a big laugh. I heard: "It's Monet, the impressionist, what a scream!" And the laughter got worse than ever. Lifting the curtain, they saw me, and they laughed in my face as they handed back my two canvases.'

RENÉ GIMPEL, *Diary of an Art Dealer*, October 1920

The first time [after the Second World War] I went to see Picasso there was an anteroom full of people reminiscent of the Spanish court sitting waiting for hours to see him. He loved these visits. That is how I got to see him by sitting and waiting. I saw Matisse by ringing the door bell and saying 'Hallo, I am starting as a dealer, may I see your work and could you possibly consign things to me? I do not have much money, but whatever money I have I can give you.'

I was trying to do something with my gallery which appealed to those artists. I was clearly so involved and so enthusiastic they trusted me.

HEINZ BERGGRUEN in an interview with Elspeth Moncrieff, *The Antique Collector*, September 1988

DEATH

So he [Raphael] made his will: and first, as a good Christian, he sent his mistress away, leaving her the means to live a decent life. Then he divided his belongings among his disciples, Giulio Romano, whom he had always loved dearly, the Florentine Giovanni Francesco, called Il Fattore, and a priest I know nothing about who was a relation of his and came from Urbino. Next he stipulated that some of his wealth should be used for restoring with new masonry one of the ancient tabernacles in Santa Maria Rotonda and for making an altar with a marble statue of Our Lady; and he chose this church, the Pantheon, as his place of rest and burial after death. He left all the rest of his possessions to Giulio and Giovanni Francesco, and he appointed as his executor Baldassare da Pescia, then the Pope's datary. Having made his confession and repented, Raphael ended his life on Good Friday, the same day he was born. He was thirty-seven when he died; and we can be sure that just as he embellished the world with his talent so his soul now adorns heaven itself.

As he lay dead in the hall where he had been working they placed at his head the picture of the Transfiguration which he had done for Cardinal de' Medici; and the sight of this living work of art along with his dead body made the hearts of everyone who saw it burst with sorrow.

GIORGIO VASARI, *'Life' of Raphael*, 1568

Once released, he [Caravaggio] could no longer find the felucca, so that raging and almost demented he strode along that shore under the merciless rays of the burning sun to try and catch sight of the ship that bore his belongings. Finally he reached a village on the shore and was put to bed with a malignant fever; without any human assistance he died within a few days as badly as he had lived.

G. BAGLIONE, *Le Vite de'pittori . . .*, 1642

Rubens writes on the death of Elsheimer.

My Illustrious and Honoured Sir:

I have received from you two letters of very different tenor and content. The first was thoroughly amusing and gay; but the second, of December 18, was the bearer of the most cruel news – that of the death of our beloved Signor Adam, – which was very bitter to me. Surely, after such a loss, our entire profession ought to clothe itself in mourning. It will not easily succeed in replacing him; in my opinion he had no equal in small figures, in Landscapes, and in many other subjects. He has died in the flower of his studies and adhuc sua messis in herba erat ['his wheat was still in the blade': Ovid, *Heroides*, 17.263]. One could have expected of him res nunquam visae numquam videndae; in summa ostenderunt terris hunc tantum fata ['things that one has never seen and never will see; in short, destiny had only shown him to the world': *Aeneid*, 6.869].

For myself, I have never felt my heart more profoundly pierced by grief than at this news, and I shall never regard with a friendly eye those who have brought him to so miserable an end. I pray that God will forgive Signor Adam his sin of sloth, by which he has deprived the world of the most beautiful things, caused himself much misery, and finally, I believe, reduced himself to despair; whereas with his own hands he could have built up a great fortune and made himself respected by all the world.

Sir Peter Paul Rubens, *Letter to Johann Faber from Antwerp*, 14 January 1611

There is another death which is not so considerable [as that of the duc d'Aumont] but which will not leave second-hand dealers uninterested. It is that of S[ieu]r Watot [*sic*], excellent painter, aged only 36. He left the great part of his studies and drawings to the Abbé Arranger, Canon of St Germain de l'Auxerrois, known among connoisseurs.

Gazette d'Utrecht, 4 August 1721

A very early public notice of the death of Watteau, who had died at Nogent-sur-Marne on 18 July. Posterity can savour the irony that now resides in the opening words.

Dear Sir Joshua,

I am just to write what I fear you will not read after lying in a dying state for 6 months. The extreme affection which I am informed of by a Friend which Sir Joshua has expresd [*sic*] induces me to beg a last favor, which is to come once under my Roof and look at my things, my woodman you never saw, if what I ask [now?] is not disagreeable to youd [*sic*] feeling that

I may have the honor to speak to you. I can from a sincere Heart say that I always admired and sincerely loved Sir Joshua Reynolds.

THOMAS GAINSBOROUGH, *Letter to Sir Joshua Reynolds, late July 1788*

Gainsborough died on 2 August 1788, having been visited by Reynolds, as Reynolds himself explained publicly a few months later.

A few days before he [Gainsborough] died, he wrote me a letter, to express his acknowledgments of the good opinion I entertained of his abilities, and the manner in which (he had been informed) I always spoke of him; and desired he might see me, once more, before he died. I am aware how flattering it is to myself to be thus connected with the dying testimony which this excellent painter bore to his art. But I cannot prevail on myself to suppress that I was not connected with him by any habits of familiarity; if any little jealousies had subsisted between us, they were forgotten, in those moments of sincerity; and he turned towards me as one, who was engrossed by the same pursuits, and who deserved his good opinion, by being sensible of his excellence. Without entering into a detail of what passed at this last interview, the impression of it upon my mind was, that his regret at losing life, was principally the regret of leaving his art.

SIR JOSHUA REYNOLDS, *Discourse XIV*, 10 December 1788

My dearest little Julie, I love you as I die; I will still love you when I am dead; I beg of you, do not cry; this parting was inevitable. I would have liked to be with you until you married . . . . Work hard and be good as you always have been; you have never caused me one sorrow in your little life. You have beauty, money; make good use of them. I think the best thing to do would be to live with your cousins in the Rue de Villejust, but I do not want to force you to do anything. Give your Tante Edma a remembrance of me; and your cousins too; and give Monet's BATEAUX EN RÉPARATION to your cousin Gabriel [Gabriel Thomas]. Tell M. Degas that if he founds a museum he is to choose a Manet. A keepsake for Monet; one for Renoir; and one of my drawings for Bartholomé. Give something to the two concierges. Do not cry. I love you more than I can tell you. Jeannie, I leave Julie in your care.

BERTHE MORISOT, *Letter to her daughter, Julie Manet, c.1 March 1895*

Berthe Morisot, widow of Manet's brother Eugène, died on 2 March 1895.

I will gladly give you some details as to the last part of the life and of the end of M. Paul Gauguin all the more willingly as I cared for him until the morning of his death, which took place on the 8th of May, 1903, towards eleven in the morning.

. . . He was a very kindly man, gentle and simple with the Marquesans. And they returned his kindness. When your friend died I heard many expressions of regret from them such as this: 'Gauguin is dead. We are lost! *Ua mate Gauguin, ua pete enata!*' They alluded to the services Gauguin had often rendered them in delivering them from the clutches of the police, who were often hard and unjust towards the natives.

. . . He had a real cult for the country here, for this nature, so wild and beautiful in itself, where his soul found its natural frame. He was able to discover almost instantly the poetry of these regions, blest by the sun, and parts of which are still inviolate. You must have seen that in the pictures he sent you from here. The Maori soul was not mysterious for him, though Gauguin felt that our islands were daily losing a part of their originality.

'The Gods are dead and Atuana dies of their death,' he wrote somewhere.

. . . I am the only European who saw Gauguin before he died. I must say that he never spoke of his family in Europe, nor did he express any last wishes.

PASTOR VERNIER, *Letter from Atuana to Georges Daniel de Monfreid in Paris, c.1903*

DECEPTION IN ART

Deception follows glare; attempts to substitute by form or colour the image for the thing, always mark the puerility of taste, though sometimes its decrepitude. The microscopic precision of Denner, and even the fastidious, though broader detail of Gherard Douw, were symptoms of its dotage. The contest of Zeuxis and Parrhasius, if not a frolic, was an effort of puerile dexterity. But Deception, though at its ultimate pitch never more than the successful mimicry of absent objects, and for itself below the aim of art, is the mother of Imitation. We must penetrate the substances of things, acquaint ourselves with their peculiar hue and texture, and colour them in detail, before we can hope to seize their principle and give their general air.

Tiziano laboured first to make facsimiles of the stuffs he copied, before he changed them into drapery, and gave them local value and a place; he learnt first to distinguish tint from tint, and give the skeleton of colour, before he emboldened himself to take the greatest quantity of colour in an object for the whole; to paint flesh which abounded in demi-tints, entirely in demi-tints, and to deprive of all, that which had but a few. It was in the school of Deception he learnt the difference of diaphanous and opaque, of firm and juicy colour; that this refracts and that absorbs the light, and hence their place; those that cut and come forward, first, and those which more or less partake of the surrounding medium in various degrees of distance. It was here he learnt the contrast of the tints, of what is called warm and cold, and by their balance, diffusion, echo, to poise a whole. His eye as musical, if I may be allowed the metaphor, as his ear, abstracted here, that colour acts, affects, delights, like sound; that stern and deep-toned tints rouse, determine, invigorate the eye, as warlike sound or a deep bass the ear; and that bland, rosy, gray, and vernal tints, soothe, charm, and melt like a sweet melody.

HENRY FUSELI, *Lecture on Colour*, 1802

DELACROIX

The studio is entirely empty. Who would believe it? This place which witnessed me surrounded by paintings of all kinds, several of which delighted me by their variety and each of which awoke a memory or an emotion, pleases me still in its emptiness. It seems double the size. In it I have a dozen small pictures that I shall take pleasure in finishing. As soon as I am awake, I rush up there hastily, hardly bothering to comb my hair; I stay there until nightfall without a single blank moment or any regret for such distractions as visits, or what are called pleasures, can give. My ambition is enclosed within these walls. I revel in the last moments left for seeing myself in this place which saw me for so many years, and in which passed in great measure the last period of the fag-end of my youth. I speak of myself in this way because – although at an advanced stage of life – my imagination and a certain *je ne sais quoi* make me experience stirrings, impulses, aspirations which indicate good years yet ahead. Inordinate ambition has not enslaved my faculties and has not made me sacrifice the pleasure of rejoicing in myself and my abilities to the vain desire of being admired by the envious in some dreamt-of post, vain bauble of last years, an absurd way of employing the mind and heart at those moments when a man in the decline of life ought rather to meditate on his memories or in healthy mental occupations, to console himself for what is escaping him and fill his final hours otherwise than with rebarbative matters in which ambitious people waste long days so as to be briefly seen, or rather see themselves, in the sun of favour. Not without keen emotion can I leave these humble surroundings where I have been sometimes sad and sometimes happy, over the course of so many years.

EUGÈNE DELACROIX, *Journal*, 20 December 1857

In comparison with the engrained nineteenth-century British attitude to non-academic French painting of the period, the two tributes below are as rare as they are perceptive.

A small picture, by Delacroix, taken from the Inferno, *Virgil and Dante in the boat*, is truly picturesque in composition and the effect, and shews a real eye for Rubens and for nature. The forms project, the colours are thrown into masses.

WILLIAM HAZLITT, *Review of the Salon, Paris*, 22 October 1824

Delacroix is a man of a very different genius [from French classicizing painters], and his 'Medea' is a genuine creation of a noble fancy .... M. Delacroix has produced a number of rude, barbarous pictures; but there is the stamp of genius on all of them, – the great poetical *intention*, which is worth all your execution.

WILLIAM MAKEPEACE THACKERAY, *On the French School of Painting* (*The Paris Sketchbook*, 1840)

DELAROCHE

It is nice horror, horror everyone can understand ... he has scrubbed, soaped, waxed and polished horror so much that he has made it pretty; the most terrible scenes become pleasing to the eye, so daintily does he arrange all their grim details.

THÉOPHILE GAUTIER in *La Presse*, 10 March 1837

This painter rejoices in such subjects [the 'Princes in the Tower'] – in what Lord Portsmouth used to call 'black jobs'. He has killed Charles I, and Lady Jane Grey, and the Duke of Guise, and I don't know whom else besides. He is, at present, occupied with a vast work at the Beaux-Arts, where the writer of this had the honour of seeing him, – a little, keen-looking man, some five feet in height. He wore, on this important occasion, a bandanna round his head, and was in the act of smoking a cigar.

WILLIAM MAKEPEACE THACKERAY, *On the French School of Painting* (*The Paris Sketchbook*, 1840)

The only man whose name had the power to wring an abusive word or two from those aristocratic lips [Delacroix's] was Paul Delaroche. In that man's works there was obviously not a single extenuating circumstance to be found, and he never rid himself of the distress which had been caused him by all that sour and muddy painting, executed with 'ink and boot-polish', as Théophile Gautier once observed in an unusual access of independence.

CHARLES BAUDELAIRE, *Letter about Delacroix to the Editor of 'Opinion Nationale'*, September–November 1863

DILATORINESS

We thought that Titian, the painter, would some day finish our picture; but he seems to take no account of us whatsoever. We therefore instruct you to tell him instantly, that we are surprised that he should not have finished our picture; that he must finish it under all circumstances or incur our great displeasure; and he may be made to feel that he is doing an ill turn to one who can resent it. We are determined that he shall complete the work he promised: if he does not, we shall see to his doing it, and you are to advise us instantly of his resolution.

ALFONSO D'ESTE, DUKE OF FERRARA, *Letter to his agent Tebaldi in Venice, 29 September 1519*

He [Leonardo da Vinci] explained that men of genius sometimes accomplish most when they work the least; for, he added, they are thinking out inventions and forming in their minds the perfect ideas which they subsequently express and reproduce with their hands.

GIORGIO VASARI, *'Life' of Leonardo da Vinci*, 1568

Lord Nugent presents his compliments to Sir Thomas Lawrence. He cannot but express his astonishment at finding that, (after Sir Thomas Lawrence's respected [*sic*] assurances to him, that Lady Nugent's picture should at length be finished in time for the Exhibition this year) not only is the picture not to be exhibited, but, that not a touch has been put to it since the assurances were first given.

His own Picture, about which Lord Nugent was never so anxious, Sir Thomas Lawrence, after repeated and unexplained delays, promised should be finished and in Lord Nugent's possession at a time which has now for several months elapsed.

Lord Nugent is extremely sorry to be obliged to be now at length explicit with Sir Thomas Lawrence, and to say that, unless he will mention a short period, at the end of which he will pass his word that both pictures shall be finished and delivered, he must consider the pictures as not his, the purchase at an end, and the half price already paid, returnable.

If however Sir Thomas Lawrence will state that, at the end of a short time named, the pictures shall be finished and delivered, Lord Nugent will still be happy to forget the numerous and unexplained difficulties and disappointments he has hitherto had to encounter in getting these pictures finished.

LORD NUGENT, *Letter to Sir Thomas Lawrence*, 22 April 1818

I've simply got to finish that damn thing. The boy keeps getting older and the woman keeps getting younger.

JOHN SARGENT *on his portrait of the Countess of Warwick and her son*

DOGS IN PICTURES

Only Ruskin could take this dangerous topic and write on it not merely eloquently but with art-historical perceptiveness, even if he expresses his perceptions with a force of feeling today unfashionable.

I stated, in speaking of Venetian religion, that the Venetians always introduced the dog as a contrast to the high aspects of humanity. They do this, not because they consider him the basest of animals, but the highest – the connecting link between men and animals; in whom the lower forms of really human feeling may be best exemplified, such as conceit, gluttony, indolence, petulance. But they saw the noble qualities of the dog, too; – all his patience, love, and faithfulness; therefore Veronese, hard as he is often on lap-dogs, has painted one great heroic poem on the dog.

Two mighty brindled mastiffs, and beyond them, darkness. You scarcely see them at first, against the gloomy green. No other sky for them – poor things. They are gray themselves, spotted with black all over; their multitudinous doggish vices may not be washed out of them, – are in grain of nature. Strong thewed and sinewed, however, – no blame on them as far as bodily strength may reach; their heads coal-black, with drooping ears and fierce eyes, bloodshot a little. Wildest of beasts perhaps they would have been, by nature. But between them stands the spirit of their human Love, dove-winged and beautiful, the resistless Greek boy, golden-quivered; his glowing breast and limbs the only light upon the sky, – purple and pure. He has cast his chain about the dogs' necks, and holds it in his strong right hand, leaning proudly a little back from them. They will never break loose.

This is Veronese's highest, or spiritual view of the dog's nature. He can only give this when looking at the creature alone. When he sees it in company with men, he subdues it, like an inferior light in presence of the sky; and generally then gives it a merely brutal nature, not insisting even on its affection. It is thus used in the Marriage of Cana to symbolise gluttony.

That great picture I have not yet had time to examine in all its bearings of thought; but the chief purpose of it is, I believe, to express the pomp and pleasure of the world, pursued without thought of the presence of Christ; therefore the Fool with the bells is put in the centre, immediately underneath the Christ; and in front are the couple of dogs in leash, one gnawing at a bone. A cat lying on her back scratches at one of the vases which holds the wine of the miracle.

In the picture of Susannah, her little pet dog is merely doing his duty, barking at the Elders. But in that of the Magdalen (at Turin) a noble piece of bye-meaning is brought out by a dog's help. On one side is the principal figure, the Mary washing Christ's feet; on the other, a dog has just come out from beneath the table (the dog under the table eating of the crumbs), and in doing so, has touched the robe of one of the Pharisees, thus making it unclean. The Pharisee gathers up his robe in a passion, and shows the hem of it to a bystander, pointing to the dog at the same time.

In the Supper at Emmaus, the dog's affection is, however, fully dwelt upon. Veronese's own two little daughters are playing, on the hither side of the table, with a great wolf-hound, larger than either of them. One with her head down, nearly touching his nose, is talking to him, – asking him questions it seems, nearly pushing him over at the same time: – the other, raising her eyes, half archly, half dreamily, – some far-away thought coming over her, – leans against him on the other side, propping him with her little hand, laid slightly on his neck. He, all passive and glad at heart, yielding himself to the pushing or sustaining hand, looks earnestly into the face of the child close to his; would answer her with the gravity of a senator, if so it might be: – can only look at her, and love her.

To Velasquez and Titian dogs seem less interesting than to Veronese; they paint them simply as noble brown beasts, but without any special character; perhaps Velasquez's dogs are sterner and more threatening than the Venetian's, as also his kings and admirals. This fierceness in the animal increases, as the spiritual power of the artist declines; and, with the fierceness, another character. One great and infallible sign of the absence of spiritual power is the presence of the slightest taint of obscenity. Dante marked this strongly in all his representations of demons, and as we pass from the Venetians and Florentines to the Dutch, the passing away of the soul-power is indicated by every animal becoming savage or foul. The dog is used by Teniers, and many other Hollanders, merely to obtain unclean jest; while by the more powerful men, Rubens, Snyders, Rembrandt, it is painted only in savage chase, or butchered agony. I know no pictures more shameful to humanity than the boar and lion hunts of Rubens and Snyders, signs of disgrace all the deeper, because the powers desecrated are so great. The painter of the village alehouse sign may, not dishonourably, paint the fox-hunt for the village squire; but the occupation of magnificent art-power in giving semblance of perpetuity to those bodily pangs which Nature has mercifully ordained to be transient, and in forcing us, by the fascination of its stormy skill, to dwell on that from which eyes of merciful men should instinctively turn away, and eyes of high-minded men scornfully, is dishonourable, alike in the power which it degrades, and the joy to which it betrays.

In our modern treatment of the dog, of which the prevailing tendency is marked by Landseer, the interest taken in him is disproportionate to that taken in man, and leads to a somewhat trivial mingling of sentiment, or warping by caricature; giving up the true nature of the animal for the sake of a pretty thought or pleasant jest. Neither Titian nor Velasquez ever jest; and though Veronese jests gracefully and tenderly, he never for an instant oversteps the absolute facts of nature. But the English painter looks for sentiment or jest primarily, and reaches both by a feebly romantic taint of fallacy, except in one or two simple and touching pictures, such as the Shepherd's Chief Mourner.

JOHN RUSKIN, *Modern Painters*, volume V, 1860

I had rather see the portrait of a dog that I know than all the allegorical paintings they can shew me in the world.

DR SAMUEL JOHNSON

DOMENICHINO

... The banquet [at Grottaferrata, on the Feast of the Annunciation] was far less substantial of course, but it had a note as of immemorial manners that couldn't fail to suggest romantic analogies to a pilgrim from the land of no cooks. There was a feast of reason close at hand, however, and I was careful to visit the famous frescoes of Domenichino in the adjoining church. It sounds rather brutal perhaps to say that, when I came back into the clamorous little piazza, the sight of the peasants swilling down their sour wine appealed to me more than the masterpieces – Murray calls them so – of the famous Bolognese. It amounts after all to saying that I prefer Teniers to Domenichino; which I am willing to let pass for the truth .... After coming out of the church I found a delightful nook – a queer little terrace before a more retired and tranquil drinking-shop – where I called for a bottle of wine to help me guess why I 'drew the line' at Domenichino ....

I don't know that I came to any very distinct conclusion about Domenichino; but it was perhaps because the view was perfection that he struck me as more than ever mediocrity. And yet I don't think it was one's bottle of wine, either, that made one after all maudlin about him; it was the sense of the foolishly usurped in his tenure of fame, of the derisive in his ever having been put forward. To say so indeed savours of flogging a dead horse, but is surely an unkind stroke of fate for him that Murray assures ten thousand

Britons every winter in the most emphatic manner that his Communion of St Jerome is the 'second finest picture in the world'. If this were so one would certainly here in Rome, where such institutions are convenient, retire into the very nearest convent; with such a world one would have a standing quarrel.

HENRY JAMES, *Italian Hours*, 1909

DRAUGHTSMANSHIP

. . . Pope Benedict IX, who was intending to have some paintings commissioned for St Peter's, sent one of his courtiers from Trevisi to Tuscany to find out what sort of man Giotto was and what his work was like.

. . . The courtier told Giotto what the Pope had in mind and the way in which he wanted to make use of his services, and, finally, he asked Giotto for a drawing which he could send to his holiness. At this Giotto, who was a very courteous man, took a sheet of paper and a brush dipped in red, closed his arm to his side, so as to make a sort of compass of it, and then with a twist of his hand drew such a perfect circle that it was a marvel to see. Then, with a smile, he said to the courtier:

'There's your drawing.'

As if he were being ridiculed, the courtier replied:

'Is this the only drawing I'm to have?'

'It's more than enough,' answered Giotto. 'Send it along with the others and you'll see whether it's understood or not.'

The Pope's messenger, seeing that that was all he was going to get, went away very dissatisfied, convinced he had been made a fool of. All the same when he sent the Pope the other drawings and the names of those who had done them, he also sent the one by Giotto, explaining the way Giotto had drawn the circle without moving his arm and without the help of a compass. This showed the Pope and a number of knowledgeable courtiers how much Giotto surpassed all the other painters of that time.

GIORGIO VASARI, *'Life' of Giotto*, 1568

But I say – and I know that I speak the truth – that the art of painting does not derive from the mathematical sciences, nor has it any need to resort to them to learn rules or means for its own art, nor even in order to reason abstractly about this art: for painting is not the daughter of mathematics but of Nature and of Drawing.

FEDERICO ZUCCARO, *L'Idea de' pittori, scultori e architetti*, 1607

He [Ingres] said to Monsieur Degas: 'Draw lines, many lines, from memory or nature: it is by this that you will become a good artist.'

MAURICE DENIS, *Théories: La doctrine d'Ingres*, 1912

On the subject of his burial, Degas had said to Forain: 'I do not want an address', then: 'Yes, Forain, you shall deliver one, you shall say: he greatly loved drawing.'

EDGAR DEGAS

The legend of the childishness of my drawing must have originated from those linear compositions of mine in which I tried to combine a concrete image, say of a man, with the pure representation of the linear element.

Had I wished to present the man 'as he is', then I should have had to use such a bewildering confusion of line that pure elementary representation would have been out of the question. The result would have been vagueness beyond recognition.

PAUL KLEE, *On Modern Art*, 1924

DREAMS

In the night between Wednesday and Thursday after Whitsunday [30–1 May] 1525, I saw this appearance in my sleep – how many great waters fell from heaven. The first struck the earth about 4 miles away from me with terrific force and tremendous noise, and it broke up and drowned the whole land. I was so sore afraid that I awoke from it. Then the other waters fell and as they fell they were very powerful and there were many of them, some further away, some nearer. And they came down from so great a height that they all seemed to fall with an equal slowness. But when the first water that touched the earth had very nearly reached it, it fell with such swiftness, with wind and roaring, and I was so sore afraid that when I awoke my whole body trembled and for a long while I could not recover myself. So when I arose in the morning I painted it above here as I saw it. God turn all things to the best.

ALBRECHT DÜRER

Dürer's inscription under a pen-and-watercolour drawing of 1525 (Kunsthistorisches Museum, Vienna).

Did you never hear Sir Godfrey's dream?

'No.' Why then I'll tell it you. A night or two ago (says Sir Godfrey) I had a very odd sort of dream. I dreamed that I was dead, and soon after found myself walking in a narrow path that led up between two hills, rising pretty equally on either side of it. Before me I saw a door, and a great number of people about it. I walked on towards them. As I drew nearer, I could distinguish Saint Peter by his keys, with some other of the Apostles. They were admitting the people as they came next the door . . . . When I had joined the company, I could see several seats every way at a little distance within the door. As the first coming after my coming up approached for admittance, St Peter asked his name, and then his religion; I am a Roman catholic, replied the spirit. Go in then, says St Peter, and sit down in those seats there on the right hand. The next was a presbyterian; he was admitted too after the usual questions, and ordered to sit down on the seat opposite to the other. My turn came next, and as I approached, St Peter very civilly asked me my name. I said 'twas Kneller. I had no sooner said so, than St Luke (who was standing just by) turned towards me, and said with a great deal of earnestness, 'What, the famous Sir Godfrey Kneller, of England?' – 'The very same, Sir,' says I, 'at your service.' On this St Luke immediately drew nearer to me, and embraced me, and made me a great many compliments on the art we both of us had followed in this world; and entered so far into the subject, that he seemed almost to have forgot the business for which I came thither. At last, however, he recollected himself, and said, 'I beg your pardon, Sir Godfrey, I was so taken up with the pleasure of conversing with you. But apropos; pray, Sir, what religion may you be of?' 'Why, truly, Sir,' says I, 'I am of no religion.' – 'O, Sir,' says he, 'you will be so good then as to go in and take your seat where you please.'

ALEXANDER POPE, from Spence's *Observations, Anecdotes, and Characters*, 1820

Dreamt Michael Angelo came to me last night in my painting-room. I talked to him, and he shook hands with me. I took him to the small medallion over my chimney-piece, and said, 'It's very like, but I do not think your nose so much broken as I imagined.' I thought it strange in my dream. I could not make it out how *he* came there. He had a brown coat and complexion. I certainly think something grand in my destiny is coming on, for all the spirits of the illustrious dead are hovering about me.

BENJAMIN ROBERT HAYDON, *Autobiography and Memoirs*, 1831

The word 'dream' is often misused concerning my painting. We certainly wish the realm of dreams to be respectable – but our works are not oneiric. *On the contrary.* If 'dreams' are concerned in this context, they are very different from those we have while sleeping. It is a question rather of *self-willed* 'dreams', in which nothing is as vague as those feelings one has when escaping in dreams . . . . 'Dreams' which are not intended to make you sleep but wake you up.

RENÉ MAGRITTE

DUCCIO

He is much greater [than Giotto] as a colourist. He has a finer technique in tempera painting. He can give more poignant expression to deep emotion. He has a more subtle sense of beauty. He is not inferior to Giotto as a master of lineal design. He shows a more accurate observation of nature in his drawings of the nude, as in his representations of rocks and trees. In a measure he anticipates the discoveries of the quattrocentists in his treatment of landscape.

[ROBERT] LANGTON DOUGLAS, *A History of Siena*, 1902

DÜRER

And then by Durers rules survay the state
Of his each limbe, and with strings the odds trye
Of his necke to his legge, and waste to thighe.

JOHN DONNE, *Satyres*, III

. . . the most exquisite man that ever leaft [*sic*] us lines to vieue.

NICHOLAS HILLIARD, *The Arte of Limning*, *c.* 1600

When I contemplate the noble Albrecht Dürer, he seems so like his own evocation of his father: an artistic and pure man. And looking at his works which are imbued with a heavenly simplicity, demonstrating his pure intentions, I am firmly convinced that virtue is the path which leads one on the way to becoming a truly great painter.

FRANZ PFORR (1788–1812)

At Mr Cross's [in Winchester] is a very interresting [*sic*] picture of Albert Durer, who, being alive in such warlike times, was perhaps forced to paint in his gauntlets, so we must make all allowances.

JOHN KEATS, *Letter to Benjamin Robert Haydon, 1819*

DUTCH PAINTING

As for the Dutch painters, those drudging mimics of nature's most uncomely coarseness, don't their earthen pots and brass kettles carry away prices only due to the sweet neatness of Albano, and to the attractive delicacy of Carlo Maratti . . .

Horace Walpole, *Aedes Walpolianae*, 1747

It is for this rare, precious quality of truthfulness that I delight in many Dutch paintings, which lofty-minded people despise. I find a source of delicious sympathy in these faithful pictures of a monotonous homely existence, which has been the fate of so many more among my fellow-mortals than a life of pomp or absolute indigence, of tragic suffering or of world-stirring actions. I turn, without shrinking, from cloud-borne angels, from prophets, sibyls, and heroic warriors, to an old woman bending over her flower-pot, or eating her solitary dinner, while the noonday light, softened perhaps by a screen of leaves, falls on her mob-cap, and just touches the rim of her spinning-wheel, and her stone jug, and all those cheap common things, which are the precious necessaries of life to her.

George Eliot, *Adam Bede*, 1859

The assembly of Dutch painters imagined below has an almost naïve air, somewhat surprising, if charming, given the writer.

The Burgomaster van Storck entertained a party of friends, consisting chiefly of his favourite artists, one summer evening. The guests were seen arriving on foot in the fine weather, some of them accompanied by their wives and daughters, against the light of the low sun, falling red on the old trees of the avenue and the faces of those who advanced along it: – Willem van Aelst, expecting to find hints for a flower-portrait in the exotics which would decorate the banqueting-room; Gerard Dow, to feed his eye, amid all that glittering luxury, on the combat between candle-light and the last rays of the setting sun; Thomas de Keyser, to catch by stealth the likeness of Sebastian the younger. Albert Cuyp was there, who, developing the latent gold in Rembrandt, had brought into his native Dordrecht a heavy wealth of sunshine, as exotic as those flowers or the eastern carpets on the Burgomaster's tables, with Hooch, the indoor Cuyp, and Willem van de Velde, who painted those shore-pieces with gay ships of war, such as he loved, for his patron's cabinet. Thomas de Keyser came, in company with his brother Peter, his niece, and young Mr Nicholas Stone from England, pupil of that brother Peter, who afterwards married the niece. For the life of Dutch artists, too, was exemplary in matters of domestic relationship, its history telling many a cheering story of mutual faith in misfortune . . . .

A little way behind the other guests, three of them together, son, grandson, and the grandfather, moving slowly, came the Hondecoeters – Giles, Gybrecht, and Melchior. They led the party before the house was entered, by fading light, to see the curious poultry of the Burgomaster go to roost; and it was almost night when the supper-room was reached at last.

WALTER PATER, 'Sebastian van Storck' in *Imaginary Portraits*, 1887

You're a baby grand of a lady and a gent,
You're an old Dutch master,
You're Mrs Astor,
You're Pepsodent.

COLE PORTER, 'You're the Top', 1934

VAN DYCK

Nor was his *Life* less perfect than his *Art*,
Nor was his *Hand* less *erring* than his *Heart*,
There was no false, or fading *Colour* there,
The *Figures* sweet and well proportion'd were.
Most other men, set next to him in view,
Appear'd more *shadows* then the Men he *drew*.
Thus still he liv'd till heav'n did for him call,
Where reverent *Luke* salutes him first of all:
Where he beholds new sights, divinely faire;
And could almost wish for his *Pencil* there;
Did he not gladly see how all things shine,
Wondrously *painted* in the *Mind Divine*,
Whilst he forever ravisht with the show
Scorns his own *Art* which we admire below.

ABRAHAM COWLEY, *On the Death of Sir Anthony Vandike*, 1668

He was still young, his beard hardly sprouted, but his youthfulness was accompanied by a grave modesty of mind and a noble appearance, despite his small stature. His manners were lordly rather than those of an ordinary man, and he was resplendent in a rich array of clothes and accessories, since he had been accustomed in Rubens's studio to noble persons; and being distinguished by nature, and eager to be illustrious, he decked himself out with feathers and sashes, with chains of gold across his chest, and had a train of servants. Thus he imitated the pomp of Zeuxis and attracted everyone's attention: this, which ought to have brought him esteem among the Flemish painters living in Rome, excited rancour and tremendous dislike of him.

GIOVANNI PIETRO BELLORI: *'Life' of Van Dyck* in *Le Vite de' pittori*, 1672

If his Performances are not alike perfect, all in the last degree, they carry with them, however, a *Great Character of Spirit, Nobleness, Grace* and *Truth*, insomuch as one may say of him, that excepting *Titian* only *Vandyck* surpasses all the *Painters* that went before him, or have come after him, in *Portraits*.

ROGER DE PILES, *The Art of Painting*, 1706

THE ENGLISH SCHOOL

Very skilfully does Disraeli in 'Coningsby' contrast the Frenchified taste of the dissolute Lord Monmouth, Coningsby's grandfather, with that of the Lancastrian manufacturer, Millbank, whose character is well conveyed by the pictures he collects.

The walls of the dining-room were covered with pictures of great merit, all of the modern English school. Mr Millbank understood no other, he was wont to say! and he found that many of his friends who did, bought a great many pleasing pictures that were copies, and many originals that were very displeasing. He loved a fine free landscape by Lee that gave him the broad plains, the green lanes, and running streams of his own land; a group of animals by Landseer, as full of speech and sentiment as if they were designed by Æsop; above all, he delighted in the household humour and homely pathos of Wilkie. And if a higher tone of imagination pleased him, he could gratify it without difficulty among his favourite masters. He possessed some specimens of Etty worthy of Venice when it was alive; he could muse amid the twilight ruins of ancient cities raised by the magic pencil of Danby; or accompany a group of fair Neapolitans to a festival by the genial aid of Uwins.

BENJAMIN DISRAELI, *Coningsby*, 1844

MAX ERNST

One day when I went into his studio I had a great shock. There on his easel was a little painting I had never seen before. In it was portrayed a strange figure with the head of a horse, which was Max's own head, and the body of a man dressed in shining armor. Facing this strange creature, and with her hand between his legs, was a portrait of me. Not of me as Max had ever known me, but of me as my face appeared as a child of eight. I have photographs of myself at this age and the likeness is unquestionable. I burst into tears the minute I recognized it and rushed to tell Max that he had at last painted my portrait. He was rather surprised as he had never seen the photos. Because my hand was where it was and because it was between two spears, I named the picture *The Mystic Marriage*. I asked for it as a present, telling Max that now he need never marry me, as this sufficed. I have still to describe the rest of the painting, as this was only one-third of it. In the center was a figure which Max admitted to be Pegeen's back, and on the left hand side was a terrifying sort of monster. It portrayed a woman in a red dress with her stomach exposed. This was undoubtedly my stomach, but the figure had two heads which resembled nobody. They were animal heads and one looked like a skeleton. Sidney Janis claimed that I was this monster. . . .

PEGGY GUGGENHEIM, *Out of This Century*, 1980

ETTY

Etty has [at the Royal Academy exhibition] a revel rout of Satyrs and lady bums as usual, very clear and sweetly scented with otter of roses – bought by an old Marquis (Ld Stafford) – coveted by the King (from description) but too late.

JOHN CONSTABLE, *Letter to Archdeacon Fisher, 11 June 1828*

EXHIBITIONS

Of this portrait [of Juan de Pareja] (which is half-length, from life) a story is related by Andreas Schmidt, a Flemish painter now at the Spanish court, who was in Rome at the time. In accordance with decorating the cloister of the Rotunda (where Raphael of Urbino is buried) on Saint Joseph's day, with famous paintings, ancient and modern, this portrait was exhibited. It gained such universal applause that in the opinion of all the painters of the different nations everything else seemed like painting, but this alone like truth. In view of this Velázquez was received as Roman Academician in the year 1650.

ANTONIO PALOMINO, *Life of Velázquez*, 1724

Velázquez' portrait of Juan de Pareja is now in the Metropolitan Museum of Art, New York.

Every year we have referred in this magazine [*Mercure de France*] to the paintings put on exhibition in the Place Dauphine on the feast of Corpus Christi. We have spoken of the pleasure given to the public and of the usefulness of these exhibitions, which – apart from the taste for and love of the fine arts which they engender – also stimulate most valuable emulation among artists.

We are far from failing in our duty to our readers, that is to say, to provide a review of the exhibition of pictures and other works of sculpture and engraving by the accomplished persons who make up the Royal Academy of Painting and Sculpture. This year it opened on the feast-day of St Louis, in the great salon of the old Louvre, and lasted ten days. A debt is owed to M. de Boullongne, Esquire, Knight of the order of St Michael, First Painter to the King, Head and Director of the Academy who, with the active support of M. le Duc d'Antin, Peer of France, Overseer of the Royal Buildings and Protector of the Academy, [someone] always disposed to keep the arts flourishing in the kingdom, received his instructions and carried them out with general approval.

We shall try to give some idea of this magnificent display, so as to preserve its memory, noting the items shown and providing at least this pleasure for interested and artistically-inclined people who had no opportunity to see a show as delightful and varied as it was sophisticated and choice.

No observations are passed on the beauties and defects which resulted in praise or censure of this or that painting. We cannot be sufficiently confident of the public's feelings to go into such detail; we would be afraid of damaging the scrupulous impartiality on which we pride ourselves; but we will omit nothing factual and interesting that can be known about either the works or their creators, to serve one day for the memoirs of the history of the Fine Arts and for writing the lives of the illustrious figures who today form the French School. . . .

If anything was lacking in the public's satisfaction with the exhibition, it was not seeing in it any works by Messieurs de Boullongne, de Troye [*sic*], Largillière, and Rigault, who, having nothing to add to their reputations, acquired fresh renown by believing they should not appear at this celebration so that justice could be done to the work of the young academicians, most of whom are their pupils.

Le Mercure de France, September 1725

View the exhibition, at the Louvre, of the Academy's paintings. For one history piece in our exhibitions at London here are ten; abundantly more than to balance the difference between the annual and biennial exhibition.

ARTHUR YOUNG, Paris, 1787: *Travels in France and Italy*, 1792

. . . Henry and I went to the Exhibition in Spring Gardens. It is not thought a good collection, but I was very well pleased – particularly (pray tell Fanny) with a small portrait of Mrs Bingley, excessively like her. I went in hopes of seeing one of her Sister, but there was no Mrs Darcy; – perhaps however, I may find her in the Great Exhibition [Royal Academy] which we shall go to, if we have time; I have no chance of her in the collection of Sir Joshua Reynolds's Paintings which is now shewing in Pall Mall, & which we are also to visit. – Mrs Bingley's is exactly herself, size, shaped face, features &

sweetness; there never was a greater likeness. She is dressed in a white gown, with green ornaments, which convinces me of what I had always supposed, that green was a favourite colour with her. I dare say Mrs D. will be in Yellow.

. . . We have been both to the Exhibition & Sir J. Reynolds', – and I am disappointed, for there was nothing like Mrs D. at either. I can only imagine that Mr D. prizes any Picture of her too much to like it should be exposed to the public eye. – I can imagine he w[d] have that sort of feeling – that mixture of Love, Pride and Delicacy. – Setting aside this disappointment, I had great amusement among the Pictures.

JANE AUSTEN, *Letter from London to her sister Cassandra*, 24 May 1813

I was today at three exhibitions: the Symbolists', the Impressionists' and the Neo-Impressionists'. I looked at the pictures conscientiously and carefully, but again felt the same stupefaction and ultimate indignation. The first exhibition, that of Camille Pissarro, was comparatively the most comprehensible, though the pictures were out of drawing, had no content, and the colourings were mostly improbable. . . . In the same gallery – that of Durand-Ruel – were other pictures: by Puvis de Chavannes, Manet, Monet, Renoir, Sisley, who are all Impressionists. One of them, whose name I could not make out – it was something like Redon – had painted a blue face in profile. . . . From there I went to see the Symbolists. I looked at them long without asking anyone for an explanation, trying to guess the meaning; but it is beyond human comprehension.

TATIANA TOLSTOY, *Letter from Paris*, 1894

This exhibition will be epoch-making in the history of American art. Tonight will be the red-letter night in the history not only of American, *but of all modern art.* Now that the exhibition is a fact, we can say with pride that it is the most *complete* art exhibition that has been held in the world during the last quarter century. We do not except any country or any capital.

JOHN QUINN *at the opening of the Armory Show, New York*, 17 February 1913

On the whole Dr Goebbels must be congratulated on a timely exposure [in the exhibition, 'Degenerate Art', Munich, 1937] of many art tendencies that are pure nonsense. Skilfully selected and arranged, satirically interlarded with large-print quotations from the critics who praised them, the Degenerates cut a sorry and even a comic figure.

J. B. C. GRUNDY, 'Art Tendencies in the Third Reich' in *German Life and Art*, 1937–8

. . . and I dread all the terrible horrors being brewd up over this Tate affair [retrospective exhibition] – surely they have *everything* they want by now but me and they can leave me alone. its like a night mare to me – very wrong Im sure but there it is.

EDWARD BURRA, *Letter to William Chappell, April 1973*

EXPORT OF PICTURES

Henry James dealt with this subject, already topical in Edwardian England, in his little-known novel, 'The Outcry', originally written as a play in 1909. The cast of characters includes members of the British aristocracy (among whom is Lord Theign, the owner of a picture which may or may not be by Moretto) and an acquisitive American connoisseur-cum-dealer, Breckenridge Bender.

This version of the case had its effect, for the moment, on his fair associate. 'Does he want to buy *their* pride and glory?'

The young man, however, struck on his own side, became at first but the bright reflector of her thought. 'Is that wonder for sale?'

She closed her eyes as with the shudder of hearing such words. 'Not, surely, by *any* monstrous chance! Fancy dear, proud Theign—!'

'I can't fancy him – no!' And Lord John appeared to renounce the effort. 'But a cat may look at a king and a funny sharp Yankee at anything.'

These things might be, Lady Sandgate's face and gesture apparently signified; but another question diverted her. 'You're clearly a wonderful showman, but do you mind my asking you whether you're on such an occasion a – well, a closely interested one?'

'"Interested"?' he echoed; though it wasn't to gain time, he showed, for he would in that case have taken more. 'To the extent, you mean, of any little percentage?' And then as in silence she but kept a slightly grim smile on him: 'Why do you ask if – with your high delicacy about your great-grandmother – you've nothing to place?'

It took her a minute to say, while her fine eye only rolled; but when she spoke that organ boldly rested and the truth vividly appeared. 'I ask because people like you, Lord John, strike me as dangerous to the – how shall I name it? – the common weal; and because of my general strong feeling that we don't want any more of our national treasures (for I regard my great-grandmother as national) to be scattered about the world.'

HENRY JAMES, *The Outcry*, 1911

The King asks if, when you are considering possible new forms of taxation, it has occurred to you that a tax might be put upon works of art which leave this country? It would have the double effect of bringing money, though perhaps only a small amount into the Revenue, and prevent a process, which if persisted in, will gradually result in denuding these Islands of some of their most priceless artistic possessions.

LORD STAMFORDHAM, *Letter to the Chancellor of the Exchequer*, 1921

Lord Stamfordham was writing on behalf of George V, who is shown here to be far from indifferent to the visual arts and who pointed to a serious problem which has never been adequately resolved by any British government.

JAN VAN EYCK

To our beloved and faithful keepers of our accounts at Lille –

Very dear and beloved, – we have heard that you do not readily verify certain of our letters granting life pension to our well beloved equerry and painter, Jan van Eyck, whereby he cannot be paid said pension; and for this reason he will find it necessary to leave our service, which would cause us great displeasure, for we would retain him for certain great works with which we intend henceforth to occupy him and we would not find his like more to our taste, nor one so excellent in his art and science [*son art et science*]. Therefore we desire and expressly order that, according to these wishes, you do verify and ratify our said letters of pension and have this pension paid to the said Jan van Eyck, all according to the content of our said letters with no further talk or argument from you nor any omission, change, variation, or difficulty, as much as you would not anger and disobey [us].

For once and for all do so much so that we have no further need to write. This we would only do with great displeasure.

Very dear and well beloved, may the Holy Spirit have you in his Holy care. Written in our city of Dijon, the xii day of March 1435.

PHILIP, DUKE OF BURGUNDY

Then I saw Jan's picture [the 'Adoration of the Lamb' polyptych, St Bavon, Ghent]; it is a most precious painting, full of thought, and the Eve, Mary and God the Father are especially good.

ALBRECHT DÜRER, *Journal*, April 1521

Besides the money she procured him [Gerard] for the journey, Margaret van Eyck gave him money's worth. Said she, 'I will tell you secrets that I learned from masters that are gone from me, and have left no fellow behind. Even the Italians know them not; and what I tell you now in Tergou you shall sell dear in Florence. Note my brother Jan's pictures: time, which fades all other paintings, leaves his colours bright as the day they left the easel. The reason is, he did nothing blindly, nothing in a hurry. He trusted to no hireling to grind his colours; he did it himself, or saw it done. His panel was prepared, and prepared again – I will show you how – a year before he laid his colour on. Most of them are quite content to have their work sucked up and lost, sooner than not be in a hurry. Bad painters are always in a hurry. Above all, Gerard, I warn you use but little oil, and never boil it: boiling it melts that vegetable dross into its very heart which it is our business to clear away; for impure oil is death to colour. . . . When your oil has been washed in bottle, put it into this trough with water and put the trough in the sun all day. You will soon see the water turbid again. But mark, you must not carry this game too far, or the sun will turn your oil to varnish. When it is as clear as crystal, and not too luscious, drain carefully and cork it up tight. Grind your own primary colours, and lay them on with this oil, and they shall live. Hubert would put sand or salt in the water to clear the oil quicker. But Jan used to say, "Water will do it best; give water time." Jan van Eyck was never in a hurry, and that is why the world will not forget *him* in a hurry.'

CHARLES READE, *The Cloister and the Hearth*, 1861

In reality, it seems unlikely that Jan van Eyck had a sister Margaret active as a painter; she seems to have been invented in the sixteenth century.

CAREL FABRITIUS

I have never heard mention in Holland of the paintings of Carel Fabritius, and I have only ever seen one, a small modest piece, but fine and indeed precious because of the signature of the man to whom Jan van der Meer of Delft attached himself. It is at Brussels in the collection of M. le Chevalier Camberlyn. It is a simple studio sketch, or rather a study, after nature, of a goldfinch perched on his box, hung up on a pale wall, which recalls the clear pale backgrounds that van der Meer seems to have liked. It is painted with beautiful touches, very strong in accent and luminous in colour. Below the bird is the signature C. FABRITIUS, and the date 1654, the exact year of the explosion of the powder-magazine at Delft.

W. BÜRGER (pseudonym of E. J. TH. THORÉ),
Galerie d'Arenberg, 1859

Fabritius had been killed in the explosion of 1654. Thoré's is one of the earliest appreciations of his rare work; he later received as a gift from Camberlyn 'The Goldfinch' (now in the Mauritshuis, The Hague).

FAILURE

The Academy assembled, and the picture, exhibited on an easel, was submitted to the criticism of the Academicians, while Greuze, in no great state of anxiety, waited in an adjoining room. At the end of an hour, the double doors of the exhibition room were thrown open. Greuze entered. 'Monsieur,' said the Director, 'you have been received into the Academy. Approach, and take the oath.' When the formalities of the reception were over, the Director added: 'Monsieur, you have been received into the Academy, but it is as a painter of genre. The Academy took into consideration the excellence of your previous productions; it has closed its eyes to the present work, unworthy both of it and of you.' Greuze felt the force of this rebuff; the words pierced him. Professorial appointments, honours, titles – with a word, the Academy had denied to his ambitions all that was the exclusive privilege of the painter of history. Dazed, unhinged, Greuze, who had at the same time the pride and the timidity of a child, started to reply, to defend himself, to assert the excellence of his picture. The Academy listened smiling, and in the end Lagrenée, drawing a pencil from his pocket, went up to the picture and demonstrated the faults in the drawing.

EDMOND AND JULES DE GONCOURT, 'Greuze' in
French XVIII Century Painters

The picture was Greuze's only history picture, 'Septimius Severus reproaching his Son Caracalla' (1769), now in the Louvre, Paris.

I can hardly say that I was surprised at what I found – a canvas that was a mere dead blank, cracked and discoloured by time. This was his immortal work! Though not surprised, I confess I was powerfully moved, and I think that for five minutes I could not have trusted myself to speak. At last my silent nearness affected him; he stirred and turned, and then rose and looked at me with a slowly kindling eye. I murmured some kind ineffective nothings about his being ill and needing advice and care, but he seemed absorbed in the effort to recall distinctly what had last passed between us. 'You were right,' he said, with a pitiful smile, 'I am a dawdler! I am a failure! I shall do nothing more in this world. . . . Look at that canvas,' he went on, as I relieved my emotion in an urgent request that he would come home with me and dine. 'That was to have contained my masterpiece! Isn't it a promising foundation? The elements of it all are *here*.' And he tapped his forehead with that mystic confidence which had marked the gesture before. 'If I could only transpose them into some brain that has the hand, the will! Since I have been sitting here taking stock of my intellects, I have come to believe that I have the material for a hundred masterpieces. But my hand is paralysed now, and they will never be painted. . . .'

HENRY JAMES. *The Madonna of the Future*, 1873

Tuesday, 27 May [1884] – It is over. I have nothing.

But it is fearfully annoying; I went on hoping up to this morning. And if you knew the things to which they have given medals!!!

Why is that not disheartening for me? I am very surprised – if my painting is good, why is it not rewarded?

Intrigues . . . it will be said.

All the same, since it is good, how then does it happen that it is not rewarded? I don't want to pose as a simple child, unaware that intrigues exist; however, it seems to me that given a good thing. . . .

Is it, then, that it is bad? Not at all.

I have eyes even for what is my own . . . and, besides, the others!

And the forty periodicals!

Saturday, 31 May – Villevieille comes to tell me that I was not given a medal because I made some noise over the mention last year and that I haughtily treated the jury as idiots. . . . It's true that I did say that . . .

My picture is not perhaps very big and very bold, but if it were, *le Meeting* would be a masterpiece. Do they have to be masterpieces for small third medals? Baude's engraving has appeared with an article where it says that the public is disappointed to see me without a medal. . . . There is neither integrity nor justice. In the end, what can you believe? I feel absolutely at sea.

MARIE BASHKIRTSEFF, *Journal*

'Le Meeting' (of two Parisian urchins) had a great public success and became French state property. Marie Bashkirtseff, born in 1860, died later in 1884.

Indeed I was so sure of my success that the news of my rejection [by the Academy of Fine Arts in Vienna] took me completely by surprise, like a bolt from the blue. It was true, all the same. When I called on the director and asked to know on what grounds I had been denied admission to the general school of painting at the Academy, he assured me that the drawings I had submitted showed clearly that I was not equipped to become a painter, but that my talents evidently lay in the field of architecture. . . .

ADOLF HITLER, *Mein Kampf*, 1925

FAME

Once, Cimabue thought to hold the field
In painting; Giotto's all the rage today;
The other's fame lies in the dust concealed.

DANTE, *The Divine Comedy: Purgatory*, Canto XI

The first great care of one who seeks to obtain eminence in painting is to acquire the fame and renown of the ancients. It is useful to remember that avarice is always the enemy of virtue. Rarely can anyone given to acquisition of wealth acquire renown. I have seen many in the first flower of learning suddenly sink to money-making. As a result they acquire neither riches nor praise. However, if they had increased their talent with study they would easily have soared into great renown. Then they would have acquired much riches and pleasure.

LEON BATTISTA ALBERTI, *On Painting*, 1435–6

In fact, I maintain that it is fortunate for Parrhasius and the other ancient painters of the ancient world, that time has not allowed what they did to survive to our own day; for this is the reason why we who give credit to what the written page claims for them refrain from conceding you the palm which they would give you if they could judge with our eyes and hail you as the supreme sculptor, supreme painter and supreme architect.

In view of this, however, why are you not content with the glory you have already acquired? I believe it should be enough for you to have vanquished the others with the works you have already done. But I hear that with the *Last Judgement* which you are painting at present, you intend to outdo the *Creation of the World* which you have already painted, so that vanquishing with your own paintings what you have painted, you will triumph over yourself. . . .

But now, Sir, you must realise that the vow I made never to see Rome again will have to be broken because of my desire to see this great painting.

I would rather make a liar of myself than slight your genius, which I hope will approve the desire I have to spread its fame through the world.

PIETRO ARETINO, *Letter to Michelangelo*, 15 September 1537

. . . I have resolved to go down to posterity upon the hem of your garment.

SIR JOSHUA REYNOLDS

To Mrs Siddons on her posing for his prominently signed portrait of her as 'The Tragic Muse', 1784

The sanctuary's gloom at least shall ward
  Vain tongues from where my pictures stand apart:
Only prayer breaks the silence of the shrine
  While, blackening in the daily candle-smoke,
They moulder on the damp wall's travertine,
  'Mid echoes the light footstep never woke.
So, die my pictures! surely, gently die!
  O youth, men praise so, – holds their praise its worth?
Blown harshly, keeps the trump its golden cry?
  Tastes sweet the water with such specks of earth?

ROBERT BROWNING, 'Pictor Ignotus' (*Dramatic Lyrics*, 1842)

The 'youth' is Raphael.

I should like to be illustrious and unknown.

EDGAR DEGAS

FANTIN-LATOUR

I found Fantin in a modest studio, in the Rue des Beaux-Arts. The studio walls were covered with canvases, mostly unframed; these were flower and still-life studies, small nudes, interiors, several self-portraits at different ages, many studies and copies after the old masters, including a superb copy of the *Marriage at Cana* by Paul Veronese, and two large paintings – the *Hommage à Delacroix* and a portrait of two ladies – his wife and sister-in-law, I found out later.

Fantin lived quietly with his wife, seeing scarcely anyone, occupied with his painting, or pottering over prints and drawings, or else going to the

Louvre, where he had passed so much of his life, copying. Everything about him was simple and unpretentious; a few commonplace chairs, a sofa, a small table, and many shabby, ample portfolios ranged against the walls. Here was just such a studio as Daumier drew and painted. And Fantin himself, stout, baggily dressed, with list slippers on his feet and a green shade over his eyes, looked like one of Daumier's artists. His talk was quiet and unpretentious; there were no fireworks nor sharp wit, as with Whistler or Degas, yet what he said was wise and to the point. I wish I had made notes of his talk; it would have been worth while; for he probably knew more about methods of painting than any other artist living. And he had been associated with, and had painted, the most gifted men of his time, Manet and Baudelaire – and how many others! In spite of his remarkable patient compositions, one of which, hanging in the Luxembourg, had long been familiar – no one, he said, ever asked him to paint a portrait. But for his friend, Mrs Edwin Edwards, he had scarcely been able to continue painting; through Mrs Edwards he sold many of his flower pieces to English collectors, and this made him feel very friendly towards England. He had a high opinion of Millais – of his earlier work especially. Fantin had been one of the pioneers of modern painting, but though he knew his own paintings were out of fashion, I never heard him complain. When Degas and others acquired his *Hommage à Delacroix*, and offered it to the Louvre, Fantin was quietly pleased. He knew the world and its vanities too well to be elated.

What pleased me most was that Fantin, being a middle-class Frenchman, painted middle-class life. He was of the company of Chardin, Daumier and Cézanne. In the portraits he painted there were no Coromandel screens or Louis XV settees; they were of ordinary men and women sitting in the rooms where they lived. So in his still-life paintings, the bottles of wine, the bread, fruit and knives on the rough linen table cloths, were usual on any French bourgeois table.

Fantin's studio always gave me a sense of rest and security; and his active encouragement of my own efforts (he actually offered to sit to me, although he said he had never before been model to anyone save himself) was generous and heartening.

William Rothenstein, *Men and Memories*, 1931

Rothenstein's visit to Fantin-Latour took place in or around 1895.

FOIBLES

He could not stand babies crying, men coughing, bells ringing, or friars chanting, and when the rain was pouring down from the sky, he loved to watch it as it ricocheted off the roof-tops and hurtled on to the ground. He went in terror of lightning, and when the thunder roared he would wrap himself up in his cloak, shut fast the doors and windows, and crouch in a corner of the room till the storm abated.

GIORGIO VASARI, *'Life' of Piero di Cosimo*, 1568

Pontormo had some very odd traits, and was so fearful of death that he would not even hear it mentioned, and he fled from having to encounter dead bodies. He never went to festivals, or to any places where people get together, to avoid being caught in a crowd; and he was solitary beyond all belief.

GIORGIO VASARI, *'Life' of Pontormo*, 1568

He was by nature acquisitive and thrifty, and he was also very faint-hearted, in fact, he was so timid that he would climb on top of the church spire in order to watch the parade of the militia because he was afraid of the shooting, thinking he might not be safe elsewhere.

CAREL VAN MANDER, *'Life' of Maerten Heemskerck*, 1604

He always had a fear of poison and of witchcraft. Because of this he did not want any woman in his house. He hated to deal with them, but when he had to he pulled himself away quickly. He was afraid of old women and fled from them, complaining that every time he went shopping or stopped to do business he always found one near him. He wanted to have servants who were extremely simple if not actually simple-minded. . . .

Having lost one of his slippers about the house he went into a rage because of his suspicion of sorcery. The same thing happened when he found a woman's blouse among his linens. He quickly had the linens rinsed in pure water and dried, and from then on he wanted his Marco to do the laundry himself at the house.

C. C. MALVASIA, *'Life' of Guido Reni*, 1678

The spirit of isolation belonged markedly to Sargent. He had . . . no business instinct whatever; he left the management of his affairs to others and was ignorant of the way they were conducted. He extended this ignorance, coupled with considerable indifference, to the administration of the world's affairs. He read no newspapers; he had the sketchiest knowledge of current movements outside art; his receptive credulity made him accept fabulous items of information without question. He would have been puzzled to answer if he were asked how nine-tenths of the population lived; he would have been dumbfounded if asked how they were governed.

EVAN CHARTERIS, *John Sargent*, 1927

FORGERY

A forgery done by a contemporary is not infrequently successful from being pleasant and plausible, precisely because something in it responds to our natural habit of vision; because the forger has understood, and misunderstood, the old master in the same way as ourselves. Here is, say, a 'Jan van Eyck' – thus the great venerable name, and yet something that has attractiveness in conformity with the taste linked up with our own time: how could it fail to gain applause under such circumstances? To many lovers of art a false Memling is the first Memling that gave pleasure.

I remember how, years ago, an art dealer submitted to me drawings after Holbein's *Dance of Death*, claiming them as originals from the master's hand and referring to the fact that pathos and emotional expression made a stronger appeal in the drawings than in the woodcuts. The observation was accurate; the drawings were, however, imitations of recent date. Holbein, in the woodcut, in the design upon a small scale, has made the motifs of movement – not the facial features – the vehicle of expression: and in this he followed the sure sense of style characteristic of him. The copyist took as his starting-point neither vision nor the requirements of the woodcut, but the intellectual significance of the tragic theme; and, by petty strokes of the pen, he heightened the expression of fear and distress in the heads.

Above all things I would not wish that my argument produced the impression that I feel sure of myself. This is by no means the case. Not only I, but also my teachers – for whom I have the greatest regard – have been taken in – though in truth, it seemed impossible to understand, later on, how this had come about.

The eye sleeps until the spirit awakes it with a question. And the question 'Is this work ancient or not?' will at times not be asked, especially not when a dealer deserving of confidence submits the object with the power of suggestion springing from a good conscience and a demand for a high price.

Novel forgeries tend to be most immediately successful. It is easier to deduce from certain characteristics 'This is the work of a forger I know' than to argue negatively 'This cannot be genuine'. In order to give pictures the look of age, the forgers imitate the cracks of the stratum of colour, and this all the more keenly since the wrinkles in the skin of the picture are noted by less gifted amateurs as the only indication of age and genuineness. There exist many genuine pictures which show no cracks, but these are never absent in false ones. The *craquelure* caused by age differs more or less clearly from the one achieved artificially. The primitive method of making cracks by drawing or scratching with pencil or brush is held in contempt by the forgers of our day. It is customary to resort to the trick of producing false cracks by a chemical action – say by sudden heating which causes a coating and breaks up the colour surface lattice-fashion. . . .

More danger has come to attach to the falsification – a defiling of works of art which is difficult to combat – than to the forgery in the strict sense of the word. Let us say that a dealer possesses a Dutch 17th century landscape which has suffered greatly. From certain indications he considers it – though wrongly – to be a work by Hercules Seghers, all the more gladly as the works by this master are scarce and valuable. He hands the picture over to an able restorer, supervises its cleaning, and supplies reproductions of genuine works in support of his attribution and in order to instruct the restorer. The latter, without any evil intention, is thus inspired to re-interpret certain passages in the picture 'in the style of Seghers'. Under the delusion that he has in front of him a work by the master, he restores it. By slow degrees, proceeding from case to case, the *bona fide* restoration approaches the malevolent falsification. At times pictures in poor condition have been shown to me. Of one such I will have said for instance: 'This is in the manner of Holbein.' And before long it was once again submitted to me, neatly completed and with beautiful clearness showing the style of Holbein.

MAX J. FRIEDLÄNDER, *On Art and Connoisseurship*, 1942

FRAMES

When you receive yours [picture of 'The Israelites Gathering Manna'], I beg of you, if you like it, to provide it with a small frame; it needs one so that, in considering it in all its parts, the eyesight may remain concentrated, and not distracted beyond the limits of the picture by receiving impressions of objects which, seen pell-mell with the painted objects, confuse the light.

It would be very suitable if the said frame were gilded quite simply with dull gold, as it blends very softly with the colours without disturbing them.

NICOLAS POUSSIN, *Letter from Rome to Paul de Fréart, sieur de Chantelou*, 28 April 1639

Derby, 6 June, 1774

Sir,

I shall be obliged if you will inform Mr Martin that the picture of *The Earth Stopper* is to be delivered to Lord Hardwicke without the frame. The shabby price his Lordship is to pay for it will leave no room for his Lordship to expect the frame with it; but if he should say anything about it pray inform his Lordship that *The Earth Stopper* was exhibited in an old Italian moulding frame which I have had by me for many years and keep for the use of the exhibition, and on no account let him have it.

I am, your very humble servant

JOH. WRIGHT

Joseph Wright's lively letter was addressed to the Secretary of the Incorporated Society of Artists in London. Wright was an early supporter of it.

FRAME is a decoration, which like every other decoration must not spoil the subject decorated. And it will spoil [it] if through too great lavishness and the multiplicity of its richness it distracts attention from the principal object. The fine arts are like fine ladies, whose beauty gives emphasis to their adornment.

The chief merit of *frames* is to be in proportion to the work they serve; to be simple, and suitable for the works and the locations.

FRANCESCO MILIZIA, *Dizionario delle Belle Arti del disegno . . . dalla Enciclopedia Metodica*, Volume I, 1797

I am not too sure how this study ['Cypresses'] ought to be framed, but seeing that it makes one think of those delightful Scottish materials I have noticed that a *very simple flat frame* of BRIGHT ORANGE LEAD achieves the desired effect with the blues of the background and the dark greens of the trees. Without that there would not perhaps be sufficient red in the picture and the upper part might look a little cold.

VINCENT VAN GOGH, *Letter to his brother Theo*, 1890

THE FRENCH SCHOOL

In writing on the Salon of 1767 for his friend, Baron Grimm, Diderot drew up a detailed account of the current state of the French School which is both acute and tart in its end-of-term tone, while tending to be too gloomy. The extract below conveys the flavour, though somewhat shortened.

MICHEL VAN LOO, *Director of the School*. – He possesses draughtsmanship, colour, good sense and truth. He is excellent for large family groups. He paints fabrics wonderfully, and there are good portraits by him.
HALLÉ. – Poor creature.
VIEN. – Beyond dispute the prime painter of the school, for technique, I mean. For the ideal and for poetry, it is another matter. He can draw and colour, he is sensible – too sensible perhaps, but in all his compositions there reign a style and harmony that enchant you. *Sapit antiquum* ['He knows antiquity']. He is capable of both easel pictures and large-scale works.
LA GRENÉE. – Frigid artist, but excellent in small subjects. It is as with Guido. One day his small pictures will be worth their weight in gold. He can draw, he has a feeling for colour. But the larger his canvas becomes, the more his talent dwindles.

BELLE. – Belle is a nonentity.

BACHELIER. – Was formerly a good painter of flowers and animals. Since he became a leading painter of the school, he has become nothing. There are pictures of animals by this artist in our royal palaces that are painted with great vigour.

CHARDIN. – The greatest magician that we have had. His early small pictures are already sought after, as if he were no longer alive. Admirable painter of genre; but he is passing away.

VERNET. – Excellent man in every aspect of painting; great painter of seascapes and landscapes.

MILLET. – Nonentity.

LUNDBERG. – Nonentity.

LE BEL. – Nonentity.

PERRONEAU. – Did previously achieve something in pastel painting.

JULLIART. – Nothing.

VOIRIOT. – Like Julliart.

DOYEN. – Takes second place for large-scale work; but I fear he will never take first.

CASANOVA. – Good, very good for landscape and battle-pictures.

BAUDOIN. – Our friend Baudoin – negligible.

ROLAND DE LA PORTE. – Not without merit. There are some paintings by him of fruit and animals that it would be wrong to despise.

ROBERT. – Excellent painter of ancient ruins. Great artist.

MADAME THERBOUCHE. – Excellent, if she had talent equivalent to a tenth part of her vanity. Her colouring and warmth cannot be denied. Everything militates against the good she would have attained had she been young and amenable. Her talent is not commonplace for woman, and for a woman who is self-taught.

PARROCEL. – Nothing; less than nothing.

BRENET. – Overcome by domestic cares.

BOUCHER. – I almost forgot him. He will scarcely leave a name, and yet he could have been the best of all, had he so wished.

DESHAYS. – Bad.

LEPICIÉ. – Poor artist.

FRAGONARD. – He has painted one very fine picture. Can he paint a second? I don't at all know.

RESTOUT. – One must wait and see. Perhaps there will be something; perhaps nothing.

JOLLAIN. – Very definitely nothing.

DURAMEAU. – I had the highest opinion of this man; he could let me down.

RENOU. – Your humble servant, Monsieur Renou.

CARESME. – I recall poor paintings and very good drawings by him.

BEAUFORT. – I am not aware of him. Bad sign.

DENIS DIDEROT, 'The Salon of 1767'

CASPAR DAVID FRIEDRICH

Friedrich has now been given a task: someone wants to have two pictures – one representing an Italian landscape in all its luxuriant and magnificent beauty, the other – the awe-inspiring nature of the North. It is the second that Friedrich has undertaken to paint; he does not know what it will be. He is waiting for the moment of inspiration, which frequently comes to him, as he told me, in a dream. 'Sometimes,' he said, 'I try to think and nothing comes of it; but it happens that I doze off and suddenly feel as though someone is rousing me. I am startled, open my eyes, and what my mind was looking for stands before me like an apparition – at once I seize my pencil and draw; the main thing has been done.'

V. A. ZHUKOVSKY, *Letter from Dresden to the Grand Duchess Alexandra Fedorovna of Russia*, 23 June 1821

The artist should not only paint what he sees before him, but also what he sees within him. If, however, he sees nothing within him, then he should also omit to paint that which he sees before him. Otherwise his pictures will resemble those folding screens behind which one expects to find only the sick or even the dead.

C. D. FRIEDRICH, *Observations*, c.1830

GAINSBOROUGH

If ever this nation should produce genius sufficient to acquire to us the honorable distinction of an English School, the name of Gainsborough will be transmitted to posterity, in the history of the Art, among the very first of that rising name.

Sir Joshua Reynolds, *Discourse XIV*, 10 December 1788

The fact is that Gainsborough never even painted his men as men or his women as women. He painted individuals; he did not underline the fact that they were men or women, or lords or ladies, or his own bourgeois daughters. All that comes out by the way; he is at no pains to tell us about it. He paints human beings, and he makes them live for us in their particular personal characters. But even *that* is not underlined – it emanates from the image as we contemplate it. For it would be a mistake to suppose that Gainsborough was intensely preoccupied with the psychological aspect of his sitters. He had nothing of the intense and penetrating curiosity about the drama of human life of a Rembrandt, nor even that half pathetic, comedic sense which animates Watteau's figures. It is rather that the clarity and sincerity of his vision inevitably bring their character before us. And one guesses too that he never dictated a pose to his sitters; he let his design and his general conception of the picture grow out of whatever appeared most easy and natural to them. . . .

And with all that easy simplicity of presentment there is, none the less, a mood superadded. However plain and direct a statement Gainsborough makes, he can never make it in prose. Always there is just that heightening of the emotional pitch which makes poetry.

Roger Fry, *Reflections on British Painting*, 1934

GAUGUIN'S ISLAND

The venerable frangipani tree growing from the head of Gauguin's grave was putting forth such a stupendous show of blooms that it may have taken root in his skull. One of the branches bore a length of knotted rag which, on closer examination, turned out to be a silk scarf inscribed with strange, gnomic verses. Written in English and addressed to the artist, they contained reproachful reminders of his desertion of his family and presumed insanity – but concluded on a conciliatory note:

'Now Mette brings you flowers

The first you ever got
From Denmark, where you're still alive
In our flesh and blood.'

The scarf, signed 'On behalf of your descendants in Denmark, Alice and Mette', was dated October 1987.

This was a personal matter, of course (Mette had also been the name of Gauguin's Danish wife), but I felt his remains would rest a little easier when the climate had finally disposed of the scarf, just as it disposed of Mette's Danish flowers. I imagined them lying here, wintry, Nordic, utterly eclipsed by the wild eruption of primary colours all around.

In this respect the islanders of Hiva Oa, in the Marquesas, have served him well, turning the quiet little hill-top cemetery into a remarkable natural garden. The frangipani by the grave was one of many planted in his immediate vicinity, carpeting the ground with white and gold blossoms that gave off tiny vortices of fragrance when trodden on. There were also massed banks of hibiscus, bougainvillaea, poinsettia, wild orchids and tiger lilies, which filtered and deepened the light around the grave, giving it the pellucid quality of stained glass.

Crouching beside the head of the tomb – slabs of heavy rust-coloured island rock with the legend 'Paul Gauguin 1903' inscribed in pink paint – I looked along his lines of sight, as it were, and noted the 4,000-foot-high spire of Mount Temetiu, soaring overhead. Frigate birds rode the thermals like lifts. Thunder rumbled somewhere in the cloud forest (marked 'nuage' and left blank on the map). Orange butterflies with the wingspan of pigeons drifted by. In a small house down the hill someone strummed a ukelele. I could hear children's voices. Cooling air indicated rain within the hour. It was ironic, I reflected, that the aggrieved Danes waited so long to make their journey when it would have taken them only two minutes here to understand Gauguin's reasons for coming.

Today the island lives casually with his memory. There are no monuments and, aside from the grave, nothing overt to indicate he had ever passed this way. But during my week-long visit, the Magasin Pierre Shan, a two-storeyed wooden shop once patronised by the artist himself, received a shipment of Gauguin T-shirts and suddenly, all over the place, people were wearing his paintings.

ALEXANDER FRATER in the *Observer Magazine*, 8 January 1989

GENIUS

Gentlemen,
The highest ambition of every Artist is to be thought a man of Genius. As long as this flattering quality is joined to his name, he can bear with patience

the imputation of carelessness, incorrectness, or defects of whatever kind.

So far indeed is the presence of Genius from implying the absence of faults, that they are considered by many as its inseparable companions. Some go such lengths as to take indications from them, and not only excuse faults on account of Genius, but presume Genius from the existence of certain faults.

It is certainly true, that a work may justly claim the character of Genius, though full of errors; and it is equally true, that it may be faultless, and yet not exhibit the least spark of Genius. This naturally suggests an enquiry, a desire at least of enquiring, what qualities of a work and of a workman may justly entitle a Painter to that character.

I have in a former discourse [III] endeavoured to impress you with a fixed opinion, that a comprehensive and critical knowledge of the works of nature is the only source of beauty and grandeur. But when we speak to Painters we must always consider this rule, and all rules, with a reference to the mechanical practice of their own particular Art. It is not properly in the learning, the taste, and the dignity of the ideas, that Genius appears as belonging to a painter. There is a Genius particular and appropriated to his own trade, (as I may call it,) distinguished from all others. For that power, which enables the Artist to conceive his subject with dignity, may be said to belong to general education; and is as much the Genius of a Poet, or the professor of any other liberal Art, or even a good Critick in any of those arts, as of a Painter. Whatever sublime ideas may fill his mind, he is a Painter only as he can put in practice what he knows, and communicate those ideas by visible representation.

SIR JOSHUA REYNOLDS, *Discourse XI*,
10 December 1782

GENTILE DA FABRIANO

I stopped before a Gentile da Fabriano, a master I adore because he was so respectful of the things he painted; he takes us into a paradise always simple but not without a radiance of glory. His Christ and his Virgin have the innocence of those who are so good that they fall victim to scoundrels, but at the same time they are armed with the grace that made lions recoil in past ages, when human beasts persecuted the new believers. He doesn't give us an exact image of paradise like Fra Angelico, he doesn't paint God the Father with a white silken beard of real hair, and pink cheeks; he doesn't give us groupings of angels touched by the miracle of adolescence and dressed in trains made of silk rent from the heavens in their flight; he doesn't bathe his world in a blue haze peculiar to himself and the monk caught in his ecstatic reverie; Gentile da Fabriano's paradise is not really seen. He paints on a golden background, and it is in this gold, or behind this crackled metal veil, or before it perhaps, or before us – who can tell? – that his paradise is found; I would say that he pours it into us, the beholders, whereas we are ourselves drawn into that of Fra Angelico. To attain Fra Angelico's paradise, we would make any promise, but to enter Gentile da Fabriano's we must have been good all our lives.

René Gimpel, *Diary of an Art Dealer*, 16 May 1924

Gimpel is writing of visiting the Brera, in Milan; the picture is the polyptych of the Coronation of the Virgin.

ARTISTIC GEOGRAPHY

It is singular that Collinson should, throughout his composition, speak of Nazareth as being on the sea-shore – which is the reverse of the fact. The Præraphaelites, with all their love of exact truth to nature, were a little arbitrary in applying the principle; and Collinson seems to have regarded it as quite superfluous to look into a map, and see whether Nazareth was near the sea or not. Or possibly he trusted to Dante Rossetti's poem 'Ave', in which likewise Nazareth is a marine town. My brother advisedly stuck to this in 1869, when I pointed out the error to him: he replied, 'I fear the sea must remain at Nazareth: you know an old painter would have made no bones if he wanted it for his background.'

William Michael Rossetti, 1901

The painter James Collinson's 'composition' was a poem, 'The Child Jesus', published in The Germ, *no. 2, February 1850, accompanied by an etching of his; he resigned from the Pre-Raphaelite Brotherhood after being converted to Roman Catholicism.*

GIFTS

Your Excellency – If a feeling of delicacy on your part will not admit of accepting the offer I made you, on behalf of the nation, of such trifles in the Royal Palace of San Ildefonso as might have been most agreeable to you, I cannot overlook the deep obligation of my country to the hero of Great Britain, and the Regent would justly resent any indifference on my part in showing the gratitude due to the Liberator of Spain. As I believe you take a particular interest in pictures, I take the liberty of presenting to you the twelve best and most artistic pictures which I have been able to find.

In the name of the Spanish Nation and the Government I beg that you will deign to accept this very small offering – the chief object of which is to show the gratitude and recognition of the Nation.

I pray the God of Armies to keep you in perfect health, and beg that you will favour me with the expression of your wishes on the subject.

RAMON LUIS ESCOVEDO, *Letter to the future Duke of Wellington*, 15 August 1812

Wellington had entered Madrid on 12 August, having defeated the French at the battle of Salamanca. Only two of these twelve pictures have been identified among the Duke's collection, but this was the first gift of its kind from Spain to him. Escovedo was Intendant of the Province of Segovia.

Would you be inclined to give Fritz and me an object for our birthdays which I saw at Rome and which would give us the very greatest pleasure? It is a picture. I do not know whether it is still to be had but I know the price was not outrageous. Would you telegraph to me whether you would do such a thing? Then I might leave directions at Rome for someone to see about it as I am afraid it will be gone.

You are always so very generous to us that I am almost ashamed of asking, but so early in the year I thought that you might not have settled birthday gifts yet, and that you might not mind fixing on this for us which would be the thing of all others to delight us, I fancy the picture is by Tintoretto (it is not much damaged). I shall only be three days at Rome therefore your telegram would have just time to reach me.

THE CROWN PRINCESS FREDERICK OF GERMANY, *Letter to Queen Victoria*, 18 April 1880

The following 1930s incident might come from a play by Noël Coward, though in fact he was merely one of the guests of Eleonora von Mendelssohn at Schloss Kammer, in upper Austria, when it took place.

Eleonora was, or gave the effect of being, romantically beautiful and she was also, perhaps, a little too intense. . . . Her great love at this time was for Toscanini; he was at Kammer and so, to Noël's joy, was Fritzi Massary, whom he had seen and adored in operette in Berlin. It was from Fritzi that I heard of Toscanini playing the piano at Kammer one evening after dinner. He played exquisitely, and cast a spell so strong that he ended in a hush too complete to be broken. Eleonora, typically, rose to her feet during the hush, then walked across the room, theatrically took a painting off the wall, brought it back in homage to the Maestro and said, 'This is my Guardi. It is for you.' Then the hubbub and applause did break out, only to subside when Toscanini consented to play once more. But the expectant silence was shattered by Eleonora's mother's loud cry: 'All ze ozzer pictures on ze wall are mine.'

COLE LESLEY, *The Life of Noël Coward*, 1976

GIORGIONE

My most illustrious and most Excellent, respected lady. I understood from what your Excellency wrote to me in your letter of the 25th of last month that you had heard that among the possessions and things left by the late Giorgio of Castelfranco there was a picture of a *Night-scene*, extremely beautiful and unusual; that being so, you would like to see about obtaining it. To which I answer your Excellency that the said Giorgio died some while ago of plague, and in order to serve you I have talked with several of my friends who were on very familiar terms with him, who assure me that in that estate there is no such picture. It is indeed true that the said Giorgio executed one such for Messer Taddeo Contarini, which as far as I can learn is not as fine as you would desire. Another Night-scene was done by the said Giorgio for a certain Vittorio Becharo, which – as far as I can learn – is better designed and executed than the Contarini one. But that Becharo is not at present to be found here, and from what I have been told, neither picture is for sale at any price, moreover both were done because their owners wanted to have them; so I regret not being able to meet the wish of your excellency. Venice, 7 November 1510.

[Your] Servant,

THADEUS ALBANUS

This very early letter from Taddeo Albano to Isabella d'Este, Marchioness of Mantua, not actually published until 1888, marks the start of the quest for Giorgione's rare pictures, and by chance initiates the myth around them and their creator.

Byron claimed to have little eye for paintings, and still less time for those who enthused over them. Nevertheless, he gave his old school friend, William Bankes, shrewd and perceptive advice when he encouraged him to buy the 'Judgement of Solomon', traditionally thought to be by Giorgione, though almost certainly by Sebastiano del Piombo: a fine Venetian painting of a rare kind, now in the Bankes Collection, Kingston Lacy (National Trust).

Ravenna, February 26th, 1820

Pulci and I are waiting for you with impatience; but I suppose we must give way to the attraction of the Bolognese galleries for a time. I know nothing of pictures myself, and care almost as little: but to me there are none like the Venetian – above all, Giorgione. I remember well his Judgment of Solomon in the Mariscalchi [collection] in Bologna. The real mother is beautiful, exquisitely beautiful. Buy her by all means, if you can, and take her home with you: put her in safety: for be assured there are troublous times brewing for Italy; and as I never could keep out of a row in my life, it will be my fate, I dare say, to be over head and ears in it; but no matter, these are the stronger reasons for coming to see me soon.

BYRON, *Letter to William Bankes*

I am not saying, mark you, that all passionate people are good painters, but I *do* say that all great artists have been men of passion. This is equally true of all the arts, from Giorgione dying of love at thirty-three because his pupil, Morto da Feltre, had run away with his mistress, to Mozart. . . .

STENDHAL, 'The Salon of 1824'

One of the wedges of light traced by the sun on the wall chanced to be projected against the window, and the scene acquired a gilded tint, warm and translucent, with which Giorgione's most sparkling canvas could not vie.

THÉOPHILE GAUTIER, *Mademoiselle de Maupin*, 1835

At last, with final mastery of all the technical secrets of his art, and with somewhat more than 'a spark of the divine fire' to his share, comes Giorgione. He is the inventor of *genre*, of those easily movable pictures which serve neither for uses of devotion, nor of allegorical or historic teaching – little groups of real men and women, amid congruous furniture or landscape – morsels of actual life, conversation or music or play, but refined upon or idealised, till they come to seem like glimpses of life from afar. Those spaces of more cunningly blent colour, obediently filling their places, hitherto, in a mere architectural scheme, Giorgione detaches from the wall. He frames them by the hands of some skilful carver, so that people may move them readily and take with them where they go, as one might a poem in manuscript, or a musical instrument, to be used, at will, as a means of self-education, stimulus or solace, coming like an animated presence, into one's cabinet, to enrich the air as if with some choice aroma, and, like persons, live with us, for a day or a lifetime. Of all art such as this, art which has played so large a part in men's culture since that time. Giorgione is the initiator. Yet in him too that old Venetian clearness or justice, in the apprehension of the essential limitations of the pictorial art, is still undisturbed. While he interfuses his painted work with a high-strung sort of poetry, caught directly from a singularly rich and high-strung sort of life, yet in his selection of subject, or phase of subject, in the subordination of mere subject to pictorial design, to the main purpose of a picture, he is typical of that aspiration of all the arts towards music, which I have endeavoured to explain, – towards the perfect identification of matter and form.

WALTER PATER, 'The School of Giorgione' in
The Fortnightly Review, 1877

GIOTTO

I turn now to the disposal of my other possessions. To my lord of Padua aforementioned, both since he by God's grace is not in want, and since I have nothing else worthy of him, I leave my portrait or rather representation of the Blessed Virgin Mary by the great painter Giotto, which was left to me by my friend Michele Vannis of Florence; the ignorant do not comprehend its beauty but the masters of art wonder at it.

PETRARCH, *His Will*, quoted in Vasari's 'Life' of Giotto, 1568

Petrarch died in 1374.

After dinner and rest from our dusty journeying, we took a carriage and went out to see the town, desiring most of all to see the Arena Chapel.

It stands apart, and is approached at present through a pretty garden. Here one is uninterruptedly with Giotto. The whole chapel was designed and painted by himself alone; and it is said that while he was at work on it, Dante lodged with him in Padua. The nave of the chapel is in tolerably good preservation, but the apsis has suffered severely from damp. It is in this apsis that the lovely Madonna, with the Infant at her breast, is painted in a niche, now quite hidden by some altarpiece or woodwork, which one has to push by in order to see the tenderest bit of Giotto's painting. This chapel must have been a blessed vision when it was fresh from Giotto's hand – the blue vaulted roof; the exquisite bands of which he was so fond, representing inlaid marble, uniting roofs and walls and forming the divisions between the various frescoes which cover the upper part of the wall. The glory of Paradise at one end, and the histories of Mary and Jesus on the two sides; and the subdued effect of the series of monochromes representing the Virtues and Vices below.

GEORGE ELIOT, *Journal*, June 1860

VAN GOGH

Ah, I shall never be able to convey my impressions of some faces I have seen here [Saint-Rémy]. Certainly this is the road on which there is something new, the road to the South, but men of the North have difficulty in penetrating it. And already I can see myself in the future, when I shall have had some success, regretting my solitude and my wretchedness here, when I saw between the iron bars of the cell the reaper in the field below. Misfortune is good for something.

To succeed, to have lasting prosperity, you must have a temperament different from mine; I shall never do what I might have done and ought to have wished and pursued.

But I cannot live, since I have this dizziness so often, except in a fourth or fifth rate condition. When I realize the worth and the originality and the superiority of Delacroix and Millet, for instance, then I am bold to say – yes, I am something. I can do something. But I must have a foundation in those artists, and then produce the little which I am capable of in the same direction.

VINCENT VAN GOGH, *Letter to his brother Theo*, early September 1889

We chose as example a common sort of equipment – a pair of peasant shoes. We do not even need to exhibit actual pieces of this sort of useful article in order to describe them. Everyone is acquainted with them. But since it is a matter here of direct description, it may be well to facilitate the visual realization of them. For this purpose a pictorial representation suffices. We shall choose a well-known painting by Van Gogh, who painted such shoes several times. But what is there to see here? Everyone knows what shoes consist of. If they are not wooden or bast shoes, there will be leather soles and uppers, joined together by thread and nails. Such gear serves to clothe the feet. Depending on the use to which the shoes are to be put, whether to work in the field or for dancing, matter and form will differ.

Such statements, no doubt correct, only implicate what we already know. The equipmental quality of equipment consists in its usefulness. But what about this usefulness itself? In conceiving it, do we already conceive along with it the equipmental character of equipment? In order to succeed in doing this, must we not look out for useful equipment in its use? The peasant woman wears her shoes in the field. Only here are they what they are. They are all the more genuinely so, the less the peasant woman thinks about the shoes while she is at work, or looks at them at all, or is even aware of them. She stands and walks in them. That is how shoes actually serve. It is in this process of the use of equipment that we must actually encounter the character of equipment.

As long as we only imagine a pair of shoes in general, or simply look at the empty, unused shoes as they merely stand there in the picture, we shall never discover what the equipmental being of the equipment in truth is. From Van Gogh's painting we cannot even tell where these shoes stand. There is nothing surrounding this pair of peasant shoes to which they might belong – only an undefined space. There are not even clods of soil from the field or the field-path sticking to them, which could at least hint at their use. A pair of peasant shoes and nothing more. And yet –

From the dark opening of the worn insides of the shoes the toilsome tread of the worker stares forth. In the stiffly rugged heaviness of the shoes there is the accumulated tenacity of her slow trudge through the far-spreading and ever-uniform furrows of the field swept by a raw wind. On the leather lie the dampness and richness of the soil. Under the soles slides the loneliness of the field-path as evening falls. In the shoes vibrates the silent call of the earth, its quiet gift of the ripening grain and its unexplained self-refusal in the fallow desolation of the wintry field. This equipment is pervaded by uncomplaining anxiety as to the certainty of bread, the wordless joy of having once more withstood want, the trembling before the impending childbed and shivering at the surrounding menace of death. This equipment belongs to the *earth*, and it is protected in the *world* of the peasant woman. From out of this protected belonging the equipment itself rises to its resting-within-itself. . . .

The repose of equipment resting within itself consists in its reliability. Only in this reliability do we discern what equipment in truth is. But we still know nothing of what we first sought: the thing's thingly character. And we know nothing at all of what we really and solely seek: the workly character of the work in the sense of the work of art.

Or have we already learned something unwittingly, in passing so to speak, about the work-being of the work?

The equipmental quality of equipment was discovered. But how? Not by a description and explanation of a pair of shoes actually present; not by a report about the process of making shoes; and also not by the observation of the actual use of shoes occurring here and there; but only by bringing ourselves before Van Gogh's painting. This painting spoke. In the vicinity of the work we were suddenly somewhere else than we usually tend to be.

MARTIN HEIDEGGER, *The Origin of the Work of Art*, 1950

GOYA

Don Francisco Goya has also worked for the Royal Tapestry Factory. He is a man of talent and spirit, who should make great progress in art if he continues to receive financial support from the Crown. He is already proving useful in the royal service.

A. R. MENGS

Goya was thirty when Mengs wrote this report, dated 18 June 1776; his work for the Royal Tapestry Factory was a series of cartoons chiefly of country subjects, now recognized as brilliant works of art in themselves.

A Collection of Prints of Capricious Subjects, Invented and Etched by Don Francisco Goya. Since the artist is convinced that the censure of human errors and vices (though they may seem to be the province of Eloquence and Poetry) may also be the object of Painting, he has chosen as subjects adequate for his work, from the multitude of follies and blunders common in every civil society, as well as from the vulgar prejudices and lies authorized by custom, ignorance or interest, those that he has thought most suitable matter for ridicule as well as for exercising the artificer's fancy [*fantasia*].

Diario de Madrid, 6 February 1799

First paragraph of the public announcement of Goya's 'Caprichos', probably written by himself.

Goya, nightmare full of things unknown,
Of foetuses cooking in the midst of witches' sabbaths,
Of old women at the glass and of young girls quite naked,
Adjusting their stockings nicely to tempt the demons.

CHARLES BAUDELAIRE, 'Les Phares': *Les Fleurs du Mal*, 1857

I asked her [Marie Laurencin] if she was influenced by her painter friends when she started; she said she wasn't and added: 'The greatest influence in my life has been Goya's. Many of my works on these walls are influenced by him. I lived with him a great deal during my five years of exile in Spain. I knew him before going there. Ah, I suffered deeply in Spain and painted only four canvases there.'

RENÉ GIMPEL, *Diary of an Art Dealer*, 25 May 1939

After Morocco, we'd gone to Madrid, my first time, to see the Velasquez pictures. I found the Goyas more stunning – all those rooms full of Goyas, they're fabulous; about six rooms in the Prado, beginning with the early works, when he painted pretty pictures of people dancing in sylvan glades, happy pictures, beautifully painted; then the portraits of the royal family, and finally those marvellous pictures he did in his old age, almost like Bacons. It's wonderful to go from the young, free, happy-go-lucky early Goyas, the pretty little scenes, to the late paintings. Marvellous! Great effect, wonderful effect. Much more impressive to me, than the Velasquez pictures. This was something I didn't expect.

DAVID HOCKNEY, *My Early Years*, 1988

EL GRECO

The works of this artist are almost entirely confined to Spain, where he passed the greater part of his life. His best productions are those he painted in imitation of his master [Titian], though he occasionally attempted an originality of style, in which he was totally unsuccessful. When he departs from the principles of Titian, he sinks into an extravagance of composition, with so impoverished a mode, both of drawing and colouring, that he no longer appears the same painter.

Bryan's Dictionary of Painters and Engravers, 1853 edn.

The artist, or lover of art, who has once beheld it ['The Burial of Count Orgaz' in Toledo], will never, as he rambles among the winding streets of the ancient city, pass the pretty belfry of that church [San Tomé] – full of horse-shoe niches and Moorish reticulations – without turning aside to gaze upon its superb picture once more. It hangs to your left, on the wall opposite to the high altar. Gonzalo Ruiz, Count of Orgaz – head of a house famous in romance – rebuilt the fabric of the church, and was in all respects so religious and gracious a grandee, that when he was buried in 1323 within these very walls, St Stephen and St Augustine came down from heaven, and laid his body in the tomb with their own holy hands, an incident which forms the subject of the picture. St Stephen is represented as a dark-haired youth of noble countenance, and St Augustine as a hoary old man wearing a mitre, both of them arrayed in rich pontifical vestments of gold tissue, embroidered with coloured figures, and at the bottom of St Stephen's robe a large piece of work representing his martyrdom. They support the dead count in their arms, and gently lower him into grave, shrouded, like a baron of Roslin, 'in his iron panoply'. Nothing can be finer than the execution and the contrast of these three heads; never was the image of the peaceful death of 'the just man' more happily conveyed than in the placid face and powerless form of the warrior; nor did Giorgione or Titian ever excel the splendid colouring of his black armour, rich with gold damascening.

Sir William Stirling-Maxwell, *Annals of the Artists of Spain*, 1891 edn.

In looking at any of the great compositions of El Greco's maturity, we must always remember that the intention of the artist was neither to imitate nature nor to tell a story with dramatic verisimilitude. Like the Post-Impressionists three centuries later, El Greco used natural objects as the raw material out of which, by the process of calculated distortion, he might create his own world of pictorial forms in pictorial space under pictorial illumination. Within this private universe he situated his religious subject-matter, using it as a vehicle for expressing what he wanted to say about life.

And what *did* El Greco want to say? The answer can only be inferred; but to me, at least, it seems sufficiently clear. Those faces with their uniformly rapturous expression, those hands clasped in devotion or lifted towards heaven, those figures stretched out to the point where the whole inordinately elongated anatomy becomes a living symbol of upward aspiration – all these bear witness to the artist's constant preoccupation with the ideas of mystical religion. His aim is to assert the soul's capacity to come, through effort and through grace, to ecstatic union with the divine Spirit. This idea of union is more and more emphatically stressed as the painter advances in years. The frontier between earth and heaven which is clearly defined in such works as *The Burial of Count Orgaz* and *The Dream of Philip II*, grows fainter and finally disappears. In the latest version of Christ's Baptism there is no separation of any kind. The forms and colours flow continuously from the bottom of the picture to the top. The two realms are totally fused.

ALDOUS HUXLEY, 'Variations on El Greco' in
Themes and Variations, 1950

THE GREEKS

Nothing would demonstrate more clearly the advantage of following the ancients rather than nature than to take two equally gifted youngsters and have one study the antique, the other nature alone. The second would depict nature as he found it; were he an Italian, he would perhaps paint like Caravaggio; were he a Fleming, he might at best approach Jordaens; as a Frenchman, he would paint like [Jacques] Stella. The first, however, would recreate nature in its essence; his figures would be like Raphael's.

Even if the imitation of nature could give the artist everything else, it would not yield him the essential truth of forms. That he can acquire only from the Greeks. In the statuary of the Greeks all aspects of natural and ideal beauty are merged and defined by the most noble of contours; or rather, this contour represents the highest concept of both. Euphranos, who flourished after the time of Zeuxis, is regarded as the first artist to have developed the grander style of contour. Among the modern artists, many have attempted to imitate the contour of the Greeks, but hardly anyone has succeeded. The great Rubens nowhere approached the Greek proportions, and those of his works that he did before his Italian journey and his study of antique art are the farthest removed from the Greek ideal . . .

However, it must be said in justice to some great artists, especially modern painters, that in certain cases they have deviated from the manner most common in the drapery of Greek figures without sacrifice of nature and truth. The Greek drapery, for the most part, imitates thin and wet garments; these, as the artist knows, cling closely to the skin, revealing the body beneath. The entire outer garment of the Greek woman consisted of very thin material; therefore it was called 'peplon', a veil. That the ancients did not always employ drapery broken with minute folds is shown in their high reliefs, their paintings, and especially, their busts. The splendid bust of

Caracalla among the Royal Antiquities at Dresden confirms this. In modern times artists have had to arrange one garment over another and at times have had to portray heavy garments that do not fall into folds as gently and flowingly as those of the ancients. This gave rise to the modern treatment of large drapery schemes in which the artist can display his mastery no less than in the customary style of the ancients. Carlo Maratta and Francesco Solimena may be said to have attained greatest perfection here. The new modern Venetian School has exaggerated this style and, by showing nothing but bold drapery schemes, has succeeded only in producing rigid and tinny garments.

Finally, the most prominent general characteristic of the Greek masterpieces is a noble simplicity and silent greatness in pose as well as in expression. As the depths of the sea remain always at rest, however the surface may be agitated, so the expression in the figures of the Greeks reveals in the midst of passion a great and steadfast soul.

J. J. WINCKELMANN, *Thoughts on the Imitation of Greek Art in Painting and Sculpture*, 1755

It was then that there was formed the sect of *thinkers* or *primitives*, for they were given indifferently both these names. Without speaking as yet of the singular principles on which they meant to practise the art of painting, it was agreed between them that, to protect themselves more firmly from the mannered and mincing customs of society in modern times, they would adopt Greek dress, and among those costumes, the ones that had been worn in ancient Greece; for, among them, Pericles was another Louis XIV and his century already savoured of decadence. In brief, they had their clothes tailored on the pattern of those covering the figures represented on Sicilian vases, reputed to be the oldest of all, and they let their hair and beards grow.

The number of those who had the strong will-power and the means to fulfil this desire was not large; it amounted to five or six; but they excited curiosity; and doubtless there are still people in Paris who must recall having seen, around 1799, two young men wearing beards, one dressed as Agamemnon, the other as Paris, in a Phrygian costume. I was on friendly terms with them both, but more especially with Agamemnon, who often came to my lodgings, to the great astonishment of the house-porter and my neighbours. . . .

Agamemnon gave me a striking proof [of his mind] by a judgment, no doubt exaggerated in its expression but true at bottom. After having spoken of Homer, one of our favourite topics of conversation, the name of Sophocles was pronounced and his tragedies passed under review with the respect due to a disciple of Homer, to a poet who had had the power to preserve intact the elevated traditions of Greek antiquity. But when by bad luck the name of Euripides escaped from my lips, at that name, my painter Agamemnon got up and angrily shouted in a scornful tone: '*Euripides? Vanloo! Pompadour! Rococo! It's like M. de Voltaire!*'

M. E. J. DELÉCLUZE, *Louis David, son école et son temps*, 1855

As Delécluze, himself a pupil of David, explains, these studio terms of abuse, using eighteenth-century names derisively, including that of a one-time premier peintre, *Carle van Loo, were to be applied to David when he exhibited 'The Rape of the Sabines' (Louvre, Paris).*

Me, I am a Greek.

J. A. D. INGRES

GRÜNEWALD

Into his novel 'Là-Bas' (1891) J.-K. Huysmans, art critic as well as novelist, inserted what is still the most hallucinatory description of the horrific aspect of Grünewald's art – writing at a time when the painter and his achievements were very little known or appreciated. What follows is only part of a lengthy passage on a Crucifixion by Grünewald.

The hour of putrefaction had arrived; the watery wound in the side streamed more thickly, soaking the hip with blood dark like the juice of mulberries; pinkish liquid, a sort of diluted whey resembling the Moselle *vins gris*, oozed from the chest and soaked the belly below which undulated a puffed-out patch of loin-cloth; then the knees, drawn together convulsively, brought the knee-caps into collision, and the twisted legs arched out all the way to the feet which, one crossed over the other, stretched and sprouted in full decay, turning green amid the torrents of blood. Those feet, spongy and distended, were horrible; their flesh swelled over the nail-head and their shrivelled toes conflicted with the imploring gesture of the hands, threatening, almost scratching at the iron-filled, ochre soil, like the purple earth of Thuringia, with the blue horn of their toe-nails.

This corpse in eruption was topped by a head huge and tormented; encircled by a shaggy crown of thorns, it hung, exhausted, with one sunken, barely-opened eye where still quivered a look of pain and fear; the face was distorted, the forehead creased, the cheeks drained, every battered feature dissolved, while the slack mouth grimaced, its jaw contracted in appalling, tetanus-like shock.

The agony must have been terrible, and the death throes had quenched the joy of the executioners as they fled.

Now, in a sky of nocturnal blueness, the Cross appeared to bend very low, almost touching the ground, watched over by two figures standing either side of Christ. One is the Virgin, her head covered by a rose-coloured hood the tone of watered blood, falling in serried pleats on top of an azure robe of long trailing folds: the Virgin rigid and with a face blanched and swollen from weeping, who sobs with staring eyes as her finger-nails press into her hands. The other figure is St John, looking like a vagrant or swarthy Swabian peasant, tall in stature, his beard frizzled into tiny curls, and wearing materials broadly scalloped as if carved from the bark of a tree, with a scarlet tunic and a cloak of leathery yellow whose lining, tucked up at the sleeves, showed the feverish green of unripe lemons. Drained by his tears but better able to endure than Mary, herself shattered and desolate though yet upright, he clasps his hands in a transport of emotion, straining up towards that corpse at which he gazes with raw, bloodshot eyes, and he chokes on a silent cry in the constriction of his hollow throat.

J.-K. Huysmans, *Là-Bas*, 1891

HANGING OF PICTURES

The Secretary read out a letter addressed by M. Oudry, Academician, to M. Chardin, Councillor, deputed by the King to arrange the pictures at the Salon, in which the Sieur Oudry complained of the judgment of the Academy's stewards in terms insulting both to it and to M. Chardin. Having heard the letter read, the Academy ordered its Secretary to write on its behalf to the Sr Oudry to inform him that he was forbidden to attend its meetings until, by proper amends, he had satisfied the Academy no less than M. Chardin; first, the Academy ordered that the two pictures by him which were in the Salon should be removed.

ACADÉMIE ROYALE, PARIS, *Procès-Verbaux*, 5 September 1761

Oudry was Jacques-Charles, son of the famous painter; on 26 September 1761, Chardin was present at the session of the Academy when a letter of apology from Oudry was read and accepted. Chardin's hanging of pictures at the Salon was usually praised.

Mr Gainsborough's Compls to the Gentlemen of the [Hanging] Committee, and begs pardon for giving them so much trouble; but he has painted the Picture of the Princesses, in so tender a light, that notwithstanding he approves very much of the established Line for strong Effects, he cannot possibly consent to have it placed higher than five feet & a half, because the likenesses & Work of the Picture will not be seen any higher; therefore at a word, he will not trouble the Gentlemen against their Inclination, but will beg the rest of his Pictures back again. Saturday Evening.

THOMAS GAINSBOROUGH, *Letter to the Hanging Committee of the Royal Academy*, 10 April 1784

Gainsborough's pictures were returned; he never again exhibited at the Royal Academy.

Lawrence is very anxious about the arrangements [for hanging at the Royal Academy exhibition]. He has placed two very bad half lengths over his *Circular picture* on acct. of their being *low in tone*. He removed his picture of Mr Baker from the *fire* side of the room thinking His portrait of Sir Joseph Banks wd. appear better there. When the exchange had been made Westall told Him that the picture of Sir Joseph hurt a picture of his but as Lawrence was not moved by that Westall sd. it might remain & He wd. work upon his picture to make it suit the other better. – Some time after

Lawrence came into the room and found a picture of Northcote's placed by His of Mr Baker at the head of the room, against which he exclaimed as injuring the effect of his picture. He wished to have Northcote's removed, but Westall did not think it injured His picture & sd. there was no place for Northcote's. On this he removed Mr Bakers picture to its former situation & placed Sir Joseph's as before next to Northcote's. – His portrait of Lord Ellenborough was on the door side between a whole length by Opie & one by Shee, but He placed the whole lengths together & put Lord Ellenborough next to Shee. – Rigaud & Cosway have been anxious to have the Historical Pictures by [Dubost] the Frenchman, well placed. Lawrence has nearly the whole of the half length portrait of Lord Malmsbury to finish & something to do to others. – He is there constantly.

Thomson is also there but not for the purpose of painting. He is afraid the *light through the door* may affect His large picture which is placed on that side of the room.

JOSEPH FARINGTON, *Diary*, 12 April 1806

At the end of the day we were asking ourselves how on earth everything was going to be ready by the next day [the opening of the Berthe Morisot memorial exhibition], and we arranged to meet in the morning, but a decision had to be made as to whether the screen should be put with the drawings and water-colours in the middle of the big gallery where it cut the room into two and prevented one being able to view the large paintings such as the CERISIERS, the copy after Boucher, L'OIE, etc., in proper perspective, as well as other smaller ones whose tones look so harmonious next to each other when seen from a distance. Monsieur Degas would not hear a word about the general effect. 'There's no such thing as the general effect,' he said. 'Only imbeciles see a general effect. What on earth is it supposed to mean when one writes in a newspaper that the general impression of this year's salon is much better than that of last year's?' Towards 6 o'clock, night began to fall, only the paintings retaining a few rays of light which illuminated them; all those portraits of young girls seeming more and more alive and the screen even more of a barrier than ever. Monsieur Monet asked M. Degas if he wouldn't mind trying the infamous screen in the end gallery the next day, but M. Degas claimed that the drawings on it wouldn't be visible – 'Those drawings are superb, I think more of them than of all these paintings.' 'The screen in the gallery full of drawings would give it an intimate, quite charming atmosphere,' said Monsieur Mallarmé. 'It will confuse the public to see drawings in the middle of the paintings.'

'Do I care a jot about the public,' shouted M. Degas. 'They see nothing – it's for myself, for ourselves, that we are mounting this exhibition; you can't honestly mean that you want to teach the public to see?'

'Certainly I do,' replied M. Monet, 'we want to try. If we put on this exhibition just for ourselves, it won't be worth going to the trouble of hanging all these paintings; we could quite simply look at them on the floor.'

During this discussion M. Renoir told us that what he wanted to do was put the couch in the middle of the room; in fact it would be rather pleasant to be able to sit down while viewing but M. Degas wouldn't hear of it. 'I would stay on my feet for thirteen hours at a time if I had to,' he shouted.

It was dark by then, and, as he spoke, M. Degas paced back and forth in his great hooded cape and top hat, his silhouette looking very comical; M. Monet, also on his feet, was beginning to shout; Mallarmé was trying to smooth things over; M. Renoir, exhausted, was stranded on a chair. The Durand-Ruel men were laughing, and declared, 'He'll never give in.' Mlle Blanche, Jeannie, and I were just listening.

'You want me to remove this screen which I *adore*,' M. Degas said, emphasizing the last word.

'*We* adore Mme Manet,' retorted M. Monet. 'It's not a question of the screen but one of Mme Manet's exhibition. Let's have it understood that we'll try the screen in the other room tomorrow.'

JULIE MANET, *Diary*, 4–6 March 1896

HISTORY PAINTING

The *istoria* which merits both praise and admiration will be so agreeably and pleasantly attractive that it will capture the eye of whatever learned or unlearned person is looking at it and will move his soul. That which first gives pleasure in the *istoria* comes from copiousness and variety of things. In food and in music novelty and abundance please, as they are different from the old and the usual. So the soul is delighted by all copiousness and variety. For this reason copiousness and variety please in painting. I say that *istoria* is most copious in which in their places are mixed old, young, maidens, women, youths, young boys, fowls, small dogs, birds, horses, sheep, buildings, landscapes and all similar things. I will praise any copiousness which belongs in that *istoria*. Frequently the copiousness of the painter begets much pleasure when the beholder stands staring at all the things there. However, I prefer this copiousness to be embellished with a certain variety, yet moderate and grave with dignity and truth. I blame those painters who, where they wish to appear copious, leave nothing vacant. It is not composition but dissolute confusion which they disseminate. There the *istoria* does not appear to aim to do something worthy but rather to be in tumult.

LEON BATTISTA ALBERTI, *On Painting*, 1435–6

Before I had done any thing of much consequence in this work [modern moral subjects], I entertained some hopes of succeeding in what the puffers in books call *the great style of History painting*; so that without having had a stroke of this *grand* business before, I quitted small portraits and familiar conversations, and, with a smile at my own temerity, commenced history painter, and on a great staircase at St Bartholomew's Hospital, painted two Scripture stories, *the Pool of Bethesda* and the *Good Samaritan*, with figures seven feet high. These I presented to the Charity, and thought they might serve as a specimen to shew that, were there an inclination in England for encouraging historical pictures, such a first essay might prove the painting them more easily attainable than is generally imagined. But as religion, the great promoter of this style in other countries, rejected it in England, I was unwilling to sink into a *portrait manufacturer*; and, still ambitious of being singular, dropped all expectation of advantage from that source, and returned to the pursuit of my former dealings with the public at large.

William Hogarth, *Anecdotes of William Hogarth, written by himself*, 1833

HOGARTH

It is the force of these kindly admixtures [of comedy and tragedy], which assimilates the scenes of Hogarth and of Shakespeare to the drama of real life, where no such thing as pure tragedy is to be found; but merriment and infelicity, ponderous crime and feather-light vanity, like twi-formed births, disagreeing complexions of one intexture, perpetually unite to shew forth motley spectacles to the world. Then it is that the poet or painter shows his art, when in the selection of these comic adjuncts he chooses such circumstances as shall relieve, contrast with, or fall into, without forming a violent opposition to, his principal subject. Who sees not the Grave-digger in *Hamlet*, the Fool in *Lear*, have a kind of corresponding to, and fall in with, the subjects which they seem to interrupt; while the comic stuff in *Venice Preserved*, and the doggerel nonsense of the Cook and his poisoning associates in the *Rollo* of Beaumont and Fletcher, are pure, irrelevant, impertinent discords, – as bad as the quarrelling dog and cat under the table of the *Lord and the Disciples at Emmaus* of Titian?

Charles Lamb, 'Essay on the Genius and Character of Hogarth', 1811

His lively conversation – his knowledge of character – his readiness of speech – and quickness of retort, made many covet his company, who were sometimes the objects of his satire; but he employed his wit on those who were present, and spared or defended the absent. His personal spirit was equal to his satiric talents; he provoked, with his pencil, the temper of those whom it was not prudent to offend; with him no vice nor folly found shelter behind wealth, or rank, or power. As to the license of his tongue, he himself often said that he never uttered that sentence about a living man which he would not repeat gladly to his face: as to his works, he always felt conscious of their merit, and predicted with equal openness that his name would descend with no decrease of honour to posterity. He loved state in his dress, good order in his household, and the success of his works enabled him to indulge in the luxuries of a good table and pleasant guests.

ALLAN CUNNINGHAM, *Lives of the Most Eminent British Painters . . .*, 1829

HANS HOLBEIN THE YOUNGER

My most bounden duty remembered unto Your good Lordship. Pleaseth the same to be advertised, that the 10th of this present month in the evening arrived here [Brussels] your Lordship's servant Philip Hoby, accompanied with a servant of the King's Majesty's named Mr Hans, by which Philip I received your Lordship's letter bearing date at St James's the second day of this present. The effect whereof perceived, having the day before sent one of my servants towards your Lordship with a picture of the Duchess of Milan, I thought it very necessary to stay the same, for that in my opinion it was not so perfect as the cause required, neither as the said Mr Hans could make it. . . .

And for as much as your Lordship had heard great commendation of the form, beauty, wisdom and other virtuous qualities the which God had indued the said Duchess with, you could perceive no mean more meet for the advancement of the same [the project of her marriage to Henry VIII], than to procure her perfect picture; for which your Lordship had sent, in company of your said servant, a man very excellent in the making of physiognomies; so that your Lordship's desire was that your said servant might in most humblest wise salute the Duchess' Grace, requiring that her pleasure might be to appoint the time and place, where the said painter might accomplish his charge. . . . The next day following, at one of the clock in the afternoon, the said Lord Benedict came for Mr Hans; who having but three hours' space hath shown himself to be master of that science, for it is very perfect; the other [portrait] is but slobbered in comparison to it, as by the sight of both your Lordship shall well perceive.

JOHN HUTTON, *Letter to Thomas Cromwell*, 14 March 1538

Hutton was English agent in Brussels. This letter to Cromwell in London is probably the most vivid contemporary tribute to Holbein's art. From what must have been a drawing or watercolour of the Duchess, he afterwards painted the full-length portrait of her now in the National Gallery. She did not marry Henry VIII.

We saw the Munster and the Museum [at Basel] – where there is a noble dead Christ by the younger Holbein, but the other Holbeins were unimpressive.

GERARD MANLEY HOPKINS, *Journal*, 1868

I turned into the National Gallery yesterday where I saw for the first time the new acquisition, Holbein's *Ambassadors*, a damned ugly picture I assure you.

AUBREY BEARDSLEY, *Letter to G. F. Scotson-Clark*, 9 August 1891

I am beginning to feel somewhat ashamed of what I said about Holbein's *Ambassadors*. I have seen it several times since.

AUBREY BEARDSLEY, *Letter to G. F. Scotson-Clark*, *c.* September 1891

WINSLOW HOMER

He not only has no imagination, but he contrives to elevate this rather blighting negative into a blooming and honourable positive. He is almost barbarously simple, and, to our eye, he is horribly ugly; but there is nevertheless something one likes about him. What is it? For ourselves, it is not his subjects. We frankly confess that we detest his subjects – his barren plank fences, his glaring, bald, blue skies, his big, dreary, vacant lots of meadows, his freckled, straight-haired Yankee urchins, his flat-breasted maidens, suggestive of a dish of rural doughnuts and pie, his calico sun-bonnets, his flannel shirts, his cowhide boots. He has chosen the least pictorial features of the least pictorial range of scenery and civilization; he has resolutely treated them as if they *were* pictorial, as if they were every inch as good as Capri or Tangier; and, to reward his audacity, he has incontestably succeeded. It makes one feel the value of consistency; it is a proof that if you will only be doggedly literal, though you may often be unpleasing, you will at least have a stamp of your own.

HENRY JAMES, 'On Some Pictures Lately Exhibited', 1875

HONOURS

In the year 1658, when Don Diego Velázquez was at the Escorial with the King, His Majesty, considering that the genius, ability, personal merits, and other services performed by Don Diego Velázquez made him deserving of further promotion, one day during Holy Week, conferred on him the honour of membership of whichever he wished to choose of the three Military Orders. Velázquez chose the Military Order of the Knights of Santiago. If death had not overtaken him, it would have been the beginning of a rise to the greater honours due to his personal fitness for them, which offered material for cultivating more elevated fortunes.

I have heard it said by a person of high standing that when the Proofs [of Nobility] were delayed through some impediment due to jealousy, of which there was a great deal, the King, learning of the matter, commanded the President of Orders, the Marqués de Tabara, to send him the statement which His Majesty had to testify to in the Proofs of Velázquez, and when they came the King said: 'Write that I am certain of his nobility.' At this, no further inquiry was necessary.

ANTONIO PALOMINO, *'Life' of Velázquez* in *El Museo Pitórico*, 1724

FOREIGN OFFICE, *16th Dec. 1891* – Lord Salisbury with his humble duty respectfully submits the enclosed lists of honours for New Year's Day.

There are more peers than usual; but two of them have no children, and the occasion of the marriage of Prince Albert Victor should be in some degree marked.

But Lord Salisbury owes to your Majesty an explanation for again submitting two names to which on previous occasions your Majesty had in conversation expressed some objection. He has thought a great deal over the matter; and as the result of that reflection ventures with some earnestness to press the names upon your Majesty's gracious consideration.

Sir Frederick [*sic*] Leighton and Sir William Thomson are, whatever their merits, respectively at the head of the Art and Science of England. It is very desirable to give the feeling that the House of Lords contains something besides rich men and politicians . . . and the more the House of Lords can be provided, as occasion serves, with elements of convenience of a different kind, the greater will be its moral authority and its chance of doing useful service, when the necessity arises, to your Majesty, and to the institutions of this country.

THE MARQUIS OF SALISBURY, *Letter to Queen Victoria*

19th Dec. 1891 – . . . I am very sorry for the Queen's decision about Leighton. A desperate effort is being made to reduce the House of Lords to practical impotence, without abolishing it. . . . It is very difficult to find men who can speak, and who will go into the House of Lords. . . . I wanted Sir A. Hood, who can speak on naval matters, and Sir F. Leighton, who can speak on art; and they are both childless. But the Queen objects to both of them. As the House of Commons will not give Life peerages, it is difficult to know where to look. . . .

THE MARQUIS OF SALISBURY, *Letter to Sir Henry Ponsonby*

Although Lord Salisbury failed on this occasion, and obviously felt his failure, Leighton was made a peer in January 1896, a few days before his death.

PIETER DE HOOCH

Hoping to amuse Constable, I had sent him a copy of a small picture by De Hooge [*sic*], of which a sunbeam, and that alone, may be considered the subject; but it shines through a window on the wall of a clean little Dutch room, from which it is reflected on the return of the wall and other objects with extreme elegance, and a degree of truth perfectly illusive.

'September 22nd [1832]. My dear Leslie, I came here last evening, and saw the pictures. I am delighted with the copy of De Hooge. How completely has he overcome the art, and trampled it under foot, yet how full of art it is. No painter that ever lived could change a single thing in it, either in place, or light or dark, or colour, warm or cold. Such things are in short quite above the art, and it is a blessing they are done. I must take the De Hooge to Hampstead.'

C. R. LESLIE, *Memoirs of the Life of John Constable*, 1845 edition

Then pause before the 'Interior' of Pieter de Hooch [in the Louvre, Paris], go into this deep picture, stuffy and shut up, in which the light is so sifted, in which there is a fire, a silence, an appearance of comfort, a pleasant mystery – and notice, near to the woman with bright eyes, red lips, dainty teeth, that big boy, rather foolish looking, who reminds us of the son of Molière's M. Diafoirus, standing straight up on his spindle shanks, awkward in his big stiff clothes, so strange with his rapier, so awkward on his false balance, so right for the part he plays, so marvellously created that we cannot forget him. Here again is the same hidden art, the same impersonal drawing, the same incomprehensible mixture of nature and art. There is not an inkling of any set purpose, in this expression of things – so ingenuously sincere that no formula for it could be found, no *knack*, which means, in the language of the studio, no bad habits, no ignorance affecting capability, and no mania.

EUGÈNE FROMENTIN, *The Masters of Past Time*, 1876

Then they [English barristers in a hotel in Ypres] spoke of the tricks of light practised by De Hooghe [*sic*]; so we rebelled, and said De Hooghe had no tricks – no one less – and what they called trick was only observation and direct rendering of nature.

SAMUEL BUTLER, *Notebooks*, 1887

ILLNESS

Rarely do age and illness serve to diminish our defects. Watteau, older than others because of the cast of his mind, and always getting iller after his return [from England], became yet more dissatisfied with himself than he had been before. The places which had previously pleased him most, the people, and his very friends, became unbearable to him. He imagined that country air would do him good. The abbé Haranger, who was among those friends, had him lent by M. Le Fevre, then in charge of the *Menus Plaisirs* and now one of your honorary members, his house at Nogent, near Vincennes. At the stage his illness had reached, he could only decline away and nevertheless was still dreaming of a new move which he would have made had his strength permitted. He wanted to go and breathe again his native air. With regard to this last project, he cannot be accused of changeability. It is always the final resource of consumptives – one sanctioned by doctors when they know not what more to say, when the proposed taking of the waters, or the waters themselves, have been unsuccessful. Death left him no time and carried him off on 18 July 1721 at the age of thirty-seven.

COMTE DE CAYLUS, *Life of Antoine Watteau*, 1748

Anne-Claude-Philippe de Tubières de Grimoard de Pestels de Levis, comte de Caylus, a friend of Watteau, at least in his own estimation, read his 'Life' at the Académie Royale, Paris, 3 February 1748. His distinctly sanctimonious and would-be detached, partly critical attitude to Watteau and his genius reveals a lot about his own character.

My swelled Neck is got very painful indeed, but I hope is the [?] near coming to a Cure – How happy I should be to set out from Yarmouth and after recruiting my poor Crazy Frame, enjoy the coasting along til I reach'd Norwich and give you a call – God only knows what is for me, but hope is the Pallat of Colors we all paint with in sickness – 'tis odd how all the Childish passions hang about me in sickness, I feel such a fondness for my first imitations of little Dutch Landskips that I can't keep from working an hour or two of a Day, though with a great mixture of bodily Pain –

THOMAS GAINSBOROUGH, *Letter to Thomas Harvey*, 22 May 1788

Gainsborough died on 2 August 1788. Harvey, who lived in Norwich, had a good collection of old master paintings and at least one Gainsborough ('The Cottage Door').

When the King [George IV] was informed, which he was in the summer of 1825, that Wilkie's physicians apprehended him to be labouring under a paralytic affection, which did not indeed obscure the rational faculties, but made it impossible for him to exert his mind on any serious subject for more than a very short interval, his Majesty sent his private secretary, Sir W. Knighton (himself a physician of eminence, and much attached to Wilkie), to convey to him the regret with which he had received such intelligence, and his anxiety that no thought about the two or three pictures for the Royal Gallery left unfinished, or about anything else in the shape of business or money, should be allowed to disturb him in the arrangements judged most advisable with a view to his health. As we heard Sir William Knighton himself tell the story – the King said to him, 'Go to Wilkie – he is proud and shy – he may not want money at all, and it would not do to offer him that: say to him, however, that on your report I entertain a confident expectation of his recovery by-and-by, and have no fear on that score – if he will consent to be idle for the period recommended by his medical men. Tell him I am so sure of this, that he has my permission to consider me as his banker – so long as he continues to travel, and *does not work*. . . .'

J. G. LOCKHART, *Life of Sir Walter Scott*, 1843

This incident typifies the human thoughtfulness and keen artistic sympathies of George IV, the most unfairly traduced of British monarchs – perhaps partly because of his combination of qualities rarely otherwise united in our sovereigns.

My dear Bernard,
My cerebral disturbance is so great and I am so confused that I feared at one moment for my frail reason. After the terrible heat that we have just had a milder temperature has brought a little refreshment to our minds, and it was not too soon either; now it seems to me that I am better and I think more correctly along the lines of my studies. Will I ever attain the end for which I have striven so much and so long? I hope so. . . .

I should have liked to have you here near me, for the solitude weighs rather heavily on me. But I am old and ill, and I have sworn to myself to die painting, rather than to go under in the debasing paralysis which threatens old men who are dominated by passions that coarsen their senses.

PAUL CÉZANNE, *Letter to Emile Bernard*, 24 September 1906

Cézanne died on 22 October 1906.

ILLUSIONISM

In the upper room where the best portraits hang, the last room in the wing, you may have noticed a door which seems to lead somewhere. In fact it is a false door, and when you opened it, you were greeted by something that was more surprising than agreeable. My father seemed to be stepping forward, with my mother on his arm, and the sight startled you by its realism, which was partly the result of the situation and partly of art. Father was shown as if returning from a dinner or a *soirée*, dressed as he usually was on such occasions. The picture was painted with the greatest care, on the spot, and specifically for that situation. The figures were in perfect perspective for the point of view and the effect of the clothes was most carefully worked out. A window had to be moved so that the light might fall properly from the side to perfect the illusion.

J. W. VON GOETHE in *Propyläen*, 1799

This letter, from a certain Julie, is one of a series making up a short letter-novel, written jointly by Goethe and Schiller. It has been suggested that Goethe may have been thinking of the trompe l'œil *portraits of J. D. Bager (1734–1815), active in Frankfurt, Goethe's birthplace.*

IMAGINARY PAINTERS

Thus [from Sardou's *Tosca*] we learn that Mario Cavaradossi is the descendant of an ancient family of Roman patricians. (In the play he is addressed as 'Excellency'.) He inherited his great fortune as well as his liberal, anti-Royalist outlook from his father who frequented in Paris the society of Diderot and d'Alembert and stood on terms of friendship with Voltaire. Cavaradossi's mother was French and a great-niece of the philosopher Helvetius. He himself was brought up in Paris during the time of the Revolution when he worked in the studio of the great painter David. Family affairs brought him to Rome, but the chief reason for his prolonged stay there is Tosca, the great singer and idol of the Roman populace whom he met at the Teatro Argentina about a year before the drama takes place. Cavaradossi is an intellectual who tries to bring some enlightenment to the mind of his piously devout Tosca; he gives her *la nouvelle Héloïse* to read, but it bores her since the characters 'do nothing but talk and never make love'. Soon he will be leaving with Tosca for Venice where she is to fulfil a season's engagement, and thus turn his back on Rome for good. The Eternal City is not a safe place for him. Although he does not engage in any revolutionary activities, he is suspect in Royalist circles on account of his upbringing and his sympathy for Napoleonic France. He dresses in the French style and wears a goatee which, as the Sacristan avers with horror in Act I, is an outward sign of atheism.

In order to mislead the authorities as to his true political convictions, Cavaradossi has offered his services to the Jesuit chapter of Sant' Andrea della Valle to paint a mural in the church.

MOSCO CARNER, *Puccini: A Critical Biography*, 1958

In the opera Cavaradossi is painting an easel-picture of the Magdalen, whose appearance is inspired by an unknown blonde woman – as the dark-eyed Tosca jealously points out when she arrives in the church. Sardou's play Tosca *was first performed in 1887; the première of Puccini's opera, the libretto of which had been worked on by Sardou, took place in 1900. Sant' Andrea della Valle contains famous 'murals' by Reni and Domenichino.*

A miniature painter [Miss La Creevy] lived there, for there was a large gilt frame screwed upon the street-door, in which were displayed, upon a black velvet ground, two portraits of naval dress coats with faces looking out of them and telescopes attached; one of a young gentleman in a very vermilion uniform, flourishing a sabre; and one of a literary character with a high forehead, a pen and ink, six books, and a curtain. There was moreover a touching representation of a young lady reading a manuscript in an unfathomable forest, and a charming whole-length of a large-headed little boy, sitting on a stool with his legs foreshortened to the size of salt-spoons. Besides these works of art, there were a great many heads of old ladies and gentlemen smirking at each other out of the blue and brown skies, and an elegantly-written card of terms with an embossed border.

CHARLES DICKENS, *Nicholas Nickleby*, 1838–9

Dickens is satirizing the style of late eighteenth- and early nineteenth-century miniatures, an art form then much in vogue, and in Miss La Creevy's name seems to be raising obvious associations of the period with the diarist Thomas Creevey, who died in 1838.

That's my last Duchess painted on the wall,
Looking as if she were alive. I call
That piece a wonder, now: Frà Pandolf's hands
Worked busily a day, and there she stands.
Will't please you sit and look at her? I said
'Frà Pandolf' by design, for never read
Strangers like you that pictured countenance,
The depth and passion of its earnest glance,
But to myself they turned (since none puts by
The curtain I have drawn for you, but I)
And seemed as they would ask me, if they durst,
How such a glance came there; so, not the first
Are you to turn and ask thus. Sir, 'twas not

Her husband's presence only, called that spot
Of joy into the Duchess' cheek: perhaps
Frà Pandolf chanced to say 'Her mantle laps
Over my lady's wrist too much', or 'Paint
Must never hope to reproduce the faint
Half-flush that dies along her throat'; such stuff
Was courtesy, she thought, and cause enough
For calling up that spot of joy.

ROBERT BROWNING, 'My Last Duchess', *Poems*, 1849

It was here, and at this time that Chiaro painted the Dresden pictures, as also, in all likelihood, the one – inferior in merit, but certainly his – which is now at Munich. For the most part, he was calm and regular in his manner of study; though often he would remain at work through the whole of a day, not resting once so long as the light lasted; flushed and with the hair from his face. Or, at times, when he could not paint, he would sit for hours in thought of all the greatness the world had known from of old; until he was weak with yearning, like one who gazes upon a path of stars.

He continued in this patient endeavour for about three years, at the end of which his name was spoken throughout all Tuscany. As his fame waxed, he began to be employed, besides easel-pictures, upon paintings in fresco: but I believe that no traces remain to us of any of these latter. He is said to have painted in the Duomo: and D'Agincourt mentions having seen some portions of a fresco by him which originally had its place above the high altar in the Church of the Certosa; but which, at the time he saw it, being very dilapidated, had been hewn out of the wall, and was preserved in the stores of the convent. Before the period of Dr Aemmster's researches, however, it had been entirely destroyed.

DANTE GABRIEL ROSSETTI: 'Hand and Soul', *The Germ*, No. 1, January 1850

Rossetti invented a thirteenth-century Tuscan painter, Chiaro di Messer Bello dell' Erma, who learns that the artist must seek within himself for inspiration. In proto-Nabokovian manner the inner core of the tale is given an outer apparatus of apparent facts, with the insertion of Dr Aemmster, and so on, and the reference to Seroux d'Agincourt's 'Histoire de l'art par les monumens . . .' (1823), which is exactly where Chiaro's work would have been mentioned – had it existed.

IMAGINARY PICTURES BY REAL PAINTERS

A double flight of steps led into a circular and marble hall adorned with colossal busts of the Caesars; the staircase in fresco by Sir James Thornhill, breathed with the loves and wars of gods and heroes. It led into a vestibule painted in arabesque, hung with Venetian girandoles, and looking into gardens. . . . Mr Rigby opened a door and ushered Coningsby through an antechamber into a small saloon of beautiful proportion, and furnished in a brilliant and delicate taste. . . . The walls of the saloon, which were covered with light blue satin, held in silver panels portraits of beautiful women painted by Boucher.

BENJAMIN DISRAELI, *Coningsby*, 1844

As he was speaking, Piero [di Cosimo] laid down the book and went to look among some paintings, propped with their faces against the wall. He returned with an oil-sketch in his hand.

'I call this as good a bit of portrait as I ever did,' he said, looking at it as he advanced. 'Yours is a face that expresses fear well, because it's naturally a bright one. I noticed it the first time I saw you. The rest of the picture is hardly sketched; but I've painted *you* in thoroughly.'

Piero turned the sketch and held it towards Tito's eyes. He saw himself with his right hand uplifted, holding a wine-cup, in the attitude of triumphant joy, but with his face turned away from the cup with an expression of such intense fear in the dilated eyes and pallid lips, that he felt a cold stream through his veins, as if he were being thrown into sympathy with his imagined self.

'You are beginning to look like it already,' said Piero, with a short laugh, moving the picture away again. 'He's seeing a ghost, that fine young man. I shall finish it some day, when I've settled what ghost is the most terrible – whether it should look solid, like a dead man come to life, or half transparent, like a mist.'

Tito, rather ashamed of himself for a sudden sensitiveness strangely opposed to his usual easy self-command, said carelessly –

'That is a subject after your own heart, Messer Piero – a revel interrupted by a ghost. You seem to love the blending of the terrible with the gay. . . . I begin to think you are a Cynic philosopher in the pleasant disguise of a cunning painter.'

GEORGE ELIOT, *Romola*, 1863

Romola is set in late fifteenth-century Florence, and for her concept of Piero di Cosimo's character and art George Eliot relies greatly on Vasari. (See also under FOIBLES.*)*

The thing somehow, with the aid of the Bronzino, was done. . . . She found herself, for the first moment, looking at the mysterious portrait through tears. Perhaps it was her tears that made it just then so strange and fair – as wonderful as he had said; the face of a young woman, all magnificently drawn, down to the hands, and magnificently dressed; a face almost livid in hue, yet handsome in sadness and crowned with a mass of hair rolled back and high, that must, before fading with time, have had a family resemblance to her own. The lady in question, at all events, with her slightly Michelangelesque squareness, her eyes of other days, her full lips, her long neck, her recorded jewels, her brocaded and wasted reds, was a very great personage – only unaccompanied by a joy. And she was dead, dead, dead.

HENRY JAMES, *The Wings of the Dove*, 1902

Although James places this Bronzino portrait in an English country-house setting, he based his description on the portrait of Lucrezia Panciatichi, by Bronzino, in the Uffizi, Florence.

The Princess raised her eyes sleepily to an oval portrait of an ancestress, known to history as 'Queen Beryl the Bad'. The Queen, with a star in her hair, clad in a French dinner-gown, was leading by a chain of frail convolvulus, a prancing war-horse. The portrait was by Nattier.

RONALD FIRBANK, *The Artificial Princess*, 1934

IMPRESSIONISM

Smear a panel with grey, slap on a few black or yellow lines at random, and those in the know will say to you: Well! Well! What a good impression that gives of the woods at Meudon!

But when it comes to the human figure, it is quite another matter; the artist's aim is no longer to render the form, the modelling or the expression; it is sufficient to render the *impression* without a definite line, without colour, without shadow or light; in order to put such a far-fetched theory into execution, the practitioners fall into a senseless, mad, grotesque mess, fortunately without precedent in the history of art, for it is quite simply the negation of the most elementary rules of drawing and painting. A child's scrawls have a naïveté and a sincerity that make you smile, but the excesses of this school are nauseating or revolting.

EMILE CARDON, reviewing the first Impressionist exhibition in *La Presse*, 29 April 1874

The exhibition was held on the premises of the famous photographer Nadar, 35 Boulevard des Capucines, Paris, and opened on 15 April 1874. Although there were plenty of reviews even more violent than Cardon's, there were also a few neither stupid nor totally unfavourable. The exhibitors – of whom there were thirty – exhibited as the Anonymous Society of Artists, Painters, Sculptors and Engravers (a neutral-sounding title proposed by Renoir).

A new style of art has arisen, which seems to gratify a public ever craving for novelty. Very likely I am posing as an old-fashioned Academician, who declines to acknowledge that eccentricity is a proof of genius, or audacity an evidence of power; and I may be justly, or unjustly, accused of unfairness when I declare that the *bizarre*, French, 'impressionist' style of painting recently imported into this country will do incalculable damage to the modern school of English art. But I claim the right of judgement that half a century's constant practice of my art must give, and I wish the last words of these reminiscences to be those of warning to the rising generation of painters.

Be impressionist by all means, but let your impressions be as complete and as true to nature as those received by the great old masters. Let it not be possible for anyone to say of your impressions, as was well said of some impressionist work now popular, 'If nature made that impression upon the man, how much wiser he would have been if he had kept it to himself.'

W. P. FRITH, *My Autobiography and Reminiscences*, 1887

We ourselves are inclined to think that the craze for the impressionist landscapes will not last, but that people will continue to admire Degas for his unique gift of rendering certain movements and certain textures, and Manet for the extraordinary vitality of some of his portraits, such as the wonderful full-length of the engraver Marcelin Desboutin. But that the world, even the cultivated world, will ever see beauty in 'Le Déjeuner sur l'Herbe' – the picture made famous by the well-known novel of Zola's, is not to be believed.

'The Craze for the Impressionists', *The Times*, 5 June 1900

Hardly for the last time, the olympian assurance of 'The Times' proved devastatingly wrong.

The name which came, as it were, spontaneously to the lips of those who visited the exhibition, was within a few days taken and applied by *La Charivari*. This paper published an article dealing with the exhibition, under the heading *Exposition des Impressionistes*. The new name was used in a strictly depreciatory sense, with an implication of ignorance and presumption. The article was simply a series of sneers and sarcasms. The term Impressionist took time to spread; it was not until after the lapse of several years that it came into general use. At first the artists to whom it was applied paid no attention to it; then when it had become so common that they were no longer able to ignore it, they repudiated it, since it was always used disparagingly. Eventually, however, as the name had become established in popular speech, and as they themselves were unable to find a better one, they adopted it, and began to make use of it themselves. Thus the exhibition of April 1874 in the Boulevard des Capucines, although at the time it had been regarded as negligible, and had only attracted the unintelligent curiosity of passers-by, is now seen to mark an important date in the history of French art in the nineteenth century. There, for the first time, were to be found side by side those painters whose technique, system, and methods constituted a new contribution to art, and there originated the words 'Impressionist' and 'Impressionism' that are now known all over the world.

THÉODORE DURET, *Manet and the French Impressionists*, 1910

We do not want to change the appearance of the world, because we are not Naturalists, Impressionists, or Futurists (the latest form of Impressionism), and do not depend on the appearance of the world for our art.

PERCY WYNDHAM LEWIS, *Blast*, 1915

INGRES

And you also, my dear friends, would you abandon me to all that is crushing me? What are the horrors I have just learnt of? I am aware of all that is happening in Paris as far as I am concerned. The Salon is thus the theatre of my shame? I am the victim of ignorance, bad faith, calumny – and I get no consolation from you, my dear friends! The criminals, they waited until I left to assassinate my reputation. From one day to another have I changed from a distinguished painter into a man whose works cannot be looked at, which infuriate people, which all Paris is talking of in a frightful way? And I am not there, I cannot defend myself.

J. A. D. INGRES, *Letter to Monsieur Forestier*, 22 October 1806

Ingres was writing from Rome, maddened by the published criticisms of the pictures he exhibited at the Salon of 1806, which included 'Napoleon Enthroned' (Musée des Invalides, Paris). Violent though the criticisms tended to be, they paid tribute, in their way, to the artist's originality, and Ingres' own equally violent reaction reveals his susceptible, vulnerable nature.

A rather distinctive fact about M. Ingres's talent, and one which I believe has been overlooked, is that he is happier in dealing with female subjects. He depicts them as he sees them, for it would appear he loves them too much to change them; he fastens upon their slightest beauties with the keenness of a surgeon, he follows the gentlest sinuosities of their line with the humble devotion of a lover.

CHARLES BAUDELAIRE, 'The Salon of 1846'

I would have greatly liked to see you, good and kindly lady, to talk of your portrait which for too long has tormented us both. I must first tell you, as doubtless you know, that I am engaged on a major work for the Hôtel-de-Ville, and I have *promised positively* to finish it by the first of next January; you will realise from that, Madame, that I cannot occupy myself with other things this year. What is more, dare I frankly confess, that the successful outcome of this portrait is a painful preoccupation of mine! I see, the more I work at it, that I am not reaching the desired end, and that makes me feel despondent and extremely discouraged!

Had I not been so determined to fulfil my promise, I would some time ago have communicated to you the discouragement which has taken hold of me but I always worked on, in the hope of reaching a happy conclusion – which I now no longer hope for.

Do believe, good and kindly lady, that it pains me greatly to abandon this portrait, which I would have been so glad to offer M. Moitessier worthy of you and of him; but I prefer to obliterate it rather than present it to you inferior to what it should be.

INGRES, *Letter to Madame Moitessier*, 9 March 1853

This superb portrait (National Gallery, London) had been begun by Ingres in 1844 and was finally completed only in 1856. The delays produced a masterpiece: 'une œuvre'. Ingres wrote after having worked desperately on it seven years, 'certainement la plus importante parmi tous mes ouvrages'.

. . . and I have further made the acquaintance of Ingres, who, though sometimes bearish beyond measure, was by a piece of luck exceedingly courteous the day I was presented to him. He has just finished a beautiful figure of Nymph [*sic*], which I was able to admire loudly and sincerely.

FREDERIC LEIGHTON, Letter to his mother from Paris, 1856

The 'Nymph' is almost certainly 'La Source' (Louvre, Paris), which Ingres finished in 1856.

Degas described a scene at the studio of Ingres when the master had a kind of private view of a number of his pictures which were hung on the walls. There were such subjects as Jupiter, and, I think, Homer, and so on, and also the *Bain turc*, an agglomeration of nudes. A burgess of some importance, passing with the master from the bearded heroes to the nudities, ventured on some gesture approaching a chuckle or a nudge, as who should say 'Sly dog', or words to that effect. '*Monsieur*,' Degas heard Ingres say, as he drew himself up to his full height and bowed stiffly, '*j'ai plusieurs pinceaux*.'

'*Voilà un monsieur avec lequel on ne plaisantait pas,*'* Degas said to me in the Louvre, before the portrait of Ingres. . . .

WALTER SICKERT, 'Degas': *Burlington Magazine*, 1917

* 'Monsieur, I have several brushes.'
'There is a gentleman one didn't joke with.'

INSTRUCTIONS TO A PAINTER

First, draw the sea, that portion which between
The greater world and this of ours is seen;
Here place the British, there the Holland Fleet,
Vast floating armies! both prepared to meet.
Draw the whole world, expecting who should reign,
After this combat, o'er the conquered main.
Make Heaven concerned, and an unusual star
Declare the importance of the approaching war . . .
Let thy bold pencil hope and courage spread
Through the whole navy, by that hero led;
Make all appear, where such a Prince is by,
Resolved to conquer, or resolved to die . . .
Paint an east wind, and make it blow away
The excuse of Holland for their navy's stay;
Make them look pale, and, the bold Prince to shun,
Through the cold north and rocky regions run . . .
Painter! excuse me if I have awhile
Forgot thy art, and used another style;
For, though you draw armed heroes as they sit,
The task in battle does the Muses fit;
They, in the dark confusion of a fight,
Discover all, instruct us how to write;
And light and honour to brave actions yield,
Hid in the smoke and tumult of a field,
Ages to come shall know that leader's toil,
And his great name, on whom the Muses smile;
Their dictates here let thy famed pencil trace,
And this relation with thy colours grace.

EDMUND WALLER, 'For the drawing of His Majesty's forces at sea . . . together with the battle and victory obtained over the Dutch, 3 June 1665'

The 'Prince' is James, Duke of York, Charles II's brother; the naval battle of Solebay, a victory over the Dutch, was not, however, complete.

AN INVITATION

Few more pressing and more flatteringly grand invitations are documented as explicitly as that issued by Louis XIII to Poussin, resulting in the artist returning for a none too happy period, in reality, to his native France from Italy.

Dear and well-beloved,
Having learnt from some of our personal servants of the repute you have gained and the rank you hold among the most famous and most gifted painters in all Italy, and wishing to imitate our predecessors by doing all We can for the adornment and decoration of our royal residences, in summoning to us those who are distinguished in the arts, and whose consequence is established in the places where they appear most cherished, We are writing this letter to tell you that We have chosen and appointed you one of our painters-in-ordinary, and wish henceforward to employ you accordingly. To that end, our intention is that on receipt of this letter, you make arrangements for coming here, where the services you render us will be as much appreciated as are your works and your merits where you now live, We meanwhile instructing the Sieur de Noyers, Councillor of our Council of State, our Private Secretary and the Overseer of our Buildings, to emphasise to you the respect in which We hold you and the benefit and profit which We plan for you. We shall add nothing further to this letter than to pray God to have you in his holy care. Given at Fontainebleau, 15 January 1639.

LOUIS XIII, *Letter to Nicolas Poussin*

JEALOUSY

So then, after he [Castagno] had very successfully brought this work to a finish, blinded by his envy of the praises that he heard of Domenico's talent, he determined to get rid of him; and having thought of many different methods of doing this, he adopted one of them as follows. One summer evening, in his usual manner, Domenico took his lute and made his way out of Santa Maria Nuova, where he left Andrea drawing in his room after Andrea had declined the invitation to go for a walk with him, on the pretext that he had to do some important drawings. So after Domenico had gone off by himself to seek his pleasure, Andrea went to wait for him unseen round a street corner, and when Domenico came across him on his way home, he ruptured both his lute and his stomach at the same time with some lead weights; but as he thought he had not achieved what he wanted, he then beat him wickedly about the head with the same weapon. And then, leaving him lying on the ground, Andrea returned to his room in Santa Maria Nuova, where he left the door ajar and sat down to draw just as he had been left doing by Domenico. Meanwhile after great commotion, all the servants, on realizing what had happened, ran to summon Andrea and to give the bad news to the murderer and traitor himself. And Andrea running to where the others were clustered round Domenico, kept crying out inconsolably: 'Oh alas, my brother, alas, my brother!' Finally Domenico died in his arms, and, despite all the diligent enquiries that were made, it was never discovered who had done him to death. And if Andrea had not revealed it in confession when he himself was nearing death, it would still not be known.

GIORGIO VASARI. *'Life' of Andrea del Castagno and Domenico Veneziano*, 1568

This tale, one of Vasari's most vivid, happens to be totally untrue. Whether or not Castagno was jealous of Domenico Veneziano, he died some years before him.

GWEN JOHN

He [Rodin] admired and acclaimed her gifts. 'Vous êtes bel artiste,' were the words she reported to me with natural elation.

AUGUSTUS JOHN, *Chiaroscuro*, 1954

As to me, I cannot imagine why my vision will have some value in the world – and yet I know it will. . . . I think I will count because I am patient and recueillé.

GWEN JOHN, *undated letter to Ursula Tyrwhitt*

The recipient was a fellow-student of Gwen John at the Slade School of Art, and a close, lifelong friend.

. . . it would take much more than this to give you the measure of the impression she made on me and especially the beauty of that last afternoon I spent with her when she gave me tea under those great brooding trees at the back of that wild garden. We talked of Proust and of saints and anges [*sic*] and sinners and painters, and I came away filled with the wonder of her spirit and the keenness of her intellect.

MAYNARD WALKER, *Letter to Edwin John, Gwen John's nephew and heir, 6 May 1946*

Maynard Walker was then affiliated to a New York gallery, Ferargil. The 'last afternoon' was in 1937. Gwen John died in 1939. Walker seems one of the few people to have noticed how keen her intellect was.

JOKES

He [Botticelli] was a very good-humoured man and much given to playing jokes on his pupils and friends. For example, the story goes that one of his pupils, called Biagio, painted a circular picture exactly like one of Botticelli's mentioned above, and that Sandro sold it for him to one of the citizens for six gold florins; then he found Biagio and told him:

'I've finally sold this picture of yours. So now you must hang it up high this evening so that it looks better, and then tomorrow morning go along and find the man who bought it so that you can show it to him properly displayed in a good light, and then he'll give you your money.'

'Oh, you've done marvellously,' said Biagio, who then went along to the shop, hung his picture at a good height, and left. In the mean time, Sandro and another of his pupils, Jacopo, had made several paper hats (like the ones the citizens wore) which they stuck with white wax over the heads of the eight angels that surrounded the Madonna in his picture. Then, when the morning came, Biagio arrived with the citizen who had bought the painting (and who had been let into the joke). They went into the shop, where Biagio looked up and saw his Madonna seated not in the midst of angels but in the middle of the councillors of Florence, all wearing their paper hats! He was just about to roar out in anger and make excuses when he noticed the man he was with had said nothing at all and was in fact starting to praise the picture . . . so Biagio kept quiet himself. And at length he went home with him and was given his six florins, as the price agreed by Botticelli. Then he went back to the shop, a moment or two after Sandro and Jacopo had removed those paper hats, and he found that the angels he had painted were angels after all and was so stupefied that he was at a loss for words. Eventually he turned to Sandro and said:

'Sir, I don't know if I'm dreaming or if this is reality, but when I was here earlier those angels were wearing red hats, and now they're not. What's the meaning of it?'

'You've taken leave of your senses,' said Sandro. 'All that money has gone to your head. If what you say were true, do you think he'd have bought your picture?'

'That's so,' said Biagio. 'He didn't say a word. But all the same it struck me as very strange.'

Then all the other apprentices flocked round him and convinced him he had had some kind of giddy spell.

GIORGIO VASARI, *'Life' of Botticelli*, 1568

One day, at Windsor, after Rebecca had received a considerable sum of money, he proposed to share the expense of a post-chaise to London with Mr West; and just as they had reached Hounslow Heath, the King, who was returning to Windsor, looked into their chaise. The next time Mr West was in the Royal presence, the King asked him who the foreign nobleman was that he had in the chaise with him the last time they met on Hounslow Heath. Mr West declared Rebecca was his only companion. 'Oh, no,' observed his Majesty, 'it was a person of distinction.' Mr West, upon inquiry, found out that Rebecca, who expected to meet the King, and knew his Majesty to be near-sighted, had the impudence to fix a paper star on his coat, which he had cut out for the purpose of attracting the King's notice, supposing he would certainly laugh at it as a jest. – Rebecca, being fully aware of the great fondness people have for money, would, in whatever company he was, pass his jokes, purposely to amuse the frivolous part of them; and the following trick in particular he was sure to practise. He had prepared a drawing in imitation of a half-crown piece, which he would unobserved place upon the floor, and then laugh immoderately at the eagerness with which even a gentleman in full dress, with his sword and bag, would sometimes run and scuffle to pick it up.

J. T. SMITH, *Nollekens and His Times*, 1828

Biagio Rebecca (1735–1808), Italian-born, worked in England most successfully as a decorative painter (employed by George III at Windsor).

One day when Ducis, Alexandre and Langlois, who then assisted David and subsequently did a very good copy of the equestrian portrait of Bonaparte, were, along with Etienne, in the studio with their master, they were all standing around the lay figure clad in Bonaparte's clothes, examining with compulsive curiosity those epaulettes, that hat, that coat and that sword, deaf and dumb witnesses of the famous campaign of Marengo. Everybody was making his observations, more or less suitable, more or less lively, when David, whose hands and feet were quite slight, began to say, having drawn attention to the smallness of Bonaparte's boots, that usually great men had slender extremities. This remark, which could be aptly applied to the painter, was rapidly applauded by his pupils, one of whom added: 'And they have huge heads.' David, with his good nature that sometimes verged on the childish, immediately said, picking up the hat that belonged to the victor of Marengo: 'He's quite right, that one, let's just see.' Then, putting the hat on his head, which was very small, he burst out laughing as he realised that the large headgear fell down over his eyes.

M. E. J. Delécluze, *Louis David, son école et son temps*, 1855

The pupil Etienne is Delécluze himself; the picture David was working on was 'Napoleon Crossing the Alps'.

ASGER JORN

People often ask me what I hope to achieve by my writings. They tell me that my intentions are not always very clear. But I am not aware of having any very definite intentions in this matter. When my intentions are too clear, it makes me feel rather sad. One reason why I write is to oppose any clear-cut schemes or directions about art, whether the motives are moral, scientific or apparently liberal: like the attempt to *free* art by cutting it off from the rest of human activity.

Asger Jorn

Jorn (1914–1973) is one of the few modern examples of an outstanding painter interested also in writing seriously about art. Danish by birth, he was a founding figure in the COBRA group: CO[penhagen], BR[ussels], A[msterdam].

JUDAS ISCARIOT

Summon all Italy, summon whatever remains from remotest antiquity that is beautiful or wonderful, the portrayal of the despairing Judas alone, leaving aside so many other stupendous figures in this one single work [Rembrandt's 'Judas and the Thirty Pieces of Silver'], the figure of Judas only, I repeat, a Judas demented, wailing, beseeching forgiveness but not hoping to receive it or displaying any hope in his features, the awful face, the torn hair, the clothes rent to shreds, the twisted limbs, the hands clenched so that they bleed, the knee outstretched in an impulsive surge forward, the entire body contorted in pitiable anguish, I set against all the elegance of the ages. . . .

CONSTANTIJN HUYGENS, *Autobiography*, 1629–31

This vivid tribute to the impact of Rembrandt's picture (dated 1629: private collection, Great Britain) comes from a multi-talented, influential and cosmopolitan figure, secretary to the Prince of Orange, who goes on to write of the painter as 'a mere youth, a Batavian [that is, Dutch], a miller, a beardless boy . . . a Dutchman who has still hardly ever left the confines of his native town [Leyden]'.

JUDGEMENT

There is nothing that deceives us more than our own judgement when used to give an opinion on our own works. It is sound in judging the works of our enemies but not that of our friends, for hate and love are two of the most powerfully motivating factors found among living things. Thus, O painter, be eager to hear no less willingly what your enemies say about your work than what your friends say. Hate is more powerful than love for hate ruins and destroys love. If he is a true friend he is like another self to you and you find the opposite of this in an enemy. A friend could be deceived. There is a third kind of judgement, which is moved by jealousy and gives rise to flattery, praising the early stage of a good work so that the lie may blind the painter.

LEONARDO DA VINCI, 'Codex Urbinas' ('Book on Painting . . .')

He [Tintoretto] also said that in making a judgement of a painting one ought to note whether the eye was satisfied at first glance, and whether the painter had observed the precepts of art, but that in so far as details were concerned, everyone made errors. He further said that when exhibiting works in public one should wait for many days before going to see them, since by then all the darts would have been thrown and people would have become accustomed to them.

CARLO RIDOLFI, *'Life' of Tintoretto*, 1642

KANDINSKY

The contact between the acute angle of a triangle and a circle has no less effect than that of God's finger touching Adam's in Michelangelo.

And if fingers are not only anatomy or physiology, but more – namely, pictorial means – the triangle and the circle are not only geometry, but more – pictorial means.

WASSILY KANDINSKY, *Reflections on Abstract Art*, 1931

On the first part of this aphorism, Keith Vaughan commented: 'Not to me, boy.' ('Journals, 1939–1977', 1989, p. 134).

KITAJ

When I was sixteen, what I did attend was an art school in New York where everyone was painting with house-painters' brushes in the first flush of 'action painting', the masters of which were working two blocks away in 10th Street. My provincial heart was set on learning to paint like Hans Memlinc. No one could teach me how to do that and although I did have the strength to leave that place quickly, I never did chase down those Flemish secrets. They had been dumped into the respectable waste bins of history in the aftermath of new sets of instructions by ideologues like Roger Fry who mistrusted Flemish 'realism' for now shopworn 20th century reasons. Now that our century is closing, those fears still set me dreaming, still stand for the adventure I was looking for when I began, because the narrow terms of the face, the demands of verisimilitude are like the confining rules of mountain-climbing and lead towards the stars in *any* time. Faces are very special. (Giacometti said that the head is sovereign.) I always expect and often fail to find something in a face which will make me happy. Expectation is conducted by drawing (in my life) and drawing of a very high order is like an epiphany.

R. B. KITAJ, Introduction to 'The Artist's Eye' exhibition catalogue, National Gallery, 1980

KLEE

Bach, and particularly Mozart, were in his opinion the greatest composers, and there are musicians who claim that they have never heard Mozart played in a bolder or more congenial way than by Paul Klee.

WERNER HAFTMANN, *The Life and Work of Paul Klee*, 1954

KLIMT

I'm not good with words, written or spoken, especially not when I'm supposed to pronounce on myself or my work. . . . Anybody who wants to find out about me – as an artist, the only thing that deserves any interest – is advised to look attentively at my paintings, and try to find out from them what I am and what I want to do.

GUSTAV KLIMT

KNOWLEDGE

Perhaps no more astounding and all-embracing assertion of knowledge was made by any artist than by Leonardo da Vinci in the draft of a letter of c.1481–2 to Ludovico Sforza, de facto ruler and later Duke of Milan.

My Most Illustrious Lord, having now sufficiently seen and considered the achievements of all those who count themselves masters and artificers of instruments of war, and having noted that the invention and performance of the said instruments is in no way different from that in common usage, I shall endeavour, while intending no discredit to anyone else to bring myself to the attention of Your Excellency for the purpose of unfolding to you my secrets, and thereafter offering them at your complete disposal, and when the time is right bringing into effective operation all those things which are in part briefly listed below:

1. I have plans for very light, strong and easily portable bridges with which to pursue and, on some occasions, flee the enemy, and others, sturdy and indestructible either by fire or in battle, easy and convenient to lift and place in position. Also means of burning and destroying those of the enemy.
2. I know how, in the course of the siege of a terrain, to remove water from the moats and how to make an infinite number of bridges, mantlets and scaling ladders and other instruments necessary to such an enterprise.

3. Also, if one cannot, when besieging a terrain, proceed by bombardment either because of the height of the glacis or the strength of its situation or location, I have methods of destroying every fortress or other stronghold unless it has been founded upon rock or so forth.
4. I have also types of cannon, most convenient and easily portable, with which to hurl small stones almost like a hail-storm; and the smoke from the cannon will instil a great fear in the enemy on account of the grave damage and confusion.
5. Also, I have means of arriving at a designated spot through mines and secret winding passages constructed completely without noise, even if it should be necessary to pass underneath moats or any river.
6. Also, I will make covered vehicles, safe and unassailable, which will penetrate the enemy and their artillery, and there is no host of armed men so great that they would not break through it. And behind these the infantry will be able to follow, quite uninjured and unimpeded.
7. Also, should the need arise, I will make cannon, mortar and light ordnance of very beautiful and functional design that are quite out of the ordinary.
8. Where the use of cannon is impractical, I will assemble catapults, mangonels, trebuckets [old war engines] and other instruments of wonderful efficiency not in general use. In short, as the variety of circumstances dictate, I will make an infinite number of items for attack and defence.
9. And should a sea battle be occasioned, I have examples of many instruments which are highly suitable either in attack or defence, and craft which will resist the fire of all the heaviest cannon and powder and smoke.
10. In time of peace I believe I can give as complete satisfaction as any other in the field of architecture, and the construction of both public and private buildings, and in conducting water from one place to another.

Also I can execute sculpture in marble, bronze and clay. Likewise in painting I can do everything possible as well as any other, whosoever he may be.

Moreover, work could be undertaken on the bronze horse which will be to the immortal glory and eternal honour of the auspicious memory of His Lordship your father, and of the illustrious house of Sforza.

And if any of the above-mentioned things seems impossible or impracticable to anyone, I am most readily disposed to demonstrate them in your park or in whatever place shall please Your Excellency, to whom I commend myself with all possible humility.

LEONARDO DA VINCI

KØBKE

Believe me, my dear sister, this has been a struggle for me [work on his picture of the North Gate of the Citadel, Copenhagen]; for no less than three months I have fought with it every day; and on occasion it has been a hard fight, but then again I have been blessed with lighter moments. . . . I can assure you I have been working up to the very end. I've woken up every morning and yearned for the light to come so that I might get to work, and then painted all day long until evening, when I was tired but grumpy at having to tear myself away. . . .

CHRISTEN KØBKE, *Letter to his sister Conradine*,
27 October 1834

Købke (1810–48), still too little known outside Denmark, is an artist of European rank. The picture, one of his most remarkable masterpieces, is in the Ny Carlsberg Glyptotek, Copenhagen; it had been commissioned in January 1834 for the Kunstforening there, and by the rules had to be started no later than 1 July and completed before the end of October.

'KUNST'

May 20th

Well today Mr Spoffard is going to take me [Lorelei Lee] all round to all of the museums in Munchen, which are full of Kunst that I really ought to look at, but Dorothy said she had been punished for all of her sins last night, so now she is going to begin life all over again by going out with her German gentleman friend, who is going to take her to a house called the Half Brow house which is the worlds largest size of a Beer Hall. So Dorothy said I could be a high brow and get full of Kunst, but she is satisfide to be a Half brow and get full of beer. But Dorothy will really never be full of anything else but unrefinement.

ANITA LOOS, *Gentlemen Prefer Blondes*, 1925

LANDSCAPE

Paint a landscape at winter time; in a section of the background one should see Phoebus with Ocyrrhoe, and near them their little son Phasis. Nearer the front show Ocyrrhoe killed by the thrust of a sword, and the man who had been caught with her, fleeing and saving himself by hiding. Still closer show Phasis throwing himself into a river; and at this spot one should see a plant with white leaves growing here and there along the river like the reeds at our streams. This picture might be painted as a nocturne; and there should be depicted the northernmost region of the sky, with the Polar Star at the zenith, the Bears and other northern stars painted according to their sizes and constellations, done gracefully and not without display of great diligence.

PONTUS DE TYARD, *Twelve Fables of Rivers or Fountains . . .*, 1586

Pontus de Tyard (1521–1605) was Bishop of Chalon-sur-Saône and a member of the Pléiade; his twelve 'fables', or descriptions, were apparently intended to provide subjects for pictures in a room of the château at Anet. The instruction to paint a winter landscape is striking, and such a picture executed at so early a date would be unusual, though not unique.

Phasis, son of Apollo and Ocyroe, is here associated with one of the ancient rivers called Phasis, of which the most famous occurs in the story of the Argonauts.

Speaking of me, he [Fuseli] says, 'I like de landscapes of Constable; he is always picturesque, of a fine colour, and de lights always in de right places; but he makes me call for my greatcoat and umbrella'.

JOHN CONSTABLE, *Letter to Archdeacon John Fisher*, 9 May 1823

And now the trembling light
Glimmers behind the little hills, and corn,
Lingring [*sic*], as loth to part; yet part thou must
And though than open day far pleasing more
(Ere yet the fields, and pearled cups of flowers
Twinkle in the parting light;)
Thee night shall hide, sweet visionary gleam
That softly lookest through the rising dew:
Till all like silver bright;
The Faithful Witness, pure, and white,

Shall look o'er yonder grassy hill,
At this village, safe, and still.

From the sketchbook of SAMUEL PALMER, 1824

This landscape painted in words is wonderfully akin to Palmer's unforced visionary pastoral pictures of the same period.

The smallest corner of the forest with its manifold stirring vegetation, the simplest grassy hill with its delicate plants, before the bluish distance arched by a misty blue sky, will offer the most beautiful earth-life-picture, which, done in a small or large space, will leave nothing to be wished for, if only it is grasped by the soul.

CARL CARUS, *Nine Letters on Landscape Painting*, 1831, Letter VII

Carus (1789–1869), a naturalist, doctor and part-mystic in attitude to nature, stated that the word 'landscape' is banal and inadequate for the ideals of the genre and so coined the alternative 'earth-life-picture'. His description here not only relates to much nineteenth-century German landscape painting but also recalls certain works by the sixteenth-century 'Danube School' artists. He signed his 'Nine Letters' 'Albertus' to indicate a kinship with Dürer.

I made as if to go, but he [Degas] stopped me. 'Oh, you can come with me. I'm only doing landscape at present.'

I followed him into a little studio he had fixed up for himself on the grounds. He turned his back to the window and began to work on one of his extraordinary out-of-door studies.

I could not get over my surprise at this method of doing a landscape indoors, and when I mentioned the fact, Degas replied:

'Just an occasional glance out of the window is enough when I am travelling. I can get along very well without even going out of my own house. With a bowl of soup and three old brushes, you can make the finest landscape ever painted. . . .

'You know what I think of people who work out in the open. If I were the government I would have a special brigade of gendarmes to keep an eye on artists who paint landscapes from nature. Oh, I don't mean kill anyone; just a little dose of bird-shot now and then as a warning.'

AMBROISE VOLLARD, *Degas, An Intimate Portrait*, 1924

SIR THOMAS LAWRENCE

Again we have to think of Rubens for anything like the assurance and ease with which this composition [portrait of Pope Pius VII] is designed and carried through. How tactfully and yet effectively he has suggested the immense vistas of the Vatican behind; how right is the proportion of the figure to the space, and what character in the movements of the hands and feet! It is in the grand tradition, and really no unworthy successor to the great papal portraits of the past. A strange thing about Lawrence is that, the more exacting the task; the more he is expected to do a grand ceremonial portrait – something that is at once a portrait and a public monument – the better he succeeds.

ROGER FRY, *Reflections on British Painting*, 1934

LORD LEIGHTON

From the conversations of Burne-Jones with Thomas Rooke, his faithful studio assistant, as recorded by Rooke:

18 November 1896

I: There's such a bad reproduction in a Christmas paper of a figure of Lord Leighton's, wrong and bad everywhere – only with a look of his soft handling.

EB-J: He always did like a bed of down as much as I did a bed of thorns. But I never could care for his work, though perhaps it isn't quite kind of me to say so – But it can't hurt him now. It never seemed to me to be inspired by anything else than the Opera. As though he'd been to that entertainment, and been so pleased with it he couldn't get it out of his head, and that rather low. It was like bad rhetoric to me – not quite believable – very much in fact like his speeches on public occasions that his friends could never listen to without feeling ashamed. Nothing to be done but to hang down your heads and hide your feelings under applause. Remember a very funny thing that Millais said once after having seen Leighton's pictures. It was to Mr Prinsep I think, in his exceedingly simple, childlike way – for he was always more like a schoolboy than anything else. He said 'You know, my dear fellow, when I came back to my own work I quite felt like a giant.' It's no wonder he felt like a giant. A giant he *was*.

SIR EDWARD BURNE-JONES, Bt.

Lord Leighton had died early in 1896. In its quiet way, Burne-Jones's critique of his work is devastatingly perceptive.

LEONARDO DA VINCI

We have another advantage over earlier generations in our wider range of aesthetic comparison. We are no longer bound to assess Leonardo's work by classical standards of correctness, nor to admire only those drawings which resemble the style taught in academies. A freer approach to the problems of creation, born of our acquaintance with primitive and oriental art, has revealed the expressive qualities of work which earlier critics regarded as merely eccentric; and we see that Leonardo's personal, liberated drawings bring us closer to the sources of his genius than the wrecks of his great, formal achievements in painting. Finally, we may claim that our knowledge of psychology is fuller than it was. Whether or not we believe in the more elaborate doctrines of psychoanalysis, we are all aware that symbols come to the mind unsought, from some depths of unconscious memory and that even the greatest intellect draws part of its strength from a dark centre of animal vitality. We can no longer offer a simple explanation of every motive. In particular is this true of the character and work of Leonardo. The grand generalizations, the words of praise and blame, the categories of excellence in which older criticism abounds, cannot be applied to him without absurdity. He is a standing refutation of the comfortable belief that all good men are simple. No more complex and mysterious character ever existed, and any attempt at simplification would run contrary to the whole action of his mind. He had such a strong sense of organic life, of growth and decay, of the infinitely small and the infinitely big, in short of the nature of the physical world, that he rarely attempted an abstract proposition which was not mathematical; and we must observe the same caution in our attempts to study him.

KENNETH CLARK, *Leonardo da Vinci*, 1939

LIKENESS

10th [July 1668] To Cooper's; and there find my wife (and W. Hewer and Deb.), sitting and painting: and here he do work finely, though I fear it will not be so like as I expected: but now I understand his great skill in musick, his playing and setting to the French lute most excellently: and he speaks French, and indeed is an excellent man.

SAMUEL PEPYS, *The Diary*

Pepys's compliments are amusingly back-handed to Samuel Cooper, a distinguished and accomplished miniaturist.

After a little while I murmured to Picasso that I liked his portrait of Gertrude Stein. Yes, he said, everybody says that she does not look like it but that does not make any difference, she will, he said.

GERTRUDE STEIN, *The Autobiography of Alice B. Toklas*, 1933

FRA FILIPPO LIPPI

Well, all these
Secured at their devotion, up shall come
Out of a corner when you least expect,
As one by a dark stair into a great light,
Music and talking, who but Lippo! I! –
Mazed, motionless and moonstruck – I'm the man!
Back I shrink – what is this I see and hear?
I, caught up by my monk's-things by mistake,
My old serge gown and rope that goes all round,
I, in this presence, this pure company!
Where's a hole, where's a corner for escape?
Then steps a sweet angelic slip of a thing
Forward, puts out a soft palm – 'Not so fast!'
– Addresses the celestial presence, 'nay –
He made you and devised you, after all,
Though he's none of you! Could Saint John there, draw –
His camel-hair make up a painting-brush?
We come to brother Lippo for all that,
Iste perfecit opus!' So, all smile –

ROBERT BROWNING, 'Fra Filippo Lippi' in *Men and Women*, 1855

LIVING PICTURES

A rather special form of the 'Tableaux vivants' (which see further, page 225) was that devised for the public stage. 'The Living Pictures' put on at the Palace Theatre in London in 1895 were declared obnoxious by the National Vigilance Association, whose Secretary unfortunately described them as 'the ideal form of indecency'. As a result of the publicity, Shaw went to see and review the spectacle, with devastating effect.

I sat out the entire list of sixteen Living Pictures. Half a dozen represented naiads, mountain sprites, peris, and Lady Godiva, all practically undraped, and all, except perhaps Lady Godiva, who was posed after a well-known picture by Van Lerius (who should have read Landor's imaginary conversation between Lady Godiva and her husband), very pretty. I need hardly say that the ladies who impersonated the figures in these pictures were not actually braving our climate without any protection. It was only too obvious to a practised art critic's eye that what was presented as flesh was really spun silk. But the illusion produced on the ordinary music-hall frequenter was that of the undraped human figure, exquisitely clean, graceful, and, in striking contrast to many of the completely draped and elaborately dressed ladies who were looking at them, perfectly modest. Many of the younger and poorer girls in the audience must have gone away with a greater respect for their own persons, a greater regard for the virtues of the bath, and a quickened sense of the repulsiveness of that personal slovenliness and gluttony which are the real indecencies of popular life, in addition to the valuable recreation of an escape for a moment into the enchanted land to which naiads and peris belong. In short, the living pictures are not only works of art: they are excellent practical sermons; and I urge every father of a family who cannot afford to send his daughters the round of the picture galleries in the Haymarket and Bond Street, to take them all (with their brothers) to the Palace Theatre.

BERNARD SHAW, *Our Theatre in the Nineties*, 1932

LONELINESS

From an interview by Noel Barber with L. S. Lowry:

BARBER: But you are a lonely man – and in a way don't you enjoy it – the freedom of loneliness?

LOWRY: I *am* a lonely man – but I don't like it. I'm a lonely and miserable man and I've been lonely most of my life. The trouble is, you know, I think I'm one of those split personalities, because I've a real desire to be alone – and yet I've a horror of it. It's doing me a world of good spending a couple of days with you – but every time I meet people I face a bit of a problem: I like to be friendly with people, but sometimes I can't give myself to them. I just can't, even when I want it most. It's a bit sad, but then you've got to remember this sort of thing grows on you as you grow up. It took me 30 years, working hard all the time, to get even *some* sort of recognition. I've been painting since I was in the twenties, but I never made a good sale – apart from an odd drawing – until I was past 50. After my father died I lived 24 years alone with my mother in Pendlebury. I have never been married, I've had no women friends – well, not really – I don't smoke or drink, you know, and though my mother didn't really understand my painting, she understood me and that was enough. She stood by me for 24 years because she had faith in me. I nursed her for 14 years and the last nine of her life she had to stay in her bed. I looked after her and painted – that's all I had time for. And that doesn't leave much time, does it, for being a man-about-town? Then when she died in 1939, I was absolutely alone, and I've stayed alone, living alone, ever since.

L. S. Lowry in Noel Barber, *Conversations with Artists*, 1964

LOOKING AT PAINTINGS

Paintings must be looked at and looked at and looked at – they, I think, the good ones, like it. They must be understood, and that's not the word either, through the eyes. No writing, no talking, no singing, no dancing will explain them. They are the final, the nth whoopee of sight. A water-melon, a kiss may be fair, but after all have other uses. 'Look at that!' is all that can be said before a great painting, at least, by those who really see it.

'And cannot words, written or spoken, help those who have partial or little sight for painting?'

My answer to this question is: No. Only prayer, and looking, and looking, and looking at painting and – prayer can help.

Charles Demuth, *Creative Art* 5, no. 3, September 1929

Demuth (1883–1935) was a delicate avant-garde watercolour painter, probably little known outside America. His view, so crisply expressed here, is one that many artists – and others – have shared and echoed.

LOST PICTURES

The same distinguished author [Grünewald] produced further three altar panels, each having two wings painted on either side, which used to stand in three separate chapels on the left-hand side of the choir of Mayence Cathedral. The first of these showed the Madonna with the Christ Child on a cloud, attended by a large number of saints standing on the ground, including St Katherine, St Barbara, St Cecilia, St Elizabeth, St Apollonia, and St Ursula, all of them drawn so nobly, naturally, charmingly, and correctly, and so beautifully coloured, that they appeared to be in heaven rather than on earth. The second panel showed a blind hermit walking across the frozen Rhine river with the aid of a boy; he is being killed by two assassins and has fallen on top of the screaming child. This picture was so rich in expression and detail that it seemed to contain a greater wealth of true observations and ideas than its area could hold. The third panel was slightly less perfect than the other two. All three of them were taken away in 1631 or 1632 during the ferocious war that was raging at that time, and dispatched to Sweden by boat, but unfortunately they were lost in a shipwreck, along with many other works of art.

JOACHIM VON SANDRART, *Teutsche Academie*, 1675

Some drawings by Grünewald seem to relate to these panels, the loss of which is the sadder since his surviving paintings are so few. Sandrart's description of the second panel suggests something of an intense nightmare quality which few painters were better equipped to express than Grünewald.

He [Velázquez] also made *en passant* a sketch of His Serene Highness, Charles Prince of Wales, titular King of Scotland, only son and heir to the kingdoms and dominions of James I, King of Great Britain, Scotland, and Ireland, who at the time was at court, lodged in the Palace. He gave Diego Velázquez 100 *escudos* and honoured him with an unusual show of affection, for this Prince was extremely fond of painting.

ANTONIO PALOMINO, *'Life' of Velázquez, in 'El Museo Pitórico . . .'*, 1724

The future Charles I arrived in Madrid in the summer of 1623, with plans to marry Philip IV of Spain's sister. Although there is a note of payment 'unto a painter' in the account-book for Charles's Spanish journey, this portrait seems early to have disappeared.

Klimt's large-scale ceiling painting of 'Jurisprudence' for the Aula of Vienna University was destroyed in 1945 when retreating SS troopers set fire to the Schloss Immendorf, to which it and many other paintings by him had, ironically, been evacuated for safety.

Photographs of it exist, as does the following perceptive description of its impact by a contemporary champion of the 'new' Austrian art.

I first saw *Jurisprudence* . . . in the master's large studio, right out in the Josefstadt. . . . A metal door, on which were chalked the letters 'G.K.', and a notice 'Knock loudly'. I hammered with my fists, but the master himself was on the *qui vive*, and was at the door straight away. It was afternoon, thirty-five degrees centigrade. He had on only his usual dark smock, and nothing underneath. His life is spent in front of the great canvas, climbing up and down the ladder, pacing up and down, looking, brooding, creating out of nothing, trying, daring. He seems as if surrounded by a mist, wrestling with this element of uncertainty, kneading it, with both arms immersed up to the shoulders. The floor covered with drawings, many drawings for each figure, variants of each pose, position, movement. Never was a painter more fantastical, and yet more true to Nature. How many times has he drawn the old sinner who appears in *Jurisprudence* as the accused. This old, emaciated man, with sunken head and hunched back . . . he stands there, his gaze averted, already condemned. On that occasion he looked like a mere shadow on the canvas, tormented by three incorporeal ghosts. These three . . . twentieth century lemurs, by Klimt out of the daughters of Toorop, yet unmistakeably with their father's features . . . and then the reddish hair, these strange, comet-like tresses around their heads, studded with gold . . . golden snakes with gleaming teeth . . . Conscience gnaws with golden fangs!

No, in fact Conscience is represented by a giant squid in whose tentacles the poor sinner is enmeshed. A mighty octopus which, pressing its body against his, wrestles with the accused. A monster of skin and slime indestructible, insuperable. . . . And yet a magnificent squid, its skin patterned with spots like a leopard. The latest design of submarine leopard. . . . There is, indeed, a black humour about the whole thing. Unsuspected, it emerges from this fantasy of grimness and gravity like the golden snakes from the hair of the Gorgons. . . .

Only the day before yesterday, I saw *Jurisprudence* again. It was Friday, 13 November. A day of moody weather. . . . Not until three o'clock in the afternoon did I get round to meeting Klimt in the Secession [building]. He was still painting, although there was no longer any hope of finishing on time. I cast an eye at the picture as it hung there in the nave-like gloom, out of which golden phantoms glistened enticingly. The colours were all there . . . but a veil of dusk lay upon them. . . . And then it dawned on me. Only four days previously, I had come back from Sicily. I was still intoxicated with the golden world of the mosaics, gleaming and glittering. . . . It came back to me as I stood there in front of Klimt's picture, with its shining gold. . . . A new style, after all the pictorial orgies of the previous centuries. More solemn, more religious in form and colour . . . *Jurisprudence* . . . is dominated by gold and black – not in fact colours at all; in compensation, line and form are raised to a level of significance for which there is no other word than monumental. This picture must be regarded as the master's final step in this particular direction.

LUDWIG HEVESY, 'The Klimt Exhibition', *Acht Jahre Secession*, 1906

LOVE OF ART

So the boy grew up past the age of childhood, and his father, realizing his talented nature, and desiring that he should attend to his letters, sent him to the school run by a teacher called Francesco da Urbino, who at that time taught grammar in Florence; but, although he drew some fruit from this, both heaven and his own nature, which are difficult to contest, pulled him back to painting. In consequence, whenever he was able to steal some time, he could not resist running off to draw in one place or another, and seeking out the company of painters; and, among these, one very familiar to him was a certain Francesco Granacci, a disciple of Domenico del Ghirlandaio, who on seeing the boy's burning will and inclination, resolved to help him, and continually encouraged him in his endeavours, now providing him with drawings, now taking him along to the workshop of the master or some place where there was some work of art, from which he could gather fruit. This course of action was so effective that, added to the constant stimulus of his own nature, it led him to abandon learning his letters altogether. This brought him the disapproval of his father and his father's brothers, who hated the art of design, and very often he was outrageously beaten: as they were ignorant of the excellence and nobility of the art, it seemed shameful to them that it should be practised in their family. Although this was extremely disagreeable to him, none the less it was not enough to make him turn back; indeed, with his resolve strengthened, he now wished to try and make use of colour.

ASCANIO CONDIVI, *Life of Michelangelo Buonarroti*, 1553

LOVE OF PICTURES

SECOND SERVANT: Dost thou love pictures? We will fetch thee straight
Adonis painted by a running brook,
And Cytherea all in sedges hid,
Which seem to move and wanton with her breath,
Even as the waving sedges play with wind.
LORD: We'll show you Io as she was a maid,
And how she was beguilèd and surpris'd,
As lively painted as the deed was done.
THIRD SERVANT: Or Daphne roaming through a thorny wood,
Scratching her legs, that one shall swear she bleeds,
And at that sight shall sad Apollo weep,
So workmanly the blood and tears are drawn.

WILLIAM SHAKESPEARE, *The Taming of the Shrew*, Induction, Scene 2

MACLISE

Daniel Maclise appears one of the most interesting and attractive personalities among English nineteenth-century painters, not least perhaps because he was Irish. In some ways he is a Regency rather than Victorian figure, whose actual paintings (apart from his brilliant portrait of the young Dickens) unfortunately tend to lack inspiration. Nor is it easy now to recover the nature of his personality, but its impact was movingly conveyed in a remarkable tribute paid to him by Dickens at the Royal Academy banquet of 1870, shortly after his death and only a few months before the speaker's own.

Of his genius in his chosen art I will venture to say nothing here, but of his prodigious fertility of mind, and wonderful wealth of intellect, I may confidently assert that they would have made him, if he had been so minded, at least as great a writer as he was a painter. The gentlest and most modest of men, the freest as to his generous appreciation of young aspirants, and the frankest and largest-hearted as to his peers, incapable of a sordid or ignoble thought, gallantly sustaining the true dignity of his vocation, without one grain of self-assertion, wholesomely natural at the last as at the first, 'in wit a man, in simplicity a child', no artist, of whatsoever denomination, I make bold to say, ever went to his rest leaving a golden memory more pure from dross, or having devoted himself with a truer chivalry to the art-goddess whom he worshipped.

W. J. O'Driscoll, *A Memoir of Daniel Maclise, R.A.*, 1871

MADNESS

Although it makes a convenient heading, the term is harsh and crude as a characterization especially of the mental illness, early documented, of a very great painter, Hugo van der Goes. A fellow-inmate of the monastery Hugo had entered at some date about 1475–8 wrote this account.

In the year of our Lord 1482 death took converse brother Hugo, who had made profession here. As a painter he enjoyed so great a reputation that people used to say he had no peer this side of the Alps. We were novices at the same time, he and I who am writing this down. Immediately upon Hugo's investiture and generally during his novitiate, the prior, Father Thomas, gave him permission to seek solace and entertainment of all kinds after the fashion of people of the world, out of regard to the fact that Hugo had been an esteemed person among them. But this had the effect that he was made more familiar with worldly pomp than with the ways of penance and humility. This did not fail to cause strong objections: novices, some people would say, ought to be taught not exaltation but humility. But since he was a great expert in the art of painting he often received visitors of high rank, including the most illustrious Archduke Maximilian; all of them had a great desire to inspect his pictures. Thus whenever such guests came to see him, the prior Father Thomas, out of respect for them, permitted him to enter the guest room and to partake of festivities held there.

Now it happened that about five or six years after he had taken the vows it fell to our brother to make a journey which – if I remember right – took him to Cologne. He was accompanied by his half-brother Nicolaes, who had also taken his vows here as a *donatus* [someone not a full monk who gave all possessions to the monastery], as well as by Brother Petrus from the Monastery of Marienthron, who was then staying in the monastery of Jericho in Brussels, and several other people. As his brother Nicolaes told me at the time, our brother Hugo, during one night of his journey home, was seized by a strange illness of his mind; he uttered unceasing laments about being doomed and sentenced to eternal damnation. He even wanted to lay murderous hands on himself and had to be prevented by force from doing so. Because of this strange illness that journey came to an extremely sad end. However, thanks to efficient help, Brussels was safely reached, and prior Thomas was immediately summoned. When he saw and heard all that had happened he suspected that Hugo was vexed by the same illness which had befallen King Saul; and remembering that Saul was relieved when David played the harp he at once permitted plenty of music to be made in the presence of Hugo and also other soothing performances to be arranged in order to chase away those fantasies. But with all this, Hugo's health did not improve; he continued to rave and to pronounce himself a child of perdition. In this sad state he came home to the monastery.

The care and succour which our brethren extended to him with charity and compassion day and night, will be remembered by our Lord in all eternity and beyond, even though at that time many people, including some magnates, talked otherwise.

There are many different opinions about the nature of the illness that had befallen this converse brother. Some said it was a special kind of 'frenesis magna', others asserted that he was possessed by a demon. Apparently some symptoms of both these calamities were present; but I have invariably heard that at no time during his illness did he ever threaten anybody except, over and again, himself. And since this is not reported either of phrenetics or of the possessed, I think God alone knows what his disease was.

Thus we can speak of two possible assumptions concerning the illness of our painter-brother converse. The first is that it was a natural one, a kind of frenzy. There exist various natural species of this disease: sometimes it is caused by 'melancholy' victuals, sometimes by imbibing strong wine; then again by passions of the soul such as anxiety, sadness, overwork, or fear. Sometimes such illness stems from the malignity of corrupt humours that predominate in the human body. As regards those passions of the soul, I know for certain that this converse brother was much afflicted by them. For he was deeply troubled by the thought of how he could ever finish the works of art he wanted to paint, and it was said at that time that nine years would hardly suffice for it. Again and again, he was steeped in reading a Flemish book. I also fear that his illness was aggravated by the drinking of wine – though this was undoubtedly done for the sake of his guests. It is therefore possible that in this way, in the course of time, the basis was laid for his grave illness.

GASPAR OFHUYS, *Originale Cenobii Rubeevallis in Zonia prope Bruxellam in Brabancia*, c.1509–13

In the National Gallery . . . [King George V] confided to the director: 'I tell you what, Turner was *mad*. My grandmother always said so.'

KENNETH ROSE, *King George V*, 1983

MANET

To understand Manet's genius, the nineteenth century would have required ten years more than usual, for in Manet there is nothing but good painting, and there is nothing that the nineteenth century dislikes as much as good painting. In Whistler there is an exquisite and inveigling sense of beauty; in Degas there is an extraordinary acute criticism of life, and so the least brutal section of the public ended by pardoning Whistler his brush-work, and Degas his beautiful drawing. But in Manet there is nothing but good painting, and it is therefore possible that he might have lived till he was eighty without obtaining recognition. Death alone could accomplish the miracle of opening the public's eyes to his merits. During his life the excuse given for the constant persecution waged against him by the 'authorities' was his excessive originality. But this was mere subterfuge; what was really hated – what made him so unpopular – was the extraordinary beauty of his handling. Whatever he painted became beautiful – his hand was dowered with the gift of quality, and there his art began and ended. His painting of still life never has been exceeded, and never will be. I remember a pear that used to hang in his studio. Hals would have taken his hat off to it.

Twenty years ago Manet's name was a folly and a byword in the Parisian studios. The students of the Beaux Arts used to stand before his *salon* pictures and sincerely wonder how anyone could paint like that; the students were quite sure that it was done for a joke, to attract attention; and then, not quite sincerely, one would say, 'But I'll undertake to paint you three pictures a week like that.' I say that the remark was never quite sincere, for I never heard it made without someone answering, 'I don't think you could; just come and look at it again – there's more in it than you think.' No doubt we thought Manet very absurd, but there was always something forced and artificial in our laughter and the ridicule we heaped upon him.

But about that time my opinions were changing, and it was a great event in my life when Manet spoke to me in the café of the Nouvelle Athène. I knew it was Manet; he had been pointed out to me, and I had admired the finely-cut face from whose prominent chin a closely-cut blonde beard came forward; and the aquiline nose, the clear grey eyes, the decisive voice, the remarkable comeliness of the well-knit figure, scrupulously but simply dressed, represented a personality curiously sympathetic. On several occasions shyness had compelled me to abandon my determination to speak to him. But once he had spoken I entered eagerly into conversation, and next day I went to his studio. It was quite a simple place. Manet expended his aestheticism on his canvases, and not upon tapestries and inlaid cabinets. There was very little in his studio except his pictures: a sofa, a rocking-chair, a table for his paints, and a marble table on iron supports, such as one sees in cafés. Being a fresh-complexioned, fair-haired young man, the type most suitable to Manet's palette, he at once asked me to sit. His first intention was to paint me in a café; he had met me in a café, and he thought he could realise his impression of me in the first surrounding he had seen me in.

The portrait did not come right; ultimately it was destroyed; but it gave me every opportunity of studying Manet's method of painting. Strictly speaking, he had no method; painting with him was a pure instinct. Painting was one of the ways his nature manifested itself. That frank, fearless, prompt nature manifested itself in everything that concerned him – in his large plain studio, full of light as a conservatory; in his simple, scrupulous clothes, and yet with a touch of the dandy about them; in decisive speech, quick, hearty, and informed with a manly and sincere understanding of life. Never was an artist's inner nature in more direct conformity with his work. There were no circumlocutions in Manet's nature, there were none in his art.

The colour of my hair never gave me a thought until Manet began to paint it. Then the blonde gold that came up under his brush filled me with admiration, and I was astonished when, a few days after, I saw him scrape off the rough paint and prepare to start afresh.

'Are you going to get a new canvas?'

'No; this will do very well.'

'But you can't paint yellow ochre on yellow ochre without getting it dirty?'

'Yes, I think I can. You go and sit down.'

Half-an-hour after he had entirely repainted the hair, and without losing anything of its brightness. He painted it again and again; every time it came out brighter and fresher, and the painting never seemed to lose anything in quality. That this portrait cost him infinite labour and was eventually destroyed matters nothing; my point is merely that he could paint yellow over yellow without getting the colour muddy. One day, seeing that I was in difficulties with a black, he took a brush from my hand, and it seemed to have barely touched the canvas when the ugly heaviness of my tiresome black began to disappear. There came into it grey and shimmering lights, the shadows filled up with air, and silk seemed to float and rustle. There was no method – there was no trick; he merely painted.

GEORGE MOORE, *Modern Painting*, 1893

MANTEGNA

At a time when the Italian 'Primitives' were not very highly esteemed, Goethe was surprised and impressed on seeing the frescoes in the Eremitani Church, Padua, largely destroyed in the Second World War.

In the church of the Eremitani I saw some astonishing paintings by Mantegna, one of the older masters. What a sharp, assured actuality they have! It was from this actuality, which does not merely appeal to the imagination, but is solid, lucid and scrupulously exact and has something austere, even laborious about it, that the later painters drew their strength. . . .

J. W. VON GOETHE, *Italian Journey*, 1786

MARRIAGE

Then there was Joy in the House! Mistress *Agnes* prepared some strong foaming Chocolate, which new Beverage she had heard much vaunted, and with long suppressed desire to partake it. During the sipping of the same, she now in her usual way spoke of everything which she could procure, as pleasantly as the Drink fell pleasantly on her Tongue. The things she now saw so sweetly in her Mind's Eye, she afterwards provided herself with; good household Furniture, pretty Dresses, Trunks, Drawers, Pewter vessels, all the requisites for Needlework. Now there was Abundance going on – cutting, sewing, trimming and putting in order! At last Master *Albert* laid down the Receipt before her, shewing that he had paid the whole of his Debts in *Venice*. She tore the *paper* for Joy. When the bright Sun shone into the Room and the polished Tin glistened, then *Agnes* sat down pleasantly and played again on the Harp. She smiled quite benignantly Night and Morning from beneath the new Bedclothes. She even allowed herself to be drawn by her Husband in a Picture which represented *Adam* and *Eve*, and the beautiful *Agnes* was the beautiful *Eve*.

LEOPOLD SCHEFER, *The Artist's Married Life: Being that of Albert Dürer*, 1848

This romantic effusion purports to be Dürer's own account of his married life, handed by him on his deathbed to his friend Willibald Pirkheimer, and its flagrant unhistoricity is part of its eccentric charm.

Rather different are the facts recorded about Carlo Dolci's approach to marriage:

It was in 1654, when he was in satisfactory circumstances, that he was advised to get married. His marriage to Teresa di Giovanni Becherelli was arranged, and then it was quite charming to see our painter in the role of bridegroom; I speak of him seen with excessively modest gravity, sprucely dressed, cheerful and joyful certainly but also absorbed by feelings and words of devotion and spirituality; and in that connection it is enough to tell how when the day arrived for his giving of the ring to the bride, with everything arranged, and the relations, and the bride herself, assembled at the agreed place, all that was lacking was the groom – no small lack, it must be said, in the circumstances. Searching and more searching went on for Carlino, at the Company [of S. Benedetto] and at home, and in various churches, but no sign of him. Finally, as the hour of the wedding grew imminent, and hope of finding him desperate, he was discovered in the church of SS. Annunziata, tucked away in a corner of the chapel of the Crucifixion, in the act of prayer. And after some upbraiding for the delay he had caused, he was led to his bride.

FILIPPO BALDINUCCI, *'Life' of Carlo Dolci* in *Notizie de' Professori del disegno da Cimabue in qua . . .*, 1773

'But what about yourself, Monsieur Degas? Why haven't you ever married?'

'I, marry? Oh, I could never bring myself to do it. I would have been in mortal misery all my life for fear my wife might say, "That's a pretty little thing", after I had finished a picture.'

AMBROISE VOLLARD, *Degas, An Intimate Portrait*, 1924

I have cried a lot in my first year of marriage. . . . I feel as lonely as I did in my childhood. . . .

It is my experience that marriage doesn't make one happier. It destroys the illusion that has been the essence of one's previous existence, that there existed something like a soul-mate. The feeling of not being understood is heightened in marriage by the fact that one's entire life beforehand had the aim of finding a being who would understand one. But isn't it better to exist without such an illusion and look this great lonely truth straight in the eye?

PAULA MODERSOHN-BECKER, *Diary*, March 1902

MARRIAGE *MANQUÉ*

Lives of the obscure Leendert van Cooghen (1610–81), a painter of Haarlem, tell an unusual, entertaining story.

This painter lived unmarried and remained *en pension* with one of his relations. One day, towards dusk, a well-known young lady asked to see him. The servant announced her jokingly, saying that a delightful person had come to seek his hand in marriage. The timid painter was confused by this jest, and would not have left his corner of the hearth had he not been obliged to see who had come asking for him; he composed himself as speedily as possible and went to find the woman waiting in one of the main rooms.

After the usual civilities, the young lady began her speech with praises which he replied to only in an embarrassed way, and she finished by requiring him to keep secret her purpose, which he promised, not knowing that their conversation was being overheard.

This is what she had to say: 'Sir, my proposal is going to surprise you, since it is not at all normal, and perhaps you will find it out of place. For myself, I see nothing unreasonable in it, for as the proverb rightly says, it does not matter who makes the request, if the request is proper. You are known to and esteemed by my family and by me; you know me and you know who I am. You and I live contentedly on the wealth our fathers have left us, but time is rapidly passing and we are not getting any younger. One after another, our friends die, and what is more distressing, it is often the best ones whom we lose. As for our relations, some are too rich to deign to live with us, while the others are poor and feel we are living too long. This is why I have decided to get married, and if I suit you, I am ready to choose you as my husband.'

The timid van der Koogen [*sic*] could not pull himself together, and could only reply, trembling: 'But, Mademoiselle . . . but, Mademoiselle, this strikes me as very peculiar!'

'I was quite prepared for that reaction,' she said. 'But think about it: our situations and our birth are equal. I have opened my heart to you; now do you consider your own. Whatever you decide, we shall always be good friends.'

He remained for a long while unable to say anything except stammer: 'But, Mademoiselle. . . . Really, I don't know! Me marry? Well, yes; but I'm extremely surprised.'

The young lady saw how her speech had disconcerted her intended husband, but she tried nevertheless to put him more at ease. She gently told him that she had not come to settle the matter but solely to propose it and that he could reflect on it as long as he thought necessary; then she left him.

Our loved-one had no sooner retreated than he was forced to endure a thousand jokes from those who were around him. Although they had heard it all, they pretended to know nothing and they teased him greatly by trying to discover from him what had happened. He kept the secret, as he had promised, and said not a word the whole evening, so dumbfounded was he. He passed a sleepless night. However, that decided his course of action. His anxiety increased as day dawned. He hastily dressed and went out to dispel his worry and take the air, but he had scarcely got into the open than the young lady passed by. That appeared extraordinary to him, and he tried to avoid her. Eventually, he came to his senses; abruptly approaching the person who had so profoundly embarrassed him the previous evening, he said, 'Mademoiselle, nothing will come of what we spoke of last night.' 'Very well, sir,' said she, curtseying to him, and they parted.

This incident did nothing to change van der Koogen's life. He always remained a bachelor.

J. B. DESCAMPS, *La Vie des peintres flamands, allemands et hollandois*, 1754

MATERIALS

One day an artist was making a great parade of the methods he employed for purifying and perfecting his pigments. M. Chardin, irritated by this chatter of someone whose sole talent appeared to him to lie in frigid and painstaking handling, said to him: 'But who told you that painting was done with pigments?' 'With what then?' the other man answered, extremely astonished. – 'One makes use of pigments,' retorted M. Chardin, 'but one paints with feeling.'

CHARLES-NICOLAS COCHIN, *Essai sur la vie de M. Chardin*, 1780

So dexterous was he [Goya] in turning all materials to artistic account, that during morning visits to his friends, he would take the sandbox from the inkstand, and, strewing the contents on the table, amuse them with caricatures, traced in an instant by his ready finger. The great subject, repeated with ever new variations in these sand-sketches, was Godoy, to whom he cherished an especial antipathy, and whose face he was never weary of depicting with every ludicrous exaggeration of its peculiarities that quick wit and ill-will could supply.*

SIR WILLIAM STIRLING-MAXWELL, *Annals of the Artists of Spain*, 1891 edn.

* This I was told by Don Bartolomé J. Gallardo, who had himself seen Goya paint and caricature in the manner described.

Another thing about chaos is that I can use the dust. I used dust from the studio in doing those paintings of the sand dunes that I saw in Brittany. It's an awful game getting all that dust up from the floor but there is plenty of it here, as you know, stuck to pictures and everything else. So I just took dust and a cloth and put it onto the wet paint and after it was dried I set it as one sets a pastel. And that early painting in the Tate Gallery of Eric Hall in which his suit looks immaculate is painted with dust. Actually there is no paint at all on the suit apart from a very thin grey wash on which I put dust from the floor. Well, dust seems to be eternal – seems to be the one thing that lasts for ever – and one of the things that I have noticed and been very pleased to see is that it doesn't seem to have changed at all; it seems to be as fresh as when I first put it on forty years ago.

FRANCIS BACON in *The Brutality of Fact: Interviews with Francis Bacon* by David Sylvester, 1987

MATISSE

Very late in life, Matisse, whose views on art had always been expressed with great clarity, summed up his vision.

To create, that is the artist's prerogative; where there is no creation, art does not exist. But it would be a mistake to attribute this creative power to an innate gift. In the matter of art, the authentic creator is not only a gifted person but someone who knows how to organise, with a view to their end, a whole bundle of activities, of which the work of art is the result. So it is that for the artist creation begins with seeing. To see – that is already a creative action, and one which requires an effort. Everything we see in ordinary life undergoes, more or less, the deformation brought about by acquired habits, and the fact is perhaps more patent in an era like ours, where the cinema, advertising and magazines impose on us daily a host of ready-made images which are to some extent equivalent – in terms of sight – to a prejudice in terms of intellect. The effort necessary to get out of this rut requires a sort of courage; and that courage is indispensable to the artist who must see things as though he saw them for the first time; you have to see the whole of life as you did when a child; and the loss of that potentiality robs you of the potentiality to express yourself in an original way – that is to say, personally.

To take an example: I think that nothing is more difficult for a true painter than to paint a rose, because, to do it, he must first forget all the roses that have been painted. I often put the question to visitors who came to see me at Vence: 'Did you see the acanthus on the banks of the roadside?' Nobody had seen them; everyone would have recognized the acanthus leaf on a corinthian capital, but in life the memory of the capital hindered them seeing the acanthus. The first step towards creativity is to see something as it really is, and that presupposes a continual effort.

To create is to express what lies inside you. Every authentic effort of creation is internal. Yet sensibility requires nourishment, and that is achieved with the aid of elements taken from the external world. This is where work comes in; through that the artist incorporates and assimilates by degrees the external world, until the object he is drawing becomes like a part of himself, until he has absorbed it into his being and can project it onto the canvas as his own creation.

HENRI MATISSE in *Le Courier de l'Unesco*, October 1953

In a postcard to her mother on 7 January 1956, Sylvia Plath movingly described a visit she made from Nice to the Matisse chapel in Vence.

To Vence – small, on a sun-warmed hill, uncommercial, slow, peaceful. Walked to Matisse cathedral [*sic*] – small, pure, clean-cut. White, with blue-tile roof sparkling in the sun. But shut! Only open to public two days a week. A kindly talkative peasant told me stories of how rich people came daily in large cars from Italy, Germany, Sweden, etc., and were not admitted, even for large sums of money. I was desolate and wandered to the back of the walled nunnery, where I could see a corner of the chapel and sketched it, feeling like Alice outside the garden, watching the white doves and orange trees. Then I went back to the front and stared with my face through the barred gate. I began to cry. I knew it was so lovely inside, pure white with the sun through blue, yellow and green stained windows.

Then I heard a voice. 'Ne pleurez plus, entrez', and the Mother Superior let me in, after denying all the wealthy people in cars.

I just knelt in the heart of the sun and the colours of sky, sea and sun, in the pure white heart of the chapel. 'Vous êtes si gentille,' I stammered. The nun smiled. 'C'est la miséricorde de Dieu'. It was.

SYLVIA PLATH

MICHELANGELO

The Sistine Chapel ceiling is one of the most extraordinary achievements of Western painting. No contract or programme for it exists, and not the least extraordinary aspect of it is the painter's terse and half-ironic attitude to what he had achieved. Thus he wrote to his father in October 1512:

I have finished the chapel I have been painting; the Pope is very well satisfied. But other things have not turned out for me as I'd hoped. For this I blame the times, which are very unfavourable to our art.

In December 1523, writing from Florence, Michelangelo expanded somewhat on this work, along with other work he had been commissioned to do by Pope Julius II; his letter (which exists in two drafts) was to his friend Giovan Francesco Fattucci, then in Rome.

When I had set up the figure on the façade of San Petronio [Bologna] and returned to Rome, Pope Julius still did not want me to do the Tomb, and set me to paint the vault of Sixtus and we made a bargain for three thousand ducats. The first design for the said work was for twelve Apostles in the lunettes and the usual ornamentations to fill the remaining area.

After the work was begun it seemed to me that it would turn out a poor affair, and I told the Pope that if the Apostles alone were put there it seemed to me that it would turn out a poor affair. He asked me why. I said, 'Because they themselves were poor.' Then he gave me a new commission to do what I liked, and said he would content me and that I should paint down to the Histories below. Meanwhile, when the vault was nearly finished the Pope returned to Bologna; whereupon I went there twice for money that was owed me, but effected nothing and wasted all that time until he returned to Rome. When I returned to Rome I began to do the cartoons for the said work, that is for the ends and the sides round the said chapel of Sixtus, in the expectation of having the money to finish the work. I was never able to obtain anything. . . .

MICHELANGELO, *Letters*

While painting the Sistine Chapel ceiling, Michelangelo sent a satirical poem about the work involved to his friend Giovanni da Pistoia.

I've grown a goitre by dwelling in this den –
    As cats from stagnant streams in Lombardy,
    Or in what other land they hap to be –
    Which drives the belly close beneath the chin:
My beard turns up to heaven; my nape falls in,
    Fixed on my spine: my breast-bone visibly
    Grows like a harp: a rich embroidery
    Bedews my face from brush-drops thick and thin.

My loins into my paunch like levers grind:
My buttock like a crupper bears my weight;
My feet unguided wander to and fro;
In front my skin grows loose and long; behind,
By bending it becomes more taut and strait;
Crosswise I strain me like a Syrian bow:
Whence false and quaint, I know,
Must be the fruit of squinting brain and eye;
For ill can aim the gun that bends awry.
Come then, Giovanni, try
To succour my dead pictures and my fame;
Since foul I fare and painting is my shame.

MICHELANGELO

MODELS

It having been asserted that Angelica Kauffmann studied from an exposed male living model, which Mr Nollekens said he believed, – I was determined to gain the best information on the subject, by going to Mr Charles Cranmer, one of the original models of the Royal Academy, now living, in his eighty-second year; at No 13, in Regent-street, Vauxhall-bridge; and he assured me, that he did frequently sit before Angelica Kauffmann at her house on the south side of Golden-square, but that he only exposed his arms, shoulders and legs, and that her father, who was also an artist and likewise an exhibitor at the Royal Academy, was always present.

J. T. SMITH, *Nollekens and his Times*, 1828

I received this morning [30 May 1849] a note, dated yesterday, from Wells, apprizing me that the Model was to come that evening. On going to the Class in the afternoon, I was told that, on her unrobing, she was unanimously requested not to give herself so much trouble; and we have determined, as the preferable alternative, to draw her dressed almost entirely. She is very fat and at least 45.

WILLIAM MICHAEL ROSSETTI

It seems typical of W. M. Rossetti that when he published his journal of the Pre-Raphaelite Brotherhood he omitted this passage as indecorous. Today, it is more likely to strike the reader as sad, not least from the point of view of the model.

Manzi the Model

They had promised him sittings at the Royal Academy and then refused him on the ground that his legs were too hairy. He complained to Gogin:

'Why,' said he, 'I sat at the Slade School for the figure only last week, and there were five ladies, but not one of them told me my legs were too hairy.'

SAMUEL BUTLER, 'Written Sketches' in *The Notebooks*

THE MONA LISA

'La Gioconda' is, in the truest sense, Lionardo's masterpiece, the revealing instance of his mode of thought and work. In suggestiveness, only the Melancholia of Dürer is comparable to it; and no crude symbolism disturbs the effect of its subdued and graceful mystery. We all know the face and hands of the figure, set in its marble chair, in that cirque of fantastic rocks, as in some faint light under sea. Perhaps of all ancient pictures time has chilled it least.* As often happens with works in which invention seems to reach its limit, there is an element in it given to, not invented by, the master. In that inestimable folio of drawings, once in the possession of Vasari, were certain designs by Verrocchio, faces of such impressive beauty that Lionardo in his boyhood copied them many times. It is hard not to connect with these designs of the elder by-past master, as with its germinal principle, the unfathomable smile, always with a touch of something sinister in it, which plays over all Lionardo's work. Besides, the picture is a portrait. From childhood we see this image defining itself on the fabric of his dreams; and but for express historical testimony, we might fancy that this was but his ideal lady, embodied and beheld at last. What was the relationship of a living Florentine to this creature of his thought? By what strange affinities had she and the dream grown thus apart, yet so closely together? Present from the first, incorporeal in Lionardo's thought, dimly traced in the designs of Verrocchio, she is found present at last in Il Giocondo's house. That there is much of mere portraiture in the picture is attested by the legend that by artificial means, the presence of mimes and flute-players, that subtle expression was protracted on the face. Again, was it in four years and by renewed labour never really completed, or in four months and as by stroke of magic, that the image was projected?

The presence that thus so strangely rose beside the waters is expressive of what in the ways of a thousand years man had come to desire. Hers is the head upon which all 'the ends of the world are come', and the eyelids are a little weary. It is a beauty wrought out from within upon the flesh, the

* Yet for Vasari there was some further magic of crimson in the lips and cheeks, lost for us.

deposit, little cell by cell, of strange thoughts and fantastic reveries and exquisite passions. Set it for a moment beside one of those white Greek goddesses or beautiful women of antiquity, and how they would be troubled by this beauty, into which the soul with all its maladies has passed? All the thoughts and experience of the world have etched and moulded there in that which they have of power to refine and make expressive the outward form, the animalism of Greece, the lust of Rome, the reverie of the middle age with its spiritual ambition and imaginative loves, the return of the Pagan world, the sins of the Borgias. She is older than the rocks among which she sits; like the vampire, she has been dead many times, and learned the secrets of the grave; and has been a diver in deep seas, and keeps their fallen day about her; and trafficked for strange webs with Eastern merchants; and, as Leda, was the mother of Helen of Troy, and, as Saint Anne, the mother of Mary; and all this has been to her but as the sound of lyres and flutes, and lives only in the delicacy with which it has moulded the changing lineaments and tinged the eyelids and the hands. The fancy of a perpetual life, sweeping together ten thousand experiences, is an old one; and modern thought has conceived the idea of humanity as wrought upon by, and summing up in itself, all modes of thought and life. Certainly Lady Lisa might stand as the embodiment of the old fancy, the symbol of the modern idea.

WALTER PATER, 'Lionardo da Vinci' in *Studies in the History of the Renaissance*, 1873

This is perhaps the most famous passage of writing that exists about a single great picture – quoted here in the text of its first book publication. Fame and familiarity may have staled it, but a careful reading shows it is no mere rhapsody; it is psychologically acute about both the picture and its creator, as such an expert on Leonardo as Kenneth Clark frequently stressed.

MONET

A visit to Monet on 19 August 1918:

A servant took our cards and told us that she'd go and see. Bernheim was nervous and whispered: 'Don't be surprised if we aren't received.' I asked him if that was not Monet coming towards us.

'Where? What's he look like?'

'There, under a big straw peasant's hat. With a large white beard.'

'Why, yes, it is he: he's coming.'

We advanced. Bernheim shook his hand, introduced me, and Monet said: 'Ah, gentlemen, I don't receive when I'm working, no, I don't receive. When I'm working, if I'm interrupted, it just finishes me, I'm lost. You'll understand, I'm sure, that I'm chasing the merest sliver of colour. It's my own fault, I want to grasp the intangible. It's terrible how the light runs out, taking colour with it. Colour, any colour, lasts a second, sometimes three or four minutes at most. What to do, what to paint in three or four minutes? They've gone, you have to stop. Ah, how I suffer, how painting makes me suffer! It tortures me. The pain it causes me!'

Monet had come to the end of his monologue. I thought he would shake me by the hand and return to his work. I wanted him to stay a few minutes longer, and I said to him: 'Excuse me, M. Monet, I'm the guilty one, it's I who wished to come. Georges Bernheim warned me, but I've been looking forward to this for so long! I sell old paintings but adore the moderns. I adore your work. I get furious with my collectors when they tell me, "It's finished, no one knows how to paint any more, the ancients will never be equalled!" What idiots!' Then, looking at his flowers: 'How pretty your garden is. Mary Cassatt has so often spoken to me of it.' 'How is she?' he asked. I told him that she is nearly blind, and I sensed in the painter an old man's indifference. At this point Georges Bernheim said to notice how young M. Monet looked. I asked him his age, and he answered that he was seventy-eight. I complimented him, and indeed it's astonishing; I've never seen a man of that age look so young. He can't be taller than about five foot five, but he is absolutely erect. He looks like a young father on Christmas Day wearing a false white beard to make his children believe in old Father Christmas. His face is softly coloured and unblotched. His small round chestnut eyes, full of vivacity, add emphasis to whatever he says. 'Come into the studio,' he said. It's a large rectangular room. About a hundred paintings are hung on the wall in three or four graduated rows. For the most part they are paintings of little interest, rather flat, without colour: just foundations. But here and there a picture stands out from the others. I see one which seems to me to represent a thick forest with rifts of startling light, a forest of flowers which could be his garden.

My remark about modern painting had pleased him, for he brought it up again, saying: 'I prefer a still life by Delacroix to a Chardin painting.' As the conversation touched on landscape, I said: 'You and your colleagues of the nineteenth century, you're the masters who brought the art of landscape to heights never attained.' Monet cried: 'Don't call me a master: I don't like it.' Protesting that I hadn't called him a master, I added: 'You remind me of Renoir, who won't hear the word "master" uttered.' 'I suppose,' he observed, 'that those Dutch didn't see nature as all yellow. Their colours must have changed. When we were young, we went round the Louvre comparing our cuffs with the linen of Rembrandt's people, and decided that his canvases were far from the original colours. Rubens, now, did beautiful landscapes.'

René Gimpel, *Diary of an Art Dealer*

MONEY

Any jokes about the subject and the Scots in particular are silenced by the punctilious behaviour of Raeburn in the following instance.

My Dear Sir,

I return you my best thanks for the very handsome manner in which you have paid me for Mrs Bell's picture. You have enclosed 25 guineas, I return you five of them, which I have no right to accept, my price having been raised since I painted that picture, and my obligations to you are such, that, were it not for the peculiar situation in which I find myself at present, and the great demand I have for money, I believe (great as the regard is which I have for you) I would almost have quarrelled with you sooner than I would have accepted of one farthing.

SIR HENRY RAEBURN, *Letter to George Joseph Bell*, 8 December 1810

By the time I left the Royal College of Art I'd become a kind of rich student. I got a grant of three hundred pounds a year and perhaps I got another three or four hundred a year from pictures. It was enough, and I didn't have to work during the holidays. I'd met Kasmin in about January 1961, when he was working for Marlborough Fine Art. He was interested in my pictures; he said Bring some more into the Marlborough, and I did, and they *hated* them. Harry Fischer thought they were awful, and told Kas These are dreadful; what are you doing with all this junk? But James Kirkman, who worked there then, bought them for about ten pounds each, still has them, I think. Kas, in the late summer of 1961 when I'd gone to America, had given me a little bit of money to go, about forty pounds, and he said When you come back, if you want some, I'll give you a bit more. In America I got a letter from him saying I've left the Marlborough Gallery; when you come back don't go there, come and see me. And so I did. And he said I'm going to open a gallery soon and I'd like to deal in these pictures. I'll buy some pictures from you. He was the only person that said that then, so I said Very nice; yes, all right. And he kept buying pictures. They were incredibly cheap then. Even paintings were only fifteen pounds. He sold them for fifteen pounds and took about three himself. Then in my last year at the Royal College of Art, from September 1961 to July 1962, Kas bought all the pictures I painted, so I'd quite a bit of money. I thought I was rich; and I was, really. I could buy canvas, real paint, and I began to travel a bit. Instead of hitchhiking I could go on the train. That was the Christmas I went to Italy. It was the first Christmas I hadn't worked at the post office delivering Christmas mail. When I left the College Kas said, I will give you a six hundred pound a year contract, which was twice what the grant had been. And I thought, even if I don't get anything else, I've got six hundred pounds, twice what I've been living on – that's fine; I don't need much more and I can paint every day too. And then I thought, well, one day a week teaching is all right, and so I took this job in Maidstone. But I gave it up six or eight months after. I've never taught in England since.

Kasmin's contract in practice turned out to be more than six hundred pounds a year because I painted more pictures, and he'd buy them and sell them. So I was getting money in. I began to earn about fifteen hundred pounds a year, which was very good if you had just left college. It was as good as any teaching would bring in. And I was making it from my work, which was even better.

DAVID HOCKNEY, *My Early Years*, 1988

MOODS

The mood of creativity coming on a supreme artist is vividly conveyed in the following passage by someone who must have witnessed it.

In a *draught of designe*, the Artist must *fancie* every circumstance of his matter in hand; as usually *Rubens* would (with his Arms a cross) sit musing upon his work for some time, and in an instant in the liveliness of spirit, with a nimble hand, would force out his overcharged *brain* into description so as not to be contained in the Compass of ordinary practice, but by a violent driving on of passion. The *Commotions* of the mind, are not to be cooled by slow performance.

SIR WILLIAM SANDERSON, *Graphice*, 1658

GIOVAN BATTISTA MORONI

Little literary homage seems to have been paid to this great sixteenth-century portrait-painter, nowhere better represented outside his native North Italy than in the National Gallery, London. The first picture of his acquired for the collection has become one of his most famous, 'The Tailor', bought in 1862. Someone who did, typically, respond to his sober, penetrating art was George Eliot.

The chair of red-brown velvet brocade was a becoming background for his pale-tinted well-cut features and exquisite long hands: omitting the cigar, you might have imagined him a portrait by Moroni, who would have rendered wonderfully the impenetrable gaze and air of distinction; and a portrait by that great master would have been quite as lively a companion as Grandcourt was disposed to be.

GEORGE ELIOT, *Daniel Deronda*, 1876

Its ['The Tailor's'] great quality is a certain refined and dignified simplicity. The pose and expression are perfectly natural; the colouring is a harmony in grey, the background is a plain tone, and there are no accessories beyond the scissors he is holding in his hand and a small piece of drapery on the table. The execution is smooth, but not tame. Altogether a wonderfully fine example of portraiture pure and simple.

But then what a charming person to paint – really we poor moderns are rather severely handicapped! Where shall we find sitters like this amongst our tailors – or elsewhere?

THE HON. JOHN COLLIER, *The Art of Portrait Painting*, 1905

MORTAL SINS

It was probably to live up to his 'legend' and cause a proto-Byronic frisson, rather than to admit any serious guilt, that Caravaggio spoke as he did (if indeed he actually did) in the following anecdote recorded by someone both painter and priest, writing many years later.

One day he entered the church of the Madonna del Pilero with certain gentlemen, and the most courteous among them stepped forward to offer him some holy water; he asked what purpose it served, and was told that it absolved venial sins. 'I don't need it,' said he, 'because my sins are all mortal.'

FRANCESCO SUSINNO, *Le vite de' pittori messinesi*, 1724

MOSCOW

Seldom has a painter seized the essence of a city so brilliantly in words, quite apart from pictures, as did Kandinsky in writing of this city in which he was brought up.

Even in this picture, I was actually hunting for a particular hour, which always was and remains the most beautiful hour of the Moscow day. The sun is already getting low and has attained its full intensity which it has been seeking all day, for which it has striven all day. This image does not last long: a few minutes, and the sunlight grows red with effort, redder and redder, cold at first, and then increasing in warmth. The sun dissolves the whole of Moscow into a single spot, which, like a wild tuba, sets all one's soul vibrating. No, this red fusion is not the most beautiful hour! It is only the final chord of the symphony, which brings every color vividly to life, which allows and forces the whole of Moscow to resound like the *fff* of a giant orchestra. Pink, lilac, yellow, white, blue, pistachio green, flame red houses, churches, each an independent song – the garish green of the grass, the deeper tremolo of the trees, the singing snow with its thousand voices, or the *allegretto* of the bare branches, the red, stiff, silent ring of the Kremlin walls, and above, towering over everything, like a shout of triumph, like a self-oblivious hallelujah, the long, white, graceful, serious line of the Bell Tower of Ivan the Great. And upon its tall, tense neck, stretched up toward heaven in eternal yearning, the golden head of the cupola, which among the golden and colored stars of the other cupolas, is Moscow's sun.

To paint this hour, I thought, must be for an artist the most impossible, the greatest joy.

WASSILY KANDINSKY, *Reminiscences*, 1913

MURILLO

In Andalusia Murillo holds a place in the affections of the people hardly lower than Cervantes. Like Correggio at Parma, and like Rubens at Antwerp, he is still the pride and idol of Seville. When the great drama of Corneille was yet in the morning of its glory, it became a common expression of praise in France to say of anything admirable that it was *'beau comme le Cid'*. In Castile, when the most fertile and versatile of writers was daily astonishing the world with some new masterpiece, the word Lope came to be used in common speech as synonymous with excellent. The metaphor, in the course of time, has fallen into desuetude in spoken French, and the epithet has become obsolete in the Castilian. But a. Seville, to this day, they call any picture of extraordinary merit, a Murillo; not that it may pass for one of his works, but to express its beauty in a word which suggests beauty more vividly than any other in that copious language. Seville owes a monument to her great painter, whose modest grave has been desecrated by the fury of the French. Should the proposed statue ever be erected, may the glorious subject call forth the genius of some new Montañes or Cano! Meanwhile his works in the Cathedral, and at the hospital of Charity, are noble and sufficient memorials of that fame which has been ratified by the common voice of Europe.

SIR WILLIAM STIRLING-MAXWELL, *Annals of the Artists of Spain*, 1891 edn.

PAUL NASH

Last summer I walked in a field near Avebury where two rough monoliths stand up, sixteen feet high, miraculously patterned with black and orange lichen, remnants of an avenue of stones which led to the Great Circle. A mile away, a green pyramid casts a gigantic shadow. In the hedge, at hand, the white trumpet of a convolvulus turns from its spiral stem, following the sun. In my art I would solve such an equation.

PAUL NASH, Statement in *Unit One: the Modern Movement in English Architecture, Painting and Sculpture*, 1934

NATURE

For her own person,
It beggar'd all description: she did lie
In her pavilion – cloth of gold, of tissue –
O'er-picturing that Venus where we see
The fancy outwork nature.

WILLIAM SHAKESPEARE, *Antony and Cleopatra*, Act II, Scene 2

Moreover, he [Caravaggio] claimed that he imitated his models so closely that he never made a single brushstroke that he called his own, but said rather that it was nature's. Repudiating all other rules, he considered the highest achievement not to be bound by art. For this innovation he was greatly acclaimed, and many talented and educated artists seemed compelled to follow him, as is the case of Guido Reni, who adopted much of his manner and demonstrated himself a realist . . . and so did also Giovan Franceso [Guercino] da Cento. Such praise caused Caravaggio to appreciate himself alone, and he claimed to be the only faithful imitator of nature. . . .

Just as certain herbs produce both beneficial medicine and most pernicious poison, in the same way, though he produced some good, Caravaggio has been most harmful and wrought havoc with every ornament and good tradition of painting. It is true that painters who strayed too far from nature needed someone to set them on the right path again – but how easy it is to fall into one extreme while fleeing from another. By departing from the *maniera* in order to follow nature too closely, they moved away from art altogether and remained in error and darkness until Annibale Carracci came to enlighten their minds and restore beauty to the imitation of nature.

GIOVANNI PIETRO BELLORI, 'Life' of Caravaggio in
Le Vite dei pittori, scultori et architetti moderni, 1672

For a long time Art and Nature
Stopped inhabitating the same locales;
They fled each other, and their rupture
Was of concern to both men and gods.
Nature reproached Art for her finery
And a certain air of excessive affectation;
Polished Art on her side
Accused rough Nature
Of too much rusticity . . .
It was coming to a matter of blows,
And of settling their debate as humans do;
WATTEAU appeared and first he separated them.
WATTEAU whom they both respected,
Was listened to calmly.
Such fury, said he, to possess you,
Art and Nature, delightful deities,
You do harm to yourselves; less hastiness,
For it is in your interest to combine;
You are made to live together;
I want you to unite for ever,
Come and live peaceably with me.
Art and Nature were reconciled,
While the Talents applauded.
Your counsels were appreciated,
Charming WATTEAU, and peace was made:
Art gained beauties therefrom,
And Nature thereby became more perfect.

THE ABBÉ DE LA MARRE, *L'Art et la Nature réunis par Wateaux*, 1736

From the time that man first sought to represent nature and succeeded in transmitting its faithful image to paper or canvas with pencils and colours, many landscape painters have acquired a doubtless merited reputation; but of this number very few have had a genius susceptible to being kindled by the enthusiasm that inspires ideal beauty, which, raising nature to a plane beyond itself, conveys profound and delightful sensations to our souls.

There are several whom we have admired for their truth of colour, the freshness and softness of tint, the subtle harmony of different effects of light and dark, their lightness of touch and variety of execution. Without a doubt these painters are great men. But have they known how to speak to the heart and to the mind? Have they known how to inspire feeling? Claude Lorrain rendered with the most exact truth and even in a moving fashion the quiet rise and the brilliant descent of the star of day. He admirably painted atmospheric air; no one has sensed better than he that beautiful mist, that vagueness and indecision which give nature its charm and which are so difficult to render. Gaspard [Dughet] copied the most beautiful sights of Italy; he adjusted nature with all possible taste; he chose from it the most beautiful details; he knew how to arrange and combine these alterations of objects so well that he seemed to have made an exact copy without permitting himself the least change. He seized upon all the nuances of nature; he painted her tranquil, agitated, and in the convulsions of storm. He joined a strong colour to vigorously pronounced effects. He varied her superb productions infinitely; he is, in sum, as great a landscape painter as Claude Lorrain. But it must be said, both copied nature selectively such as it is, such as one might find it in Italy and also perhaps in some other places, but have they moved the imagination? have they been able to make the soul appreciate any feeling other than admiration? Their works quite simply offer landscapes in which one might desire to have a house, for it would be situated with a beautiful view; one could breathe in the coolness at midday; one might walk along the shady banks of a river, or lose oneself in the thickness of a forest and give oneself over to sentimental reveries. Yet, in the end, all the sensations that their works produce are related to ourselves and do not evoke anything beyond.

There is not in all of their painting a single tree wherein the imagination might expect a hamadryad to dwell; no fountain where a naiad might arise; the gods, the half-gods, the nymphs, satyrs, even heroes are strangers to these beautiful sites, which do not portray their birth or dwelling places. These charming landscapes can be nothing but the dwelling places of modern shepherds and peasants. It is not to them that Tityrus would come to contest for the singing prize with other shepherds whom Virgil gave him as rivals. If that poet had created a landscape he would not have painted a locale by Gaspard or Claude; he would have chosen one appropriate to the shepherds of whom he sang, which would have an entirely different natural tone than the one we see every day.

Nicolas Poussin, Annibale Carracci, Titian, Domenichino, and some others created what Homer, Virgil, Theocritus and all the famous poets would have created had they painted with colour. These painters were themselves immersed in the reading of these sublime poets; they meditated on them, and when they closed their eyes they saw that ideal nature, that nature adorned with the treasures of the imagination that only genius can conceive of and represent. . . .

Some pretended authorities will object perhaps that these great men did not include in their works all the truth of nature. One will compare the paintings of Poussin with those of Wynants or Karel du Jardin; one will say that Wouwermans painted horses better, that Berghem painted cows better, that Panini rendered architecture better, that Ruysdael gave a truer idea of the tree, and so on. This would be incontestable if Poussin had been only a painter of horses, trees, livestock, architecture and the like. But he was more than that: when he painted the horses of Castor and Pollux, he did not think of a prince's horse or, even less, of a farmer's. He did not make truth consist of rendering the galling on the animal's neck and back, calluses on the leg, or the reddish tone on the belly caused by the dirty litter on which the animal rested. It was the horse of a god that he wanted to paint, and he made it as it ought to be.

PIERRE-HENRI DE VALENCIENNES, *Elémens de perspective pratique à l'usage des artistes . . .*, 1820

Nature contains the elements, in colour and form, of all pictures, as the keyboard contains the notes of all music.

But the artist is born to pick, and choose, and group with science, these elements, that the result may be beautiful – as the musician gathers his notes, and forms his chords, until he bring forth from chaos glorious harmony.

To say to the painter, that Nature is to be taken as she is, is to say to the player, that he may sit on the piano.

That Nature is always right, is an assertion, artistically, as untrue, as it is one whose truth is universally taken for granted. Nature is very rarely right, to such an extent even, that it might almost be said that Nature is usually wrong: that is to say, the condition of things that shall bring about the perfection of harmony worthy a picture is rare, and not common at all.

This would seem, even to the most intelligent, a doctrine almost blasphemous. So incorporated with our education has the supposed aphorism become, that its belief is held to be part of our moral being, and the words themselves have, in our ear, the ring of religion. Still, seldom does Nature succeed in producing a picture.

The sun blares, the wind blows from the east, the sky is bereft of cloud, and without, all is of iron. The windows of the Crystal Palace are seen from all points of London. The holiday-maker rejoices in the glorious day, and the painter turns aside to shut his eyes.

How little this is understood, and how dutifully the casual in Nature is accepted as sublime, may be gathered from the unlimited admiration daily produced by a very foolish sunset.

The dignity of the snow-capped mountain is lost in distinctness, but the joy of the tourist is to recognise the traveller on the top. The desire to see, for the sake of seeing, is, with the mass, alone the one to be gratified, hence the delight in detail.

And when the evening mist clothes the riverside with poetry, as with a veil, and the poor buildings lose themselves in the dim sky, and the tall chimneys become campanili, and the warehouses are palaces in the night, and the whole city hangs in the heavens, and fairy-land is before us – then the wayfarer hastens home; and the working man and the cultured one, the wise man and the one of pleasure, cease to understand, as they have ceased to see, and Nature, who, for once, has sung in tune, sings her exquisite song to the artist alone, her son and her master – her son in that he loves her, her master in that he knows her.

JAMES WHISTLER, *The Gentle Art of Making Enemies*

Whistler first included these now famous sentiments in the public lecture he gave in London at the unusual hour of 10 p.m. on 20 February 1885. 'The Gentle Art' was first published in 1890.

NEGLECT

Perhaps more intolerable for the artist than total neglect is decline into it from great success. Such was the fate, in his old age, of the once fashionable French portrait-painter Nattier, a painter of real charm and accomplishment who remains under-valued. After his death in 1766, at the age of eighty-one, his daughter (married to another gifted portraitist, Tocqué) made a memoir of her father.

He had so unfortunately disregarded the means of ensuring a prosperous lot for his old age that there is every reason to think that without the long illness which in snatching him from his studio forced him to keep his bed for four years, he would have been compelled to work up to the last moment, if he wanted to go on living as respectably as he had always done. Bearing in mind this kind of pressure to work, one can realise how much it must have increased his susceptibility at a time when he found himself facing the harsh reality of outliving his reputation. For, well before becoming incapable of touching a brush, he suffered the fate of a majority of famous men in every century: he was unfortunate. War (that scourge of the arts), the fickleness of the public, the taste for novelty – all united to cause him to experience neglect of the saddest kind. The vast flow of work to which he was accustomed was replaced by an almost total dearth. In the end, all that remained of those great labours was the finishing for the court of a few pictures begun in far happier times.

MADAME TOCQUÉ, *Abrégé de la vie de M. Nattier*, 1767

In one way or another, many Scottish painters have tended to be neglected or under-appreciated – at least until very recently. A good example is Alexander Runciman, elder brother of another talented painter, John Runciman, who died very young. An obituary of Alexander in 1785 spoke of him 'labouring under every possible disadvantage', and his case was eloquently put by a mid-nineteenth-century writer.

High indeed in the great republic of genius was the ill-starred Runciman. He was one of those who had not the good fortune, or the skill, as it may be, to make their light shine before men: and it is in obscure corners that people stumble on his best works, wondering whence came the deep artistic power, and the whole simplicity of pictures so unknown to fame. I have seen portraits of his own esteemed friends – of some of those for instance who made his student circle at Rome – which I question if even Raeburn – who took his tone from Runciman, and is generally reputed to have much improved on it – could have excelled in truth and dignified simplicity.

J. H. BENTON, *The Scot Abroad*, 1864

Cleared out my exhibition. Removed Aristides and Themistocles, and all my drawings. Next to a victory is a skilful retreat, and I marched out before General Tom Thumb, a beaten but not a conquered exhibitor.

BENJAMIN ROBERT HAYDON, *Diary*, May 1846

These few brave words crystallize the culminating failure of Haydon's career – and life. He had opened an exhibition of his pictures and drawings at the Egyptian Hall in London in April 1846, poorly attended from the first. In the great room of the same hall Barnum concurrently put on show the dwarf General Tom Thumb. Twelve thousand people went to see Barnum's exhibition, paying £600. Haydon recorded visits by 133½ (sic) people, with total receipts of £5 13s 6d (£5.68). He closed his exhibition on 18 May, having lost £111 11s 5d (£111.58). After a month of agonizing experiences as much mental as physical and practical (Sir Robert Peel had sent him £50 which he never used), Haydon killed himself on 22 June 1846.

In the London art world until recently the name 'Carrington' struck only a vaguely familiar note and that because of her strange relations with Lytton Strachey, Mark Gertler and others, but as painter and draughtsman, it might well have been asked 'What has she done?' During my long years as Director of the Tate I neither saw an example of her work nor heard allusions to it serious enough to make me attempt to see it. It was never mentioned by any Trustee at our meetings. I must confess therefore to a certain shame when I was invited (as one who had made a study of the art of her period) to contribute a few words by way of introduction to the present volume and was able to see examples of her original work as well as many reproductions.

Carrington's achievement is the more extraordinary in the light of the circumstances of her life. She died aged thirty-nine; apart from her three Slade [School] years her closest friends were, with the exception of Gertler, literary rather than visual in their outlook. Thus she had few of those contacts with painters that would have satisfied her desire to study and discuss painting. It is true that throughout her life she remained friends with Augustus John and Henry Lamb, often visiting the Johns' home at Fryern, while Lamb was a regular visitor at Ham Spray, but her letters do not suggest that in either case there was much communication about painting. . . .

Her remoteness from the impulses which moved the most considerable of her contemporaries is at least one of the reasons why she has been the most neglected serious painter of her time.

SIR JOHN ROTHENSTEIN, Foreword to N. Carrington, *Carrington*, 1980

NETHERLANDISH PAINTING

The size of a picture and the scale of the figures have their share in determining method and style of the painter. Compelled by some commission probably every Netherlandish painter of the fifteenth century undertook small, medium and large-sized panels and, to a greater or lesser degree according to his nature, yielded to the dictates of the size on his style. In many cases art critics were unable to surmount the obstacle of a change of scale and, confused by the difference in style resulting from this change, failed to perceive the identity of the artists, as in the case of Dieric Bouts. A particular size is suitable and natural for every talent even though adaptability to a greater or lesser degree must be assumed and is apparent. Generally speaking a small size is appropriate for early Netherlandish panel painting, which is akin to miniature painting. And for the production of not a few Netherlandish painters the verdict stands: the quality rises and falls in 'inverse proportion' to the measurements of the picture. This certainly applies to Petrus Christus and to the Bruges painter we call Adriaen Ysenbrandt. Others, among them famous masters, do not pass unscathed beyond a medium size, as for instance Memlinc and Gerard David, whose religious works done for Spanish patrons (the organ panels from Najera in the Antwerp Museum and the altarpiece of *St. Anne* in the J. E. Widener Collection, Philadelphia [National Gallery of Art, Washington]) are felt to be too big. Here as in many other cases the feeling intrudes that we are looking at enlarged rather than large figures, the uneasy feeling that execution and size are not suited to one another, that the knowledge of form, the observation and content do not suffice to fill out the enlarged boundaries.

Dieric Bouts seems to grow timid as soon as he approaches life-size. His, as it were, short-sighted piecemeal method of execution shies at extensive surfaces. As regards inventive power and conception, Memlinc and Gerard David seem more able to cope with large surfaces but not as regards the formal content. Finally there is a mysterious connection between intellectual power and picture size. Only if his talent is profound and deep-rooted has the artist the power to fill large surfaces of a canvas in such a way that the proportions appear natural and that no disturbing contrast arises between content and form.

Hugo van der Goes gave wings to Eyckian painting and made it supple enough to cover wide spaces. Conception and execution, all creative forces are ample, they combine and radiate from the centre of his personality to produce a monumentality that is new in Netherlandish panel painting and of a different order from what we might describe as monumentality in certain productions by the Master of Flémalle and by Rogier [van der Weyden].

MAX J. FRIEDLÄNDER, *From Van Eyck to Bruegel*, 1956 edn.

NIGHT SCENES

How to represent a night scene.

That which is wholly deprived of light is all in darkness. Such being the condition of night, if you wish to represent a night scene, have a great fire in it, for then the object which is closest to this fire will be most tinged with its colours, because that which is nearest to an object most shares in its nature. And in making the fire tend towards a red colour, make everything illuminated by it reddish in colour too. Those things which are furthest from this fire are more tinted by the black colour of the night. The figures which are drawn towards the fire appear dark against the brightness of the fire because the part of the object which you see is coloured with the darkness of the night and not by the brightness of the fire. Those who stand at the sides will be half dark and half reddish, while those who can be seen beyond the edges of the flames will all be lit by the reddish light against a black background. As for their gestures, show those which are near the fire shielding themselves with their hands and cloaks as protection against the intense heat, with their faces turned in the opposite direction as if to flee. Show many of those further away with their hands raised to their eyes which are smarting from the intolerable glare.

LEONARDO DA VINCI, *Notebooks*

An artist in his criminal revenge, Lodovico boasts of the massacre on the stage at the end of 'The White Devil' in pictorial terms:

Here's my rest;
I limned this night-piece, and it was my best.

JOHN WEBSTER, *The White Devil* (1612), Act V, sc. 6

But now it is evening. It is that strange, equivocal hour when the curtains of heaven are drawn and cities light up. The gas-light makes a stain upon the crimson of the sunset. Honest men and rogues, sane men and mad, are all saying to themselves, 'The end of another day!' The thoughts of all, whether good men or knaves, turn to pleasure, and each one hastens to the place of his choice to drink the cup of oblivion. Monsieur G[uys] will be the last to linger wherever there can be a glow of light, an echo of poetry, a quiver of life or a chord of music; wherever a passion can *pose* before him, wherever natural man and conventional man display themselves in a strange beauty, wherever the sun lights up the swift joys of the *depraved animal.*

CHARLES BAUDELAIRE, 'The Painter of Modern Life' in *Le Figaro*, 1863

The highly original and serenely beautiful night scenes painted by late-nineteenth-century Norwegian painters like Kitty Kielland (1843–1914) were singled out for praise by some contemporary French critics. In Britain awareness of these painters and their achievements is still sadly inadequate.

They speak to us above all with a vibrant tenderness of their homeland, of the brilliant, icy waters, the splendours of the harsh winters, of the sweet magic of the slow twilight and the clear summer nights . . . where the twilight of summer lingers in the skies with an exquisite sweetness, the clear nights give the painters, late-comers, a singularly alluring motive, admirably suited to capture the eye of an artist.

ANDRÉ MICHEL in *Journal des Débats*, 27 August, 1889

NOLDE

Nolde's extraordinarily fierce empathy with nature – not so much mystic as passionately sensuous – has never been better conveyed than by the painter himself, in a letter to a friend that effortlessly evokes the very images of his art.

I lie constantly by the slope of this dune, listening to the rustling grass and the wind playing. The grass interweaves with my clothes and sand settles on me. In one pocket lives an old toad and wild bees gather honey in my hat. Hands and fingers form roots deep down in the sand, the toes have already doubled in length and will soon grow into great trees, which will then flower in some strange colour. When the sea breeze scatters the petals of the blossoms, strange fruit is formed, which everyone admires but no one dares touch.

EMIL NOLDE, *Letter to Hans Fehr*, 1901

NUDITY

The unbalancing effect that nudity in a picture can have is vividly exemplified by the fate of Guido Reni's 'Bacchus and Ariadne', a large late mythology of his which, judging from an etching based on it, was in fact entirely decorous in its treatment of the nude. Its fate occurred in 1650.

[It] was composed of almost twenty figures, the poses of which, and the character of the heads, were admirable; but too many of the beauties revealed, which had caused the picture to be admired in Italy, caused it to be destroyed in France. No sooner had M. d'Emery died, than Madame d'Emery – little swayed by the merits of the painter and the quality of the painting – was no longer able to endure in her house the nudities that distressed her in this picture; and having ordered it to be chopped up, she was so punctually obeyed that her servants reduced it to fragments without sparing a single figure.

A. FÉLIBIEN, *Entretiens sur les vies et sur les ouvrages des plus excellens peintres . . .*, 1725

A more robust view of nudity was to be taken over a century later.

In the portrait of the Duchess [of Gloucester], the painter had decently covered the nudity of the male child which she holds in her arms; but the Duke did not like this covering & would have all the world see he was a Boy: the Duke was gratified & the child exposed without the least covering whatsoever.

FATHER THORPE, *Letter from Rome, 8 January 1777.*

The painter was Batoni.

A Victorian prelate typified his period and would also have reassured Madame d'Emery.

My mind had been considerably exercised this season by the exhibition of Alma-Tadema's nude Venus. . . . [there might] be artistic reasons which justify such public exposure of the female form. . . . In the case of the nude of an old master much allowance has been made . . . for old masters it might be assumed knew no better . . . but for a living artist to exhibit a life-size, life-like, almost photographic representation of a beautiful naked woman strikes my inartistic mind as somewhat if not very mischievous.

THE BISHOP OF CARLISLE, 1877

The painting, entitled 'A Sculptor's Model' (Opus CLXXIX), is now lost but is known from reproductions.

It is widely supposed that the naked human body is in itself an object upon which the eye dwells with pleasure and which we are glad to see depicted. But anyone who has frequented art schools and seen the shapeless, pitiful model which the students are industriously drawing will know that this is an illusion. The body is not one of those subjects which can be made into art by direct transcription – like a tiger or a snowy landscape. Often in looking at the natural and animal world we joyfully identify ourselves with what we see and from this happy union create a work of art. This is the process students of aesthetics call empathy, and it is at the opposite pole of creative activity to the state of mind which has produced the nude. A mass of naked figures does not move us to empathy, but to disillusion and dismay. We do not wish to imitate; we wish to perfect. We become, in the physical sphere, like Diogenes with his lantern looking for an honest man; and, like him, we may never be rewarded. Photographers of the nude are presumably engaged in this search, with every advantage; and having found a model who pleases them, they are free to pose and light her in conformity with their notions of beauty; finally they can tone down and accentuate by retouching. But in spite of all their taste and skill, the result is hardly ever satisfactory to those whose eyes have grown accustomed to the harmonious simplifications of antiquity. We are immediately disturbed by wrinkles, pouches and other small imperfections which, in the classical scheme, are eliminated. By long habit we do not judge it as a living organism, but as a design; and we discover that the transitions are inconclusive, the outline faltering. We are bothered because the various parts of the body cannot be perceived as simple units and have no clear relationship to one another. In almost every detail the body is not the shape which art had led us to believe that it would be. Yet we can look with pleasure at photographs of trees and animals, where the canon of perfection is less strict. Consciously, or unconsciously, photographers have usually recognised that in a photograph of the nude their real object is not to reproduce the naked body but to imitate some artist's view of what the naked body should be like.

KENNETH CLARK, *The Nude*, 1956

OLD MASTERS

The Victorian fondness for dressing up and the Victorian sense of history meet in the 'sort of masque to represent different epochs of art' organised in 1885 to inaugurate the reorganization of the Institute of Painters in Water Colour in London, partly recorded by Walter Crane in a watercolour and also in his memoirs.

I designed a group to represent the art of Italy, arranging it as a triptych of round-arched Renascence arches. Through the centre one were seen the towers of Florence, with a group in front, including Dante and Beatrice, Petrarch and Laura, Fiammetta and an early Italian angel, Niccolo Pisano, Cimabue and the [*sic*] Giotto as the shepherd boy. Under the right-hand arch was the dome of St Peter's, and the group consisted of Pope Julius II examining a plan presented by Michael Angelo, while in front the young Raphael and a cardinal completed the group. On the left Venetian art was suggested by a group in a balcony . . . while in front stood Titian with Paolo Veronese, and Giovanni Bellini played a lute, seated on the steps.

Of the sort of difficulties encountered in getting together suitable impersonations, and keeping them together when caught, further increased by the postponement, the following extracts from a letter from Mr E. J. Gregory gives a glimpse (he was to have arranged a separate Venetian group, but eventually handed it over to me to be included in my triptych). . . .

'Pilleau was to have been my Titian, but chucked me up on the ground of ill-health. He may be better now.

'Herkomer was to have been Giorgione, but *he* threw me over.

'Henry Moore promised to come in the group, and asked me again about it recently.

'My Bellini (clean-shaved) was Lewis Jarvis – I expect he is still game.' . . .

I was fortunate enough to have some beautiful ladies in my Florentine and Venetian groups. . . . Mr W. A. S. Benson was Niccolo Pisano. My wife took the part of Laura. My little daughter was an early Italian angel. My eldest son personated the young Giotto, and I represented Cimabue myself, in the white costume in which Leighton painted him, taken from the fresco of Simone Memmi.

Sir James Linton was Veronese in my Venetian group, the late Mr John O'Connor made an excellent Michael Angelo, and Mr E. R. Hughes presented a lifelike and artistic portrait of the young Raphael.

WALTER CRANE, *An Artist's Reminiscences*, 1907

The Louvre is the book in which we learn to read. We must not, however, be satisfied with retaining the beautiful formulas of our illustrious predecessors. Let us go forth to study beautiful nature, let us free our minds from them, let us strive to express ourselves according to our personal temperaments. Time and reflection, moreover, modify little by little our vision, and at last comprehension comes to us.

PAUL CÉZANNE, *Letter to Emile Bernard (undated, but 1905)*

Emile Bernard (in 'Une Conversation avec Cézanne', published in 1921) recorded that when he enquired what Cézanne thought of 'the Masters' Cézanne replied: 'They are good. I went to the Louvre every morning when I was in Paris; but I ended up by attaching myself to nature more than they did.' Unknown to Bernard, Cézanne described him as 'an intellectual engorged by the memory of the museums . . . who does not look at nature enough'.

Musée des Beaux Arts

About suffering they were never wrong,
The Old Masters: how well they understood
Its human position; how it takes place
While someone else is eating or opening a window or just walking
  dully along;
How, when the aged are reverently, passionately waiting
For the miraculous birth, there always must be
Children who did not specially want it to happen, skating
On a pond at the edge of the wood:
They never forgot
That even the dreadful martyrdom must run its course
Anyhow in a corner, some untidy spot
Where the dogs go on with their doggy life and the torturer's horse
Scratches its innocent behind on a tree.
In Brueghel's *Icarus*, for instance: how everything turns away
Quite leisurely from the disaster; the ploughman may
Have heard the splash, the forsaken cry,
But for him it was not an important failure; the sun shone
As it had to on the white legs disappearing into the green
Water; and the expensive delicate ship that must have seen
Something amazing, a boy falling out of the sky,
Had somewhere to get to and sailed calmly on.

W. H. AUDEN, December 1938

Among the great Masters some are like Fighters, others like Victors. The fighters are perhaps: Michelangelo, Dürer, Rembrandt, Grünewald, Greco,

Cézanne; victors: Raphael, Memling, Holbein, Rubens (?) – the historians are more interested in the fighters than in the victors.

MAX J. FRIEDLÄNDER, *Reminiscences and Reflections*, 1969

Edouard Roditi questioned Giorgio Morandi in 1958 about old master influence on his paintings, and the name of Cézanne was interestingly introduced into the conversation by the painter.

ER: Many critics seem to stress your reliance on old-masterly lighting effects to create an atmosphere in your pictures. Have you consciously imitated the devices of any of the old masters?

MORANDI: I wouldn't really agree with any of these critics, though I have often found it very useful to study the works of some great artists of the past. But I have never lost my interest in the experiments of my contemporaries either. I believe, however, that Giotto, Masaccio, Paolo Uccello, Piero della Francesca and Fouquet can still teach a lot to any modern painter.

ER: Might I add Giorgione and Leonardo da Vinci to this list? Their names might explain to some extent your reliance on *sfumato* effects as opposed to the more clear-cut outlines of *chiaroscuro*.

MORANDI: Most certainly, though I have never been as interested in their works as in those of the artists whom I have just mentioned.

ER: I have also wondered whether you might not have studied the still-life arrangements which one finds in some of Antonello da Messina's interiors with figures.

MORANDI: Of course, Antonello interests me very much, but it was only much later in my life that I became aware of his great qualities. You see, Antonello worked in a different tradition, that of the Van Eyck brothers and the Flemish masters whose art we have little opportunity to study here in Italy. Still, I must add that I also owe much of my understanding of the art of the masters of the Italian Renaissance to Cézanne and to Seurat.

EDOUARD RODITI, *Dialogues on Art*, 1960

I repeat that Modernist art does not offer theoretical demonstrations. It could be said, rather, that it converts all the theoretical possibilities into empirical ones, and in doing so tests, inadvertently, all the theories about art for their relevance to the actual practice and experience of art. Modernism is subversive in this respect alone. Ever so many factors thought to be essential to the making and experiencing of art have been shown not to be so by the fact that Modernist art has been able to dispense with them and yet continue to provide the experience of art in all its essentials. That this 'demonstration' has left most of our old *value* judgments intact only makes it the more conclusive. Modernism may have had something to do with the revival of the reputations of Uccello, Piero, El Greco, Georges de la Tour, and even Vermeer, and it certainly confirmed if it did not start other revivals like that of Giotto; but Modernism has not lowered thereby the standing of Leonardo, Raphael, Titian, Rubens, Rembrandt or Watteau. What Modernism has made clear is that, though the past did appreciate masters like these justly, it often gave wrong or irrelevant reasons for doing so.

CLEMENT GREENBERG in *Art and Literature*, no. 4, Spring 1963

OPEN AIR

. . . I should like to comment somewhat on that truism of tomorrow, that paradox of today, which in studio slang is called 'the theory of open air' or at least on that which it becomes with the authoritative evidence of the later efforts of Manet. But here is first of all an objection to overcome. Why is it needful to represent the open air of gardens, shore or street when it must be owned that the chief part of modern existence is passed within doors? There are many answers; among these I hold the first, that in the atmosphere of any interior, bare or furnished, the reflected lights are mixed and broken and too often discolour the flesh tints. For instance, I would remind you of a painting in the Salon of 1873 which our painter justly called a *Rêverie* [*recte*: 'Le Repos']. There a young woman reclines on a divan exhaling all the lassitude of summertime; the jalousies of her room are almost closed, the dreamer's face is dim with shadow, but a vague, deadened daylight suffuses her figure and her muslin dress. This work is altogether exceptional and sympathetic. . . .

The search after truth, peculiar to modern artists, which enables them to see Nature and reproduce her, such as she appears to just and pure eyes, must lead them to adopt air almost exclusively as their medium, or at all events habituate themselves to work in it freely and without restraint: there should at least be in the revival of such a medium, if nothing more, an incentive to a new manner of painting. This is the result of our reasoning, and the end I wish to establish. As no artist has on his palette a transparent and neutral colour answering to open air, the desired effect can only be obtained by lightness or heaviness of touch, or by the regulation of tone. Now Manet and his school use simple colour, fresh, or lightly laid on, and their results appear to have been attained at the first stroke, that the ever-present light blends with and vivifies all things. As to the details of the picture, nothing should be absolutely fixed in order that we may feel that the bright gleam which lights the picture, or the diaphanous shadow which veils it, are seen only in passing, and just when the spectator beholds the represented subject, which being composed of a harmony of reflected and ever-changing lights, cannot be supposed always to look the same but palpitates with movement, light and life.

STÉPHANE MALLARMÉ in *Art Monthly Review*,
30 September, 1876

Mallarmé's article, 'The Impressionists and Edouard Manet', appeared in English, as above, with no translator credited: a French translation was published in the 'Gazette des Beaux-Arts' in 1975. Manet's 'Le Repos' (Rhode Island School of Design, Museum of Art, Providence) is a portrait of Berthe Morisot.

OPULENCE

Many successful artists, especially nineteenth-century ones, have demonstrated their success by their houses. Perhaps the most splendid of all were Alma-Tadema's two houses, the first Townshend House, Regent's Park; the second Grove End House, St John's Wood, a residence of a rather different kind from the little yellow house in Arles inhabited contemporaneously for a period by another Dutch painter.

It was reported that he [Alma-Tadema] spent £70,000 on the residence – approximately the equivalent of £1,000,000 today.

The remodelling of the house took a great deal of time. In fact, so much of 1886 was spent supervising the renovation that Alma-Tadema finished only three pictures all year. Most of the articles on Tadema at this period contain more copy about his home than his art, the 'Palace of the Beautiful' or 'Casa Tadema' becoming the most astonishing house in all London. In many ways it was Townshend House all over again, but on a grander scale, including among its decorative features Mexican onyx, medieval Dutch rooms, bronze doors (after those of the Eumactia House, Pompeii), fountains, walls of sea-green marble, a mosaic atrium and marble floors so valuable and highly polished that visitors were requested to don special slippers before walking on them. . . .

His house was, remembered one visitor, '. . . quite literally, like nothing on earth, because to enter any of its rooms was apparently to walk into a picture. Lady Tadema's studio, for instance, might have been a perfect Dutch interior by Vermeer or de Hooch! Tadema's on the other hand, conjured up visions of all the luxury, the ivory, apes and peacocks of the Roman civilization with which his art was largely pre-occupied.'

Another visitor commented, 'His house is a glimpse of his work, it is his soul seen from the interior. Whoever understands his house learns to cherish his art.'

Sadly, the house no longer stands in its former glory; today apartments have divided the rooms and almost all the rich trappings have long since vanished.

VERN G. SWANSON, *Sir Lawrence Alma-Tadema*, 1977

ORNANS

At this small French town near the Swiss border Courbet was born; he swept it out of its quiet obscurity with his large-scale painting of 'A Burial at Ornans' (Paris, Musée d'Orsay), which created a scandal at the Salon of 1850–1. In the passage below, Champfleury (Jules-François-Félix Husson), an art critic and defender of Courbet, imagines the stir created among the characters depicted in the painting.

The inhabitants of Ornans tremble on reading in the papers that they might later be suspected of complicity with the 'monster' for having lent their faces and costumes to his brush for a moment. I understand the terror of Proudhon, cousin of the revolutionary economist and vice-judge of the peace, who saw no crime in entering the painter's studio, his mourning clothes well brushed, a black coat, polished shoes, his hat in his hand. The youngest Marlet, who studied law at Paris, tries uselessly to calm him.

Tête, the mayor of Ornans, a great jovial man, goes to the café to find out what his administrators have to say. Old man Cardet, who was at the burial in short trousers and blue stockings, goes to find his colleague Secrétan, who lives in the Rue de la Peteuse, and the two worthy vine growers, who are withdrawn from the affairs of this world and do not read newspapers, are astonished at the noise made over the three-cornered hat of the one and the grey coat of the other. Unfortunately, the vine grower Sage's son is in Africa at the moment; he would warmly defend his friend the painter. Max Büchon, the poet, is not there either, but he will defend Courbet in Salin's newspaper. Why is Jean-Antoine Oudot, the painter's grandfather, dead? He was a man of prudent counsel whom all Ornans consulted; he would have brought everyone to their senses.

Only Alphonse Bon remains in town and meets Célestine Garmont the lame, the wife of Alexandre the hunchback. 'Everyone in the market is talking about nothing except the painting of the vine grower Courbet's son,' she says. 'It seems he has not flattered us any. They say he has caricatured us. But when he gets back, just wait. Madame Beurey's son has prepared something . . . You can't make fun of people that way. He is a great devil. . . .'

Actually, what makes the citizens of Ornans angry is that last year they led the painter into town with a band. Promayer, who directs the music of the National Guard, arranged the surprise for the Parisian. And how has the painter paid back his fellow citizens for this triumphant acclaim? By amusing all Paris at the expense of the vergers of Ornans, the vine grower Jean-Baptiste Muselier, and the shoemaker Pierre Clément.

The parish curate, Monsieur Bounet, does not like his vergers mocked in this way, because they belong to an extent to the Church, and nothing respecting the clergy must be held up to ridicule. Why did the newspapers not mention Cauchi, the sacristan, or the vine grower Colart who bore the cross? There is nothing ridiculous about them, while Pierre Clément's red nose indicates too prolonged conversations with the bottle. The curate thinks that the broad-brimmed hats that the *chapelin* Cuenot rents for funerals are the reason too that no one has bothered with Etienne Nodier, who carries the body with Crevot.

Courbet's sisters do not know what to think of the newspapers their brother sends them from Paris. They are so sure of his intentions that they try in every way to prove that 'Gustave' did not dream of making fun of anyone in town. They go to see Fili Caillot, who posed in the painting, and Joséphine Bocquin, the one weeping with a *capuchon* on her head, and show them a newspaper in which a critic calls them pretty. The women, happy to see the compliment in print, are almost convinced when big Marlet comes in. He has received the *Presse* and reads an article in which the critic states that the painter expressly caricatured his fellow townsmen in order to appear handsomer himself.

'The paper is right,' says big Marlet. 'Since Courbet knows how to make himself handsomer, he could have made us like himself.'

'He is not so handsome, with his pipe!' exclaims Mother Promayer.

Only the gravedigger Cassart says nothing. His practice of burying people has taught him to reflect, and he does not unleash his words like a magpie. He listens to Tony Marlet's reproaches while stroking his dog, then goes off whistling along the valley of Manbouc.

CHAMPFLEURY, *Grandes Figures d'hier et d'aujourd'hui*, 1861

PAINTING

Because this [process of] learning may perhaps appear a fatiguing thing to young people, I ought to prove here that painting is not unworthy of consuming all our time and study.

Painting contains a divine force which not only makes absent men present, as friendship is said to do, but moreover makes the dead seem almost alive. Even after many centuries they are recognised with great pleasure and with great admiration for the painter. Plutarch says that Cassander, one of the captains of Alexander, trembled through all his body because he saw a portrait of his King. Agesilaos, the Lacedaemonian, never permitted anyone to paint him or to represent him in sculpture; his own form so displeased him that he avoided being known by those who would come after him. Thus the face of a man who is already dead certainly lives a long life through painting. Some think that painting shaped the gods who were adored by the nations. It certainly was their greatest gift to mortals, for painting is most useful to that piety which joins us to the gods and keeps our souls full of religion. They say that Phidias made in Aulis a god Jove so beautiful that it considerably strengthened the religion then current.

The extent to which painting contributes to the most honourable delights of the soul and to the dignified beauty of things can be clearly seen not only from other things but especially from this: you can conceive of almost nothing so precious which is not made far richer and much more beautiful by association with painting.

LEON BATTISTA ALBERTI, *On Painting*, 1435–6

The art of painting is hard to acquire. Therefore, who does not find himself gifted therefor should not undertake it, for it will come from influence from above [*öbere Eingiessungen*: approximately, 'influences of the stars']. . . . This great art of painting has been held in high esteem by the mighty kings many hundreds of years ago. They made the outstanding artists rich and treated them with distinction because they felt that the great masters had an equality with God, as it is written. For, a good painter is inwardly full of figures [*inwendig voller Figur*], and if it were possible for him to live on forever he would always have to pour forth something new from the inner ideas of which Plato writes.

ALBRECHT DÜRER

Painting, *n.*, The art of protecting flat surfaces from the weather and exposing them to the critic.

Formerly, painting and sculpture were combined in the same work: the ancients painted their statues. The only present alliance between the two arts is that the modern painter chisels his patrons.

AMBROSE BIERCE, *The Devil's Dictionary*, 1911

PATINIR'S RIVER

Brimming and shining river, pale crags, and trees richly dark, slopes where the turf is the colour of whitened verdigris – I took these things for fancies. Peering into the little pictures, each painted with a million tiny strokes of a four-haired sable brush, I laughed with pleasure at the beauty of the charming invention. This Joachim Patinir, I thought, imagines delicately. For years I was accustomed to float along that crag-reflecting river as down a river of the mind, out of the world.

And then one day – one wet day in autumn – driving out of Namur towards Dinant through the rain, suddenly I found myself rolling, as fast as ten horses ventured to take me through the slippery mud, along the bank of this imaginary stream. The rain, it is true, a little blurred the scene. Greyly it hung, like a dirty glass, between the picture and the beholder's eye. But through it, unmistakably, I distinguished the fabulous landscape of the Fleming's little paintings. Crags, river, emerald green slopes, dark woods were there, indubitably real. I had given Joachim Patinir the credit that was due to God. What I had taken for his exquisite invention was the real and actual Meuse.

ALDOUS HUXLEY, *Along the Road*, 1925

PATRONAGE

One of the most famous of all patrons of painters is Isabella d'Este, Marchioness of Mantua; her patronage was not, however, always exercised successfully, or without considerable strain on both herself and the painter, and also on her agents, as is shown by the following exchanges over obtaining work from Giovanni Bellini in Venice.

Isabella set out the position in a letter of 10 April 1504 to Alvise Marcello, a Venetian patrician and ex-ambassador to Mantua.

Three years ago I gave Giovanni Bellini, the painter, 25 ducats as part payment of a subject which he had promised to do for my studio. Afterwards, since he declined to paint this *Storia*, he agreed to execute a Nativity of Our Lord for the said sum, as Michele Vianello and Lorenzo da Pavia are aware. The master has never kept any of his promises, and does not, it is plain, intend to keep them. We hardly know what steps to take next, but we see clearly how little is the respect which the painter has shown us. Bellini has never considered his obligations to us, and we are determined to have our money back. As there is no one in Venice whom we trust more than Your Magnificence, we have thought it best to ask you to desire Bellini to return our 25 ducats, without accepting either excuses or promises, for we will have no more of his work. If he refuses, I beg of you not to shrink in this extremity from saying words to the Prince [the Doge], or to any magistrate who can order an execution, so that he may not be allowed to insult us in this fashion. If he refuses to give back the money, which we can hardly believe, you might appeal to Michele Vianello or Lorenzo da Pavia; and Your Magnificence may rest assured that you can do us no greater service than to recover our money, and, what is of far more importance, prevent Bellini from doing us so great an injury.

Marcello responded more subtly, by putting pressure on Bellini to finish the picture, which was three parts done, and the painter himself wrote to Isabella on 2 July:

Most illustrious Excellency, – If I have been slow to satisfy the wish of Your Highness, which was no less my own, and you have found it tedious to wait so long for the promised picture, I beg your pardon on bended knees, praying you of your wonted kindness to attribute this delay to my innumerable occupations, and not to any forgetfulness of Your Excellency's orders, which are graven in my heart continually, since I am your most devoted servant; and I pray God that if I have not satisfied Your Highness in point of time, you may at least be content with the work, and if this does not satisfy your great wisdom and experience, you will ascribe my failure to the weakness of my own poor powers. – Humbly commending myself to Your Excellency, your most humble servant. . . .

Isabella's agent in Venice, Lorenzo da Pavia, reported to her a few days later that the picture was 'really finished . . . and a beautiful thing'. She thereupon wrote to Bellini:

Messer Zuan Bellini, – If the picture you have painted for us agrees, as we believe and hope, with your fame, we shall be satisfied, and are ready to forgive you the wrong which your long delays have caused us. Therefore, I beg you to give the canvas to Lorenzo da Pavia, who will pay you the 25 ducats that are still owing, and we pray you to pack it in such a manner that it may be brought here conveniently and without risk. If we can oblige you in any way we will do so gladly, when we have seen if you have served us well.

So well did she find Bellini had served her, when the picture duly arrived, that she wrote – rather less grandly – to him on 19 October 1505, reverting to the question of his painting a 'Storia' for her studio:

Messer Joanne, – You will no doubt remember how greatly we desired to have a painted *Storia* from your hand to hang near those of your brother-in-law, Mantegna, and how earnestly we formerly begged you to gratify our wish. But since, by reason of your numerous engagements, you were unable to gratify us, we were content to accept, instead of the *Storia*, a Nativity, which pleased us greatly and is as dear to us as any picture we possess. But the Magnifico Pietro Bembo, when he was here a few months ago, heard of this our great desire, and gave us hopes that it might be gratified, since he believed that many of the works upon which you were engaged are now finished, and, knowing the sweetness of your nature and your readiness to oblige all men, more especially persons in authority, he assured us that you might be willing to satisfy us. Since then, however, we have been constantly ill with fever, and unable to attend to business, but now that we are in better health we write to ask if you will paint this picture, and choose the poetic invention yourself, if you do not wish us to give it to you. And besides giving you full and honourable payment, we shall remain under eternal obligations to you. When we hear that you agree to this, we will send you the measure of the canvas and the earnest money.

from JULIA CARTWRIGHT, *Isabella d'Este, Marchioness of Mantua*, 1903

Just how great a concession Isabella was making in leaving Bellini free to choose his subject is revealed by comparison with an earlier letter of hers, to Perugino, which set out a fearfully elaborate programme for a picture and ended ominously: '. . . you are forbidden to introduce anything of your own invention.'

But it appears that Bellini never, in fact, painted a 'Storia' for her.

Even when helpful in practical, financial ways to a painter, patronage has often had in it an element of condescension, well illustrated by letters from two English patrons of Canaletto. Owen McSwiney, a bankrupt Irish impresario, living in Italy, wrote thus of the up-and-coming young view-painter in 1727:

The pieces wch Mr Southwell has (of Canal's painting) were done for me, & they cost me *70: Sequeens*. The fellow is whimsical, and vary's his prices, every day: and he that has Mind to have any of his Work, must not seem to be too fond of it, for he'l be ye worse treated for it, both in the price, & in the painting too.

He has more work than he can doe, in any reasonable time, and well; but by the assistance of a particular Friend, of his, I get once in Two months a piece sketch'd out and in a little time afterwards finished by force of Bribery.

OWEN MCSWINEY, *Letter to the Duke of Richmond*, 28 November 1727

The 'Friend' mentioned was probably Joseph Smith, the future British Consul in Venice, who became Canaletto's greatest patron. This is how he wrote of the painter in 1730:

At last Ive got Canal under articles to finish your 2 peices within a twelvemonth; he's so much follow'd and all are so ready to pay him his own price for his work (and which he vallues himself as much as anybody) that he would be thought in this to have much obliged me, nor is it the first time I have been glad to submitt to a painter's impertinence to serve myself and friends, for besides that resentment is lost upon them, a rupture with such as are excellent in their profession resolves 'em either not to work for you at all, or which is worse, one gets from them only slight and labour'd productions, and so our taste and generosity is censured – tho' both unjustly.

JOSEPH SMITH, *Letter to Samuel Hill*, 17 July 1730

PARMIGIANINO

But what shall I say of Francesco Parmigiano? He is someone who gave such gracefulness to his works that whoever sees them falls in love with them. Besides, he used colour attractively, and was so charming and accomplished a draughtsman that every sheet of his drawings incites astonishment in the eyes of the beholder, since you see there an assiduousness that is wonderful.

LODOVICO DOLCE, *Dialogo della pittura . . .*, 1557

PERSPECTIVE

He [Uccello] left a daughter, who had some knowledge of drawing, and a wife who told people that Paolo used to stay up all night in his study, trying to work out the vanishing points of his perspective, and that when she called him to come to bed he would say: 'Oh, what a lovely thing this perspective is!'

And indeed, if perspective was dear to Uccello it also proved, thanks to his works, attractive and rewarding to those who have used it since.

GIORGIO VASARI, *'Life' of Uccello*, 1568

He delighted, in addition, to have about the house many kinds of extraordinary animals; badgers, squirrels, apes, marmosets, dwarf asses, horses, barbs for running races, little horses from Elba, jays, dwarf fowls, Indian turtle-doves, and other suchlike animals, as many as he could lay his hands on. But, besides all these beasts, he had a raven, which had learned from him to speak so well, that in some things it imitated exactly the voice of Giovanni Antonio, and particularly to anyone who knocked at the door, doing this so excellently that it seemed like Giovanni Antonio himself, as all the people of Siena know very well. In like manner, the other animals were so tame that they always flocked round anybody in the house, playing the strangest pranks and the maddest tricks in the world, insomuch that the man's house looked like a real Noah's Ark.

GIORGIO VASARI, *'Life' of Giovanni Antonio Bazzi, called Il Sodoma*, 1568

While I am occupied in mentioning the companions of the artist's home, I must not omit to notice one who was ever as ready to offer his small aid and humble obedience as were many of his superiors, to confer the benefit of their penetrating advice – I refer to Mr Collins's dog 'Prinny' (Prince). This docile and affectionate animal had been trained by his master to sit in any attitude which the introduction of a dog in his pictures (a frequent occurrence) might happen to demand. So strict was 'Prinny's' sense of duty that he never ventured to move from his set position, until his master's signal gave him permission to approach his chair, when he was generally rewarded with a lump of sugar, placed, not between his teeth, but on his nose, where he continued to balance it, until he was desired to throw it into the air and catch it in his mouth – a feat which he very seldom failed to perform. On one occasion, his extraordinary integrity in the performance of his duties was thus pleasantly exemplified: – My father had placed him on the backs of two chairs – his fore legs on the rails of one, and his hind legs on the rails of the other – and, in this rather arduous position, had painted from him for a considerable time, when a friend was announced as waiting for him in another apartment. Particularly desirous of seeing this visitor immediately, the painter hurried from the room, entirely forgetting to tell 'Prinny' to get down; and remained in conversation with his friend for full half an hour. On returning to his study, the first object that greeted him was poor 'Prinny', standing on his 'bad eminence' exactly in the position in which he had been left, trembling with fatigue, and occasionally venting his anger and distress in a low, piteous moan, but not moving a limb, or venturing even to turn his head. Not having received the usual signal, he had never once attempted to get down, but had remained disconsolate in his position 'sitting' hard, with nobody to paint him, during the long half hour that had delayed his master's return.

WILKIE COLLINS, *Memoirs of the Life of William Collins, Esq., R.A.*, 1848

Rosa Bonheur's 'Noah's Ark' was hardly less remarkable than Sodoma's, and at various times included lions, stags, a gazelle, an eagle and an otter. She herself reports on an arrival in Nice in 1888:

Everything is in good order in the villa. Ratata [her monkey] is in her fine cage out in the sun and rolling herself in the hay. Gamine [her dog] puts on her lovely airs as soon as she gets to Nice. My little bull-finch is just now singing his ditty 'Father Bugeaud's Cap', while Green Cocotte [her parrot] is swearing in Spanish. You see I give you every item of news. . . .

ROSA BONHEUR, *Letter to Madame Peyrol*

He [Rossetti] collected almost anything that attracted his attention, particularly china, furniture, and animals.

Of the last he had at one time or another a Pomeranian puppy called Punch, an Irish Wolfhound called Wolf, two brown owls called Jenny and Bobby, some rabbits, dormice, hedgehogs, white mice, squirrels, a mole, a chameleon, some salamanders, a deer, a wallaby, some kangaroos, two wombats, a Canadian marmot, a wood-chuck, an armadillo, a racoon, a Brahmin Bull, a jackass, and numerous birds including peacocks, Chinese horned owls, talking grey parrots, a raven, and a grass parakeet. These lived a life of conflict and depredation in and about the house and gardens and those of his neighbours. The armadillo disappeared for several weeks, and suddenly appeared through the floor of a basement kitchen some distance away, to the great alarm of the cook, 'who opined that if it was not the devil there was no knowing what it was'; the deer stamped out all the tail feathers of the peacock, who in turn made so much noise that a clause was in future introduced into all the leases on the Cadogan Estate forbidding them to be kept in the neighbourhood. The racoon was particularly ferocious and destructive.

It does not appear that Rossetti lavished any personal affection upon his various pets, except perhaps upon the first of the wombats; he met their frequent deaths and disappearances with fortitude; some indeed died or disappeared almost the moment they were acquired, and some, such as the Brahmin Bull, which Rossetti bought for twenty pounds at Cremorne Gardens because it had eyes that reminded him of Janey Morris, proved quite unmanageable. But he liked to have them about the place, and he particularly delighted in visits to Jamrack's shop, where in an acrid atmosphere, beasts from all countries chattered and rattled against their bars.

EVELYN WAUGH, *Rossetti, his Life and Works*, 1928

PHOTOGRAPHY

Certainly photography is an interesting art, or can be, but I think it's been – not overpraised, but relied on too much, so that in painting and drawing people have used photographs and abandoned actually looking at the world. I think it will all recur when we begin to sort out what photography truly is. After all, photography is a quite recent development. It does coincide in a sense with the modern period in art, and that's probably no accident. Surely the decline in portrait painting and the rise of the portrait photograph isn't coincidental. Yet it seems to me that a really good drawing or painting of a figure is infinitely more interesting than any photograph. Picasso's portrait of Gertrude Stein is more interesting than any photograph I've ever seen of her, and for us to think not is foolish. And if that's the case, what does it mean? We tend to think the information a photographer provides is true. Just as you can make a drawing of somebody and then the friends of the person say It's not like him, you can take a photograph and you can eventually say You know it's not like him, he doesn't look like that. So the information in a photograph is not always true. We've tended to think the camera cannot lie, and I think it probably can lie just as much as a painting.

DAVID HOCKNEY, *My Early Years*, 1988

PICASSO

In 1900, at the age of nineteen, Picasso held his first exhibition, at the Els Quatre Gats café, Barcelona, which got some shrewdly appreciative reviews in local newspapers. Perhaps the most favourable was the 'notice' below by an unidentified visitor, probably written for publication but apparently not printed at the time.

Having been cordially invited by our good friend Pablo Ruiz Picasso, we went to see his exhibition in the big hall of the Quatre Gats. We went with the assurance of seeing something good, because we know the artist and we were delighted to look at more than 150 works, each one of them worthy of being a passport to the realm of art. We have never seen so rich an exhibition, and seldom one with so many good things. Picasso is an artist from head to toe. He has a genuine feeling for art and he knows how to project his feelings with good taste, which is a rare quality in our artists. In painting he is a revolutionary and an enthusiastic campaigner for the new school.

All his paintings are full of great strength and ease and, down to the most insignificant drawings, they convey a deep philosophy, a need to unite the psychological aspect of the work to the materiality of the craft. In each stroke of the pencil or of charcoal, in each brushstroke, one can see a profound faith in the art he is making, and a kind of inspired fever reminiscent of the best works of El Greco and Goya, the only indisputable masters or divinities for Picasso. His portraits can be rated as masterpieces; they are all true embodiments of those pipe-smoking characters we have seen walking down the Ramblas, but this collection presents more than personalities, it is a portrait of the present age. The exhibition may become a special testimonial and historical document. In the same way, in the Casas exhibition one saw a gallery of personalities, who are, with a few exceptions, representatives of intellectual society.

ANONYMOUS (Barcelona, 1900)

Ramon Casas was an older Catalan artist who had exhibited in Barcelona in 1899 a large number of charcoal drawings of local personalities.

Picasso speaks.

I can hardly understand the importance given to the word *research* in connection with modern painting. In my opinion to search means nothing in painting. To find, is the thing. Nobody is interested in following a man who, with his eyes fixed on the ground, spends his life looking for the pocketbook [*sic*] that fortune should put in his path. The one who finds something no matter what it might be, even if his intention were not to search for it, at least arouses our curiosity, if not our admiration.

Among the several sins that I have been accused of committing, none is more false than the one that I have, as the principal objective in my work, the spirit of research. When I paint any object it is to show what I have found and not what I am looking for. In art intentions are not sufficient and, as we say in Spanish: love must be proved by facts and not by reasons. What one does is what counts and not what one had the intention of doing.

We all know that Art is not truth. Art is a lie that makes us realise truth, at least the truth that is given us to understand. The artist must know the manner whereby to convince others of the truthfulness of his lies. If he only shows in his work that he has searched, and re-searched, for the way to put over lies, he would never accomplish anything.

The idea of research has often made painting go astray, and made the artist lose himself in mental lucubrations. Perhaps this has been the principal fault of modern art. The spirit of research has poisoned those who have not fully understood all the positive and conclusive elements in modern art and has made them attempt to paint the invisible and, therefore, the unpaintable.

They speak of naturalism in opposition to modern painting. I would like to know if anyone has ever seen a natural work of art. Nature and art, being two different things, cannot be the same thing. Through art we express our conception of what nature is not.

PABLO PICASSO, 1923

PIERO DELLA FRANCESCA

England can claim a significant part in 'rediscovery' of this supreme Renaissance painter. Thanks to that English interest, three of his rare panel paintings, including two altarpieces, were acquired for the National Gallery well before the end of the nineteenth century; and, in 1877, John Addington Symonds was among the first people to pay literary tribute to what is now one of the most famous pictures in the world.

Those who have once seen his fresco of the 'Resurrection' in the hall of the Compagnia della Misericordia at Borgo San Sepolcro, will never forget the deep impression of solitude and aloofness from all earthly things produced by it. It is not so much the admirable grouping and masterly drawing of the four sleeping soldiers, or even the majestic type of the Christ emergent from the grave, as the communication of a mood felt by the painter and instilled into our souls, that makes this by far the grandest, most poetic, and most awe-inspiring picture of the Resurrection. The landscape is simple and severe, with the cold light upon it of the dawn before the sun is risen. The drapery of the ascending Christ is tinged with auroral colours like the earliest clouds of the morning; and His level eyes, with the mystery of the slumber of the grave still upon them, seem gazing, far beyond our scope of vision, into the region of the eternal and illimitable.

JOHN ADDINGTON SYMONDS, *Renaissance in Italy: The Fine Arts*, 1877

The best picture in the world is painted in fresco on the wall of a room in the town hall [at Borgo San Sepolcro]. Some unwittingly beneficent vandal had it covered, some time after it was painted, with a thick layer of plaster, under which it lay hidden for a century or two, to be revealed at last in a state of preservation remarkably perfect for a fresco of its date. Thanks to the vandals, the visitor who now enters the Palazzo dei Conservatori at Borgo San Sepolcro finds the stupendous Resurrection almost as Piero della Francesca left it. Its clear, yet subtly sober colours shine out from the wall with scarcely impaired freshness. Damp has blotted out nothing of the design, nor dirt obscured it. We need no imagination to help us figure forth its beauty; it stands there before us in entire and actual splendour, the greatest picture in the world.

ALDOUS HUXLEY, *Along the Road*, 1925

CAMILLE PISSARRO

Pissarro was aged sixty when he wrote this letter to his eldest son. The most kindly and generously appreciative of the group of Impressionist painters, he probably remained the poorest, despite being enormously productive in a variety of media.

Paris, 9 May 1891

My dear Lucien,
Tell me if you have received my etchings and whether you like them. The landscape has had some success, Degas liked *The Market* very much. He advised me to leave it as it was, but I have not yet made up my mind whether I want to try to give it more clarity after I have made a few prints. You will notice it is quite strong.

Times are hard, I can't sell anything. I have had five rather old canvases done in 1872–1873 belonging to a banker [Achille Arosa], who commissioned them from me, on auction, besides four door panels, (measurements 22 × 52 inches). The five canvases are well preserved, grey and delicate, particularly *Snow Effect* done at Louveciennes which is very good. There is also a small canvas, *Street of Louveciennes* which seemed very fine to me. The lot was sold for a song, eleven hundred francs for the four panels and three hundred and seventy francs for the small canvas of 18 × 15 inches. The latter was bought to be sent to New York. The buyer had seen my new things and had suggested them without being able to get them taken – his backers claim they are done 'in dots' and won't hear of them. Only Théo van Gogh was able to have the collectors here accept them. It's hopeless now, they are more stubborn than ever.

Durand [Ruel] was at the auction. He let my paintings go at the most ridiculous prices! However, they were works done long ago! The strangest thing is that this devil of a Durand praised my *Serpentine* with Effect of Fog which belongs to M. Gallimard and a small canvas of 21 × 18 inches done completely in the divisionist technique, a field in a white, setting sun, which had been sold to poor Dupuis who committed suicide. And didn't he say to me yesterday, right in front of Zandomeneghi at the Monet show: 'Monsieur Pissarro, it's your turn now to have a good show!'

CAMILLE PISSARRO, *Letter to his son Lucien*

PORTRAITURE

To Messer Titian
Painting of a little girl
I have seen portrayed by you, my dearest friend, the little girl of Roberto Strozzi, that grave and splendid gentleman. And since you seek my serious opinion, I tell you that if I were a painter myself I should despair; although it would be necessary for my vision to partake of the knowledge of God in order to understand just why I ought to despair. Undoubtedly your brush has kept its miracles for the ripeness of your old age.

So I, who am not blind when it comes to such genius, solemnly swear in conscience that it is impossible to believe, let alone easy to do such a thing; and so it deserves to be placed before all the paintings that ever were or ever will be. Thus Nature must swear that this likeness is not simulated, if Art asserts that it is not alive. I would also praise the puppy that she strokes, if it were not enough to exclaim on the liveliness that animates it. But this too leaves me speechless for want of words to express my stupor.

PIETRO ARETINO, *Letter to Titian*, 1542

Titian's portrait of the very young Clarice Strozzi, dated 1542, is in the Gemäldegalerie, Berlin-Dahlem, and deserves all the praise Aretino gives it. Aretino is himself a personality more complex than is always realized, and one of his most genuine qualities was his response to paintings – above all, to Titian's. (See also SKY.*)*

'Ha, what's this?' asked Napoleon, noticing that all the courtiers were looking at something concealed under a cloth.

With courtly adroitness de Bausset half turned, and without turning his back to the Emperor retired two steps, twitching off the cloth at the same time, and said:

'A present to your Majesty from the Empress.'

It was a portrait, painted in bright colours by Gérard, of the son borne to Napoleon by the daughter of the Emperor of Austria, the boy whom for some reason every one called 'The King of Rome'.

A very pretty curly-headed boy, with a look of the Christ in the Sistine Madonna, was depicted playing at stick and ball. The ball represented the terrestrial globe and the stick in his hand a sceptre.

Though it was not clear what the artist meant to express by depicting the so-called King of Rome spiking the earth with a stick, the allegory apparently seemed to Napoleon, as it had done to all who had seen it in Paris, quite clear and very pleasing.

'The King of Rome!' he said, pointing to the portrait with a graceful gesture. 'Admirable!'

With the natural capacity of an Italian for changing the expression of his face at will, he drew nearer to the portrait and assumed a look of pensive tenderness. He felt that what he said now and did would be historical, and it seemed to him that it would now be best for him – whose grandeur enabled his son to play stick and ball with the terrestrial globe – to show, in contrast to that grandeur, the simplest paternal tenderness. His eyes grew dim, he moved forward, glanced round at a chair (which seemed to place itself under him), and sat down on it before the portrait. At a single gesture from him every one went out on tiptoe, leaving the great man to himself and his emotion.

Having sat still for a while he touched – himself not knowing why – the thick spot of paint representing the highest light in the portrait, rose, and recalled de Bausset and the officer on duty. He ordered the portrait to be carried outside his tent, that the Old Guard, stationed round it, might not be deprived of the pleasure of seeing the King of Rome, the son and heir of their adored monarch.

And while he was doing M. de Bausset the honour of breakfasting with him, they heard, as Napoleon had anticipated, the rapturous cries of the officers and men of the Old Guard who had run up to see the portrait.

'*Vive l'Empéreur! Vive le Roi de Rome! Vive l'Empéreur!*' came those ecstatic cries.

LEO TOLSTOY, *War and Peace*, 1863–9

Tolstoy did not entirely invent this scene, but drew the facts of it from the memoirs of de Bausset.

As he was turning the handle of the door, his eye fell upon the portrait Basil Hallward had painted of him. He started back as if in surprise. Then he went on into his own room, looking somewhat puzzled. After he had taken the buttonhole out of his coat, he seemed to hesitate. Finally he came back, went over to the picture, and examined it. In the dim arrested light that struggled through the cream-coloured silk blinds, the face appeared to him to be a little changed. The expression looked different. One would have said that there was a touch of cruelty in the mouth. It was certainly strange.

He turned round, and, walking to the window, drew up the blind. The bright dawn flooded the room, and swept the fantastic shadows into dusky corners, where they lay shuddering. The strange expression he had noticed in the face of the portrait seemed to linger there, to be more intensified even. The quivering, ardent sunlight showed him the lines of cruelty round the mouth as clearly as if he had been looking into a mirror after he had done some dreadful thing.

He winced, and, taking up from the table an oval glass framed in ivory Cupids, one of Lord Henry's many presents to him, glanced hurriedly into the polished depths. No line like that warped his red lips. What did it mean?

He rubbed his eyes, and came close to the picture, and examined it again.

There were no signs of any change when he looked into the actual painting, and yet there was no doubt that the whole expression had altered. It was not a mere fancy of his own. The thing was horribly apparent.

He threw himself into a chair, and began to think. Suddenly there flashed across his mind what he had said in Basil Hallward's studio the day the picture had been finished. Yes, he remembered it perfectly. He had uttered a mad wish that he himself might remain young, and the portrait grow old; that his own beauty might be untarnished, and the face on the canvas bear the burden of his passions and his sins; that the painted image might be seared with the lines of suffering and thought, and that he might keep all the delicate bloom and loveliness of his just then conscious boyhood. Surely his wish had not been fulfilled? Such things were impossible. It seemed monstrous even to think of them. And, yet, there was the picture before him, with a touch of cruelty in the mouth.

OSCAR WILDE, *The Picture of Dorian Gray*, 1891

A great and fashionable portrait-painter, one admittedly tiring of that aspect of his own art, gave this wise advice to a student (later Director of the Tate Gallery):

You say you are studying painting to become a portrait painter. I think you would be making a great mistake if you kept that only in view during the time you intend to work in a life class – where the object of the student should be to acquire sufficient command over his material to do whatever nature presents to him. The conventionalities of portrait painting are only tolerable in one who is a good *painter* – if he is only a good *portrait-painter* he is nobody. Try to become a painter first and then apply your knowledge to a special branch – but do not begin by learning what is required for a special branch, or you will become a mannerist.

JOHN SARGENT, *Letter to J. B. Manson*, 1901

You know, if one paints someone's portrait, one should not know him if at all possible. No knowledge! I do not want to know him at all, want only to see what is there, the outside. The inner follows by itself. It is mirrored in the visible. As soon as one knows him too long, one gets irritated. The visual immediacy is lost. The first impression is the right one. Once I have finished his picture, I can perhaps revise my impression and say, he really isn't such a beast as it seemed. Or he is not as decadent or as greedy as Flechtheim was at that time, or not so naïve as the Trillhaases. . . . It's all the same to me. I must keep the first impression fresh. If it is lost, I must find it again.

OTTO DIX, *c.* 1965

POUSSIN

I often admired the extreme devotion that this excellent painter had to perfecting his art. I encountered him, at the age he had reached, among the ruins of ancient Rome and sometimes in the countryside and on the banks of the Tiber where he drew what he found most to his taste. I have also seen him collecting in his handkerchief pebbles, moss, flowers and other such things, that he wished to paint exactly from nature. I asked him one day by what route he had reached that lofty eminence which gave him a notable place among the greatest painters of Italy; he replied modestly: 'I have neglected nothing.'

ANONYMOUS, *Mélanges d'Histoire et de Littérature . . .*, 1699–1700

This crisply vivid eyewitness account probably refers to the period around 1658, when Poussin was sixty-four.

Bernini's comment, after looking long at Poussin's 'Gathering of the Ashes of Phocion' [Walker Art Gallery, Liverpool] is one of the most succinctly perceptive tributes ever paid by one great artist to another:

Signor Poussin is a painter who works up there [*indicating his forehead*].

P. FRÉART DE CHANTELOU, *Journal du voyage du Cavalier Bernin en France*, 1665

. . . and there is a noble N. Poussin at the Academy [now National Gallery, no. 40], a solemn, deep, still summer's noon, with large umbrageous trees, and a man washing his feet at a fountain near them. Through the breaks in the trees are mountains, and the clouds collecting about them with the most enchanting effects possible. It cannot be too much to say that this landscape is full of religious and moral feeling.

JOHN CONSTABLE, *Letter to Archdeacon Fisher*, 20 September 1821

Poussin had to wait two hundred and fifty years for that famous fund to raise a statue to him, which I believe still does not exist, owing to the inadequacy of the subscription. If he had merely burned a couple of villages he would not have waited so long.

EUGÈNE DELACROIX, *Letter to Théophile Silvestre*, 1858

POVERTY

Few examples of sad circumstances at a great painter's death are more poignant and vivid than that of Piazzetta's family, following his death in Venice in 1754. Famous and respected, as is shown by the family's petition to the Doge given below, and never inactive – though notoriously slow – he yet died destitute.

Most Serene Prince,
The poor afflicted family of Giovanni Battista Piazzetta appeal as supplicants at the feet of your Serenity, left as they are following his recent death in a condition truly deserving of mercy and compassion. While he lived, he justly enjoyed through his labours in the highly noble art of painting, in this most Serene Republic and also beyond, the sympathy and praise which his work attracts and will always attract. More than once, his service was sought, with handsome proposals, by foreign princes. But content and proud to live under the protection of his own respected ruler, he not only had the courage to refuse all such offers from abroad, but was determined to remain in this Most Serene Republic, and wished moreover to train under him a number of pupils who will one day be a credit to their master and also to their country. He lived in the hope of at some time being eventually the recipient of state benevolence, through an act of graciousness, as in the past was Paolo Veronese and were other famous painters. Always therefore toiling in his studio, and mentally preoccupied with succeeding in the most inventive aspects of art, seeking glory more than gain, he was reduced at the close of his advanced years to a condition so straitened and miserable that it hastened his end; he died tormented by distress at having to leave, after so many labours, a numerous family, a mother and three daughters (two of them unmarried) and four sons, all deprived of any means of support. For that reason, prostrate at the throne of their respected Prince, with tears in their eyes, they beg your Serenity's indulgence for relief of some sort in their extreme want.

REGISTRO DE SUPPLICHE E CARTE PUBBLICHE
CONCERNENTI LE ARTI, Venice, 1751–9

That this petition was no exaggerated account was confirmed by other people, including Piazzetta's parish priest, and was eloquently expanded on and supported by the Inquisitor for the Arts, Marc' Antonio Dolfin.

PRISON

Among painters put into prison, Haydon seems to have survived the ordeal, undergone several times, remarkably well. Almost like a sketch for some scene in 'Little Dorrit' is his characterization in 1836 of the head turnkey of the King's Bench Prison, with short thighs that poked out from under his belly, who claimed to be able to prove that Abraham was circumcised 'the very day before Sodom and Gomorrah were burnt!'

When he came in he seemed labouring with deep thoughts, and he left me relieved, as if he had done his duty. He was the first man I saw in 1823 when I paid my fees. The hideous look of his dark globular eyes, one of them awry like [Edward] Irving's, gave me a horror. He looked a perfect Schidone; but I have caught him in perpetual acts of benevolence, where he little thought my eye would find him out.

There is not a worthier heart, and never was a rougher case for it. Strange to find such sensibilities in a gaol.

BENJAMIN ROBERT HAYDON, *Autobiography and Memoirs*

In 1912, Egon Schiele was arrested in the small Austrian town of Neulengbach on charges of 'immorality' and 'seduction of a minor', and imprisoned for twenty-four days before being tried. He kept a diary of his days in prison.

The key-jangling guard put a bucket, a broom, brush etc., in the cell and ordered me to scrub the floor. Is that allowed? Indecent, this demand. And yet I was happy about it; just to be busy is a blessing. I scrubbed and scoured, washed and wiped with all my strength. Knees, spine and arms still hurt long afterwards and my fingers are raw, the nails broken. Almost proud of what I had done, I waited for the guard and believed that he would praise me. He came, looked at the floor, then spat, here and there he spat, ugly puddles, and growled: 'D'you call this scrubbed? It's nothin' but pig's smear. Scrub it again, right away, but good this time I'm tellin' you!' And I dragged water over and knelt down again and scrubbed and scrubbed.

EGON SCHIELE, *Diary*, 1912

PIERRE PRUD'HON

May I venture, dear sir, to express my surprise that in so conscientious a work (and one in which for my own part I find nothing to blame save an excessively generous partiality where I am concerned) I find no reference among the painters of this century whom you consider most remarkable, to one admirable man who ranks very high in my esteem and whose name you do not ever mention: I mean Prud'hon, perhaps the most original of all the men with whom you deal, and one whom posterity will undoubtedly set high above a good many of those you have discussed. I can only ascribe this omission to a deliberate bias, for which you no doubt have grounds but which I am sorry you have not taken the trouble to explain to the art-lover reader, to whom you promise a sort of history of painting in our time.

EUGÈNE DELACROIX, *Letter to Ernest Chesneau*, 1862

Chesneau had just published and sent Delacroix a copy of his book 'La Peinture française au 19e siècle'.

PUPIL AND MASTER

After five years of education and training, impressed by his virtue, integrity and excellent qualities, and also by the promise of his great natural genius, I gave him [Velázquez] my daughter in marriage. And since a master is more to be honoured than a father-in-law, it is only right to attack the effrontery of one who wishes to take to himself this honour, robbing me of the glory of my old age. I consider it no disgrace for the pupil to surpass the master; it is more important to tell the truth. Leonardo da Vinci was none the worse for having Raphael for a pupil, nor Giorgio da Castelfranco for Titian, nor Plato for Aristotle, since none affected the renown of the teacher for excellence.

I write this not only for the sake of extolling the present subject, which will be done elsewhere (in my Eulogy of him), but much more out of gratitude and reverence to his Catholic Majesty, our great King Philip IV, whom heaven protect for many years, for it is from his liberal hand that Velázquez has received and continues to receive the greatest honours.

FRANCISCO PACHECO, *Arte de Pintura*, 1649

. . . and in the end he [Testa] was strongly taken with Pietro da Cortona's way of colouring; whereupon he left the first school and settled with the latter, being so impressed that he entirely adopted his style. But because Testa had, in addition to an exceptionally tall figure, with an imposing presence, a certain complacency about himself and anything to do with himself, the result was that he sometimes showed less respect than he should have for the works of that great painter who was his master. Things reached the point where he began to make his attitude obvious; it could no longer be concealed or left unperceived by Pietro da Cortona. And so, one day, taking I know not what pretext, he turned to Testa and said: 'My dear Pietro, I realise that my work fails to satisfy you because it doesn't reach the mark that would suffice for teaching art to someone of your high standards of taste. Therefore, the best thing will be for you to get another master, who may be better than I am, and more suited to your requirements: and so please feel free to seek your fortune elsewhere.' The young man, who knew his master's character, did not wait for a second warning; and with an embarrassment that can be imagined, he took himself off from that school.

FILIPPO BALDINUCCI, *'Life' of Pietro Testa* in *Notizie de' Professori del disegno da Cimabue in qua*, 1773

QUALITY

On reading – impatiently or with a patient smile – elaborate dissertations which 'prove' that a picture is by such and such a master, at the end we generally, after many arguments and references, come upon the word 'quality'. This means that the decisive point, which also brings things to a dead end, has been reached. You derive the impression that the entire letterpress – lengthy, spasmodic, crowded with quotations – is just counsel's pleading, while the judge who condemns or acquits solely uses the word 'quality'. The concept of 'quality' arrests the flow of words of even the most garrulous.

When the impression fills us with pleasurable satisfaction – with 'disinterested pleasure' as the aestheticians say – it springs from a pure, individual and hence uniform vision and also from a successful realization of this vision, thanks to which the emotional values are communicated to us without any considerable loss. We have an individually coloured voice which says something that we know, but says it in such a fashion that we think we hear it for the first time.

A pleasurable sensation of a definite degree and a definite kind is, in our experience, associated with the works of this or that master. We stand in expectation of some such kind of delight as a work of art can produce – a sense of elevation, of shock, of revelation, of disclosure, of rapture, or whatever the case may be – and we decide on authorship and authenticity according as such an experience does or does not take place.

The connoisseur of wine determines with full certainty brand and vintage from a particular flavour: in the same way, the connoisseur of art recognizes the author on the strength of the sensually spiritualized impression that he receives. Sometimes it is a question of lovely equipoise, sometimes of stark, exciting vividness, sometimes again of an intensification of the sense of life, or a sense of pathos, of boundless abundance, of heroic exaltation – and every time the accent is unmistakeable. Always quality shows itself in this, that emotional values experienced by the artist in his vision are interpreted in visible terms.

I must anticipate the query whether the quality of, say, a still-life or a slight scene from passing life is due to a successful interpretation of spiritual emotion. The answer is, Yes; only if it is necessary fully to understand what has happened. When Chardin saw a fruit this visual experience filled him with delicate enjoyment, and this sensation invested eye and hand with the capacity to paint as he did. Again, when Pieter de Hooch painted the roof of a house, so deeply did he feel the marvel of light in the wealth of colours and tonal values, that he was able to communicate to the spectator, in full purity and completeness, the delight, the peaceful pleasure that the world, as he had seen it, had given him.

It is only the line put down at the dictate of feeling, only the brushstroke guided by instinct – nothing that is taught, calculated, selected or painstakingly improved upon – which communicates the vibrations of feeling and thereby that experience for the sake of which art has value to us. No wonder that the differences between good and bad, measured or weighed, appear infinitesimal.

An unsatisfactory column, shall we say, is the one which is drawn as with a ruler. To the good architect the column is an organism with a soul, suffering, triumphant, carrying and burdened; and in the scarcely measureable, delicate life of the outline there are expressed strength, tension, pressure and resistance.

The notion of quality is brought out by a comparison between an original and a copy better than by the best definition. Such a comparison makes us penetrate deep into the essence of artistic production.

MAX J. FRIEDLÄNDER, *On Art and Connoisseurship*, 1942

RAEBURN

At least until recently Raeburn – along with other fine Scottish painters – suffered undeserved neglect in England. That he himself felt his isolation, and the indifference, is confirmed by this dignified letter to a friend in London.

I observe what you say respecting the election of RA, but what am I to do here? they know I am on the list; if they choose to elect me without solicitation, it will be the more honourable to me, and I will think the more of it; but if it can only be obtained by means of solicitation and canvassing, I must give up all hope of it, for I would think it unfair to employ those means. I am besides out of the way, and have no opportunity. I rejoice in the worthy president's increasing reputation; it is pleasing and consolatory to see that additional powers come with the increase of years. Write and tell me what artists are about, and whether anything be indispensable for a person who desires to become a member of the Royal Academy. Were you in sufficient health to see Somerset House during the last exhibition? I had some things there, but no artist of my acquaintance has been kind enough to write me one syllable on the subject, to say either what he thought himself or what others thought.

SIR HENRY RAEBURN, *Letter of 1814*

The President was Benjamin West. Raeburn was elected an RA in 1815, but his sense of isolation remained and he wrote to David Wilkie four years later, in 1819:

I send up generally a picture or two to the exhibition, which serve merely as an advertisement that I am still in the land of the living, but nor have I the least conception how they look beside others. I know not in what London papers any critiques of that kind are made, and our Edinburgh ones (at least those that I see) take no notice of these matters. At anyrate I would prefer a candid observation or two from an artist like you, conveying not only your own opinion but perhaps that of others, before any of them.

SIR HENRY RAEBURN, *Letter of 12 September 1819*

'And I suppose I must have a hobby; I shall probably collect Raeburns.'

SAKI, 'The Treasure-Ship' in *Beasts and Super-Beasts*, 1914

This is one of the agreeable ways that Vasco Honiton proposes to spend the money acquired through blackmailing his aunt, Lulu, Duchess of Dulverton, and other well-known people, as a result of the papers he has found in the sunken treasure-ship.

ALLAN RAMSAY

With pride in his own literary art, and pride also in his son's in a different medium, the elder Allan Ramsay thus apostrophized the younger: 'On His Drawing a Fine Gentleman's Picture'.

Young Painter, thy Attempt is fair,
And may'st thou finish with a Grace,
The happy Smile unmix'd with Care,
That ever shines in —— Face.
So far thy Labour, well design'd,
May all thy outward Form display,
But Pencils cannot paint the Mind,
In this, to me, thou must give way.
With glowing Colours thou canst show,
Th'embroider'd Coat and nice *Tupee*:
Draw him a first Rate blazing Beau,
Easy and airy, gay and free.
But I can place him in a Light,
That will his higher Merits hit;
Display, what makes him much more bright,
His Courage, Learning, and his Wit.

ALLAN RAMSAY in *The Scarborough Miscellany*, 1732

RAPHAEL

What has been remarked of Leonardo da Vinci, is still more true of Raphael, that there is an angelic sweetness and tenderness in his faces, peculiarly adapted to his subjects, in which natural frailty and passion are purified by the sanctity of religion. They answer exactly to Milton's description of the 'human face divine'. The ancient statues are finer objects for the eye to contemplate: they represent a more perfect race of physical beings, but we have no sympathy with them. In Raphael, all our natural sensibilities are raised and refined by pointing mysteriously to the interests of another world. The same intensity of passion appears also to distinguish Raphael from Michael Angelo. Michael Angelo's forms are grander, but they are not so full of expression. Raphael's, however ordinary in themselves, are full of expression even to o'erflowing: every nerve and muscle is impregnated with feeling, or bursting with meaning. . . . It has been said that Michael Angelo painted *man*, and Raphael *men*; that the one was an epic, the other a dramatic painter. But the distinction we have made is perhaps truer and more intelligible, *viz.* that the former gave greater dignity of form, and the latter greater force and refinement of expression.

WILLIAM HAZLITT in *The Champion*, 1814

I should need a book – several volumes – to expatiate on the qualities of Raphael and on his incomparable compositions; but I will say that the Vatican frescoes are in themselves worth more than all the galleries of pictures together. That splendid museum is so varied, so skilfully has its creator touched every chord – so well caught the versatility of nature even to the diversity of effects! And all that has been painted by Raphael from drawings!

So let us contrive – trying to imitate him – to comprehend him, being myself quite wretched at having all my life to deplore not being born in his century. When I think that three hundred years ago I should have been able to become truly his pupil!

J. A. D. INGRES, 1814

Three mornings in the week we went to the Picture Gallery [in Dresden] from twelve till one. The first day we went was a Sunday, when there is always a crowd in the Sistine Madonna Cabinet. I sat down on a sofa opposite the picture for an instant, but a sort of awe, as if I were suddenly in the living presence of some glorious being, made my heart swell too much for me to remain comfortably, and we hurried out of the room. On subsequent mornings we always came, in the last minutes of our stay, to look at this sublimest picture; and while the others, except the 'Christo della Moneta' [by Titian] and Holbein's Madonna, lost much of their first interest, this becomes harder and harder to leave.

GEORGE ELIOT, *Journal*, July 1858

I shall be told that Raffaelle did come to draw and paint much better than he has done here [the Ansidei Madonna]. I demur to this. He did a little better; he just took so much pains as to prevent him from going down-hill headlong, and, with practice, he gained facility, but he was never any good, either as a draughtsman or as a painter. His reputation, indeed, rests mainly on his supposed exquisitely pure and tender feeling. His colour is admittedly inferior, his handling is not highly praised by any one, his drawing has been much praised, but it is of a penmanship freehand kind which is particularly apt to take people in. Of course he could draw in some ways, no one giving all his time to art and living in Raffaelle's surroundings could, with even ordinary pains, help becoming a facile draughtsman, but it is the expression and sentiment of his pictures which are supposed to be ineffable and to make him the prince of painters.

I do not think this reputation will be maintained much longer.

SAMUEL BUTLER, *Notebooks*, 1885, revised 1897

'READYMADES'

In 1913 I had the happy idea to fasten a bicycle wheel to a kitchen stool and watch it turn.

A few months later I bought a cheap reproduction of a winter evening landscape, which I called *Pharmacy* after adding two small dots, one red and one yellow, in the horizon.

In New York in 1915 I bought at a hardware store a snow shovel on which I wrote 'in advance of the broken arm'.

It was around this time that the word 'readymade' came to mind to designate this form of manifestation.

A point which I want very much to establish is that the choice of these 'readymades' was never dictated by aesthetic delectation.

This choice was based on a reaction of visual indifference with at the same time a total absence of good or bad taste . . . in fact a complete anaesthesia.

One important characteristic was the short sentence which I occasionally inscribed on the 'readymade'.

That sentence instead of describing the object like a title was meant to carry the mind of the spectator toward other regions more verbal.

Sometimes I would add a graphic detail of presentation which, in order to satisfy my craving for alliteration, would be called 'readymade aided'.

At another time wanting to expose the basic antinomy between art and readymades I imagined a 'reciprocal readymade': Use a Rembrandt as an ironing board!

I realised very soon the danger of repeating indiscriminately this form of expression and decided to limit the production of 'readymades' to a small number yearly. I was aware at that time that, for the spectator even more than for the artist, art is a habit-forming drug and I wanted to protect my 'readymades' against such contamination.

MARCEL DUCHAMP, 1961

RELIGIOUS PICTURES

At every fresh exhibition, the critics observe that religious painting is more and more deficient. I do not know if they are correct so far as numbers are concerned; but certainly they make no mistake as to quality. Religious writers, like socialist writers, naturally tend to make beauty dependent upon belief, and more than one religious writer has attributed to a simple lack of faith this difficulty in giving expression to the things of faith. This error could be philosophically demonstrated if the facts did not show us sufficient proof to the contrary, and if the history of painting did not offer us the example of impious and atheistical artists producing excellent religious works. Let us simply say then that since religion is the highest *fiction* of the human mind (I am purposely speaking as an atheistic professor of the fine arts would speak, and nothing of what I say should be inferred as arguing against my own faith), it will require the most vigorous imagination and the most concentrated efforts from those who devote themselves to the expression of its acts and its sentiments. In the same way the character of Polyeuctes demands from the poet and the actor a spiritual assent and an enthusiasm far more lively than those demanded by some vulgar character in love with a vulgar earthy creature, or even than a purely political hero. The only concession that one can reasonably make to those who hold to the theory of faith as the unique source of religious inspiration, is that at the moment of executing his work the poet, the actor and the artist must believe in the reality of what he is representing, fired as he is by necessity. Thus it is that art is the only spiritual sphere in which man can say, 'I shall believe if I wish, and if I do not wish, I shall not believe.' The cruel and humiliating maxim, *Spiritus flat ubi vult*, loses its credit in matters of art.

CHARLES BAUDELAIRE, *The Salon of 1859*

REMBRANDT

The great Rembrandt who did not go to Titian nor Van Dyck,
Michelangelo nor Raphael,
Who rather chose illustriously to wander,
To be the foremost heretic in painting,
Than to subject his famous brush to any discipline.
A shame it is for Art
That such an honest hand
Did not make better use of gifts inborn!
In painting, who would have surpassed him?
Hélas, the nobler the spirit, the more it will run wild
If he build not on common ground nor recognise the rules,
But try to know it all out of himself!

ANDRIES PELS, *Gebruik en misbruik des tooneels*, 1681

Pels was a man of letters and a friend of Gérard de Lairesse, a painter-theorist who knew Rembrandt and had been portrayed by him. Pels's attitude is not untypical of early commentators, who were at least free from the blind total veneration characteristic of later approaches to the painter – of which we are probably still not entirely free.

Notice that he is the least Dutch of the Dutch painters, and that, if he is of his time, he is never altogether of it. What his fellow-countrymen noticed, he did not see; what they turned from he turned to. They had left the fable behind, he returned to it; they left the Bible behind: he illustrated it; the Gospels: he delighted in them. He clothed them in his own individual way, but he showed in them a unique, new, and universally comprehensible meaning. He dreamed of Simeon, Jacob, Laban, the Prodigal Son, Tobias, the Apostles, the Holy Family, King David, Calvary, the Samaritan, Lazarus, the Evangelists. He haunts Jerusalem and Emmaus; we can feel always that he is tempted by the synagogue. These time-honoured themes he brings forward in nameless surroundings and in senseless costumes. He conceives them and formulates them with as little care for tradition as regard for total truth. And yet such is his creative power that this very special and individual mind gives the subjects it treats a general expression, an inner and typical meaning that great thinkers and epic draughtsmen do not always reach.

I have told you somewhere in this study that his principle was to extract from things one element from among all the others, or rather to take them all away to seize expressly only one of them. He has thus done the work of an analyst, a distiller, or, to speak in nobler terms, of a metaphysician even more than of a poet. Never did reality in the whole take possession of him. Judging from the way he treated bodies, one might well doubt whether he took an interest in the outside of things at all. He liked women, and has painted only misshapen ones; he liked fabrics, and never imitated them; to make up for this, in default of grace, beauty, purity of line, and fineness of flesh, he expressed the nude body by suppleness, curves, elasticity, with a love of substance, a sense of the living being, which are the delight of the craftsman. He decomposed and reduced everything, colour as well as light, so that by eliminating from appearances all that was composite, by condensing all that was dispersed, he came to be able to draw without outline, to paint a portrait almost without apparent traits, to colour without colouring, to concentrate the light of the solar world into a single ray. It is not possible in plastic art to push any farther the interest of a human being as a human being. For physical beauty he substituted moral expression, for the imitation of things their almost complete metamorphosis, for examination the speculations of the psychologist, for clear, wise, simple observation the visionary's glimpse and such sincere apparitions that he himself was their dupe. By this faculty of double sight, thanks to this somnambulist's intuition, he saw farther into the supernatural than anyone else. The life he perceives in thought has an indescribable flavour of the other world, which makes real life seem cold and pale. Look at his 'Portrait of a Woman' in the Louvre, two paces from the 'Mistress' of Titian. Compare the two beings, question the two paintings, and you will understand the difference between the two brains. His ideal, pursued as in a dream with closed eyes, is light: the halo round the objects is phosphorescence against a dark background. It is fugitive, uncertain, composed of imperceptible lines, quite ready to disappear before they can be fixed, ephemeral, and dazzling. To arrest the vision, fix it on canvas, give it its form, its relief, preserve its fragile texture, render its brilliancy so that the result might be a solid, masculine, and substantial painting, more real than any other, that could stand comparison with Rubens, Titian, Veronese, Giorgione, Van Dyck – that is what Rembrandt attempted. Did he succeed in doing it? Universal testimony is there to say that he did.

EUGÈNE FROMENTIN, *The Masters of Past Time*, 1876

. . . Rembrandt reverses the normal procedure of idealising artists. Whereas they transform the essence of things and leave a reminder of nature in the details, he preserves reality in the essence and clothes its outward forms with a mysterious beauty and suggestiveness.

It is useful to begin thus by recalling some of the aesthetic characteristics of Rembrandt's paintings, because for over a hundred years the praise of Rembrandt has often been less aesthetic than moral. His work has been treated as the product not so much of a visual artist as of a superior, almost God-like personality. The emphasis has fallen on his possession of qualities of character: dedication, humanity, compassion, spiritual and psychological insight, courage to ignore fashion and to refuse to flatter patrons, above all, unswerving devotion to 'the truth' – the truth about himself, his sitters and the events and characters of the Bible. These qualities are immediately attractive nowadays. We admire integrity and the spirit of independence in artists. Nor is it intrinsically an error to see Rembrandt in this light, although it is possible to exaggerate the extent to which he possessed some of the virtues attributed to him. Nevertheless it is important to be aware of what has happened, so to speak. That is to say, we should realise that much of the modern bias in Rembrandt appreciation is due to developments in art criticism since his time, and that what we see in his work may not have been present, either to the minds and eyes of his contemporaries, or in the consciousness of Rembrandt himself. For some reason this problem is particularly acute where Rembrandt is concerned. It may be so partly because contemporary information about his *art* is very hard to obtain, whereas his personality – and hence by unconscious inference his mind – is deceptively accessible, through documents relating to his life, through his self-portraits, through his portraits of his family, and so on. But whatever the reason, the result has been to divert attention from Rembrandt the artist to Rembrandt the man. Thus there has emerged a sentimental cult of Rembrandt, which is not by any means confined to popular or old-fashioned literature; this cult presents us with Rembrandt the home-lover, the paragon of virtue and the sage.

It is not easy to tell how far the modern Rembrandt, even without the sentimental distortions, is the invention, and how far the discovery of later critics. It would be as foolish to ignore the insights of the past hundred and fifty years as it would be to accept them without question. What is certain is that they were made possible by a radical shift in the methods of criticism which began in the Romantic period. The practice of previous critics had been to assess the qualities of a work of art by examining the work itself; the tendency now was to look beyond the work and to seek for the key to its qualities in the artist's mind. The significance of this for the understanding of Rembrandt is so great that it is worth discussing a little further.

Until the Romantics works of art had been judged by more or less objective standards: whether they were beautiful or ugly, true or false to nature, and whether or not they were treated in accordance with certain rules. They were examined piecemeal, under the headings of drawing, colour, composition, etc. With the coming of Romanticism, standards became at once more comprehensive and more subjective. Sincerity was used as a criterion of artistic judgement for the first time and new kinds of truth were brought into the argument. Was the artist true to his own inner vision and experience (that is, was he sincere)? Did he, as Goethe expressed it, 'love what he painted and paint only what he loved'? Was he true not just to the letter but to the spirit of his subject matter? In this way the critical interest was shifted from the work of art to the artist's total attitude.

MICHAEL KITSON, *Rembrandt*, 1969

Rembrandt Tulips Mixed

Mid-season specialities of traditional Darwin form but with petals 'brush marked' in an endless array of colour combinations – as if by the great artist himself!

HORTICO GARDENING CATALOGUE, Autumn 1988

THE RENAISSANCE

Long time the Sister Arts, in Iron sleep,
A heavy Sabbath did supinely keep;
At length, in *Raphael's* Age, at once they rise;
Stretch all their Limbs, and open all their Eyes.

Thence rose the *Roman*, and the *Lombard* Line,
One colour'd best, and one did best design.
Raphael's like *Homer's*, was the Nobler part;
But *Titian's* painting, look'd like *Virgil's* Art.

JOHN DRYDEN, 'To Sir Godfrey Kneller', 1694

By the end of the fourteenth century, then, the art of Italy was nearly as radically estranged from the Antique as was that of the North; and it was only by beginning, as it were, from zero that the real Renaissance could come into being.

In contrast to the various mediaeval 'renascences' this Renaissance amounted to what the biologists would call a mutational as opposed to an evolutional change: a change both sudden and permanent. And an analogous and simultaneous mutation – viz. the emergence of a new style of painting, based on the apparently trivial yet, at the same time, essential novel conviction that, to quote Leonardo, 'that picture is the most praise-worthy which most closely resembles the thing to be imitated' and determined by what was to become a Cartesian, or at least Cusanian, interpretation of space – took place on the other side of the Alps. To be specific, it took place in the Netherlands which, after the battle of Agincourt in 1415 and the subsequent transmigration of the Burgundian court from Dijon to Bruges and Lille, had ceased to export its native talent to France and England and from 1420–25 emerged as the second Great Power in European Art.

Like nearly all great innovatory movements in the history of art, these two concurrent phenomena – the *ars nova* or *nouvelle pratique* of Jan van Eyck, the Master of Flémalle and Roger van der Weyden, and the *buona maniera moderna* of Brunelleschi, Donatello and Masaccio – disengaged themselves from the antecedent tradition by way of cross-fertilisation, on the one hand, and by way of reversion, on the other: across the boundaries of professional parochialism their pioneers looked for guidance to such sister arts as had achieved remarkable results in a different medium; across the boundaries of time they looked for guidance to the distant past.

The Netherlandish painters evolved their new style in intimate contact with nearly all other visual arts and, in a manner of speaking, learned to practice them vicariously. From major statuary which, in the works of the mighty Claus Sluter (d.1406), had broken the spell of the International Style as early as about 1400, they learned to impart to their figures a plastic solidity which makes them look like sculpture turned into flesh; we happen to know that even the greatest painters did not disdain to coat and gild reliefs and statues in stone, wood or brass, thus seeing them in the nude, as it were, and observing the action of light on solid bodies as under laboratory conditions. When they began to adorn the exteriors of their altarpieces with simulated statues in grisaille – 'stone-coloured figures', as Dürer calls them – they not only showed off their ability to produce a *trompe-l'œil* effect but also tacitly acknowledged an indebtedness to the sculptors. They repaid this debt, with interest, by providing the sculptors with prototypes, not infrequently even drawings, for their works until, towards the end of the fifteenth century, sculpture became more dependent on painting than painting had been on sculpture at the beginning.

And since the Netherlandish 'primitives', deservedly famous for endowing the products of human hands, from 'ornate halls and porticoes' to 'multicoloured garments' and 'gold that looked like gold', with the same semblance of reality as the products of nature, often included in their compositions all kinds of buildings and artifacts conforming to the requirements of a given iconographical context (it would not have been easy, for example, to find a throne whose sculptured decoration included, all at once, the Sacrifice of Isaac, the Victory of David over Goliath, the Pelican in her Piety and the Phoenix [as in the Madonna's throne in Jan van Eyck's triptych in Dresden]), they had to construct, without a loss in verisimilitude, what they wished to be seen. They had to become, as it were, their own carpenters, coppersmiths, jewellers, tapestry weavers, sculptors and architects, using the brush instead of hammers, tongs and chisels.

Similarly, Donatello and Masaccio turned to Brunelleschi, either directly or indirectly through Alberti, in matters of perspective and architectural settings. . . .

While the *ars nova* of the North and the Italian Renaissance thus agreed in principle – in the acceptance of verisimilitude as a general and basic postulate, in the interpretation of space as a three-dimensional continuum and in a tendency toward cross-fertilization as well as reversion – they differed (apart from such important technical matters as the emergence of the oil technique in Northern painting and the virtual disappearance of bronze from Northern sculpture) in the distribution and direction of what may be called mutational energy.

The first of these differences consists in the fact that the various arts or media responded to the spirit of innovation that swept over Europe in the first quarter of the fifteenth century in inverse order, so to speak. In the Netherlands, the earliest and most unequivocal departure from the immediate past occurred in painting and music; it was, in fact, in order to glorify two great composers, Guillaume Dufay and Gilles Binchois (both natives of the Hainaut and born about 1400), that the expressions *ars nova* and *nouvelle pratique*, which I have appropriated for the new style of painting, were coined. Sculpture, we recall, had had a kind of prenatal headstart over painting, but this situation was reversed once Eyckian and Rogerian painting had been born. And the development of architecture – no less Late Gothic after than before the otherwise crucial years of 1420–25 – remained essentially unaltered until it was deflected, like all other arts, by the impact of the transalpine Renaissance.

In Italy, on the other hand, the architects and sculptors broke with the prevailing tradition not only at a slightly earlier date but also, which is more important, with more assistance from the Antique than did the painters. And Italian music, unable to find support in classical prototypes and (therefore?) playing a surprisingly insignificant role in the transition from the Middle Ages to the modern era, did not achieve international importance until the middle of the sixteenth century and did not participate in the mutational process at all.

ERWIN PANOFSKY, *Renaissance and Renascences in Western Art*, 1965

GUIDO RENI

Nobody could accuse Smollett of gushing over works of art – or indeed over anything else – encountered abroad; and it is surprising to find him being so enthusiastic about such a universal subject of praise at the period as Reni's pictures, though, Smollett-like, the enthusiasm is quickly tempered.

I am extremely fond of all this artist's pieces. There is a tenderness and delicacy in his manner; and his figures are all exquisitely beautiful, though his expression is often erroneous, and his attitudes are always affected and unnatural. In this very piece ['St Michael'] the archangel has all the air of a French dancing-master; and I have seen a Madonna by the same hand, I think it is in the Palazzo di Barberini, in which, though the figures are enchanting, the Virgin is represented holding up the drapery of the Infant, with the ridiculous affectation of a singer on the stage of our Italian opera.

TOBIAS SMOLLETT, *Travels Through France and Italy*, 1766

RENOIR

23 April 1918, at Renoir's, in Nice.

In this small apartment he paints sometimes in the dining room and at other times in his drawing room, as at Cagnes, where every room in his house is a studio. Today his devoted servant and nurse, Mme Petit, ushered me into his drawing room. He has a model, a beautiful plump girl of twenty, rather short, with golden hair, large blue eyes, and a fine skin, with a purity of blood suffusing her face; a daughter of the fields, to judge by her fine health, but already of the town as well, with a dusting of rice powder and a tailor-made suit. I looked at the small painting which I'd seen last time and in which Renoir has seated this woman in a landscape. The other day he'd captured, as a soap bubble does, the sun's thousand colours in a falling sleeve of transparent tulle. Today it was a botch, a mess, and he knew it and said to me: 'Twenty-seven times I've had this woman pose and I can't get it to work; my picture was much better the other week; I ought to have left it. What do you think of these flowers I did yesterday but haven't finished?'

'I think they're magnificent and I wouldn't do another thing to them. Looking at them, I'm reminded of a phrase I read once in an astronomy book: "The sun throws out flames thousands of miles long." These flowers too cast immense flames; they blaze. Would you sell them to me?'

'Yes.'

'How much?'

'Three thousand.'

'That's a lot.'

'I know, but these are my flowers, which cost more. I can't sell cheaply because of the dealers; I don't want to hamper their business. I have, for example, an old debt of gratitude to Durand Ruel, who alone helped me to eat when I was hungry.'

'I'll take your flowers. Why don't you sell me as well this portrait of the woman with the hat, your model? Ten thousand, you say? Done. And this woman in a glade? Let's add five thousand for that one. And if ever you'd agree to sell these washerwomen, let me know; I adore the olive trees at the edge of that stream. When I leave you and return to Cannes, I look at nature and think of your paintings. You've shown me how differently each tree contains the sun. I marvel at the rightness of your olive tree coming up out of the ground, the trunk contained in the funny little hillock that rises with such dignity.'

Renoir answered: 'The olive tree, what a fiend! If you knew the trouble it gave me. A tree full of colours, not grey at all. Its little leaves, how they made me sweat! A gust of wind, and my tree changes in tonality. The colour isn't on the leaves but in the empty spaces. I can't paint nature, I know, but the hand-to-hand struggle with her stimulates me. A painter can't be great if he doesn't understand landscape. At one time the term "landscapist" was one of scorn, especially in the eighteenth century. And yet, that century which I adore produced great landscape artists. I am of the eighteenth century. I humbly consider not only that my art descends from Watteau, Fragonard, Hubert Robert, but even that I am one of them. Watteau, what a genius! To have possessed all knowledge so young! Watteau, Raphael, giants departed in the prime of life. I swear to you, they knew they would die. So their talent advanced with giant's steps.'

RENÉ GIMPEL, *Diary of an Art Dealer*

RESTORATION OF PICTURES

. . . You ask for my opinion on the restoration of the Rubens paintings. On the whole I think it has been well done, remarkably so indeed compared to the usual methods of cleaning pictures. What has happened is this: the complete removal of the varnish, particularly on the lighter colours, has revealed a freshness of tone which might have been expected. Novices in painting, who imagine that they only have to paint in thick oils and to produce, with the help of bitumen, what they call warm tones in their pictures, must have been disappointed. People will realise now that it's possible to paint very warmly and yet to reproduce the true tones of nature. The only drawback of this process is doubtless due to the way the pictures were painted. Rubens probably produced his shadows by means of scumble. This was done with a coating of transparent colour which has since turned blackish. The yellow tint of the varnish, accumulated during the years, which affected the lighter tones as well, spread a sort of unity between the light and dark tones. Today the proportion is disturbed. I mean the shadows look darker and the light tones gleam so brightly – as the painter intended – that the pictures have a somewhat metallic and monotonous appearance, due to the uniformly dark effect of the parts in shadow. This moreover is the effect almost invariably produced by cleaning. I wish pictures need never be varnished. Our descendants would certainly have a more accurate idea of our paintings; but how can anyone resist the desire to give his contemporaries the best possible opinion of himself and his works? . . .

EUGÈNE DELACROIX, *Letter to Constant Dutilleux, 8 August 1858*

Dutilleux (1817–65) was a painter and an admirer of Delacroix. It is no surprise to learn that cleaning of the Rubens pictures – the 'Marie de Médicis' cycle in the Louvre – was violently criticized and that the curator involved, Frédéric Villot, was forced to resign.

. . . Degas talked to me about the Louvre: 'What do I want? I want them not to restore the paintings. If you were to scratch a painting you would be arrested. If M. Kaempfen were to restore the *Gioconda* they'd decorate him. . . . Time has to take its course with paintings as with everything else, that's the beauty of it. A man who touches a picture ought to be deported. To touch a picture! You don't know what that does to me. These paintings are the joy of my life; they beautify it, they soothe it. To touch a Rembrandt! It's as though—'

We were at the door of his studio. He disappeared.

DANIEL HALÉVY, *My Friend Degas*, 1966

Albert Kaempfen was a curator of the Louvre. 'What is Kaempfen?' Degas asked at dinner at the Halévys', answering: 'A journalist!' The Rembrandt in question was the 'Supper at Emmaus'.

SIR JOSHUA REYNOLDS

Here Reynolds is laid, and, to tell you my mind,
He has not left a better or wiser behind;
His pencil was striking, resistless and grand,
His manners were gentle, complying and bland;
Still born to improve us in every part,
His pencil our faces, his manners our heart:
To coxcombs averse, yet most civilly steering,
When they judg'd without skill he was still hard of hearing:
When they talked of their Raphaels, Corregios and stuff,

He shifted his trumpet, and only took snuff.

OLIVER GOLDSMITH, 'Retaliation', 1774

'Retaliation', an unfinished poem, was published shortly after Goldsmith's death; it contains a number of premature epitaphs, of which the one on Reynolds is the last.

When Sir Joshua Reynolds died
All Nature was degraded;
The King drop'd a tear into the Queen's Ear,
And all his Pictures Faded.

WILLIAM BLAKE, *Annotation to an account of Reynolds' death* (1792)

RIVALRY

Some cases of rivalry between painters in the seventeenth century grew so intense that one would avoid buying the kind of cheese bought by another (as did Albani when going to a shop in Bologna where Guido Reni had previously been). More destructive and damaging was the rivalry stirred up by Domenichino when he went to Naples to work in the important chapel of St Januarius in the cathedral there, which is documented by the artist himself and his early biographers.

What Domenichino undoubtedly had not counted on was the strength and determination of the opposition he encountered in Naples, and the constraints of the contract. Passeri, who talked with him during his stay in Frascati in 1634 about his recent experiences in Naples, writes that 'barely arrived in Naples . . . he began to get a taste of the bitter fruit of rivalry and of envy, because the Neapolitan painters, finding themselves dissatisfied that a foreigner could get the job despite their claim as natives of the City, fumed about it anxiously, and tormented themselves with resentment and suffering'. Passeri further relates that the second day in Naples Domenichino discovered a note in his keyhole threatening his life if he did not return to Rome. Malvasia later talked with the artist's widow, who also reported that twice her husband had received threatening anonymous letters. Aware of Cesari's and Reni's [earlier] difficulties and worried about the threats, Domenichino sought the Viceroy's protection, but nonetheless was so frightened that he would not leave his rooms other than to go to work in the adjacent chapel. Confirmation of his serious anxieties and regrets for agreeing not to accept any other jobs is provided by a letter he wrote to Cassiano dal Pozzo as early as 23 January 1632, only a half-year after he settled in Naples. He wrote: 'Finding myself with my hands bound by iron chains, I do not know where to turn. These *Signori* have wanted me to obligate myself not to take up brush during the job; they have compelled me to promise this with caution money [*cautele*]; they persuaded me to submit to not light penalties when I was contumacious; and rivals are around already with their teeth sharpened to damage me.'

RICHARD E. SPEAR, *Domenichino*, 1982

Domenichino eventually fled from Naples but was persuaded to return, though he suffered fresh persecution from local artists: he died in Naples in 1641 – 'not,' recorded his biographer Passeri, 'without suspicion of poison'.

ROMNEY

Tennyson prefaced his surprisingly Browning-like monologue of Romney on his death-bed (what follows is only an extract) with a passage from his old friend Edward FitzGerald, which had probably prompted the poem.

Romney's Remorse

'I read Hayley's Life of Romney the other day – Romney wanted but education and reading to make him a very fine painter; but his ideal was not high nor fixed. How touching is the close of his life! He married at nineteen, and because Sir Joshua and others had said that 'marriage spoilt an artist' almost immediately left his wife in the North and scarce saw her till the end of his life; when old, nearly mad and quite desolate, he went back to her and she received him and nursed him till he died. This quiet act of hers is worth all Romney's pictures! even as a matter of Art, I am sure.' (*Letters and Literary Remains of Edward FitzGerald*, vol. i)

'Beat, little heart – I give you this and this.'
Who are you? What! the Lady Hamilton!
Good, I am never weary painting you.
To sit once more? Cassandra, Hebe, Joan,
Or spinning at your wheel beside the vine –
Bacchante, what you will; and if I fail
To conjure and concentrate into form
And colour all you are, the fault is less
In me than Art. What Artist ever yet
Could make pure light live on the canvas? Art!
Why should I so disrelish that short word?
    Where am I? snow on all the hills! so hot,
So fever'd! never colt would more delight
To roll himself in meadow grass than I

To wallow in that winter of the hills.
    Nurse, were you hired? or came of your own will
To wait on one so broken, so forlorn?
Have I not met you somewhere long ago?
I am all but sure I have – in Kendal church –
O yes! I hired you for a season there,
And then we parted; but you look so kind
That you will not deny my sultry throat
One draught of icy water. There – you spill
The drops upon my forehead. Your hand shakes.
I am ashamed. I am a trouble to you,
Could kneel for your forgiveness. Are they tears?
For me – they do me too much grace – for me?
O Mary, Mary!
                    Vexing you with words!
Words only, born of fever, or the fumes
Of that dark opiate dose you gave me, – words,
Wild babble. I have stumbled back again
Into the common day, the sounder self.
God stay me there, if only for your sake,
The truest, kindliest, noblest-hearted wife
That ever wore a Christian marriage-ring.
    My curse upon the Master's apothegm,
That wife and children drag an Artist down!
This seem'd my lodestar in the Heaven of Art,
And lured me from the household fire on earth.
To you my days have been a life-long lie,
Grafted on half a truth, and tho' you say
'Take comfort, you have won the Painter's fame',
The best in me that sees the worst in me,
And groans to see it, finds no comfort there.
    What fame? I am not Raphaël, Titian – no
Nor even a Sir Joshua, some will cry.
Wrong there! The painter's fame? but mine, that grew
Blown into glittering by the popular breath,
May float awhile beneath the sun, may roll
The rainbow hues of heaven about it –
                                        There!
The colour'd bubble bursts above the abyss
Of Darkness, utter Lethe.

ALFRED TENNYSON, 'Romney's Remorse' in *Demeter and Other Poems*, 1889

SALVATOR ROSA

My pictures all Salvator's, save a few
Of Titian's portraiture. . . .

JOHN KEATS, 'The Castle Builder'

One of the two persons in what was intended to be a dialogue evokes an ideally luxurious room; Keats adds a further picture: 'one, though new,/Of Haydon's in its fresh magnificence'.

But, while thus laboriously devoted to business and to pleasure, insatiate in the pursuit of fame, and seeking to obtain it alike from contemporaries and from posterity by the cultivation of the most opposite talents; his susceptible spirits too frequently sunk under the exertions of his overworked mind; and fits of moody melancholy, the natural concomitants of the disease called genius, shadowed the settled sunshine of this portion of his life, and left him no solace but such as he could find in solitude or in friendship. Long and lonely walks amid the forest gloom of Volterra, or pensive saunterings in the more lovely scenery of the Val d' Arno, with the friend of his most intimate selection, were the sure remedies to which he applied, when his temperament led him to view life in its own true colours, or when, the fervour of some transient excitement having died away, he felt a full conviction of the truth of his painted adage '*Nasci pena*, etc., etc., etc.' succeed to every brighter dream and more flattering illusion.

The friend *par excellence*, chosen to accompany him in these wanderings, was Lorenzo Lippi, a man who seems to have been cast in the same mould with himself, though formed perhaps of an inferior clay. A painter by profession, a poet by taste, a philosopher upon system, and an epicurean from temperament: he yet was all these in a lower degree than Salvator; and this very inequality rendered their accordance but the more perfect: for Lippi looked up to Rosa; and Rosa liked to be respected, even by those by whom he was beloved. There was also another point of similitude between these eminent geniuses: they were both alive

'To every sense of ridicule in things';

and both indulged in the dangerous propensity with a most hazardous indiscretion; too happy when they could laugh at a world, over which they were more frequently compelled to weep.

LADY MORGAN, *The Life and Times of Salvator Rosa*, 1824

Lady Morgan's book on Rosa is much more scholarly than is often supposed; she printed several of his letters – and some of his music – and cited her sources with un-Romantic attention to facts.

THE DOUANIER ROUSSEAU

Picasso and his friends organized a famous banquet in Picasso's studio for Henri Rousseau ('the Douanier') in November 1908, when the painter was aged sixty-four. Two accounts of the evening were published, both in 1933. Gertrude Stein's, in 'The Autobiography of Alice B. Toklas', was later criticized by at least one of the participants, André Salmon, who said that Fernande Olivier, Picasso's mistress, had described the occasion much better.

After dinner there were speeches and songs composed especially for the occasion; then a few words from Rousseau, who was so moved that he spluttered with pleasure. Indeed, so happy was he that he accepted with the greatest stoicism the regular dripping of wax tears on to his brow from a large lantern above him. The wax droppings accumulated to form a small pyramid like a clown's cap on his head, which stayed there until the lantern eventually caught fire. It didn't take much to persuade Rousseau that this was his apotheosis. Then Rousseau, who had brought his violin, started to play a little tune.

What a colourful evening that was! Two or three American couples, who had got there by accident, had to make the most excruciating efforts to keep a straight face. The men in their dark suits and the women in pale evening-dresses seemed a bit out of their element amongst us.

The wives and mistresses of the painters were wearing simple dresses of undeniable originality. Madame Agero looked like a schoolgirl in a black smock. Her husband hadn't a care in the world, and though he probably imagined he was taking it all in he seemed to be oblivious of everything. There were the Pichots, the Fornerods, André Salmon and Cremnitz, who at the end of the evening did an imitation of *delirium tremens*, chewing soap and making it froth out of his mouth, which horrified the Americans. Jacques Vaillant, Max Jacob, Apollinaire and Leo and Gertrude Stein were there, and many, many others.

FERNANDE OLIVIER, *Picasso et ses amis*, 1933

ROYALTY

One abrupt way of meeting royalty and getting commissions for pictures thereby is amusingly related about the obscure painter Michael W. Sharpe, a pupil of Sir William Beechey's. The king was George III.

Beechey had obtained his introduction to the Court by accident, and so it happened to his pupil, Michael W. Sharpe – known afterwards for a picture he painted, as 'Bees-wing Sharpe'. Sharpe was so pertinacious in his request to be present at a sitting of royalty that at last Beechey consented, on the express stipulation that he should be quite silent, keep out of the way, and merely sit, and from time to time hand him a fresh palette. Under these conditions, he accompanied Sir William to the palace. They had hardly reached the apartment where the sitting was to take place when the door was thrown open and the astonished pupil heard the cry of Sharp! – simply a warning to be on the *qui vive* for royalty. Nervously impulsive, he thought that he was called, and rushed forward, to hear from the domestics in the suite of rooms he traversed the same cry of 'Sharp! Sharp!' This only increased his confusion, until, at length, in passing through one of the doors, he ran right into the arms of someone. 'Hullo! hallo!, what's this, what's this? Who are you?' were uttered in quick succession. 'Who are you?' 'Sharpe, your Majesty,' said the young painter, who, though dreadfully alarmed, saw at once that it was the King. 'Sharpe, Sharpe,' said the King; 'What, son of the hautboy player of Norwich?' Now it so happened that the King had hit upon the right person, and when the youth acknowledged that Sharpe of Norwich was his father, the King at once was gracious. 'Well, Sharpe,' said he, 'you had almost knocked royalty down, but it is well it is no worse. What brought you here?' Sharpe explained that he was Sir William's pupil, had come to aid him in the sitting, etc. The story amused the King as much as it annoyed Beechey, and the accident led to a commission to Sharpe to paint the Princess Amelia and others of the royal family.

RICHARD AND SAMUEL REDGRAVE, *A Century of British Painters*, 1866

RUBENS

For a candid yet also complex verbal portrait of Rubens in middle age, retired from politics but not from art, there is no better source than the artist himself, writing to a lifelong friend, the French scholar Peiresc.

Now, by God's grace . . . I am leading a quiet life with my wife and children, and have no pretention in the world other than to live in peace.

I made up my mind to marry again, since I was not yet inclined to live the abstinent life of the celibate, thinking that, if we must give the first place to continence, *fruimur licita voluptate cum gratiarum actione* ['we may enjoy licit pleasures with thankfulness']. I have taken a young wife of honest but middle-class family, although everyone tried to persuade me to make a Court marriage. But I feared *commune illud nobilitatis malum superbiam praesertim in illo sexu* ['Pride, that inherent vice of the nobility, particularly in that sex'], and that is why I chose one who would not blush to see me take my brushes in hand. And to tell the truth it would have been hard for me to exchange the priceless treasure of liberty for the embraces of an old woman.

That is the story of my life since the interruption of our correspondence. I see you have been informed by M. Picquery about the children of my present marriage, and therefore I shall tell you only that my Albert [elder son by first marriage] is now in Venice. . . . Today I am so overburdened with the preparations for the triumphal entry of the Cardinal Infante (which takes place at the end of the month) that I have time neither to live nor to write. I am therefore cheating my art by stealing a few evening hours to write this most inadequate and negligent reply to the courteous and elegant letter of yours. The magistrates of this city have laid on my shoulders the entire burden of this festival, and I believe you would not be displeased at the invention and variety of the subjects, the novelty of the designs and the fitness of their application. Perhaps one day you will see them published, adorned with the beautiful inscriptions and verses of our friend Gevaerts (who sends you affectionate greetings). All these occupations force me to ask you for a truce, for it is really impossible for me in these circumstances, to make the necessary effort to satisfy my obligation to you and to answer the questions in your letter.

SIR PETER PAUL RUBENS, *Letter from Antwerp*, 18 December 1634

I have never spoken, and I will never speak of Rubens but with the most reverential feeling, and whatever imperfections in his art may have resulted from his unfortunate want of seriousness and incapability of true passion, his calibre of mind was originally such that I believe the world may see another Titian and another Raffaelle, before it sees another Rubens.

JOHN RUSKIN, *Modern Painters*, volume I, 1843

Rubens' will was detailed and specific. His bequests were not limited to his family, but included people from all stations of life, even down to the gift of a copy after his painting of a *Nymph and Satyr carrying a Basket of Fruit*, to 'Peter outrider of the Clarenstraat', for his help in buying a horse. To Helena Fourment, Rubens left the customary half share, as well as his portrait of her in a fur cloak. She took the opportunity to buy nine others from the estate, mainly family portraits but also a *Conversation à la mode*. To her and all his children, who were specifically granted equal rights, he left all the family portraits of both marriages. To his eldest son, Albert, who showed promise of becoming a scholar, he left his books and to both him and his brother Nicolaas his agates and medals, except the vases of agate, jasper and other precious stones. The Château de Steen was divided equally between the widow and her two stepsons. He stipulated that the pictures, statues and other works of art should, on the advice of Snyders, Wildens and another painter, Jacques Moermans, be sold either at auction or privately. An inventory was drawn up the following month and consisted of 314 specified items, plus various other items such as copies after Rubens' drawings, ivories carved after his designs and antique busts. Thirty-two pictures, fourteen by Rubens and eighteen by other artists, were sold directly to Philip IV, and others were disposed of to the family or various purchasers. The remainder of the collection was put up for auction in a series of sales the following year. But, despite the testator's careful instructions, litigation between Helena Fourment and her stepsons took place during the following years over the division of the estate.

Yet when it came to disposing of the vast collection of his own drawings, which contained the wisdom and experience of a lifetime, the true artist in him ordained that they should not be sold until the youngest of his children was eighteen, and only then if none of his sons had become a painter and none of his daughters had married one (Frans Pourbus the Elder had made a similar arrangement). But such is the chance of heredity that Rubens, a painter through and through, was unable to produce a glimmering of artistic inspiration among any of his eight children. And so, with the eventual disposal of his drawings in 1657, when his youngest daughter was enclosed in a nunnery, the remaining works of Peter Paul Rubens became hostages to fortune.

CHRISTOPHER WHITE, *Peter Paul Rubens*, 1987

JACOB VAN RUISDAEL

Jacob Ruisdael, born at Haarlem in 1635 [*in fact 1628/9*] and active until 1681, is recognized as one of the best landscape painters. His works satisfy all the demands that the senses can make of works of art: hand and brush work freely towards the most precise perfection. Light, shade, keeping and the effect of the whole leave nothing to be desired. A glance is sufficient to convince every amateur and expert of this. But here we want to look at him as a thinking artist, even as a poet, and in this respect, too, we must own that he is worth a great deal.

J. W. VON GOETHE in *Morgenblatt für gebildete Stände*, 1816

I have seen an affecting picture this morning by Ruysdael [*sic*]; it haunts my mind, and clings to my heart, and stands between you and me while I am talking to you; it is a water-mill; a man and boy are cutting rushes in the running stream (the tail-water); the whole so true, clear, and fresh, and as brisk as champagne; a shower has not long passed.

JOHN CONSTABLE, *Letter to Archdeacon Fisher*, 28 November 1826

SALES

In Sheridan's 'The School for Scandal' a scene is set in Charles Surface's 'picture room', where he is raising money by selling the portraits of his ancestors. His uncle, Sir Oliver, disguised as a broker, 'Mr Premium', is shocked to find what Charles is doing but touched when his nephew refuses to sell – at any price – one particular picture: the portrait of Sir Oliver.

CHARLES SURFACE: . . . Well, here's my great-uncle, Sir Richard Ravelin, a marvellous good general in his day, I assure you. He served in all the Duke of Marlborough's wars, and got that cut over his eye at the battle of Malplaquet. What say you, Mr Premium? look at him – there's a hero! not cut out of his feathers, as your modern clipped captains are, but enveloped in wig and regimentals, as a general should be. What do you bid?

SIR OLIVER [*aside to Moses*]: Bid him speak.

MOSES: Mr Premium would have you speak.

CHARLES SURFACE: Why, then, he shall have him for ten pounds, and I'm sure that's not dear for a staff-officer.

SIR OLIVER [*aside*]: Heaven deliver me! his famous uncle Richard for ten pounds! – [*Aloud*]: Very well, sir, I take him at that.

CHARLES SURFACE: Careless, knock down my uncle Richard. – Here, now, is a maiden sister of his, my great-aunt Deborah, done by Kneller, in his best manner, and esteemed a very formidable likeness. There she is, you see, a shepherdess feeding her flock. You shall have her for five pounds ten – the sheep are worth the money.

SIR OLIVER [*aside*]: Ah! poor Deborah! a woman who set such value on herself! – [*Aloud*]: Five pounds ten – she's mine.

CHARLES SURFACE: Knock down my aunt Deborah!

R. B. SHERIDAN, *The School for Scandal*, 1777
Act IV, Scene I

One fine morning, in the month of June, as they were perambulating with an English friend, about the east end of the town, in search of their beloved Guido, a small picture, hanging at a broker's door, attracted their notice, and they crossed a narrow street in order to inspect it more accurately. The proprietor of this shop, a good jolly-looking fellow, whose chief traffic was in old iron and lead, seeing three men genteelly dressed cross over and stop at his door in the sight of his neighbours, felt himself something elated at this distinction; and when he was asked the price of the picture, answered with one of his lowest bows, 'one guinea gemmen, and I'm sure that's cheap enough in all conscience – that it is, dog-cheap. . . . Why look ye, gemmen, I don't pretend to any great judgment in this here business, but I know my neighbour Cullender, who kept yon cook's-shop, at that there corner, gave one o' your foreigners, a capital judge, more dinners that came to three guineas, upon that there very identical picture. . . . Lord, it would ha' done one good to hear him speak about your *Tishuans, Raffles, Clods,* and your *Piss-hangs*. As for this here picture, I've heard him, many o' the time, talk about what a fine *come physician* it is, and the subject so high-learned: why this here picture, you must know gemmen, is painted by that same great *Tishuan*, it is the *three fat sisters threading the needle of life*.'

WILLIAM COLLINS, *Memoirs of a Picture*, 1805
ch. XVIII

The author of this rambling, slightly silly and yet not unentertaining story was the father of the painter William Collins and the grandfather of Wilkie Collins, and the author also of a memoir of George Morland.

From the Crown Princess

Meran, July 23, 1882

I always forget to mention the sale of the Duke of Hamilton's works of art which I think such a pity. . . . It will be the same soon with the Duke of Marlborough's pictures and library, it is said though I do not know for certain. If our great English families are obliged to sell their unique collections at least I think, if possible, the nation ought to secure them. Mr Gladstone as a lover of art and learning, would I am sure – even from a financial point of view – think money well invested that is spent on increasing the art collections of the nation. The day will come when these things can no longer be had and all is readily snapped up by the new collections of America and the Continent.

From the Queen

Osborne, July 31, 1882

Mr Robinson has been constantly looking out for pictures and things at the Hamilton Sale and I have bought a very fine original full length portrait of Edward VI by one of Holbein's best pupils. The National Gallery have bought several very fine things. I have also got another small drawing after Raphael of St George and the Dragon which had Charles I's mark on it. Other things I wished to have went too high.

from *Beloved Mama: Private Correspondence of Queen Victoria and the German Crown Princess*, ed. R. Fulford

The Crown Princess was quite right about the Blenheim sales which followed two or three years later.

An amusing and revealing tug-of-war between artist and patron took place in 1756 over the view of the Port of Sète to be painted by Claude-Joseph Vernet in his series of the 'Ports of France', which was a royal commission. Vernet felt Sète was lacking in pictorial interest and explained to Marigny, the Directeur des Bâtiments, how he would improve the facts:

There I shall have the opportunity to put in the foreground a somewhat agitated sea, and I might even paint a storm. This would create quite an unusual effect amongst the pictures I have already made for the King, for they are normally port interiors, and in consequence the sea is calm. . . .

Marigny replied:

Your pictures should unite two merits – that of pictorial beauty and that of resemblance. I can see the former in the project you propose, but I fear that this would be only at the expense of the latter. I doubt whether the port of Sète represented from the sea would be recognised by the majority of those who had only seen it from the land. The storm which you wish to introduce will render your picture even less like, given that it is rare to see the sea troubled by a storm in a port. It would mean that the foreground showed the open sea, and consequently the port would be pushed into the distance, which would prevent you from including its characteristic details . . . above all, you must not lose sight of the intention of the King, which is to see the ports of the kingdom represented realistically in your pictures.

However, Vernet emphasized in response that stormy weather was characteristic of the region and that the sea could be rough even in the harbour:

Thus, there would be nothing contrary to verisimilitude – quite the opposite. On the one hand, the picture would make for variety among the others, on the other hand a storm would make the distinguishing characteristic of this port.

Vernet won his point and painted a dramatically stormy scene, in which Sète is indeed 'pushed into the distance'; and when he exhibited the picture (now Musée de la Marine, Paris) at the Salon of 1757, the 'livret' emphasized the propriety of his depiction: 'As this port is right inside the Golphe de Lyon and as the sea is often rough there, particularly when the wind is from the south, the artist has represented stormy weather. . . .'

CLAUDE-JOSEPH VERNET AND THE MARQUIS DE MARIGNY

He [Admiral Croft] was standing by himself, at a printshop window, with his hands behind him, in earnest contemplation of some print, and she [Anne Elliot] not only might have passed him unseen, but was obliged to touch as well as address him before she could catch his notice. When he did perceive and acknowledge her, however, it was done with all his usual frankness and good humour. 'Ha! is it you? Thank you, thank you. This is treating me like a friend. Here I am, you see, staring at a picture. I can never get by this shop without stopping. But what a thing here is, by way of a boat. Do look at it. Did you ever see the like? What queer fellows your fine painters must be, to think that anybody would venture their lives in such a shapeless old cockleshell as that. And yet, here are two gentlemen stuck up in it mightily at their ease, and looking about them at the rocks and mountains, as if they were not to be upset the next moment, which they certainly must be. I wonder where that boat was built!' (laughing heartily) 'I would not venture over a horsepond in it. . . .'

JANE AUSTEN, *Persuasion*, 1817

The project of Turner painting the battle of Trafalgar for George IV promised much from the uniting of great painter, great theme and great patron, but the resulting picture was not judged a success, despite the artist's care and perhaps partly because of the plethora of nautical advice he received.

Turner's attention to detail is revealed by a letter he wrote in December 1823 to the marine painter J. C. Schetky, living at Portsmouth:

Dear Sir,
I thank you for your kind offer of the *Téméraire*; but I can bring in very little, if any of her hull, because of the *Redoubtable*. If you will make me a sketch of the *Victory* (she is in Hayle Lake or Portsmouth Harbour) three-quarter bow on starboard side, or opposite the bow port, you will much oblige; and if you have a sketch of the *Neptune*, Captain Freemantle's ship, or know any particulars of *Santissima Trinidada* or *Redoubtable*, any communication I will thank you much for. . . .

While Turner was at work on the picture, he was visited by the Duke of Clarence (later William IV) and a letter of 22 December 1824 from Henry Tijou to Sir John Leicester recounts the following incident (though Turner is subsequently recorded as having found the Duke's observations the only sensible ones he received):

He [the Duke of Clarence] immediately began as a sailor to make his observations which not being agreeable, he says that Turner was rather rough in his reply. They went on for some time and the Duke finished the conversation by saying 'I have been at sea the greater part of my life, Sir, you don't know who you are talking to, and I'll be damned if you know what you are talking about.'

Letters and documentation in M. BUTLIN and E. JOLL,
The Paintings of J. M. W. Turner, 1977

George IV gave the picture to Greenwich (now the National Maritime Museum) a few years after it was finished.

Lecturing at the Royal Institution, London, in 1836, Constable showed a marine painting by Ruisdael and declared:

The subject . . . is the mouth of a Dutch river, without a single feature of grandeur in the scenery; but the stormy sky, the grouping of the vessels, and the breaking of the sea, make the picture one of the most impressive ever painted.

JOHN CONSTABLE (C. R. Leslie, *Memoirs of the Life of John Constable*, 1845 edn.)

SEBASTIANO DEL PIOMBO

Viterbo looks picturesque. We go to *S. Francesco* to see the del Piombo Christ. It is splendid, marvellous drawing. This painting is extraordinarily impressive. The Virgin is very inferior.

GEORGES BIZET in Italy, 1860

SERVANTS

Poussin was one day visited in his studio by Monsignor Camillo Massimi, now the very worthy Cardinal, who was highly attached to him and respected him for his noble qualities, and while they talked together, night came on. At their parting, Poussin accompanied the Monsignor with a lantern in his hand down the stairs to the carriage: whereupon that gentleman, referring to the nuisance of his having to carry the light, said, 'I pity you not having any servants.' Nicolas responded, 'And I pity your Lordship having a lot of them.'

GIOVANNI PIETRO BELLORI, 'Life' of Poussin in *Le Vite de' pittori, scultori et architetti moderni*, 1672

Just before, he [Sir Thomas Lawrence] had spoken of the tender care of his servant, Jean Duts, with great gratitude: I observed that Jean's countenance at the door always told me how I should find him. He was quite affected at this.

ELIZABETH CROFT, *Memoir of Lawrence's last days* (1831)

Degas' soirées were of course somewhat different from the one the Baroness of Cl. T. gave in his honour. When the evening was over, a valet called for the attendants of the Prince of W., the English ambassador, and other gentry.

'But,' exclaimed a lady who did not know just how important a personage Degas might be, 'what about Monsieur Degas' attendants?'

'Monsieur Degas' attendants are Zoé,' replied the painter, 'and she has been asleep in bed since eight o'clock.'

AMBROISE VOLLARD, *Degas, An Intimate Portrait*, 1924

SEURAT

Of the newcomers Seurat strikes me as possessing the most talent. His large picture, 'Un Dimanche à la Grande Jatte', looks like a modernised version of ancient Egypt. The sward is yellow with sunlight, and through the yellow glare children, nursemaids, dogs, young men, and cocottes are straying. In the foreground a superb cocotte poses with the monkey, the length of whose tail has raised a clamour in the petite press.

Anonymous review of the 'Impressionist' exhibition in the rue Lafitte, published in the 'Bat', 25 May 1886

This is probably the earliest mention in an English periodical of Seurat. ('La Grande Jatte' is now a treasure of the Art Institute, Chicago.) It is possible that the reviewer was George Moore.

SHIPS

This incident of two great artists drawn into rivalry over the making of a toy ship for a small boy is at once delightful and revealing.

When we returned . . . Turner became quite chatty, rigging me a little ship, cut out of a chip, sticking masts into it, and making her sails from a leaf or two torn from a small sketchbook, in which I recollect seeing a memorandum in colour that he had made of the sky and sunset . . .

I think the foundation of *the ship* was a mere flat bit of board or chip, cut out for me by my father, and that Constable, the artist, had stuck a sail in it for me some days before (he was also at Petworth). I must have mentioned this to Turner, as I have a recollection of his saying, as he rigged it, 'Oh, he don't know nothing about ships,' or 'What does he know about ships? this is how it ought to be,' sticking up some sails which looked to my eyes really quite ship-shape at that time.

ROBERT LESLIE, *Letters to Ruskin, 1884*

Robert Leslie, son of the painter C. R. Leslie, Constable's biographer, was staying with his father at Lord Egremont's house, Petworth, in 1832, or more probably 1834, when this incident occurred.

SIGN-PAINTING

The greatest surviving example of sign-painting must be Watteau's 'Enseigne de Gersaint' (in Berlin), but Chardin and Hogarth are other famous painters who certainly painted comparable signs on occasion, as inevitably did lesser painters while work of that kind was in demand; one such was Samuel Wale (1721–86).

Mr Wale painted some signs; the principal one was a whole-length of Shakespeare, about five foot high, which was executed for, and displayed before, the door of a public house, the north-east corner of little Russel St. in Drury Lane. It was enclosed in a most sumptuous carved gilt frame, and suspended by rich iron work; but this splendid object of attraction did not hang long before it was taken down, in consequence of the act of Parliament which was passed for paving, and also for removing the signs and other obstructions in the streets of London. Such was the total change of fashion, and the consequent disuse of signs, that the above representation of our great poet was sold for a trifle . . . before this change took place, the universal use of signs furnished no little employment for the inferior rank of painters, and sometimes for the superior professors.

EDWARD EDWARDS, *Anecdotes of Painters*, 1808

SIGNORELLI

He stayed in the house of the Vasari, and as a child of eight I remember the worthy old man, so gracious and refined, and when he heard from my master who taught me my letters that I did nothing but draw figures in school, he turned to my father Antonio and said, 'Antonio, in order that Giorgio may not grow worse, get him to learn to draw, because even with his other studies this cannot fail to be of assistance and honour to him as it is to all worthy men.' Then turning to me as I stood before him, he said, 'Learn, little kinsman, learn.' He said a great deal more, which I will not repeat, because I know that I have not nearly realised the expectations which he formed of me. Knowing also that I suffered severely from bleeding at the nose, which sometimes left me in a fainting condition, he very tenderly put a jasper [charm] on my neck. This memory of Luca will remain with me for ever.

GIORGIO VASARI, 'Life' of Signorelli, 1568

Signorelli's secular masterpiece of 'Pan' (Berlin) was a casualty of the Second World War, but something of the spell it exerted is sensed in the comments of various art historians, even if to do it justice really required the gifts of Pater.

Sometimes called the 'School of Pan', it is more poetically described in the German catalogue 'Pan, as God of Natural Life, and Master of Music, with his attendants'. It is full of poetry, and of idyllic charm with all its stately solemnity. The sad beauty of the god as he listens to the music of the pipes, the golden sunlight on the moss-green grass, the quiet peace of the scene, have an entrancing effect, and we are transported in spirit to the same 'melodious plot of beechen green and shadows numberless' where Pan holds his court.

MAUD CRUTTWELL, *Luca Signorelli*, 1899

SITTING FOR A PICTURE

Miss Rehan's sittings had been interrupted by a few final rehearsals of 'Twelfth Night' before its production in London, but at last the evening arrived. I was 'in front' with a friend, J. J. Shannon, then Sargent's most formidable rival among portrait painters, and had sent round a line to the Leading Lady asking to see her when all was over.

Almost from the start her Viola had enchanted the audience, but in the midst of her triumph, and success in a great Shakespearian rôle in Shakespeare's country meant very much to her, she found time to scribble a note and send it to me.

> Yes, come by all means. I have something particular to tell you about Sargent – something he said of you – you must hear it and, I hope, act upon it. Shall I tell you before your friend? – you must bring him. This evening is so nice – it has unnerved me a little.
>
> Affectionately,
> ADA REHAN

I felt puzzled and intrigued. What could Sargent have said of me, Sargent who so very seldom said anything of anybody? It was quite exciting. We presented ourselves in due course and found Viola rather overwhelmed by her great ovation, but still eager to impart news.

'Well, he's very anxious to paint you.'

'Me?'

'Yes. He wants you to sit to him.'

'Wants *me*? But good gracious. Why?'

'I don't know,' said Ada, a little tactlessly. 'He says you are so paintable: that the lines of your long overcoat and – and the dog – and – I can't quite remember *what* he said, but he was tremendously enthusiastic.'

I did not wonder that Miss Rehan's memory had failed, but I was well able to supply the missing words. Sargent, I felt sure, had delivered himself thus – 'You know – there's a certain sort of – er – er – that is to say a kind of – er – er – in fact a – er – er –' and so on and so on. He had not the gift of tongues, but that mattered little; he was so well able to express himself otherwise.

No one had ever wanted to paint me before. Portions of me had been borrowed from time to time; hands pretty frequently by Albert Moore, hands again by Poynter, quite a good deal by Walter Crane for immortals of uncertain shape and sex, but I myself, proper (I use the word in its heraldic sense), had never been in request. Even now, as far as I could gather, the dog and the overcoat seemed to be regarded as my strong points; nevertheless, I felt very proud and – well, Sargent soon had three large canvases on hand instead of two.

Being but an amateur model, I was easily entrapped into a trying pose, turning as if to walk away, with a general twist of the whole body and all the weight on one foot. Professional models will always try to poise the weight equally on both feet and will go to any lengths of duplicity to gain this end.

I managed pretty well on the whole, but the sittings cleared up a point which had long puzzled me: why did models occasionally faint during a long pose without mentioning that they felt tired and wanted a rest? One day the answer came to me quite suddenly.

I had been standing for over an hour and saw no reason why I should not go on for another hour, when I became aware of what seemed a cold wind blowing in my face accompanied by a curious 'going' at the knees.

I tried to ask for a rest, but found that my lips were frozen stiff and refused to move. Hundreds of years passed – I suppose about twenty seconds.

Sargent glanced at me.

'What a horrid light there is just now,' he remarked. 'A sort of green –' He looked more steadily. 'Why, it's you!' he cried, and seizing me by the collar, rushed me into the street, where he propped me up against a door post . . .

The Sargent . . . was of the artist's best period and he was painting something he had 'seen' pictorially and for some unknown reason had wished to perpetuate. Why a very thin boy (I then looked no more) in a very tight coat should have struck him as a subject worthy of treatment I never discovered, but he evidently had the finished picture in his mind from the first and started it almost exactly upon its final lines.

It was hot summer weather and I feebly rebelled against the thick overcoat.

'But the coat is the picture,' said Sargent. 'You must wear it.'

'Then I can't wear anything else,' I cried in despair, and with the sacrifice of most of my wardrobe I became thinner and thinner, much to the satisfaction of the artist, who used to pull and drag the unfortunate coat more and more closely round me until it might have been draping a lamp-post.

Even before the picture was finished its fame began to grow, and friends took to dropping in, anxious for a sight of it. Sargent's old friend, Henry

James, whom I had known before very slightly, came several times and expressed high approbation.

W. Graham Robertson, *Time Was*, 1931

Sargent's portrait, one of his most successful and subtle (no doubt because it had been 'seen' and was not commissioned), was painted in 1895 and now hangs in the Tate Gallery.

SKETCHES

Why does a fine sketch please us more than a fine picture? It is because there is more life in it and fewer forms. The more the forms are defined, the more life disappears. In a dead animal, a hideous thing to see, the forms are there but life no longer is. In young birds, kittens and several other animals, the form is still muffled and there is total vitality. So they delight us greatly. Why can a young student, incapable of doing even a mediocre picture, do a marvellous sketch? It is because the sketch is the product of enthusiasm and inspiration, while the picture is the product of labour, patience, lengthy study and consummate experience in art.

The sketch might perhaps not attract us so strongly were it not that being indeterminate it leaves greater liberty to the imagination, which sees there anything it likes. It is the story of children looking at the clouds, and we are all children more or less. It is the case of vocal music and instrumental music. We hear what the former tells us, we can make the latter tell us what we wish.

Denis Diderot, 'Salon of 1767'

Diderot was writing apropos sketches, which he went on to describe in detail, by Hubert Robert.

But the Sketcher speaks directly to the mind, and thus bribes and seduces the inexperienced. A good, half-defined idea, sketched out as it were symbolically, does not detain the eye, but excites the mind, the wit, the imagination, and the amateur is taken by surprise and sees what is not really there. Drawing, proportion, form, character, expression, composition, harmony, finish are no longer in question: they are replaced by the illusion of themselves. Mind speaks to mind, and the means by which this should happen is done away with.

Good sketches by great masters, those enchanting hieroglyphs, are usually the start of an enthusiasm for art and slowly lead the amateur to the threshold of the whole of its world, from which, if he once looks onward, he will never turn back. But the aspiring artist has more to fear than the amateur if he lingers in the realm of invention and design, for, if he moves faster through the door into the realm of art, he is also the first to run the risk of staying on the threshold.

J. W. von Goethe in *Propyläen*, 1799

This extract is from the short letter-novel written by Goethe and Schiller in the fictional 'persona' of Julie, whose uncle is the proponent of the views quoted above.

This afternoon I found a quiet piazza on the hill, south bank, somewhere near S. Maria sopra Arno [Florence], where I could sketch, and I did a little water colour that took me two hours.

Arnold Bennett, *Journal*, May 1910

She travelled and sketched, and it was hard to tell which was means and which end. Her talent, very likely, was not great enough to dispense with the sensational appeal of the subjects she chose, her vivacity and initiative at the same time too great for contentment with the simple practice of her art. Thus she was perpetually on the hunt after famous names and places; and wherever possible, the sketch of a celebrity in her book would have its authenticity confirmed by the original's own signature beneath it – often obtained under incredibly trying circumstances. Charlotte was amazed to hear and see the range of the young lady's travels. She had charcoal sketches of the bridge at Arcole, the Acropolis of Athens, and the birthplace of Kant in Königsberg. She had paid fifty pounds for the hire of a jolly-boat, and while it rocked up and down in the roadstead at Plymouth she had drawn the Emperor Napoleon standing at the rail of the *Bellerophon* after dinner, taking snuff. It was not a good picture, she confessed as much. A frantic press of boats full of shouting and huzzaing men, women and children, the roughness of the sea, and the brevity of the Emperor's stay on deck had disadvantaged her efforts. The great man, with his cocked hat, his ventripotent waistcoat and spreading coat-tails, looked absurdly foreshortened and distorted, like a figure in a conjuring-glass. All the same, she had contrived to get his signature, through an officer acquaintance on board the fateful ship – or at least a hasty scrawl which passed for such. The Duke of Wellington had given her his. From the Congress of Vienna she had reaped a splendid harvest. She worked so very fast, did Miss Rose, that even the busiest man could find a moment to accommodate her. Prince Metternich, Monsieur Talleyrand, Lord Castlereagh, Herr von Hardenberg, and many another honest European broker had done the same. Czar Alexander had set his signature beneath a side-whiskered likeness adorned with a highly caricatured nose – probably because the artist had clearly given to the fringe of hair round his bald pate the semblance of a laurel wreath.

Thomas Mann, *Lotte in Weimar*, 1939

And after all these various streams of humanity applauded and went their way, you could have seen me, like a man sick of himself and not knowing what to do with his thoughts and fancies, turn my eyes up to the sky; and, ever since God created it, never had it been so embellished by such a lovely picture of light and shades. Thus the air was such that those who envy you because they cannot be like you would have longed to show it . . .

Oh, how beautiful were the strokes with which Nature's brushes pushed the air back at this point, separating it from the palaces in the way that Titian does when painting his landscapes!

In some places the colours were green-blue, and in others they appeared blue-green, finely mixed by the whims of Nature, who is the teacher of teachers. With light and shades, she gave deep perspective and high relief to what she wished to bring forward and set back, and so I, who know how your brush breathes with her spirit, cried out three or four times: 'Oh, Titian, where are you?'

PIETRO ARETINO, *Letter to Titian, May 1544*

Aretino is describing an evening scene over the Grand Canal, Venice, from his house there. At the date of the letter, Titian was presumably out of Venice or it suited Aretino's literary purpose to suppose so.

That landscape painter who does not make his skies a very material part of his composition, neglects to avail himself of one of his greatest aids. Sir Joshua Reynolds, speaking of the landscapes of Titian, of Salvator and of Claude, says: 'Even their *skies* seem to sympathise with their subjects.' I have often been advised to consider my sky as '*a white sheet thrown behind the objects*'. Certainly, if the sky is obtrusive, as mine are, it is bad; but if it is evaded, as mine are not, it is worse; it must and always shall with me make an effectual part of the composition.

JOHN CONSTABLE, *Letter to Archdeacon Fisher, 23 October 1821*

Returning to the pictures of the religious schools, we find that their open skies are also of the highest value. Their preciousness is such that no subsequent schools can by comparison be said to have painted sky at all, but only clouds, or mist, or blue canopies. The golden sky of Marco Basaiti in the Academy of Venice altogether overpowers and renders valueless that of Titian beside it. Those of Francia in the gallery of Bologna are even more wonderful, because cooler in tone and behind figures in full light. The touches of white light in the horizon of Angelico's Last Judgment are felt and wrought with equal truth . . .

It [Giovanni Bellini's 'St Jerome' altarpiece in S. Giovanni Crisostomo,

Venice] is remarkable for the absolute truth of its sky, whose blue, clear as crystal, and, though deep in tone, bright as the open air, is gradated to the horizon with a cautiousness and finish almost inconceivable; and to obtain light at the horizon without contradicting the system of chiaroscuro adopted in the figures, which are lighted from the right hand, it is barred across with some glowing white cirri, which, in their turn, are opposed by a single dark horizontal line of lower cloud; and to throw the whole further back, there is a wreath of rain cloud of warmer colour floating above the mountains, lighted on its under edge, whose faithfulness to nature, both in hue, and in its irregular and shattering form, is altogether exemplary.

JOHN RUSKIN, *Modern Painters*, Volume I, 1843

One night [at Saintes-Maries-sur-Mer] I went for a walk by the sea along the empty shore. It was not gay, but neither was it sad – it was – beautiful. The deep blue sky was flecked with clouds of a blue deeper than the fundamental blue of intense cobalt, and others of a clearer blue, like the blue whiteness of the Milky Way. In the blue depth the stars were sparkling, greenish, yellow, white, rose, brighter, flashing more like jewels, than they do at home – even in Paris: opals you might call them, emeralds, lapis, rubies, sapphires.

VINCENT VAN GOGH, *Letter to his brother Theo, June 1888*

The spectacle of the sky overwhelms me. I am overwhelmed when I see a crescent moon or the sun in an immense sky. In my paintings there are often tiny forms in vast empty spaces. Empty spaces, empty horizons, empty plains – everything that has been stripped bare has always made a strong impression on me.

JOAN MIRÓ, interviewed by Yvon Taillandier, 1959

SMOKING

Rosa Bonheur was an inveterate smoker of cigarettes. One summer's day, arriving in Paris from Fontainebleau, at ten o'clock in the morning, she hired an open cab and began making some calls. I was with her. At eleven o'clock she exclaimed:

'I can resist no longer. I haven't smoked for three hours. Give me a cigarette.'

'But it won't do to smoke in the streets,' I answered.

So she ordered the driver to pull up the cover of the cab, and when this was done, lifted up her skirt, beneath which were her men's trousers, and was soon enjoying her smoke.

BENJAMIN TEDESCO in *Reminiscences of Rosa Bonheur*, 1910

. . . Sickert always carried on him about six or seven large Manilas, in a case, and used invariably to smoke them the wrong way round. Moreover, it was Sir Walter Raleigh who had recommended them to Sickert. Sir Walter had lived several years in Manila, and had told him how no guano was put on the land where these were grown, and how they were therefore healthier, and that the natives, even the young girls, always smoked them in this way. In an essay, my friend Mr Clive Bell [in the *Cornhill* for May 1944] has suggested as a reason for it Sickert's desire to show 'how unlike he was to other men'. But a more charitable and likely explanation is one that I can produce from my own experience, that to smoke Manilas the wrong way round is the best way to smoke them, for, compared with other more expensive cigars, they are apt to draw badly, if you light the wide end. Sickert once explained this to me, and I have proved it to be true. And, since he always bought and smoked Manilas in his own house, this may have led him, if he were offered a Havana elsewhere, to smoke it from habit in the same manner. It is not an important point: but it fits with a more important subject, for, incidentally, it would seem to me that, if Sickert, for the sake of the fun, to be derived from it, ever posed, it was in precisely the opposite direction to that which Mr Clive Bell has indicated: to prove that the artist was exactly the same as other men.

SIR OSBERT SITWELL, editorial to *A Free House! or The Artist as Craftsman, being the writings of Walter Richard Sickert*, 1947

SPANISH PAINTING

It was the Napoleonic Wars that brought much greater awareness of the range of Spanish painting to European attention. The Scottish painter George Augustus Wallis went to Portugal and Spain in 1807, acting as agent for the art dealer William Buchanan. In a letter of 1808, which Buchanan printed in his 'Memoirs' (1824), Wallis reported to him from Madrid:

Of the Spanish school we have no idea whatsoever in England. If they could see the two or three best Murillos of the St Iago family, and some of the fine pictures of Velasquez, Alonzo Canno, Pereda, Zuberan, Caregni, and del Greco, really first-rate men, whose works are quite unknown out of Spain, some estimate of the high excellence of this school might then be formed. This school is rich beyond idea, and its painters are all great colourists: some of their colossal works are surprising. If you had time and could bear the horrors of travelling in Spain it would be worth while to visit the country. After all, I must own, I have, as an artist, learnt a great deal from this admirable school.

GEORGE AUGUSTUS WALLIS, *Letter of 25 September 1808*

'Caregñi' is Juan Carreno (1614–85), the favoured painter of Charles II of Spain. And it is remarkable to find 'del Greco' named at so early a date among the first-rate painters.

JAN STEEN

Others of the same [Dutch] school have shewn great power in expressing the character and passions of those vulgar people, which were the subjects of their study and attention. Among those Jean Stein [*sic*] seems to be one of the most diligent and accurate observers of what passed in those scenes which he frequented, and which were to him an academy. I can easily imagine, that if this extraordinary man had had the good fortune to have been born in Italy, instead of Holland, had he lived in Rome instead of Leyden, and been blessed with Michael Angelo and Raffaelle for his masters, instead of Brouwer and Van Gowen [*sic*], the same sagacity and penetration which distinguished so accurately the different characters and expressions in his vulgar figures, would, when exerted in the selection and imitation of what was great and elevated in nature, have been equally successful; and he now would have ranged with the great pillars and supporters of our Art.

SIR JOSHUA REYNOLDS, *Discourse VI*, 10 December 1774

STILL LIFE

. . . What the humanist doctors most admired was the beauty of sustained balance.

Is that the sort of beauty we behold in Dutch still life pictures, especially the *banketjestukken* or breakfast pieces of the 1620s and 1630s that were wholly their invention? Is there a relationship between the artlessness of Dutch cooking, of which so many travellers complained, and the easy transmutation of that plain fare into an object of art? Whatever else may be said of the Haarlem 'monochromatic' studies of Pieter Claesz. and Willem Claesz. Heda, they were certainly not exercises in profusion. They testify, rather, to the Dutch ingenuity at creating much from little. The ingredients of a simple meal (not necessarily breakfast): a wedge of cheese, a loaf of bread, a herring, the ubiquitous lemon, a scattering of nuts and fruit, a *roemer* of Rhenish or a tankard of ale – are all assembled with exquisite economy, both of hue and of composition. The *Banketjestukken* are as spare and as precise as the later *pronkstilleven* of Willem Kalf and Abraham van Beyeren in the 1650s and 1660s were flamboyant and luxuriant. Kalf's lobsters sit in vermilion brilliance reflecting against silver ewers or Ming dishes; Claesz.'s herrings offer just the merest glint of scaly light to offset the pewter monochrome of their background. Van Beyeren would play with the pellucid quality of glass and the jewel-like depth of wine within it; Heda made hock and *roemer* of the same brown-green transparency. Kalf might set his precious objects on the crimson glow of a Turkish rug; Claesz. and Floris van Schooten generally use starch-white linen on which to place their crust-brown pies and loaves. The monochrome *banketjestukken* are studies in ruminative plainness, to be taken in in the unhurried, contemplative manner of the humanist scholar rather than the cramming sensuousness of the man of fashion, the *pronker*. They are not easily disturbed. In Willem Heda's pictures in particular, the objects are so subtly disposed, their relationship with each other so delicately measured, that the least dislodging collapses the whole. The cunning intrusion of the upturned glass or the casually prostrated flagon acts to reinforce the sense of fragility with which this miraculous equilibrium is sustained.

SIMON SCHAMA, *The Embarrassment of Riches*, 1987

STUBBS

Stubbs had no gift for pictorial narrative or for the type of dramatic inventiveness demanded by history painting. If we may accept [Ozias] Humphry's report that he did not wish to study or copy other artists' work, and that in Italy he could not agree with his companions in their assessment of the past, then he would have had neither the opportunity nor the desire to teach himself the rules and conventions of a dying genre. His originality, his pictorial qualities and the peculiar poetry of his art are of a different kind. We find such qualities indeed in a Hogarth or Reynolds otherwise employed, but they eluded the canons of the 18th century taste and aesthetics which required that the poetic and suggestive element in painting should derive from the inherent associations of an historical or literary theme and that formal attributes should be amenable to description and enjoyment in terms of the Beautiful, the Sublime and the Picturesque. A generous appreciation of Stubbs' genius could only come when circumstances and prejudices had changed, for his art is more closely related to that of the 15th or the 19th centuries than to the main stylistic streams of the 16th, 17th and 18th. In his own century Chardin and the early Gainsborough are his companions. In spirit, the groom in the *Hambletonian* joins the portraits of

Goya. In spirit, the *Gimcrack* accords with the racing pictures of Degas.

BASIL TAYLOR, *Introduction to Stubbs exhibition catalogue, Whitechapel Art Gallery, 1957*

This exhibition was the first large assembly of Stubbs's pictures to be seen in London since 1885, though there was a good exhibition of his work in Liverpool in 1951, when he was still in the process of being rediscovered.

STUDIOS

The largest of these studios, and the dirtiest, was Carrel's, where some thirty or forty art students drew and painted from the nude model every day but Sunday from eight till twelve, and for two hours in the afternoon, except on Saturdays, when the afternoon was devoted to much-needed Augean sweepings and cleanings.

One week the model was male, the next female, and so on, alternating throughout the year.

A stove, a model-throne, stools, boxes, some fifty strongly-built low chairs with backs, a couple of score easels and many drawing-boards, completed the *mobilier*.

The bare walls were adorned with endless caricatures – *des charges* – in charcoal and white chalk; and also the scrapings of many palettes – a polychromous decoration not unpleasing.

For the freedom of the studio and the use of the model each student paid ten francs a month to the *massier*, or senior student, the responsible bell-wether of the flock; besides this, it was expected of you, on your entrance or initiation, that you should pay for your footing – your *bienvenue* – some thirty, forty or fifty francs, to be spent on cakes and rum punch all round.

Every Friday Monsieur Carrel, a great artist, and also a stately, well-dressed, and most courteous gentleman (duly decorated with the red rosette of the Legion of Honour), came for two or three hours and went the round, spending a few minutes at each drawing-board or easel – ten or even twelve when the pupil was an industrious and promising one.

He did this for love, not money, and deserved all the reverence with which he inspired this somewhat irreverent and most unruly company, which was made up of all sorts.

Graybeards who had been drawing and painting there for thirty years or more, and remembered other masters than Carrel, and who could draw and paint a torso almost as well as Titian or Velasquez – almost, but not quite – and who could never do anything else, and were fixtures at Carrel's for life.

Younger men who in a year or two, or three or five, or ten or twenty, were bound to make their mark, and perhaps follow in the footsteps of the master; others as conspicuously singled out for failure and future mischance

– for the hospital, the garret, the river, the Morgue, or, worse, the traveller's bag, the road, or even the paternal counter.

Irresponsible boys, mere *rapins*, all laugh and chaff and mischief – *blague et bagout Parisien*; little lords of misrule – wits, butts, bullies; the idle and industrious apprentice, the good and the bad, the clean and the dirty (especially the latter) – all more or less animated by a certain *esprit de corps*, and working very happily and genially together, on the whole, and always willing to help each other with sincere artistic counsel if it was asked for seriously, though it was not always couched in terms very flattering to one's self-love.

GEORGE DU MAURIER, *Trilby*, 1894

Du Maurier's evocation of Parisian studio life is very closely based on his own experiences as an art student there in the late 1850s.

SUPREMATISM

The name was given by the Russian painter Kasimir Malevich (1878–1935) to his liberated lyrical philosophy of art which early in the twentieth century celebrated the painter's freedom from depicting material reality. His own late pictures are unexpectedly 'realistic' in a Soviet idiom.

At the present time man's path lies through space and Suprematism is a colour semaphore in its infinite abyss.

The blue colour of the sky has been defeated by the Suprematist system, has been broken through, and entered white, as the true real conception of infinity, and therefore liberated from the colour background of the sky.

The system, hard, cold, and unsmiling, is brought into motion by philosophical thought, or else within the system its real strength is already moving.

All the colourings of utilitarian intention are insignificant and narrow, having the already completed purely applied significance of what was found by cognizance and the result of philosophic thought, on the horizon of our vision of little corners either serving a philistine taste or else creating a new one.

In one of its stages Suprematism has, through colour, a purely philosophical movement, and in a second, as a form which may be applied, formed a new style of Suprematist decoration . . .

I am only free when my will, on a critical and philosophical basis, can bring from what already exists the basis for new phenomena.

I have torn through the blue lampshade of colour limitations, and come out into the white; after me, comrade aviators, sail into the chasm – I have set up semaphores of Suprematism.

I have conquered the lining of the heavenly, have torn it down, and, making a bag, put in colours and tied it with a knot. Sail forth! The white, free chasm, infinity, is before us.

K. MALEVICH, *Tenth State Exhibition catalogue*, 1919

SURREALISM

The need of fixing visual images, whether these images exist before their fixation or not, stands out from all time and has led to the creation of a veritable language, which does not seem to me more artificial than any other, over the origins of which I do not feel it necessary to linger here. The most I can do is to consider the present state of this language from the same angle as that from which I should consider the present state of poetic language. It seems to me that I can demand a great deal from a faculty which, above almost all others, gives me advantage over the real, over what is vulgarly understood by *the real*. Why is it that I am so much at the mercy of a few lines, a few coloured patches? The object, the strange object itself draws from these things the greatest amount of its force of provocation, and God knows whether this is a good provocation, for *I* cannot understand whither it is tending. What does it matter to me whether trees are green, whether a piano is at this moment 'nearer' to me than a state-coach, whether a ball is cylindrical or round? That is how things are, nevertheless, if I am to believe my eyes, that is to say up to a certain point. In such a domain I dispose of a power of illusion whose limits, if I am not careful, I cease to perceive. If at this moment I turn to some illustration or other in a book, there is nothing to prevent the world around me ceasing to exist. In place of what was surrounding me there is now something else, since, for example, I can without difficulty take part in quite another ceremony . . . The corner formed by the ceiling and two walls in the picture can easily be substituted for the corner of this ceiling and these two walls. I turn over a few pages, and in spite of the almost uncomfortable heat, I do not in the least refuse to consent to this winter landscape. I can play with these winged children. 'He saw before him an illuminated cavern,' says a caption, and I can actually see it too. I see it in a way in which I do not at this moment see you for whom I am writing, yet all the same I am writing so as to be able to see you one day, just as truly as I have lived a second for this Christmas tree, this illuminated cavern, or these angels. It does not matter whether there is a perceptible difference between things thus involved and real beings, for this difference can at any moment be made light of. So that it is impossible for me to consider a picture as anything but a window, in which my first interest is to know what it *looks out on*, or, in other words, whether, from where I am, there is a 'beautiful view', for there is nothing I love so much as that which stretches away before me and *out of sight*. Within the frame of an *unnamed figure, land – or seascape*, I can enjoy an enormous spectacle.

What am I doing here, why have I to stare this person in the face for so long, of what enduring temptation am I the object? But apparently it is a man who is making this proposition to me! I do not refuse to follow wherever he would lead me. Only afterwards can I judge whether I was wise to take him as my guide and whether the adventure into which I have been drawn by him was worthy of me . . .

The very narrow conception of *imitation* which art has been given as its aim is at bottom of the serious misunderstanding that we see continuing right up to the present. In the belief that they are only capable of reproducing more or less fortunately the image of that which moves them, painters have been far too easy-going in their choice of models. The mistake lies in thinking that the model can only be taken from the exterior world, or even simply that it can be taken at all. Certainly human sensibility can confer a quite unforeseen distinction upon even the most vulgar-looking object; none the less, to make the magic power of figuration which certain men possess serve the purpose of preserving and reinforcing that which would exist without them anyway, is to make wretched use of it. There lies the inexcusable abdication. It is in any case impossible, under the present conditions of thought, when above all the exterior world appears more and more suspect, still to consent to such a sacrifice. The plastic work of art, in order to respond to the undisputed necessity of thoroughly revising all real values, will either refer to a *purely interior model* or cease to exist.

André Breton, *What is Surrealism?*, 1936

TABLEAUX VIVANTS

The little theatre [at Tsarskoselo] was charming, and I wished to take advantage of the place to compose some *tableaux vivants*. There was a continual stream of people from Saint Petersburg and I chose my characters from the most handsome men and the most beautiful women. I created their costumes, draping them with cashmere shawls, of which there was no shortage in Saint Petersburg. I preferred serious subjects from the Bible to any other. I also composed several well-known *tableaux* from memory, such as *The Family of Darius*, which worked extremely well; but the most successful of all was *Achilles at the court of Lycomedes*; I took care to arrange the costume of Achilles, for I was accustomed to dressing my models thus, using a helmet and a shield to create a very convincing warrior. The company were highly amused by these *tableaux*. The following winter they used them to vary the evening's entertainment in the salons of Saint Petersburg. Everyone wanted to join in, and I was often forced to deny this pleasure to several ladies who were extremely keen to display themselves.

ELISABETH VIGÉE-LE BRUN, *Memoirs*, 1835–7

'The Family of Darius' was probably based on Charles Le Brun's picture at Versailles. The subject of Achilles discovered at the court of Lycomedes was very popular in seventeenth- and eighteenth-century painting. The future hero had been disguised as a girl and sent by his mother to stay with the daughters of Lycomedes to avoid being involved in the Trojan War; the wily Odysseus contrived his discovery by mingling with gifts of female finery, armour and weapons which Achilles seized on.

The scenes were taken from old pictures, and the participators had been cleverly fitted with characters suited to their types. No one, for instance, could have made a more typical Goya than Carry Fisher, with her short dark-skinned face, the exaggerated glow of her eyes, the provocation of her frankly-painted smile. A brilliant Miss Smedden from Brooklyn showed to perfection the sumptuous curves of Titian's Daughter, lifting her gold salver laden with grapes above the harmonising gold of rippled hair and rich brocade, and a young Mrs Van Alstyne, who showed the frailer Dutch type, with high blue-veined forehead and pale eyes and lashes, made a characteristic Vandyke, in black satin, against a curtained archway. Then there were Kauffmann nymphs garlanding the altar of Love; a Veronese supper, all sheeny textures, pearl-woven heads and marble architecture; and a Watteau group of lute-playing comedians, lounging by a fountain in a sun-lit glade.

. . . so skilfully had the personality of the actors been subdued to the scenes they figured in that even the least imaginative of the audience must have felt a thrill of contrast when the curtain suddenly parted on a picture which was simply and undisguisedly the portrait of Miss Bart.

Here there could be no mistaking the predominance of personality – the unanimous 'Oh!' of the spectators was a tribute, not to the brushwork of Reynolds's 'Mrs Lloyd' but to the flesh and blood loveliness of Lily Bart. She had shown her artistic intelligence in selecting a type so like her own that she could embody the person represented without ceasing to be herself. It was as though she had stepped, not out of, but into, Reynolds's canvas, banishing the phantom of his dead beauty by the beams of her living grace. The impulse to show herself in a splendid setting – she had thought for a moment of representing Tiepolo's Cleopatra – had yielded to the truer instinct of trusting to her unassisted beauty, and she had purposely chosen a picture without distracting accessories of dress or surroundings.

EDITH WHARTON, *The House of Mirth*, 1905

Edith Wharton's doomed heroine has made a highly sophisticated choice of picture, indicative of the author's own keen visual knowledge and awareness. Reynolds's full-length portrait of Mrs Lloyd, shown carving the name 'Lloyd' on a tree, was sold at Christie's in 1869 and subsequently acquired by Baron Lionel de Rothschild, MP; it has remained in the family.

TAVERN-KEEPING

Tavern-keeping and comparable occupations by painters are normally associated with such Dutch seventeenth-century artists as Jan Steen, but Vasari tells of a much earlier painter so employed, Mariotto Albertinelli (1474–1515):

Mariotto was a restless man, a follower of Venus, and a good liver. He thus came to hate the subtleties of painting and its brain weaving, and, being frequently attacked by the envious tongues of painters, as is their custom, maintained through generations, he resolved to take up a baser, less difficult and more cheerful craft. Accordingly, he kept open for many months a fine inn outside the gate of S. Gallo, and a tavern at the Dragon, at the Ponte Vecchio. He continued there for some months, saying that he had found an art which did not need muscles, foreshortening or perspectives, and, better still, without critics, while the one he had abandoned possessed all these disadvantages; the one imitated flesh and blood, but the other created them. And now everyone praised him, for he had good wine, and he was not obliged to listen to criticisms every day. But he grew tired of this also, becoming disgusted with the baseness of the trade, and returned to painting, doing pictures for private citizens in Florence . . .

GIORGIO VASARI, *'Life' of Albertinelli*, 1568

TAXES

An enviably civilized way of dealing with such matters in the early nineteenth century is illustrated by the experience of Benjamin West, then President of the Royal Academy.

He [West] told me He had lately been called upon by the Commissioners appointed for the Property Tax at the insistence of their Surveyor who had not been satisfied with His return, & had accordingly rated Him to pay *Sixty three pounds* a quarter. He attended a Board at which Mr Collins of Berners Street presided & it was so ordered that few were present. He shewed that the Income which He receives from the King & upon which He lives is the *payment of a debt*, not a *gift*, & that it is for work done long since. That as Surveyor of Pictures, that part of His Income has 10 per cent deducted before it is paid to him. Mr Collins then asked Him what He wd. propose to pay supposed to be for the average annual gains from his profession, & He named a sum with which Mr Collins expressed himself satisfied.

JOSEPH FARINGTON, *Diary*, 15 December 1807

DAVID TENIERS THE YOUNGER

Whatever glory he might acquire by brilliant copying, he would always have to share it with the artist he copied, but Teniers was born to acquire glory which he had no need to share with anyone and which would be entirely his alone.

Convinced that there is no teacher greater than nature, he retired to the village of Perck, between Antwerp and Malines, so as to copy nature herself; and to achieve her artlessness, he studied nature in *Kermesses* and village feasts. Without lowering himself to the level of the rural inhabitants, he mingled with them in order to observe their dances and games, their rustic festivities, their joys and rages and fights. In such lively fashion did he catch their different aspects that one can recognize their ages, their characters and their disparate feelings. And it is astonishing that from such commonplace and apparently unrewarding subject-matter, he could produce an innumerable quantity of pictures, so admirable and so various. It is to him in particular that may be applied Virgil's words: he achieved great glory in a small category of art; *in tenui labor: at tenuis non gloria.* He proved that painting can encompass more themes than poetry, and that the brush can render agreeable objects which verse can hardly render tolerable.

J. B. DESCAMPS, *La Vie des peintres flamands, allemands et hollandois*, 1754

Teniers is an underrated landscape painter, because his figures, though often beautifully painted in themselves, are never properly related to the background and distract the eye. When they are inconspicuous, as in the *Brickworks* at Dulwich, or when by photography we are able to see a piece of landscape in isolation, we realise that he painted nature in rather the same spirit as Sisley in 1873. He saw the poetry of a prosaic scene and expressed it with a graceful, sensitive touch. No wonder he was a favourite painter of the English country gentleman, for his backgrounds show that half-conscious understanding of countryside beauty which one finds, so differently expressed, in the letters of Cowper, Cobbett and Edward FitzGerald.

KENNETH CLARK, *One Hundred Details from Pictures in the National Gallery*, 1938

GERARD TERBORCH

Gogin told me that Berg, an impulsive Swede whom he had known in Laurens's studio in Paris and who painted very well, came to London and was taken by an artist friend [Henry Scott Tuke, ARA] to the National Gallery where he became very enthusiastic about the Terbourgs [*sic*]. They then went for a walk and, in Kensington Gore, near one of the entrances to Hyde Park or Kensington Gardens, there was an old Irish apple-woman sitting with her feet in a basket, smoking a pipe and selling oranges.

'Arranges two a penny, sorr,' said the old woman in a general way.

And Berg, turning to her and throwing out his hands appealingly, said: 'Oh, madame, avez-vous vu les Terbourgs? Allez voir les Terbourgs.'

He felt that such a big note had been left out of the life of any one who had not seen them.

SAMUEL BUTLER, 'Written Sketches', *The Notebooks*

GIAMBATTISTA TIEPOLO

France was ahead – far ahead – of England (and perhaps of Italy, too) in posthumous appreciation of Tiepolo, whose death in 1770 inaugurated several decades of neglect of his art. Three distinguished French artists are involved in this terse tribute:

Do me the favour of leaving your two friends for a moment to go, when it is dry, to the Palazzo Labia to see, partly for yourself and partly for me, the frescoes of Tiepolo. Forain, yes Forain, gave me a glimpse of them on the table at the Café La Rochefoucauld, which he terminated by comparing them to a poster by Chéret. It is his way of admiring them. Perhaps it is no worse than any other . . .

EDGAR DEGAS, *Letter to Henri Rouart in Venice, 16 October 1883*

Jules Chéret (1836–1932) was a painter and a sculptor but chiefly famous for his lithographic posters, often of great wit and verve and subtle tonality.

It is rare – if not unique – to find Tiepolo given a full favourable chapter in any book on painting written in English before the 1930s. All the more notable is this sympathetic account of 1912:

We have already noted that to establish the significance of any period in art, it is necessary that the tendencies should unite and combine in some culminating spirits who rise triumphant over their contemporaries and soar above the age in which they live. Such a genius stands out above the eighteenth century crowd, and is not only of his century, but of every time. For two hundred years Tiepolo has been stigmatised as extravagant, mannered, as just equal to painting cupids, nymphs, and parroquets. In the last century he experienced the effect of the profound discredit into which the whole of eighteenth-century art had fallen. In France, David had obliterated Watteau; and the reputation of Pompeo Battoni, a sort of Italian David, effaced Tiepolo and his contemporaries. When the delegates of the French Republic inspected Italian churches and palaces, and decided that works of art should be sent to the Louvre, they singled out the Bolognese, the Guercinos and Guidos, the Carracci, even Pompeo Battoni and other such forgotten masters, a Gatti, a Nevelone [*sic*], a Badalocchio; but to the lasting regret of their descendants, they disdained to annex a single one of the great paintings of the Venetian, Giambattista Tiepolo.

Eastlake only vouchsafes him one line as 'an artist of fantastic imagination'. Most of the nineteenth-century critics do not even mention him. Burckhardt dismisses him with a grudging line of praise, Blanc is equally disparaging, and for Taine he is a mere mannerist, yet his influence has been felt far beyond his lifetime; only now is he coming into his own, and it is recognised that the *plein-air* artist, the luminarist, the impressionist, owe no small share of their knowledge to his inspiration . . .

Tiepolo, sincere and spontaneous even when he is sacrificing truth to caprice, struck the taste of the Venetians, and without emancipating himself from the tendencies of the time, contrives to introduce a fresh accent. All round him was a weak and self-indulgent world, but within himself he possessed a fund of buoyant and in-exhaustible energy. He evokes a throng of personages on the ceilings of the churches and palaces confided to his fancy. His creations range from mythology to religion, from the sublime to the grotesque. All Olympia appears upon his ample and luminous spaces. It is not to the cold, austere Lazzarini, or to the clashing chiaroscuro of Piazetta [*sic*], or the imaginative spirit of Battista Ricci, though he was touched by each of them, that we must turn for Tiepolo's derivation. Long before his time, the kind of decoration of ceilings which we are apt to call Tiepolesque; the foreshortened architecture, the columns and cornices, the figures peopling the edifices, or reclining upon clouds, had been used by an increasing throng of painters. The style arose, indeed, in the quattrocento; Mantegna, the Umbrians, and even Michelangelo had used it, though in a far more sober way than later generations. Correggio and the Venetians had perfected the idea, which the artists of the seventeenth century seized upon and carried to the most intemperate excess. But Tiepolo rose above them all; he abandoned the heavy, exaggerated, contorted designs, which by this time defied all laws of equilibrium, and we must go back further than his immediate predecessors for his origins. His claim to stand with Tintoretto or Veronese may be contested, but he is nearest to these, and no doubt Veronese is the artist he studied with the greatest fervour. Without copying, he seems to have a natural affinity of spirit with Veronese and assimilates the ample arrangement of his groups, the grace of his architecture and his decorative feeling for colour . . .

Tiepolo is a singular contradiction. His art suggests a strong being, held captive by butterflies. Sometimes he is joyous and limpid, sometimes turbulent and strong, but he has always sincerity, force and life. A great space serves to exhilirate him, and he asks nothing better than to cover it with angels and goddesses, white limbs among the clouds, sea-horses ridden by Tritons, patrician warriors in Roman armour, balustrades and columns and *amoretti*. He does not even need to pounce his design, but puts in all sorts of improvised modifications with a sure hand. The vastness of his frescoes, the daring poses of his countless figures, and the freedom of his line speak eloquently of the mastery to which his hand had attained. He revels, above all, in effects of light . . .

Nearly all his compositions have a serene and limpid horizon, with the figures approaching it painted in clear, silvery hues, airy and diaphanous, while the forms below are more muscular, the flesh tints are deeper, and the whole of the foreground is often enveloped in shadow. Veronese had lit up the shadows, which, under his contemporaries, were growing gloomy. Tiepolo carries his art further on the same lines. He makes his figures more graceful, his draperies more vaporous, and illumines his clouds with radiance. His faded blue and rose, his golden-greys, and pearly whites and pastel tints are not so much solid colours as caprices of light. We have remarked already that with Veronese the accessories of gleaming satin and rich brocades serve to obscure the persons. In many of Tiepolo's scenes the figures are lost in a flutter of drapery, subject and action melt away, and we are only conscious of soft harmonies of delicious colour, as ethereal as the hues of spring flowers in woodland ways and joyous meadows. With these delicious, audacious fancies, put on with a nervous hand, we forget the age of profound and ardent passion, we escape from that of pompous solemnity and studied grace, and we breathe an atmosphere of irresponsible and capricious pleasure. In this last word of her great masters Venice keeps what her temperament loved – sensuous colour and emotional chiaroscuro, used to accentuate an art adapted to a city of pleasure.

EVELYN MARCH PHILLIPS, *The Venetian School of Painting*, 1912

TINTORETTO

In about the year 1560 the members of the confraternity [of San Rocco] thought of acquiring an outstanding painting for the Albergo section of their building. To this end they sought the best painters of the city, among them Tintoretto, to make a design for the central oval panel. But Tintoretto secretly obtained from the servants the measurements of the space, and while the others were working to make their designs he with admirable speed did the painting itself, which depicts *St Roch in Glory* received by God the Father and attendant angels who hold the attributes of his pilgrimage; and without a word to anyone he put it in place.

The day after, Veronese, Andrea Schiavone, Giuseppe Salviati, and Federico Zuccaro were to appear to show their designs and Tintoretto was sought out to explain his as well; he had the painted canvas, which had been skilfully hidden with cardboard, uncovered, and said that this was the design he made, about which there could be no error, and if his quick work did not please them he would make a gift of it to St Roch, from whom he had obtained many favours. The painters were dumbfounded to see such a beautiful work carried out with such elegance in the space of a few days. Gathering up their sketches, they said to the members of the Confraternity that they could no longer have any claim to the commission, since Tintoretto through his valour had gained the honour. Nevertheless, the members of the Confraternity were angry, and insisted that his painting be removed because they had given no such order, but only wanted to see a sketch of the composition in order to give the work to the one that pleased them most. But being constrained to keep it (being unable because of their rules to refuse anything donated to the Saint), and since it was in actual fact considered excellent in the highest degree, and since, moreover, the majority of the votes were in favour of Tintoretto, it was agreed that he should be worthily recompensed. Receiving him into their order, they decreed that he alone would be given the commission for the rest of the paintings that would be needed for their rooms. He was given an annual provision of one hundred ducats for life, in return for which he was required to furnish one completed painting every year. But Tintoretto managed to dispatch them as quickly as possible, so that he drew his yearly pension for a long time after the paintings were completed (in his old age he used to say in jest that he wanted to live a thousand ducats longer). Then to complete the aforementioned ceiling he painted the insignias and habits of the six great schools of the city, including that of San Rocco.

CARLO RIDOLFI, *'Life' of Tintoretto*, 1642

Ruskin typically went too far in claiming he had virtually 'rediscovered' Tintoretto, whom he quite unnecessarily referred to as 'Tintoret'. English painters had been going admiringly to the Scuola di San Rocco and elsewhere in Venice to see Tintoretto's work long before Ruskin published a word of art criticism.

Among the pictures whose peculiar beauties he thus lastingly impressed upon his recollection [by copying], Tintoretto's mighty 'Crucifixion', pre-eminently engaged his attention. Of the noble group at the foot of the cross, and of other figures in this vast and glorious work, he made studies, in which the magical colour and composition of the original were transcribed with remarkable success. The writer of the present work happened to be with him on his first sight of this picture – as indeed he was on most other similar occasions. The day was declining as they entered the great room in the Scuolo [*sic*] di San Rocco, and beheld the light from without, falling soft and sober, upon the wall along which Tintoretto's immense composition extended. Thus seen, this sublime illustration of the Divine tragedy of Calvary assumed the grandest and highest aspect: it appeared to strike the painter speechless, as he looked at it. For some time he and his companion believed themselves to be the only occupants of the room; but a half-suppressed sob, suddenly audible from its lower and darker extremity, informed them that they were not alone. It proceeded from an old man, dressed in the worn rusty cassock of the lower order of Italian country curates, who was standing before the picture, with his wan hands clasped over his breast, the tears rolling down his cheeks, and his eyes fixed immovably on the majestic composition before him. He appeared to be perfectly unconscious that any one was looking at the picture but himself; and Mr Collins and his companion, on quitting the room, left him in the same position in which they had first discovered him. It is in such triumphs as these, that painting achieves its highest elevation; and, casting its mortal imperfections behind it, communes with universal humanity, in the mother language of that Nature from which it is derived.

WILKIE COLLINS, *Memoirs of the Life of William Collins Esq., R.A.*, 1848

Wilkie Collins and his father were in Venice in 1838. In a letter from there to Sir David Wilkie, the father writes: 'Tintoretto, too – how can one speak *of his pictures? – the "Miracle of S. Marco", the "Crucifixion"; and the many other fine things in the Scuolo [sic] di S. Rocco, and in the Church.'*

TITIAN

What was said of Virgil, that he threw even the dung about the ground with an air of dignity, may be applied to Titian: whatever he touched, however naturally mean, and habitually familiar, by a kind of magick he invested with grandeur and importance.

SIR JOSHUA REYNOLDS, *Discourse XI*, 10 December 1782

Is there any thing in modern art – we will not demand that it should be equal – but in any way analogous to what Titian has effected, in that wonderful bringing together of two times in the [Bacchus and] 'Ariadne' in the National Gallery? Precipitous, with his reeling Satyr rout about him, re-peopling and re-illumining suddenly the waste places, drunk with a new fury beyond the grape, Bacchus, born in fire, fire-like flings himself at the Cretan. This is the time present. With this telling of the story – an artist, and no ordinary one, might remain richly proud. Guido, in his harmonious version of it, saw no further. But from the depth of the imaginative spirit Titian has recalled past time, and laid it contributory with the present to one simultaneous effect. With the desert all ringing with the mad cymbals of his followers, made lucid with the presence and new offers of a god, – as if unconscious of Bacchus, or but idly casting her eyes as upon some unconcerning pageant – her soul undistracted from Theseus – Ariadne is still pacing the solitary shore in as much heart-silence, and in almost the same local solitude, with which she awoke at day-break to catch the forlorn last glances of the sail that bore away the Athenian.

Here are two points miraculously co-uniting; fierce society, with the feeling of solitude still absolute, noon-day revelations, with the accident of the dull grey dawn unquenched and lingering; the *present* Bacchus, with the *past* Ariadne; two stories with double Time; separate, and harmonising. Had the artist made the woman one shade less indifferent to the God; still more, had she expressed a rapture at his advent, where would have been the story of the mighty desolation of the heart previous? merged in the insipid accident of a flattering offer met with a welcome acceptance. The broken heart for Theseus was not lightly to be pieced up by a God.

CHARLES LAMB, 'Barrenness of the Imaginative Faculty in the Productions of Modern Art' in *Last Essays of Elia*, 1833

Titian could have put issues of life and death into the face of a man asking the way; nay, into the back of him, if he had so chosen.

John Ruskin, *Modern Painters*, Volume V 1860

And as a story of romantic love, fullest perhaps of all the motives of classic legend of the pride of life, it [the story of Bacchus and Ariadne] survived with undiminished interest to a later world, two of the greatest masters of Italian painting having poured their whole power into it; Titian with greater space of ingathered shore and mountain, and solemn foliage, and fiery animal life; Tintoret with profounder luxury of delight in nearness to each other, and imminent embrace, of glorious bodily presences; and both alike with consummate beauty of physical form.

Walter Pater, *Greek Studies*, 1895

On the whole, the consensus of approval has been more constantly on the side of Titian than on that of any other artist. Can we recognise the man behind the masterpiece? We can divine something of his aims and habits, nothing more. Titian's supreme gift was his great breadth of vision; but this is not all, there remains the lucid power which he brought to its expression. Other artists have seen as much, or possessed an even greater power of imagination, but not a greater gift in ordering their experience into a compact pictorial formula. With him a divine facility concealed a great power of concentration. There are many qualities in his work which in other channels of human endeavour would have made for success, in fact they helped him in the ordering of a singularly successful life. The vitality of the man, which enabled him to paint throughout a life of legendary length, endowed his vision with a constant energy and relish for life. Most great masters tower in the possession of some rare combination of gifts; with Titian the range is so vast, that we must turn to the qualities of a nation to find their equivalent. Viewing the major portion of his work, one is struck by the constant affirmation of splendid faculties, of a sort of optimism which colours his outlook. If the unique quality in the art of Raphael might be described as an unfailing sense of rhythm, the rhythmic sense, though great in Titian, is crossed by a greater hold upon realities, which he marshals into a rhythmic whole, without Raphael's tendency to transmute them into the terms of his own convention.

Titian's art is ardent and sensuous, but without the feverishness which such qualities would imply in a man of lesser faculties; unlike Michelangelo, Titian is wholly of this world, and by comparison untroubled by the sense of any other; at least this is true of the master's work before the age of seventy. Have I overstated the case? I think not, if we turn from the self-questioning and effort which twist Michelangelo's giants in their marble fetters to the St Sebastian or the 'Cristo della Moneta' of Titian. There is something Latin in the fibre of Titian, in his sense of reality and sense of control. The magisterial quality of his portraits lies deeper than their success, he belongs to a patrician people to whom experience is met by the force equal to control it successfully.

CHARLES RICKETTS, *Titian*, 1910

TOULOUSE-LAUTREC

Certainly he took the night life of his time and the world of brothels and prostitutes for his subject matter. Yet one only has to turn to the naturalistic novel at this period to see the difference in treatment between such writers and Lautrec. The truth is that he romanticises the scene. His glamorous handling of his subject may be appreciated when one compares his pictures with photographs of the themes on which, on occasion, they are based. In reality and when seen with the cold eye of time, the actual scenes appear infinitely tedious. The reverse process could also occur and in *A la Mie* (at Boston . . .) two harmless friends are turned into sordid creatures.

The model, however, was not necessary for Lautrec and the wonderful late drawings, *Au Cirque*, were executed from memory, while he was in the Madrid sanatorium at Neuilly in 1899. In these he attained an almost hallucinatory image of a favourite subject. And, like many of his later works, they stress that he was trying to enlarge his scope. In fact, certain of his final portraits – that of Joyant is one example – are richer in colour and suggest that he had looked closely at Titian and Rembrandt.

One of the central problems of Lautrec's personality is his attitude to women. Surely he saw the women he frequented as descendants of the 'tigresses', celebrated by the romantic generation; for them happiness was often to be found in inversion. It so happens that, except for his portraits of a few models and his mother, his most affectionate portraits of women are those which portray Sapphic pleasures. It may also be that as a relief from the complications of his own temperament he responded to the masculine world of bars and jockeys. For Lautrec could hardly escape the tragic sense of life: he wished to create an illusion but at the same time he could not forget how much is illusory.

DENYS SUTTON in the *Financial Times*, 21 February 1961

TURA

All the major Renaissance painters of Ferrara are fascinating artists, and all, for some reason, remain too little appreciated, though fine pictures by them can be seen in London, Liverpool and Edinburgh, quite apart from Ferrara.

Cosimo Tura was probably the most famous and esteemed of these painters in his lifetime, a court artist, and effectively the founder of the school.

Though this picture [the Allegorical Figure in the National Gallery] shows an attempt on Tura's part to submerge his strident personality . . . it yet bears the impress of a fantastic and deeply personal vision. Imagine the sensation of encountering such a figure at the bend of a road. Pull out the ringlets of her hair and they will spring back into place. Grope with the fingers over the brittle arch of the throne, and the blood will flow from contact with the fins and fangs of dolphins. Press gently on the red robe and it will refuse impudently to yield to the touch. Strike with a hammer on the heraldic fins, and they will ring out with a metallic clang, and snap, leaving a jagged edge. Shine a torch on a dolphin's eye and the ruby will glint in the lurid light.

BENEDICT NICOLSON, *The Painters of Ferrara*, 1950

TURNER

Turner exhibited his first oil painting at the Royal Academy in 1796, when he was twenty-one. In the following year he sent 'Fishermen Coming Ashore at Sun Set, previous to a Gale' (now lost), which was enthusiastically recognized, in the press and elsewhere, as exciting and highly original work by a virtually unknown painter. Most prophetic of all was the private comment of one visitor at the time (2 June 1797), not published until thirteen years later.

Visited the Royal Exhibition. Particularly struck with a sea view by Turner – fishing vessels coming in, with a heavy swell, in apprehension of tempest gathering in the distance, and casting, as it advances, a night of shade; while a parting glow is spread with fine effect upon the shore. The whole composition, bold in design, and masterly in execution. I am entirely unacquainted with the artist; but if he proceeds as he has begun, he cannot fail to become the first in his department.

THOMAS GREEN THE YOUNGER, *The Diary of a Lover of Literature*, 1810

The comments Turner's exhibited pictures drew from the contemporary press in his later years tended to be notoriously violent and uncomprehending. They make the comparable violence of Ruskin's defence of him in 'Modern Painters' understandable and most of today's art criticism seem remarkably bland.

'The Times' thus wrote of Turner's 'Schloss Rosenhau, Seat of HRH Prince Albert of Coburg', exhibited at the Royal Academy in 1841:

Here is a picture that represents nothing in nature beyond eggs and spinach. The lake is a composition in which salad oil abounds, and the art of cookery is more predominant than the art of painting.

The Times, 4 May 1841

But, I think, the noblest sea that Turner has ever painted, and, if so, the noblest certainly ever painted by man, is that of the slave ship, the chief Academy picture of the exhibition of 1840. It is a sunset on the Atlantic, after prolonged storm; but the storm is partially lulled, and the torn and streaming rain-clouds are moving in scarlet lines to lose themselves in the hollow of the night. The whole surface of sea included in the picture is divided into two ridges of enormous swell, not high, nor local, but a low broad heaving of the whole ocean, like the lifting of its bosom by deep-drawn breath after the torture of the storm. Between these two ridges the fire of the sunset falls along the trough of the sea, dyeing it with an awful but glorious light, the intense and lurid splendour which burns like gold, and bathes like blood. Along this fiery path and valley, the tossing waves by which the swell of the sea is restlessly divided, lift themselves in dark, indefinite, fantastic forms, each casting a faint and ghastly shadow behind it along the illuminated foam. They do not rise everywhere, but three or four together in wild groups, fitfully and furiously, as the under strength of the swell compels or permits them; leaving between them treacherous spaces of level and whirling water, now lighted with green and lamp-like fire, now flashing back the gold of the declining sun, now fearfully dyed from above with the undistinguishable images of the burning clouds, which fall upon them in flakes of crimson and scarlet, and give the reckless waves the added motion of their own fiery flying. Purple and blue, the lurid shadows of the hollow breakers are cast upon the mist of the night, which gathers cold and low, advancing like the shadow of death upon the guilty ship as it labours amidst the lightning of the sea, its thin masts written upon the sky in lines of blood, girded with condemnation in that fearful hue which signs the sky with horror and mixes its flaming flood with the sunlight, and, cast far along the desolate heave of the sepulchral waves, incarnadines the multitudinous sea.

I believe, if I were reduced to rest Turner's immortality upon any single work, I should choose this.

JOHN RUSKIN, *Modern Painters*, Volume I, 1843

Ruskin's father bought this famous picture (Museum of Fine Arts, Boston) and gave it to him as a New Year present in 1844. Eventually Ruskin found its subject too disturbingly painful to live with, and he sold it. Superb as Ruskin's description is, it interestingly omits any mention of the varieties of peculiar fish rather ludicrously prominent amid the waves.

I have passed without notice what the reader might suppose a principal event of my life, – the being introduced to him [Turner] by Mr Griffith, at Norwood dinner, June 22nd 1840.

The diary says, 'Introduced to-day to the man who beyond all doubt is the greatest of the age; greatest in every faculty of the imagination, in every branch of scenic knowledge; at once the painter and the poet of the day, J. M. W. Turner. Everybody had described him to me as coarse, boorish, unintellectual, vulgar. This I knew to be impossible. I found in him a somewhat eccentric, keen-mannered, matter-of-fact, English-minded-gentleman; good-natured evidently, bad-tempered evidently, hating humbug of all sorts, shrewd, perhaps a little selfish, highly intellectual, the powers of the mind not brought out with any delight in their manifestation, or intention of display, but flashing out occasionally in a word or a look.'

Pretty close, that, and full, to be seen at a first glimpse, and set down the same evening.

JOHN RUSKIN, *Praeterita*, 1885–9

UGLINESS

. . . shun also those things which are barbarous, shocking to the Eye, and party-colour'd, and which are all of an equal Force of Light and Shadow: as also all things which are obscene, impudent, filthy, unseemly, cruel, fantastical, poor, and wretched; and all those things which are sharp to the Feeling: In short, all things which corrupt their natural Forms, by a Confusion of their Parts which are entangled in each other: *For the Eyes have a Horror for those things, which the Hands will not condescend to touch.*

C. A. du Fresnoy, *The Art of Painting*, 1668

Because of the horror he felt for the insipid ideal, Caravaggio corrected none of the defects of the models he stopped in the streets to ask to pose for him. I have seen in Berlin some paintings of his which were refused by the persons who had commissioned them for being too ugly. The reign of ugliness was yet to come.

Stendhal, *Rome, Florence, Naples*, 1817

To a lady who, looking at an engraving of a house, called it an ugly thing, he [Constable] said, 'No, madam, there is nothing ugly; *I never saw an ugly thing in my life.*'

C. R. Leslie, *Memoirs of the Life of John Constable*, 1845 edn.

The ugly: it gets painted because people do not sufficiently see the beautiful.

J. A. D. Ingres

Real ugliness is just as rare as real beauty.

Asger Jorn, 1964

VARNISHING DAYS

These days at the Royal Academy, before the opening of the annual exhibition, were to be associated especially with Turner. The days were abandoned soon after his death, in 1851, and resumed only a decade or so later. The value of them in nineteenth-century artistic London is well testified to by several anecdotes, including that below.

Now on the 'varnishing days', when painting was going on in common, much of precept, much of practice, and much of common experience, were interchanged. The younger members gained much from the elder ones, and many useful hints and suggestions from one another. Who does not recollect the valuable remarks of David Wilkie, William Etty, C. R. Leslie, John Constable, and William Mulready, and, above all, of Turner? though from him, as has already been seen, it was conveyed in dark hints and ambiguous phrases. A little anecdote of what happened to one of the writers, on his first admission to the privilege of these meetings, which must be told with the singular pronoun will illustrate what has been said; at the same time it is quite characteristic of Turner, and of his keen perception of what a picture required to set right an apparent defect, and it is on both accounts well worth insertion here. 'The first varnishing days at the Royal Academy to which I was admitted on my election as associate, I was trying to *spoil* my picture of "The Castle Builder", when Henry Howard came up to me and said, in his most frigid manner, that the bosom of my figure was indelicately naked, and that some members thought I had better paint the dress higher. Here was a dilemma for a new associate. Of course, with due meekness, I was about to comply with his advice, although greatly against the grain, and with a sort of wonder at myself that I could possibly have been ignorantly guilty of sending an immodest contribution to the Exhibition. Meanwhile, Turner looked over my shoulder, and, in his usual sententious manner, mumbled out, "What – r – doing?" I told him the rebuke I had just received from the secretary. "Pooh, pooh," said he, "paint it lower." I thought he was intent upon leading me into a scrape. "You want white," he added, and turned on his heel. What could he mean? I pondered over his words, and after a while the truth struck me. The coloured dress came harshly on the flesh, and no linen intervened. I painted at once, over a portion of the bosom of the *dress*, a peep of the chemise. Howard came round soon after, and said, with a little more warmth, "Ah! You have covered it up – it is far better now – it will do." It was no higher however; there was just as much of the flesh seen, but the sense of nakedness and display was gone.'

RICHARD AND SAMUEL REDGRAVE, *A Century of British Painters*, 1866

The 'I' is Richard Redgrave, RA, the more distinguished of the two brothers.

VELAZQUEZ

Everything that our Velázquez did at that time [in his early years, painting *bodegones*] was in this vein, in order to distinguish himself from everyone else and follow a new trend. Knowing that Titian, Dürer, Raphael and others had the advantage over him, their fame being greater now that they were dead, he had recourse to the fertility of his invention, and took to painting with bravado rustic subjects, with strange lighting and colours. Some people remonstrated with him because he did not paint more serious subjects with delicacy and beauty, in emulation of Raphael of Urbino, and he politely replied: *That he preferred to be first in that kind of coarseness than second in delicacy.*

ANTONIO PALOMINO, *'Life' of Velázquez*, 1724

What a joy it would have been for you to see Velázquez, which for him alone is worth the trip. The painters of every school who surround him in the museum of Madrid, and who are all very well represented, seem completely like fakers. He is the painter of painters. He has astonished me, he has ravished me.

EDOUARD MANET, *Letter to Fantin-Latour*, 1865

The general principle which unites the colours of his later pictures was reached by Velasquez, neither through that feeling for decorative fitness which governed the work of his middle period nor entirely through the inborn Spanish love of dark hues that we see in Ribera. It comes from a broader and more imaginative outlook upon the values of colour as they are affected by juxtaposition, by atmospheric conditions, and, above all, by their inclination to the source of light. This view of the aspect of nature led him to study not only black and white but chromatic tone. The change of the plane on which a colour lies tends to make it not only lighter or darker, but to change its hue – to dose it with some proportions of blue, yellow or red. Velasquez recreates the aspect of a place and its conditions of lighting so convincingly that one feels able to imagine the value which any local tint would receive if introduced into any position in the picture. True, he seldom chooses a subject from nature which contains many bright local tints, but he always treats those he admits with a perfect mastery of the resources of colour. He is as subtle a colourist as real light itself, which veils even a monochromatic subject in a dress of coloured tissue. Indeed, the delicate colourist is never better proved than when he would paint the chromatic nuances of light upon a *motif* whose chief local tints are black or white.

R. A. M. STEVENSON, *Velasquez*, 1899

The scene of what follows is Velázquez' studio, where he has been painting a court lady, Dona Sol. After criticizing his picture of her, she walks round, looking at other pictures.

DONA SOL. Ah, that's the King. It's quite excellent. And that's the dear old Admiral. It's exactly like him. Oh, and that's Dona Elvira – *how* like, but *how* cruel! How could you do that? Didn't she mind dreadfully? And what a dear little girl! That's not finished, I suppose? Oh, and I do love that seapiece. It's a storm, I suppose?

VELASQUEZ. I'm afraid it's meant to be a man riding in a field. It's just a study.

DONA SOL. Of course it is. How stupid of me. I couldn't see properly. It's wonderful – quite wonderful. And what's that large picture on an easel over there with a curtain over it?

VELASQUEZ. Oh, that's nothing. It's only a sketch – it's not finished.

DONA SOL. Do let me see it.

VELASQUEZ. I'm afraid I can't, really.

DONA SOL. But I insist on seeing it. I've been such a good sitter. Now I'm going to pull the curtain off.

VELASQUEZ. It's not my picture at all. It's not by me. It's by one of my pupils. It's by Mazo.

DONA SOL. Then of course I can see it. (*She pulls away the curtain, revealing a picture of Venus looking into a glass.*) Oh, but that's my head! How dared you do such a thing? No wonder you didn't want me to see it. Oh, how could you do such a thing?

VELASQUEZ. But I assure you you're mistaken. In the first place, I never painted the picture. I never touched it. It's Mazo's work. And he did it out of his head. At least, he did it from a model. It's meant to be Eros and Psyche or Venus, I've forgotten which.

DONA SOL. How could you put my head on such a hideous body? I call it mean, odious, and cowardly, and quite unpardonable. I shall burn my picture.

VELASQUEZ. But, my dear lady, do listen to me for one moment. The picture's not my work. I flatter myself really that I can draw a little better than that. That's mere apprentice work. Just compare it with my pictures. I never use those hot reds and those dull lifeless greys. Just compare it with the other pictures.

DONA SOL (*crying*). How can I compare it with the others? You've never dared paint any one else like that.

VELASQUEZ. And then the face in the glass is no more your face than it is mine. It's not the least like you. It's a model's face. Mazo may have got a hint, a suggestion, quite unconsciously from seeing my picture, but nothing more. He's never set eyes on you.

DONA SOL. I don't believe it's by Mazo. I believe it's by you – or else you wouldn't have been so anxious for me not to see it.

MAURICE BARING, 'Velásquez and the Venus' in *Diminutive Dramas*, 1910

Velázquez eventually agrees the face shall be changed. After Dona Sol leaves, he calls Mazo out and says he must say he painted the picture (the 'Rokeby Venus') and sign it so that it becomes known to the world as a Mazo.

Obviously, he was a profoundly sophisticated man living in the society of the Court, and he was probably the only really sophisticated being existing around the Court at the time; that was the reason the King insisted on keeping him near him, because he was the only man that at least enlivened for a moment his day. But one feels in all his paintings the whole poignancy that Velasquez must have felt – even in those beautiful things where the figures have this wonderful structure and yet at the same time have the colouring of a Monet. You feel the shadow of life passing all the time.

FRANCIS BACON in *The Brutality of Fact: Interviews with Francis Bacon* by David Sylvester, 1987

WILLEM VAN DE VELDE ELDER AND YOUNGER

The two marine painters, father and son, left Holland and settled in England. Both died in London and were buried in St James's Church, Piccadilly, where a tablet to their memory was put up in 1929:

Near this Place
were Deposited the Remains of
WILLEM VAN DE VELDE THE ELDER
Born in 1610 Died in 1693
and of his Son
WILLEM VAN DE VELDE THE YOUNGER
Born in 1633 Died in 1707

After the year 1673
these two Eminent Dutch Marine Artists
Lived and Worked in this Country
as Painters of Seafights
to Their Majesties
KING CHARLES THE SECOND
AND KING JAMES THE SECOND

This tribute
Alike to their Artistic Merits
to their Faultless Craftsmanship
and to the Historical Value of their Works
through Money Publicly Subscribed
was Erected here by
The Society for Nautical Research
in the year 1929

VERMEER

The French nobleman, Balthasar de Monconys, was probably the first foreigner to mention meeting Vermeer, though he appeared none too enthusiastic about the sole picture of his he saw, in August 1663:

In Delft I saw the Painter Vermer [*sic*] who had none of his works: but we did see one at a Baker's, for which six hundred livres had been paid, although it contained only one figure, a picture I would have thought too highly priced at six pistoles.

BALTHASAR DE MONCONYS, *Journal de voyage*, 1666

... The circumstances of his death were as follows. An attack of uraemia, by no means serious, had led to his being ordered to rest. But one of the critics having written somewhere that in Vermeer's *Street in Delft* (lent by the Gallery at The Hague for an exhibition of Dutch painting), a picture which he adored and imagined that he knew by heart, a little patch of yellow wall (which he could not remember) was so well painted that it was, if one looked at it by itself, like some priceless specimen of Chinese art, of a beauty that was sufficient in itself, Bergotte ate a few potatoes, left the house, and went to the exhibition. At the first few steps that he had to climb he was overcome by giddiness. He passed in front of several pictures and was struck by the stiffness and futility of so artificial a school, nothing of which equalled the fresh air and sunshine of a Venetian palazzo, or of an ordinary house by the sea. At last he came to the Vermeer which he remembered as more striking, more different from anything else that he knew, but in which, thanks to the critic's article, he remarked for the first time some small figures in blue, that the ground was pink, and finally the precious substance of the tiny patch of yellow wall. His giddiness increased; he fixed his eyes, like a child upon a yellow butterfly which it is trying to catch, upon the precious little patch of wall. 'That is how I ought to have written,' he said. 'My last books are too dry, I ought to have gone over them with several coats of paint, made my language exquisite in itself, like this little patch of yellow wall.' Meanwhile he was not unconscious of the gravity of his condition. In a celestial balance there appeared to him, upon one of its scales, his own life, while the other contained the little patch of wall so beautifully painted in yellow. He felt that he had rashly surrendered the former for the latter. 'All the same,' he said to himself, 'I have no wish to provide the "feature" of this exhibition for the evening papers.'

He repeated to himself: 'Little patch of yellow wall, with a sloping roof, little patch of yellow wall.' While doing so he sank down upon a circular divan; and then at once he ceased to think that his life was in jeopardy and, reverting to his natural optimism, told himself: 'It is just an ordinary indigestion from those potatoes; they weren't properly cooked; it is nothing.' A fresh attack beat him down; he rolled from the divan to the floor, as visitors and attendants came hurrying to his assistance. He was dead. Permanently dead? Who shall say?

MARCEL PROUST, *Remembrance of Things Past,*
Volume 9, *The Captive*, 1923

HORACE VERNET

Horace Vernet is regarded by many as the greatest painter in France, and I would not absolutely contradict this popular opinion. He is in any case the most national of French painters, and he surpasses all by his productive ability, by his vigorously genial extravagance, by the ever-blooming self-rejuvenation of his creative force. Painting to him is innate, as spinning to the silk-worm, as singing to the bird, and his work seems like results of necessity. There is no style in him but nature, and withal a fecundity which borders on the ridiculous. There is a caricature which represents Horace Vernet riding a high horse at full gallop, brush in hand, by an immensely long canvas, and when he shall have got to the end, the picture will be finished. What an immense number of colossal battle-pieces has he painted of late for Versailles! If the pious legend be true that on the day of resurrection every man will be followed by his works to the place of judgment, then will Horace Vernet appear on that day in the valley of Jehosaphat, accompanied by some hundred thousands of infantry and cavalry. And however terrible the judges may be who will sit there to judge the quick and the dead, I do not believe that Horace Vernet will be condemned to fire eternal for the naughtiness of his Judah and Thamar.

I do not believe it; for, firstly, the picture is so admirably painted that were it but for that the culprit must needs be acquitted. Secondly, Horace Vernet is a genius, and things are permitted to geniuses which are forbidden to common sinners. And finally, unto him who comes marching at the head of some hundreds of thousands of soldiers much will be forgiven, even if he did not chance to be a genius.

HEINRICH HEINE, 'The Salon of 1843'

PAOLO VERONESE

. . . he deserved someone to write a large book in praise of him.

THE CARRACCI, *Postille to Vasari's 'Lives'*

Although these marginal notes to Vasari are traditionally credited to the two brothers Annibale and Agostino Carracci, it is likely that the writer was Agostino.

These instances [the 'Queen of Sheba before Solomon', the 'Ascent to Calvary'] are enough to explain the general character of the mind of Veronese, capable of tragic power to the utmost, if he chooses to exert it in that direction, but, by habitual preference, exquisitely graceful and playful; religious, without severity, and winningly noble; delighting in slight, sweet, every-day incident, but hiding deep meanings underneath it; rarely painting a gloomy subject, and never a base one.

JOHN RUSKIN, *Modern Painters*, Volume V, 1860

Colour expresses something by itself, one cannot do without this, one must use it; that which is beautiful, really beautiful – is also correct; when Veronese had painted the portraits of his beau-monde in the 'Marriage at Cana' [Louvre], he had spent on it all the richness of his palette in sombre violets, in splendid golden tones. Then – he thought still of a faint azure and a pearly-white – which does not appear in the foreground. He detonated it on in the background – and it was right, spontaneously it changes into the ambience of marble palaces and sky, which characteristically consummates the ordering of the figures.

VINCENT VAN GOGH, *Letter to his brother Theo*, 1885

In his later painting Veronese follows Titian and Tintoretto in a growing interest in effects of light, although he never allows chiaroscuro to subdue colour. His colours, without loss of richness or saturation, become less bright, more modulated, and more emotive. Landscape also begins to play a larger role in his painting, and in a series of mythological paintings he finds his own landscape ideal: a pastoral richness, as of an enchanted garden, which is as civilized and sophisticated as his figures. These scenes, which mostly concern the love of the gods, are set in a magic twilight, and perhaps it is the fleetingness of this magic light which gives them, in spite of their visual luxury, a tremor of mortality which is near to tragedy.

. . . Colour and paint do not lose their decorative value, but they become the instruments for a new depth of emotional expression, as, through light, Veronese's colour becomes more resonant and mysterious. The understanding of the decorative and emotional possibilities of colour which reaches its height in these later works was to be of profound importance to all future European colourists, and most particularly to Delacroix and Cézanne. It also provided an example which was to be the central factor in the final flowering of the Venetian School in the eighteenth century.

JOHN STEER, *A Concise History of Venetian Painting*, 1970

VISITING COLLECTIONS

Although a number of the finest private collections in nineteenth-century England were open to the public (within limits), visitors sometimes found themselves treated in a rather supercilious way by servants in the absence of the family. Fact and fiction record their experiences.

It was at Bowood that we were first initiated into the insolence of the English race of menservants. We had entered the portico, and my friend so far forgot himself, or rather so far remembered his German good manners, as to take off his hat, and address himself in a friendly tone to the servant. By this civility, he, however, forfeited all claim to respect in the fellow's eyes, who answered very saucily, and desired us to go round to the back door. Fortunately, I was better versed in English usages, and coming up with a lofty air, and my hat on my head, said in the appropriate drawl, 'Where's the housekeeper? I have a note from the Marchioness.' This altered his tone immediately, and we were properly admitted.*

As a further instance of the insufferable airs of this class in England, I add another anecdote. A nobleman of the highest rank, (an English Duke) on visiting the collection of the Duke of Sutherland, put a crown into the servant's hand: 'My Lord,' said the man, eyeing the piece with infinite contempt, 'from such noblemen as yourself, I am accustomed to receive gold.' The duke pocketed the crown again, adding, 'Tell your master, that you'll get neither gold nor silver from me.'

J. D. PASSAVANT, *Tour of a German Artist in England*, 1836

* To those acquainted with the excellent arrangement of Lord Lansdowne's household, nothing less than the assertion of a German would entitle this anecdote to belief. (Trans. Elizabeth Rigby)

The old housekeeper, with a gracious severity of deportment, waves her hand towards the great staircase. Mr Guppy and his friend follow Rosa, Mrs Rouncewell and her grandson follow them, a young gardener goes before to open the shutters.

As is usually the case with people who go over houses, Mr Guppy and his friend are dead beat before they have well begun. They straggle about in wrong places, look at wrong things, don't care for the right things, gape when more rooms are opened, exhibit profound depression of spirits, and are clearly knocked up. In each successive chamber that they enter, Mrs Rouncewell, who is as upright as the house itself, rests apart in a window-seat, or other such nook, and listens with stately approval to Rosa's exposition. Her grandson is so attentive to it, that Rosa is shyer than ever – and prettier. Thus they pass on from room to room, raising the pictured Dedlocks for a few brief minutes as the young gardener admits the light, and reconsigning them to their graves as he shuts it out again. It appears to the afflicted Mr Guppy and his inconsolable friend, that there is no end to the Dedlocks, whose family greatness seems to consist in their never having done anything to distinguish themselves, for seven hundred years.

Even the long drawing-room of Chesney Wold cannot revive Mr Guppy's spirits. He is so low that he droops on the threshold, and has hardly strength of mind to enter. But a portrait over the chimney-piece, painted by the fashionable artist of the day, acts upon him like a charm. He recovers in a moment. He stares at it with uncommon interest; he seems to be fixed and fascinated by it.

'Dear me!' says Mr Guppy. 'Who's that?'

'The picture over the fire-place,' says Rosa, 'is the portrait of the present Lady Dedlock. It is considered a perfect likeness, and the best work of the master.'

'Blest!' says Mr Guppy, staring in a kind of dismay at his friend, 'if I can ever have seen her. Yet I know her! Has the picture been engraved, miss?'

'The picture has never been engraved. Sir Leicester has always refused permission.'

'Well!' says Mr Guppy in a low voice, 'I'll be shot if it ain't very curious how well I know that picture! So that's Lady Dedlock, is it!'

'The picture on the right is the present Sir Leicester Dedlock. The picture on the left is his father, the late Sir Leicester.'

Mr Guppy has no eyes for either of these magnates. 'It's unaccountable to me,' he says, still staring at the portrait, 'how well I know that picture! I'm dashed!' adds Mr Guppy, looking round, 'if I don't think I must have had a dream of that picture, you know!'

As no one present takes any especial interest in Mr Guppy's dreams, the probability is not pursued. But he still remains so absorbed by the portrait, that he stands immovable before it until the young gardener has closed the shutters; when he comes out of the room in a dazed state, that is an odd though a sufficient substitute for interest, and follows into the succeeding rooms with a confused stare, as if he were looking everywhere for Lady Dedlock.

Charles Dickens, *Bleak House*, ch. 7, 1853

WAR

A German manifesto recently reprinted in the Italian newspapers congratulated German artists on having finally been wrested by the war from the grip of the new artistic ideas of France, cubism, orphism, etc. We do not give a hoot about formulas and words ending in 'ism', but artistic ideas interest us to the highest degree. Derain is in a motorcycle unit in the North, George Braque was recently in Le Havre as a second lieutenant, Fernand Léger is at the front with the supply corps, Albert Gleizes has been at the front since the outbreak of war, and Dufy is in Le Havre, waiting; he has published a pretty postcard, *The Allies*, which will take its place among the marvellous illustrations that have spontaneously bloomed in this war. R. de la Fresnaye is doubtless still in Lisieux. Groult suffered an arm wound. The sculptor Duchamp-Villon is a medical aide in Saint-Germain; the painter and engraver Laboureur is at the Château of Nantes, serving as an interpreter for the British army.

GUILLAUME APOLLINAIRE in *Le Petit Messager des Arts . . .*, 1 March 1915

Apollinaire himself served during the First World War, first in the artillery and then in the infantry, and was wounded in 1916.

I remember that summer [August 1917] a strange thing happened. One day I found, and started painting, the remains of a Britisher and a Boche – just skulls, bones, garments – up by the trenches at Thiepval. I was all alone. My faithful Howlett was about half a mile away with the car. When I had been working about a couple of hours I felt strange. I cannot say even now what I felt. Afraid? Of what? The sun shone fiercely. There was not a breath of air. Perhaps it was that – a touch of the sun. So I stopped painting and went and sat on the trunk of a blown-up tree close by, when suddenly I was thrown on the back of my head on the ground. My heavy easel was upset, and one of the skulls went through the canvas. I got up and thought a lot, but came to the conclusion I had better just go on working, which I did, and nothing further strange happened. That night I happened to meet Joffroy, and told him about these skulls, and how peculiar one was, as it had a division in the frontal bone (the Britisher's). He said he would like to go and make a study of it; so I brought him out the next morning to the place, I myself working that day in Thiepval Wood, about half a mile further up the hill. I left him, saying I would come back and bring him lunch from the car, as it was difficult for him to get about. When I did get back I found him lying down, not very near the place, saying he felt very ill and he thought it was the smell 'from those remains'. He had done no work, and refused even to try to eat until we got a long way from the skulls. I explained to him that there was no smell, and he said, 'But didn't you see one has an eye still?' But I knew that all four eyes had withered away months before. There must have been something strange about the place.

SIR WILLIAM ORPEN, *An Onlooker in France 1917–1919*, 1921

WASHINGTON'S TEETH

George Washington's false teeth gave him and painters of his portrait considerable trouble. Gilbert Stuart blamed a set of such teeth for the constrained effect of the mouth in one version of his familiar image of Washington.

The grandson of Washington's dentist, John Greenwood, received this letter on the subject from another painter of his portrait.

Philadelphia,
March 27, 1859

Dear Sir,
In answer to yours of the 22nd, Washington sat to me in the autumn of 1795, and at the same time sat to Stuart, having then in his mouth the teeth made by your grandfather in 1790. Not satisfied with this portrait, Stuart painted another in the spring of 1796, when the General had in his mouth an ivory set made by James Gardette which caused his mouth to be changed. Dr Harris of Baltimore showed me one half of your grandfather's set, small and beautifully made, telling me that the other half was in your father's possession and I have been told that the rejected set made by Gardette is in the possession of a gentleman in Savannah.

Respectfully yours
REMBRANDT PEALE

from W. T. WHITLEY, *Gilbert Stuart*, 1932

WATTEAU

Among those few people who had known Watteau well several were impelled after his premature death in 1721 to put down in writing their personal recollections of him, providing a remarkably detailed and broadly consistent sketch of his 'difficult' personality.

Perhaps the most sympathetic recollections were those of the dealer Gersaint, for whose shop Watteau painted the 'Enseigne' (now in Berlin), as Gersaint explained:

On his return to Paris, which occurred in 1721, at the time of my first becoming established, he came to see me to ask if I would lodge him and allow him, *so as to take the numbness out of his fingers* (thus he put it), if I would, as I say, allow him to paint a *plafond* that I should hang up outside. I felt some reluctance to agreeing, much preferring to give him a more important task, but seeing how greatly it would please him, I consented. Everyone knows the success this picture had. It was based entirely on nature: the poses were so true and so graceful, the arrangements so natural, the groupings so well composed that it attracted the gaze of passers-by; and even the most accomplished painters came several times to admire it. It took him eight days, even though he worked on it only in the mornings, his delicate state of health, or – to put it better – his weakness not permitting him to work any longer. It is the sole piece of his which slightly whetted his *amour-propre*; he had no difficulty in confessing as much to me. M. de Jullienne has the picture at present in his collection, and he was responsible for having it engraved.

E.-F. GERSAINT, *Abrégé de la vie d'Antoine Watteau*, 1744

Eight days after that soirée we were invited to dine at the Academy.

This extremely strange dinner became interesting only towards the end . . .

'I can't understand,' someone had said, 'anybody admiring Watteau or even pronouncing his name here.'

'What,' cried M. Ingres. 'Are you aware, sir, that Watteau is a very great painter? Are you acquainted with his work? It is vast . . . I have all of Watteau's work at home, sir, and I study it . . . Watteau! Watteau!'

Our situation can be envisaged, especially on account of the unfortunate person who had uttered that opinion. Happily, he was a friend of M. Ingres, and could quite adroitly get out of the affair; but M. Ingres would not listen to him and continued to say between his teeth: 'Very great master, sir, very great master! . . . whom I admire!'

AMAURY DUVAL, *L'Atelier d'Ingres*, 1878

For his 'imaginary portrait' of Watteau, Pater devised a journal kept at Valenciennes by the sister of Watteau's pupil, J. B. Pater – an idea partly prompted perhaps by the family tradition that the Paters in England were descended from the painter Pater.

June 1717

And at last one has actual sight of his work – what it is. He has brought with him certain long-cherished designs to finish here in quiet, as he protests he has never finished before. That charming *Noblesse* – can it be really so distinguished to the minutest point, so naturally aristocratic? Half in masquerade, playing the drawing-room or garden comedy of life, these persons have upon them, not less than the landscape he composes, and among the accidents of which they group themselves with such a perfect fittingness, a certain light we should seek for in vain upon anything real. For their framework they have around them a veritable architecture – a tree-architecture – of which those moss-grown balusters, *termes*, statues, fountains, are really but accessories. Only, as I gaze upon those windless afternoons, I find myself always saying to myself involuntarily, 'The evening will be a wet one.' The storm is always brooding through the massy splendour of the trees, above those sun-dried glades or lawns, where delicate children may be trusted thinly clad: and the secular trees themselves will hardly outlast another generation.

August 1717

. . . For in truth Antony Watteau is still the mason's boy, and deals with that world of ['patched and powdered ladies and fine cavaliers'] under a fascination, of the nature of which he is half-unconscious methinks, puzzled at 'the queer trick he possesses', to use his own phrase. You see him growing ever more and more meagre, as he goes through the world and its applause. Yet he reaches with wonderful sagacity the secret of an adjustment of colours, a *coiffure*, a toilette, setting I know not what air of real superiority on such things. He will never overcome his early training; and these light things will possess for him always a kind of worth, as characterizing that impossible or forbidden world which the mason's boy saw through the closed gateways of the enchanted garden.

WALTER PATER, 'A Prince of Court Painters' in *Imaginary Portraits*, 1887

WHISTLER

Much happened in the 'eighties of which I was not conscious till some years later. It was in 1888 that Whistler delivered his epoch-making 'Ten O'Clock' lecture, but of this I knew nothing till in 1896 I read *The Gentle Art of Making Enemies*. My father, who knew Ruskin, did not agree with everything he wrote, but he shared his enthusiasm for Turner and regarded Whistler as a charlatan.

Eavesdropping one evening in the 'eighties, when I should have been in bed and asleep, I overheard my parents and some friends discussing a visit they had paid to Mr Leyland to see his pictures. They talked at length about Rossetti and Burne-Jones, but not a word was said of Whistler, whose Peacock Room with *La Princesse du Pays de la Porcelaine* was then at Leyland's house in Prince's Gate. Whistler was regarded then as 'not quite nice', and mention of his name was avoided in polite circles.

FRANK RUTTER, *Art in My Time*, 1933

WINTERHALTER

Contemporaries commented on the contrast between Winterhalter's tremendously grand sitters and the painter's plain and modest and almost naïve nature.

I made Winterhalter's personal acquaintance in Paris in 1863. Never did a royal portrait painter correspond less to the conception one has of such a favourite of rulers. He had remained completely simple, natural and without mannerisms, and even retained something of the Southern German rural population about him. His life-style, his needs were extremely modest. His correspondingly simple studio contained only one ornament, but naturally the most exquisite and costly: a wonderful large portrait of a woman (lifesize half portrait) by P. P. Rubens that probably represents his first wife with a fur wrapper over her shoulders.

W. LANDGRAF in *Daheim*, 1908

Winterhalter's portrait by Rubens does represent Isabella Brant and is now in the Gemäldegalerie, Berlin-Dahlem.

CHRISTOPHER WOOD

Wood, who was to be killed at Salisbury station in 1930, at the age of twenty-nine, wrote this letter to his mother from Crete in 1922:

Dearest Mother, do you know that all the great modern painters who we may not quite understand through their pictures, are not trying to see things and paint them through the eyes and experience of a man of forty or fifty or whatever they may be, but rather through the eyes of the smallest child who sees nothing but those things which would strike him as being the most important. To the childish drawing they add the beauty and refinement of their own experience. This is the explanation of modern painting.

CHRISTOPHER WOOD, *Letter of July 1922*

WORK

He [Johann Liss] was in the habit of thinking a long time before he started on his work but once a problem was resolved nothing could make him sway. When we lived together in Venice he would stay away from the house for two or three days and then come back into the room by night, quickly prepare his palette, mixing the colours the way he wanted them and spend the whole night working. In the daytime he would rest a little and then continue with his work for another two or three days and nights. He hardly rested and hardly ate. No matter how many times I told him that he would ruin his health that way and shorten his life, it was no good. He continued that way, staying out several days and nights – where I do not know – until his purse was empty. Then he continued making the night into day and the day into night.

I then went to Rome. He had promised to follow me as soon as the work he had begun was completed. But luck was against him. He died along with many others during the plague which began in 1629.

JOACHIM VON SANDRART, *Teutsche Academie*, 1675

Liss was born around 1597 in the area of Oldenburg, north of Lübeck, and died in Venice around 1630. He has been rediscovered, as a painter of great originality, only in the twentieth century. Sandrart's vivid 'picture' of his working method is valuable; it is also an unconscious tribute by artistic mediocrity to artistic genius.

X-RAYS

The X-ray gives to gentlemen who in front of pictures see nothing the possibility of passing judgment on pictures.

MAX J. FRIEDLÄNDER, *Reminiscences and Reflections*, 1969

YOUTHFUL ABILITY

The childhood of the great artist is traditionally a subject for wonderful tales, and Vasari's 'Lives' are a treasure-house of such. Not all are to be dismissed as mere fantasy; what Vasari tells of, for example, Andrea del Sarto's early years has a ring of conviction.

. . . and when he [Andrea] reached the age of seven he was taken away from his reading and writing school and apprenticed to the goldsmith's craft; and in this he was always far more willing to practise designing (to which he was drawn by natural inclination) than to handle the tools for working in silver or gold. So then it came about that a Florentine painter, Gian Barile, albeit gross and common, having seen the boy's good method of drawing took him in, and having made him give up goldsmith's work, introduced him to the art of painting; and having embarked on it with great enjoyment, Andrea realized that Nature had made him for that profession. And very soon he began to work in colour so well that Gian Barile and all the other craftsmen of the city were filled with wonder.

After three years the boy had achieved a very good standard of proficiency through continuous study and work, and Gian Barile realized that if he persisted in his studies he would attain extraordinary success; so having discussed the matter with Piero di Cosimo, who was then held to be among the best painters in Florence, he placed Andrea with him; and as Andrea was desirous of learning, he never ceased studying and applying himself to his work. And Nature, having created him a painter, wrought in him so effectively that, when he handled colours, it was as if he had been doing so for fifty years; whereupon Piero came to love him very deeply, and he was incredibly pleased to hear that whenever he had any time to spare, especially on feast days, he would spend all day long with other young men drawing in the Hall of the Pope [in the Palazzo Vecchio], which housed the cartoon of Michelangelo and that of Leonardo da Vinci, and that, though still a lad, he surpassed all the other draughtsmen both native and foreign, who competed there endlessly.

GIORGIO VASARI, *'Life' of Andrea del Sarto*, 1568

Among the most precocious of later painters was Landseer (whom Fuseli used to call 'my little dog boy' when he studied at the Royal Academy schools, beginning at the age of thirteen). Landseer's father, John, an engraver, described to a friend his son's early ability as manifested in the fields along the Finchley Road.

These two fields were Edwin's first studio. Many a time have I lifted him over this very style [*sic*]. I then lived in Foley Street, and nearly all the way between Marylebone and Hampstead was open fields. It was a favourite walk with my boys; and one day when I had accompanied them, Edwin stopped by this style to admire some sheep and cows which were quietly grazing. At his request I lifted him over, and finding a scrap of paper and a pencil in my pocket, I made him sketch a cow. He was very young indeed then – not more than six or seven years old. After this we came on several occasions, and as he grew older this was one of his favourite spots for sketching.

FREDERICK G. STEPHENS, *Memoirs of Sir Edwin Landseer*, 1874

ZULOAGA

Outside Spain and France Ignacio Zuloaga (1870–1945) has remained little known and arguably under-estimated. Yet Degas appreciated his work and paid him a significant compliment (having once remarked that the air seen in old master pictures is not the air we breathe).

At least you do not put air into your canvases.

EDGAR DEGAS

In Spain Zuloaga retains the Spanish dignity. His women stand gravely before us. *Elles ont de la tenue.* The presentation they make of their bodies is so direct, so correct and so reticent that the soul is given a chance of looking forth at us. Mystery and romance are allowed to spring again from wells of freshness.

WALTER SICKERT in *The New Age*, 6 June 1910

ZURBARÁN

Zurbarán undoubtedly stands in the front rank of Spanish painters. He painted heads with admirable skill, but he had not that wonderful power which belonged to Velázquez, of producing an exact fac-simile of a group of figures at various distances; none of his large compositions equal the Meninas in airy ease and truth of effect; nor have his figures the rounded and undefined, yet truly life-like, outlines which charm in the works of Murillo. But in colouring he is not inferior to these great masters; and his tints, although always sober and subdued, have sometimes much of the brilliancy and depth of Rembrandt's style . . . He is the peculiar painter of monks, as Rafael is of Madonnas, and Ribera of martyrdoms; he studied the Spanish friar, and painted him with as high a relish as Titian painted the Venetian noble, and Vandyck the gentlemen of England. His Virgins are rare, and in general not very pleasing; but he frequently painted female saints, apparently preserving in their persons the portraits of beauties of the day, for the rouge of good society may often be detected on their cheeks.

SIR WILLIAM STIRLING-MAXWELL, *Annals of the Artists of Spain*, revised edn., 1891

SOURCES AND ACKNOWLEDGEMENTS

The author and publisher gratefully acknowledge permission to print relevant extracts

page

3 R. and M. Wittkower, *The Divine Michelangelo: The Florentine Academy's Homage on His Death in 1564* (London: Phaidon, 1964). Reprinted by permission of Phaidon Press Ltd.

3 *The Diary of Joseph Farington*, Vol. I, ed. K. Garlick & A. Macintyre (New Haven, Conn./London: Yale University Press, 1978).

3 Saki, 'Reginald on the Academy', *Reginald* (1904): *The Complete Works of Saki* (London: The Bodley Head, 1980).

4 *Literary Remains of Albrecht Dürer*, trans. and ed. W. M. Conway (Cambridge: Cambridge University Press, 1889).

4 Antonio de Beatis, *The Travel Journal . . .*, trans. J. R. Hale and J. M. A. Lindon, and ed. J. R. Hale (London: Hakluyt Society, 1979), 10 October 1517.

4 For Van Dyck's drawing and translation of his note, C. Brown, *Van Dyck* (Oxford: Phaidon, 1982).

5 Eugène Delacroix, *Selected Letters*, ed. and trans. J. Stewart (London: Eyre & Spottiswoode, 1971). Reprinted by permission of Eyre & Spottiswoode.

5 Rosamond Bernier, 'Altdorfer vu par Picasso', *L'Oeil*, 1955, trans. P. S. Falla in *A Picasso Anthology*, ed. M. McCully (Arts Council of Great Britain in association with Thames & Hudson, 1981). Reprinted by permission of Thames & Hudson.

5 *The Letters of Thomas Gainsborough*, ed. M. Woodall (London: The Cupid Press, 1963).

6 A. Vollard, *Souvenirs d'un marchand de tableaux* (Paris: Albin Michel, 1937).

6 L. L. Noble, *The Life and Works of Thomas Cole*, ed. E. S. Vessell (Cambridge, Mass.: Harvard University Press, 1964), cited in M. Baigell, *Thomas Cole* (New York: Watson-Guptill Publications, 1985).

6 William Shakespeare, *Richard II*, Act I, scene 2.

6 Dr Robert Plot, *The Natural History of Staffordshire* (1686).

7 *The Letters of Robert Browning and Elizabeth Barrett Browning* (London: John Murray, 1934), Vol. 1.

7 Lord Lindsay, *Sketches of the History of Christian Art*, 2nd edn (London, 1885), Vol. 2.

7 John Ruskin, *The Stones of Venice* (London, 1851), Vol. 1.

8 Andrew Marvell, 'The Gallery', *Miscellaneous Poems* (1681).

8 Anthony Trollope, 1861; cited in D. Robertson, *Sir Charles Eastlake and the Victorian Art World* (Princeton, NJ & Guildford, U.K.: Princeton University Press, 1978).

8 M. E. Chevreul, *The Laws of Contrast of Colour*, trans. J. Spanton (London, 1868).

9 J. Beavington Atkinson, *An Art Tour to Northern Capitals of Europe* (London, 1873).

9 *Beloved Mama: Private Correspondence of Queen Victoria and the German Crown Princess, 1878–1885*, ed. R. Fulford (London: Evans, 1981). We acknowledge the gracious permission of Her Majesty The Queen for the reproduction of material subject to copyright.

9 Prefatory notice to illustrated catalogue of the Municipal Gallery of Modern Art (Dublin, 1908).

10 Arnold Bennett, Florence, 1910, *Journals*, ed. Frank Swinnerton (Harmondsworth: Penguin, 1971).

10 W. B. Yeats, 'The Municipal Gallery

Revisited', *Last Poems* (London: Macmillan, 1940).
11 Francis Bacon, interview by Geordie Greig, *Sunday Times*, 25 September 1988. © Times Newspapers Ltd, 1988.
11 Walter Sickert in the *New Age*, 1910; in *A Free House!; or, The Artist as Craftsman: Being the Writings of Walter Richard Sickert*, ed. (Sir) Osbert Sitwell (London: Macmillan, 1947).
11 Felix Mendelssohn-Bartholdy, *Letters from Italy and Switzerland*, trans. Lady Wallace (London, 1864).
12 William Blake, annotation to Reynolds' *Discourses*, Appendix I of Sir Joshua Reynolds, *Discourses on Art*, ed. R. R. Wark (New Haven & London: Yale University Press, 1981 edn).
12 Henri Lapauze, *Ingres, sa vie et son œuvre* (Paris, 1911).
12 J. M. Whistler, notes for possible memoirs, Whistler exhibition catalogue, ed. D. Sutton, Japan, 1987–8.
12 Degas to Whistler, in D. Halévy, *Degas Parle* (Paris & Geneva: La Palatine, 1960).
12 J. W. von Goethe, 'Early Paintings and Recent Restorations in Venice' (1790), in *Goethe on Art*, ed. and trans. J. Gage (London: Scolar Press, 1980). Reprinted by permission of Scolar Press.
13 *Letters of George Meredith*, collected and edited by his son (London: Constable, 1912), Vol. 1.
13 *The Notebooks of Samuel Butler*, ed. H. Festing Jones (London: Hogarth Press, 1985).
13 Roger Fry, *Giovanni Bellini* (London: At the Sign of the Unicorn, 1899).
14 Life of Piero della Francesca, in Giorgio Vasari, *Lives of the Artists*, Vol. I, trans. G. Bull (Harmondsworth: Penguin, 1987). Reproduced by permission of Penguin Books Ltd.
14 From Alice Michel, '*Degas et Son Modèle*' (*Mercure de France*, February 1919), translated and quoted in R. Kendall, *Degas by himself* (London: Macdonald & Co. Ltd., 1987).
14 *Cassatt and Her Circle: Selected Letters*, ed. N. Mowll Mathews (New York: Abbeville Press, 1984).
14 Eugène Delacroix, *Selected Letters*, ed. and trans. J. Stewart (London: Eyre & Spottiswoode, 1971). Reprinted by permission of Eyre & Spottiswoode.
15 Cited in C. Bo & G. Mandel, *L'opera completa del Botticelli* (Milan: Rizzoli, 1967).
15 W. P. Frith, *My Autobiography and Reminiscences* (London, 1887), Vol 2; letter of 1875.
15 *Burne-Jones Talking*, ed. M. Lago (London: John Murray, 1982).
16 Preface to the *Catalogue de l'Exposition Braque* (1908), in *Apollinaire on Art: Essays and Reviews, 1902–1918*, ed. LeRoy C. Breunig, trans. S. Suleiman (New York: Viking Press, 1972; Da Capo Press paperback, 1988).
16 Ronald Firbank, *The Artificial Princess* (1934), ch. I.
17 Aldous Huxley, 'Breughel', in *Along the Road* (1925; reissued London: Chatto & Windus, 1974). Reprinted by permission of Mrs Laura Huxley and Chatto & Windus.
18 Henry James, *Italian Hours* (1909; reissued New York: Grove Press Inc., 1959).
18 R. M. Rilke, *Letters on Cézanne*, ed. C. M. Rilke, trans. J. Agee (London: Cape, 1988). Reprinted by permission of the Hogarth Press.
19 W. R. Sickert, 'Mesopotamian–Cézanne', in the *New Age*, 5 March 1914; reprinted in *A Free House!; or, The Artist as Craftsman: Being the Writings of Walter Richard Sickert*, ed. (Sir) Osbert Sitwell (London: Macmillan, 1947).
19 Interview by Tom Lubbock in *The Independent*, 12 July 1988. Reprinted by permission of The *Independent*.
19 Ronald Firbank, *Vainglory* (1915), ch. 2.
19 H. Brigstocke, *William Buchanan and the Nineteenth-Century Art Trade* (London: privately printed for the Paul Mellon Centre for Studies in British Art, 1982).
20 *John Constable's Correspondence*,

ed. R. B. Beckett (Ipswich: Suffolk Records Society), Vol. 2 (1964).
20 *Eckermann's Conversations with Goethe*, trans. R. O. Moon (London: Morgan, Laird, n.d.), 14 April 1829.
20 Roger Fry in the *Burlington Magazine*, 1907, reprinted in his *Vision and Design*, 1920 (Harmondsworth: Penguin Books, 1961 edn).
21 *The Anonimo*, trans. P. Musi and ed. G. C. Williamson (London: G. Bell, 1903).
21 Federico Borromeo, *Commentarius* (1627), quoted and translated in A. Quint, *Federico Borromeo as Patron and Critic of the Arts* (New York/London: Garland Publishing, 1986).
22 Louis-Henri de Loménie, Comte de Brienne, *Mémoires*, quoted in the original in F. Haskell, *Patrons and Painters* (New Haven/London: Yale University Press, 1980 edn).
22 S. N. Behrman, *Duveen* (London: Hamish Hamilton, 1952). Reprinted by permission of Hamish Hamilton Ltd.
23 Peggy Guggenheim, *Out of This Century* (London: André Deutsch, 1980). Reprinted by permission of André Deutsch Ltd.
24 *Goethe's Theory of Colours*, trans. C. L. Eastlake (London, 1840).
24 Eugène Delacroix, *Journal*, 2 January 1853, *Journal de Delacroix*, ed. A. Joubin (Geneva: La Palatine, 1943).
24 John Ruskin, *Modern Painters*, Vol. IV (London, 1856).
25 Max Beckmann, July 1938, cited in *Artists on Art*, ed. R. Goldwater and M. Treves (London: Kegan Paul, 1947).
25 John Dryden, 'To Sir Godfrey Kneller', in *Annual Miscellany* (1694).
25 Cited in D. Goldring, *Regency Portrait Painter, the life of Sir Thomas Lawrence, P.R.A.* (London: Macdonald, 1951).
26 M. E. J. Delécluze, *Louis David, son école et son temps* (Paris, 1855).
26 Charles Baudelaire, 'The Salon of 1846', in *Art in Paris, 1845–1862: Salons and Other Exhibitions Reviewed by Charles Baudelaire*, ed. and trans. J. Mayne (London: Phaidon, 1965). Reprinted by permission of Phaidon Press Ltd.
26 In W. Stechow, *Northern Renaissance Art, 1400–1600*, Sources and Documents in the History of Art (Englewood Cliffs, NJ: Prentice-Hall, 1966).
27 In ibid.
28 In M. Baxandall, *Painting and Experience in Fifteenth-Century Italy* (Oxford: Oxford University Press, 1986).
28 Quoted in the original in T. Besterman, *Voltaire on the Arts: unity and paradox* (Zaharoff Lecture, Oxford: Clarendon Press, 1974).
29 (Mrs Delaney): *Autobiography and Correspondence*, ed. Lady Llanover (London, 1861), Vol. III.
29 William Blake, annotation to Reynolds' *Discourses*: Appendix I of Sir Joshua Reynolds, *Discourses on Art*, ed. R. R. Wark (New Haven, Conn./London: Yale University Press, 1981 edn).
29 Henry James, *Italian Hours* (1909; reissued New York: Grove Press Inc., 1959).
30 Oscar Wilde, *An Ideal Husband* (1895), Act 1.
30 Lily McCormack, *I Hear You Calling Me: The Life of Count John McCormack* (London: W. H. Allen, n.d.).
30 Letter to Ludovico Carracci, 1580, first published in C. C. Malvasia, *Felsina Pittrice* (Bologna, 1678).
31 Letter of 1880 from Rome, quoted in V. Volkoff, *Tchaikovsky: A Self-Portrait* (London: Robert Hale, 1975).
31 Bernard Shaw, *The Doctor's Dilemma* (1908), Act 4.
31 Paul Cézanne, letter to Emile Bernard, 25 July 1904, *Paul Cézanne, Letters*, ed. J. Rewald, trans. M. Kay (London: Bruno Cassirer, 1941).
31 *Futurist Manifesto*, 1910, H. B. Chipp *et al.*, *Theories of Modern Art* (Berkeley/Los Angeles/London: University of California Press, 1968).
31 *Anecdotes of William Hogarth*, ed. J. B. Nichols (London, 1833).

32 Cited in R. Ormond, *Sir Edwin Landseer*, exhibition catalogue (Thames & Hudson, in association with the Philadelphia Museum of Art and the Tate Gallery, London, 1981).

32 J. Golding, *Cubism: A History and an Analysis 1907–14* (London: Faber and Faber, rev. edn, 1988).

33 Salvador Dali, preface to *Dali's Mustache* (New York: Simon & Schuster, 1954).

33 René Gimpel, *Diary of an Art Dealer*, trans. J. Rosenberg (London: Hamish Hamilton, 1986), October 1920. Reprinted by permission of Aitken & Stone Ltd, representing the estate of René Gimpel.

34 Heinz Berggruen, interview with Elspeth Moncrieff, *The Antique Collector*, September 1988. Reprinted by permission of *The Antique Collector.*

34 Life of Raphael, in Giorgio Vasari, *Lives of the Artists*, trans. G. Bull (Harmondsworth: Penguin, 1987), Vol. 1. Reprinted by permission of Penguin Books Ltd.

34 G. Baglione, *Le Vite de' pittori . . .* (1642), cited in M. Kitson, *The Complete Paintings of Caravaggio* (Harmondsworth: Penguin, 1985). Reprinted by permission of Penguin Books Ltd.

35 *The Letters of Peter Paul Rubens*, ed. and trans. R. S. Magurn (Cambridge, Mass.: Harvard University Press, 1955).

35 *Gazette d'Utrecht*, 4 August 1721 (letter of 28 July, from Paris), cited by F. Moureau in *Antoine Watteau (1684–1721) The Painter, His Age and His Legend*, ed. F. Moureau & M. Morgan Grasselli (Paris/Geneva: Champion-Slatkine, 1987).

35 *The Letters of Thomas Gainsborough*, ed. M. Woodall (London: Cupid Press, 1963).

36 Sir Joshua Reynolds, Discourse XIV, delivered to the students of the Royal Academy, 10 December 1788, in Sir Joshua Reynolds, *Discourses on Art*, ed. R. R. Wark (New Haven, Conn./London: Yale University Press, 1981).

36 Berthe Morisot, in *Growing Up with the Impressionists: The Diary of Julie Manet*, trans., ed. and with an introduction by Rosalind de Boland Roberts and Jane Roberts (London: Sotheby's, 1987). First published for Sotheby's Publications by Philip Wilson Publishers Ltd.

36 In *The Letters of Paul Gauguin to Georges Daniel de Monfreid*, trans. R. Pielkovo (London: Heinemann, 1923).

37 Henry Fuseli, 'Lecture on Colour', in *The Life and Writings of Henry Fuseli . . .*, written and ed. J. Knowles (London, 1831), Vol. 2.

38 Eugène Delacroix, *Journal*, 20 December 1857, *Journal de Delacroix (édition abrégée)*, ed. A. Joubin (Geneva: La Palatine, 1943).

38 William Hazlitt, in *Morning Chronicle*, 22 October 1824, reprinted in *Collected Works of William Hazlitt*, Vol. 9 (London: Dent, 1903).

39 W. M. Thackeray, 'On the French School of Painting', reprinted in his *The Paris Sketch-Book* (London, 1840).

39 Théophile Gautier in *La Presse*, 10 March 1837, trans. in R. Snell, *Théophile Gautier: A Romantic Critic of the Visual Arts* (Oxford: Oxford University Press, 1982). Reprinted by permission of Oxford University Press.

39 W. M. Thackeray, 'On the French School of Painting', reprinted in his *The Paris Sketch-Book* (1840).

39 Charles Baudelaire, letter about Delacroix to the editor of *Opinion nationale*, September–November 1863, in *The Painter of Modern Life and Other Essays by Charles Baudelaire*, trans. J. Mayne (London: Phaidon, 1964). Reproduced by permission of Phaidon Press Ltd.

40 Alfonso d'Este, in J. A. Crowe and G. B. Cavalcaselle, *The Life and Times of Titian* (London, 1881), Vol. 1.

40 Life of Leonardo da Vinci, in Giorgio Vasari, *Lives of the Artists*, trans. G. Bull (Harmondsworth: Penguin, 1987), Vol. 1. Reproduced by permission of Penguin Books Ltd.

40 Lord Nugent, in G. Somes Layard, *Sir Thomas Lawrence's Letter-Bag* (London: G. Allen, 1906).
41 C. Merrill Mount, *John Singer Sargent* (London: Cresset Press, 1957).
41 John Ruskin, *Modern Painters*, Vol. V (London, 1860).
43 Sir John Hawkins, *Life and Works of Dr Johnson* (London, 1787).
43 Henry James, *Italian Hours* (1909; reissued New York: Grove Press Inc., 1959).
44 Life of Giotto, in Giorgio Vasari, *Lives of the Artists*, trans. G. Bull (Harmondsworth: Penguin, 1987), Vol. 1. Reproduced by permission of Penguin Books Ltd.
44 Federico Zuccaro, *L'Idea de' pittori, scultori e architetti* (1607), trans. in A. Blunt, *Artistic Theory in Italy, 1450–1600* (Oxford: Oxford University Press, 1985 edn.). Reproduced by permission of Oxford University Press.
45 Maurice Denis, *Théories: La doctrine d'Ingres* (1912), trans. and quoted in E. Gilmore Holt, *From the Classicists to the Impressionists: A Documentary History of Art*, Vol. 3 (Garden City, NY: Doubleday, 1966).
45 G. Coquiot, *Degas* (1924), quoted in F. Sevin, 'Degas à travers ses mots', *Gazette des Beaux-Arts*, July–August 1975.
45 Paul Klee, *On Modern Art*, trans. P. Findlay (London: Faber & Faber, 1948). Reprinted by permission of Berteli Publishers, Berne, 1945.
45 Reproduced in C. White, *Dürer: The Artist and His Drawings* (London: Phaidon, 1971). Reprinted by permission of Phaidon Press Ltd.
45 Alexander Pope, in J. Spence, *Observations, Anecdotes, and Characters* (London, 1820).
46 B. R. Haydon, *Autobiography and Memoirs*, ed. T. Taylor (London: Peter Davies, 1926), Vol. 2, January 1831).
46 Suzi Gablik, *Magritte* (New York: New York Graphic Society, 1970), quoted in D. Ashton (ed.), *Twentieth-Century Artists on Art* (New York: Pantheon Books, 1985). Reprinted by permission of Little, Brown & Company.
47 R. Langton Douglas, *A History of Siena* (London, 1902).
47 John Donne, *Satyres*, III.
47 Nicholas Hilliard, *Treatise concerning the Arte of Limning*, ed. P. Norman (Walpole Society, Vol. 1, 1911–12).
47 Franz Pforr, quoted in K. Andrews, 'Dürer's Posthumous Fame', in C. R. Dodwell (ed.), *Essays on Dürer* (Manchester: Manchester University Press, 1973).
47 *Letters of John Keats*, selected F. Page (London: Oxford University Press, 1954).
48 Horace Walpole, *Aedes Walpolianae* (1747), quoted in I. Pears, *The Discovery of Painting* (New Haven, Conn./London: Yale University Press, 1988).
48 George Eliot, *Adam Bede* (1859), ch. 17.
48 Walter Pater, 'Sebastian van Storck', in *Imaginary Portraits* (London: Macmillan, 1887).
49 Cole Porter, 'You're the Top', in *The Complete Lyrics of Cole Porter*, ed. R. Kimball (London: Hamish Hamilton, 1983). Reproduced by permission of Hamish Hamilton Ltd.
49 Abraham Cowley, 'On the Death of Sir Anthony Vandike', *Works* (1668).
49 G. P. Bellori, Life of Van Dyck, in *Le Vite de pittori . . .* (Rome, 1672).
50 Roger de Piles, *The Art of Painting*, trans. B. Buckeridge (London, 1706).
51 Benjamin Disraeli, *Coningsby* (1844), bk 4, ch. 4.
51 Peggy Guggenheim, *Out of This Century* (London: André Deutsch, 1980). Reprinted by permission of Andre Deutsch Ltd.
52 *John Constable's Correspondence*, ed. R. B. Beckett, Vol. 6, *The Fishers* (Ipswich: Suffolk Records Society, 1968).
52 A. Palomino, *Life of Velázquez* (1724), trans. in E. Harris, *Velázquez* (Oxford: Phaidon, 1982). Reprinted by permission of Phaidon Press Ltd.
52 *Le Mercure de France*, September 1725, reprinted in G. Wildenstein, *Le*

Salon de 1725 (Paris: Les Beaux-Arts, 1924).

53 Arthur Young, *Travels in France and Italy . . .* (1792), Everyman's Library (London: Dent, 1927).

53 *Jane Austen's Letters*, ed. R. W. Chapman (London: Oxford University Press, 1959).

54 Tatiana Tolstoy, quoted by Leo Tolstoy in *What Is Art?* (1898), trans. Aylmer Maude (London: Oxford University Press, 1929). Reprinted by permission of Oxford University Press.

54 John Quinn, quoted in I. Dunlop, *The Shock of the New* (London: Weidenfeld & Nicolson, 1972).

54 J. B. C. Grundy, 'Art Tendencies in the Third Reich', in *German Life and Art* (London: Oxford University Press, 1937–8), Vol. 2, quoted in I. Dunlop, *The Shock of the New* (London: Weidenfeld & Nicolson, 1972). Reprinted by permission of Oxford University Press.

55 *Well, Dearie! The Letters of Edward Burra*, ed. William Chappell (London: Gordon Fraser, 1985).

55 Henry James, *The Outcry* (1911), bk 1, ch. 1 (reprinted New York: Howard Fertig, 1982).

55 Lord Stamfordham, quoted in Kenneth Rose, *King George V* (London: Weidenfeld & Nicolson, 1983).

56 Philip, Duke of Burgundy, trans. in E. Gilmore Holt, *A Documentary History of Art*, Vol. 1 (Garden City, NY: Doubleday, 1957).

56 Albrecht Dürer, *Journal*, April 1521: *Literary Remains . . .* trans. & ed. W. M. Conway, (Cambridge: C.U.P., 1889).

56 Charles Reade, *The Cloister and the Hearth* (1861), ch. 9.

58 W. Bürger (pseudonym of E. J. Th. Thoré), *Galerie d'Arenberg* (Paris/Brussels/Leipzig, 1859), cited in original French in C. Brown, *Carel Fabritius* (Oxford: Phaidon, 1981). Reprinted by permission of Phaidon Press Ltd.

58 E. and J. de Goncourt, 'Greuze', in *French XVIII Century Painters*, trans. R. Ironside (London: Phaidon, 1948).

59 Henry James, 'The Madonna of the Future', in *Atlantic Monthly* (March 1873), reprinted in *Transatlantic Sketches* (Boston, Mass., 1875).

59 *Journal de Marie Bashkirtseff* (Paris: Bibliothèque-Carpentier, 1919), Vol. 2.

60 Adolf Hitler, *Mein Kampf*, quoted in F. Jetzinger, *Hitler's Youth*, trans. L. Wilson (London: Hutchinson, 1958).

60 Dante, *The Divine Comedy: Purgatory*, trans. Dorothy L. Sayers (Harmondsworth: Penguin, 1955), canto 11. Reprinted by permission of David Higham Associates Ltd.

60 L. B. Alberti, *On Painting*, trans. J. R. Spencer (New Haven, Conn./London: Yale University Press, 1966).

60 Aretino: *Selected Letters*, trans. G. Bull (Harmondsworth: Penguin, 1976). Reproduced by permission of Penguin Books Ltd.

61 Sarah Siddons, *Reminiscences*, ed. W. van Lennep (Cambridge: Cambridge University Press, 1942).

61 Robert Browning, 'Pictor Ignotus', *Dramatic Lyrics* (1842).

61 P. A. Lemoisne, *Degas* (Paris: Plon, 1954).

61 William Rothenstein, *Men and Memories* (London: Faber & Faber, 1931). Reproduced by permission of Sir John Rothenstein.

62 Life of Piero di Cosimo, in Giorgio Vasari, *Lives of the Artists*, trans. G. Bull (Harmondsworth: Penguin, 1987), Vol. 2. Reproduced by permission of Penguin Books Ltd.

63 Life of Pontormo, in ibid.

63 Carel van Mander, Life of Maerten Heemskerck, from *Het Schilderboek* (1617 edn.), trans. W. Stechow in E. Gilmore Holt, *A Documentary History of Art*, Vol. 1 (Garden City, NY: Doubleday, 1957).

63 C. C. Malvasia, *The Life of Guido Reni*, trans. C. and R. Enggass (Philadelphia, Pa/London: Pennsylvania State University Press, 1980). Reproduced by permission of Pennsylvania State University Press.

63 Evan Charteris, *John Sargent* (London: Heinemann, 1927).

64 Max J. Friedländer, *On Art and*

Connoisseurship, trans. T. Borenius (London: Cassirer, 1943).
65 *Correspondance de Nicolas Poussin*, ed. C. Jouanny (Paris: Champion, 1911).
65 Joseph Wright, cited in W. Whitley, *Artists and Their Friends in England, 1700–1799* (New York/London: Blom, 1968 edn.), Vol. 1.
66 Francesco Milizia, *Dizionario delle Belle Arti del disegno . . . dalla Enciclopedia Metodica* (Bassano, 1797), Vol. 1.
66 *Versamelde Brieven van Vincent Van Gogh*, Vol. 3 (Amsterdam, 1953).
66 Denis Diderot, 'The Salon of 1767': *Oeuvres complètes de Diderot*, ed. J. Assézat, Vol. II (Paris, 1876).
68 V. A. Zhukovsky, trans. in *Caspar David Friedrich, 1774–1840*, exhibition catalogue (Tate Gallery, 1972). Reprinted by permission of the Tate Gallery.
68 C. D. Friedrich, *Observations . . .*, *c.*1830, trans. in ibid.
69 Sir Joshua Reynolds, Discourse XIV, in *Discourses on Art*, ed. R. R. Wark (New Haven, Conn./London: Yale University Press, 1981).
69 Roger Fry, *Reflections on British Painting* (London: Faber & Faber, 1934).
69 Alexander Frater, in the *Observer Magazine*, 8 January 1989. Reprinted by permission of the *Observer*.
70 Sir Joshua Reynolds, Discourse XI to the students of the Royal Academy, 10 December 1782, in *Discourses on Art*, ed. R. R. Wark (New Haven, Conn./London: Yale University Press, 1981).
71 René Gimpel, *Diary of an Art Dealer*, trans. J. Rosenberg (London: Hamish Hamilton, 1986). Reproduced by permission of Aitken & Stone Ltd, representing the estate of René Gimpel.
72 W. M. Rossetti, introduction to a reprint of *The Germ* (1901; reprinted Ashmolean Museum, Oxford/Birmingham City Museums and Art Gallery, 1979).
72 Ramon Luis Escovedo, quoted in C. M. Kauffmann, *Catalogue of Paintings in the Wellington Museum* (London: Her Majesty's Stationery Office, 1982).
73 *Beloved Mama: Private Correspondence of Queen Victoria and the German Crown Princess, 1878–1885*, ed. R. Fulford (London: Evans, 1981). We acknowledge the gracious permission of Her Majesty the Queen for the reproduction of material subject to copyright.
73 Cole Lesley, *The Life of Noël Coward* (Harmondsworth: Penguin, 1978). Reprinted by permission of Jonathan Cape.
74 Taddeo Albano, letter printed in the original in T. Pignatti, *Giorgione* (Venice: Alfieri, 1969).
74 *Byron's Letters and Journals*, ed. L. A. Marchand, Vol. 7, *Between Two Worlds* (London: John Murray, 1977).
75 Stendhal, 'The Salon of 1824', in *Stendhal and the Arts*, sel. & ed. D. Wakefield (London: Phaidon, 1975).
75 Théophile Gautier, *Mademoiselle de Maupin* (1835), ch. 9; trans. P. Selver, Novel Library (London: Hamish Hamilton, 1948).
75 Walter Pater, 'The School of Giorgione' (1877), in *The Renaissance* (London: Macmillan, 1888).
76 Quoted in Vasari's Life of Giotto, in Giorgio Vasari, *Lives of the Artists*, trans. G. Bull (Harmondsworth: Penguin, 1987), Vol. 1. Reprinted by permission of Penguin Books Ltd.
76 George Eliot, Journal, June 1860, in J. W. Cross, *George Eliot's Life as Related in Her Letters and Journals*, new edn (Edinburgh: Blackwood [1887]).
76 *The Letters of Vincent Van Gogh*, ed. M. Roskill (London: Fontana, 1985).
77 Martin Heidegger, *The Origin of the Work of Art*, trans. A. Hofstadter, Colophon edn (New York: Harper & Row, 1975).
78 A. R. Mengs, cited in N. Glendinning, *Goya and His Critics* (New Haven, Conn./London: Yale University Press, 1977).
78 *Diario de Madrid*, 6 February 1799, trans. in J. López-Rey, *Goya's Ca-*

prichos (Princeton, NJ: Princeton University Press, 1953), Vol. 1.
79 Charles Baudelaire, 'Les Phares', *Les Fleurs du mal* (1857).
79 René Gimpel, *Diary of an Art Dealer*, trans. J. Rosenberg (London: Hamish Hamilton, 1968), 25 May 1939. Reprinted by permission of Aitken & Stone Ltd, representing the estate of René Gimpel.
79 David Hockney, *My Early Years*, ed. N. Stangos (London: Thames & Hudson, 1988). Reprinted by permission of Thames & Hudson.
79 Entry for 'Greche' in *Bryan's Dictionary of Painters and Engravers*, new edn (London, 1853).
80 Sir William Stirling-Maxwell, *Annals of the Artists of Spain* (London, 1891), revised edn., Vol. 1.
80 Aldous Huxley, 'Variations on El Greco', *Themes and Variations* (London: Chatto & Windus, 1950). Reprinted by permission of Mrs Laura Huxley and Chatto & Windus.
81 J. J. Winckelmann, *Thoughts on the Imitation of Greek Art in Painting and Sculpture* (1755), trans. E. Gilmore Holt, *A Documentary History of Art*, Vol. 2 (Garden City, NY: Doubleday, 1957).
82 M. E. J. Delécluze, *Louis David, son école et son temps* (Paris, 1855).
83 M. Denis, *La Doctrine d'Ingres* (Paris, 1912).
83 J.–K. Huysmans, *Là-Bas* (Paris, 1891), ch. I.
85 Académie Royale, Paris, cited in Chardin exhibition catalogue, ed. P. Rosenberg, Paris, 1979.
85 *The Letters of Thomas Gainsborough*, ed. M. Woodall (London: Cupid Press, 1963).
85 *The Diary of Joseph Farington*, ed. K. Cave, Vol. 7 (New Haven, Conn./London: Yale University Press, 1982), 12 April 1806.
86 *Growing Up with the Impressionists: The Diary of Julie Manet*, ed. and trans. Rosalind de Boland Roberts and Jane Roberts (London: Sotheby's, 1987), 4–6 March 1896. First published for Sotheby's Publications by Philip Wilson Ltd.
87 L. B. Alberti, *On Painting*, ed. and trans. J. R. Spencer (New Haven, Conn./London: Yale University Press, 1966).
87 *Anecdotes of William Hogarth*, ed. J. B. Nichols (London, 1833).
88 Charles Lamb, 'Essay on the Genius and Character of Hogarth', first printed in *The Reflector*, no. 3 (1811); C. Lamb, *Miscellaneous Essays & Sketches* (London & Toronto: J. M. Dent, 1929).
88 Allan Cunningham, *Lives of the Most Eminent British Painters . . .* (London, 1829).
89 John Hutton, unmodernized text printed in full in A. B. Chamberlain, *Hans Holbein the Younger* (London: George Allen, 1913), Vol. 2.
90 Gerard Manley Hopkins, *Journal*, 1868, in *Selected Prose*, ed. G. Roberts (Oxford: Oxford University Press, 1980).
90 *The Letters of Aubrey Beardsley*, ed. H. Maas, J. L. Duncan and W. G. Good (London: Cassell, 1970).
90 ibid.
90 Henry James, 'On Some Pictures Lately Exhibited' (1875), in *The Painter's Eye*, ed. J. L. Sweeney (London: Hart-Davis, 1956).
90 A. Palomino, Life of Velázcuez, in *El Museo Pitórico*, Vol. 3 (1724), trans. in E. Harris, *Velázquez* (Oxford: Phaidon, 1982). Reprinted by permission of Phaidon Press Ltd.
91 *The Letters of Queen Victoria*, Third Series, Vol. 2 (London: John Murray, 1931).
91 ibid.
92 C. R. Leslie, *Memoirs of the Life of John Constable*, ed. J. Mayne (London: Phaidon, 1951). Reprinted by permission of Phaidon Press Ltd.
92 Eugène Fromentin, *The Masters of Past Time* (1876), trans. A. Boyle, ed. H. Gerson (Oxford: Phaidon, 1981).
92 *The Notebooks of Samuel Butler*, ed. H. Festing Jones (London Hogarth Press, 1985).
94 Comte de Caylus, *Life of Antoine Watteau* (1748), trans. from P. Rosen-

berg (ed.), *Vies anciennes de Watteau* (Paris: Hermann, 1984).
94 *The Letters of Thomas Gainsborough*, ed. M. Woodall (London: Cupid Press, 1963).
95 J. G. Lockhart, *Life of Sir Walter Scott* (1843), quoted in W. Bayne, *Sir David Wilkie, RA* (London: Walter Scott Publishing, 1903).
95 Paul Cézanne, Letter to Emile Bernard, *Paul Cézanne, Letters*, ed. J. Rewald, trans. M. Kay (London: Bruno Cassirer, 1941).
96 J. W. von Goethe, *Propyläen* (1799), II, ii, letter 2, in *Goethe on Art*, ed. and trans. J. Gage (London: Scolar Press, 1980). Reprinted by permission of Scolar Press.
96 Mosco Carner, *Puccini: A Critical Biography* (London: Duckworth, 1958). Reprinted by permission of Duckworth.
97 Charles Dickens, *Nicholas Nickleby* (1838–9), ch. 3.
97 Robert Browning, 'My Last Duchess', *Poems* (1849).
98 D. G. Rossetti, 'Hand and Soul', *The Germ*, No. 1 (January 1850), reprinted in *The Germ, the Literary Magazine of the Pre-Raphaelites* (1901; reprinted the Ashmolean Museum, Oxford/Birmingham City Museums and Art Gallery, 1984).
98 Benjamin Disraeli, *Coningsby* (1844), ch. 3.
99 George Eliot, *Romola* (1863), ch. 18.
99 Henry James, *The Wings of the Dove* (1902), ch. 11.
100 Ronald Firbank, *The Artificial Princess* (1934), ch. 1.
100 Emile Cardon, in *La Presse*, Paris, 29 April 1874: quoted in I. Dunlop, *The Shock of the New* (London: Weidenfeld & Nicolson, 1972).
101 W. P. Frith, *My Autobiography and Reminiscences* (London, 1887), Vol. 2.
101 'The Craze for the Impressionists', *The Times*, 5 June 1900; full text reprinted in K. Flint, *Impressionists in England: The Critical Reception* (London: Routledge & Kegan Paul, 1984).
101 Théodore Duret, *Manet and the French Impressionists*, trans. J. E. Crawford Flitch (London: Grant Richards, 1910).
102 Percy Wyndham Lewis, *Blast* (1915), cited in D. Ashton (ed.), *Twentieth-Century Artists on Art* (New York: Pantheon Books, 1985).
102 J. A. D. Ingres, quoted in original in H. Lapauze, *Ingres, sa vie et son œuvre* (Paris, 1911).
102 Charles Baudelaire, 'The Salon of 1846', in *Art in Paris, 1845–1862: Salons and Other Exhibitions Reviewed by Charles Baudelaire*, ed. and trans. J. Mayne (London: Phaidon, 1965). Reprinted by permission of Phaidon Press Ltd.
103 J. A. D. Ingres, quoted in original in H. Lapauze, *Ingres, sa vie et son œuvre* (Paris, 1911).
103 Frederic Leighton, in Mrs Russell Barrington, *The Life, Letters and Work of Frederic Leighton* (London: George Allen, 1906), Vol. 1.
103 W. R. Sickert, 'Degas', *Burlington Magazine*, 1917; reprinted in *A Free House!; or, The Artist as Craftsman: Being the Writings of Walter Richard Sickert*, ed. (Sir) Osbert Sitwell (London: Macmillan, 1947).
104 Edmund Waller, 'For the drawing of the posture and progress of His Majesty's forces at sea . . . together with the battle and victory obtained over the Dutch, 3 June 1665': *The Poems of Edmund Waller*, ed. G. Thorn Drury (London/New York: Lawrence & Bullen/Scribner's, 1893).
105 *Correspondance de Nicolas Poussin*, ed. C. Jouanny (Paris: Champion, 1911).
106 Life of Andrea del Castagno and Domenico Veneziano, in Giorgio Vasari, *Lives of the Artists*, trans. G. Bull (Harmondsworth: Penguin, 1987), Vol. 2. Reprinted by permission of Penguin Books Ltd.
106 Augustus John, *Chiaroscuro* (London: Jonathan Cape, 1954). Reprinted by permission of David Higham Associates Ltd.
107 Gwen John, in C. Langdale, *Gwen John* (New Haven, Conn./London: Yale University Press, 1987).

107 Maynard Walker, in ibid.

107 Life of Botticelli, in Giorgio Vasari, *Lives of the Artists*, trans. G. Bull (Harmondsworth: Penguin, 1987), Vol. 1. Reprinted by permission of Penguin Books Ltd.

108 J. T. Smith, *Nollekens and His Times* (1828; reissued London: Century Hutchinson, 1986).

108 M. E. J. Delécluze, *Louis David, son école et son temps* (Paris, 1855).

109 G. Atkins, *Asger Jorn* (London: Methuen, 1964), cited in D. Ashton (ed.), *Twentieth-Century Artists on Art* (New York: Pantheon Books, 1985). Reprinted by permission of Methuen & Co.

109 Constantijn Huygens, *Autobiography* (1629–31); quoted in D. Bomford, C. Brown and A. Roy, *Art in the Making: Rembrandt* (London: National Gallery, 1988–9).

110 Leonardo da Vinci, 'Codex Urbinas' ('Book on Painting . . .'), in *Leonardo on Painting*, ed. M. Kemp, trans. M. Kemp and M. Walker (New Haven, Conn./London: Yale University Press, 1989).

110 Carlo Ridolfi, *The Life of Tintoretto* (1642), trans. C. Enggass and R. Enggass (Philadelphia, Pa: Pennsylvania State University Press, 1984). Reproduced by permission of Pennsylvania State University Press.

111 Wassily Kandinsky, *Reflections on Abstract Art* (1931); *Complete Writings On Art*, ed. K. C. Lindsay and P. Vergo (London: Faber and Faber, 1982). Keith Vaughan, *Journals 1939–1977*, ed. A. Ross (London: John Murray, 1989).

111 R. B. Kitaj, introduction to *The Artist's Eye*, exhibition catalogue, (National Gallery, London, 1980).

112 Werner Haftmann, *The Mind and Work of Paul Klee* (London: Faber & Faber, 1954).

112 Gustav Klimt, quoted in O. Breicha and C. Nebehay, *Klimt, Schiele, Kokoschka: Drawings and Watercolours* (London: Thames & Hudson, 1981). Reprinted by permission of Thames & Hudson.

112 *Leonardo on Painting*, ed. M. Kemp, trans. M. Kemp and M. Walker (New Haven, Conn./London: Yale University Press, 1989).

114 Christen Købke, quoted in K. Monrad, *Danish Painting: The Golden Age*, exhibition catalogue (London: National Gallery, 1984).

114 Anita Loos, *Gentlemen Prefer Blondes* (1925; copyright © 1925, 1953, 1963; reissued London: Picador, 1982). Reprinted by permission of the Anita Loos Trust.

115 Pontus de Tyard, *Twelve Fables of Rivers or Fountains . . .* (Paris, 1586), in W. Stechow, *Northern Renaissance Art, 1400–1600*, Sources and Documents in the History of Art (Englewood Cliffs, NJ: Prentice-Hall, 1966).

115 C. R. Leslie, *Memoirs of the Life of John Constable*, ed. J. Mayne (London: Phaidon, 1951).

115 Samuel Palmer, *Sketchbook* (1824), quoted in R. Lister, *Samuel Palmer, His Life and Art* (Cambridge: Cambridge University Press, 1987).

116 Carl Carus, *Nine Letters on Landscape Painting* (1831), Letter VII, in E. Gilmore Holt, *From the Classicists to the Impressionists, A Documentary History of Art*, Vol. 3 (Garden City, NY: Doubleday, 1966).

116 A. Vollard, *Degas: An Intimate Portrait*, trans. R. T. Weaver (New York: Dover Publications, 1986). Reproduced by permission of Dover Publications

117 Roger Fry, *Reflections on British Painting* (London: Faber & Faber, 1934).

117 *Burne-Jones Talking*, ed. Mary Lago (London: John Murray, 1982).

118 Kenneth Clark, *Leonardo da Vinci* (Cambridge: Cambridge University Press, 1957). Reprinted by kind permission of the Cambridge University Press.

118 Samuel Pepys, *The Diary . . .*, ed. R. Latham & W. Matthews (London: G. Bell & Sons), Vol. IX, 1976).

119 [Gertrude Stein], *The Autobiography of Alice B. Toklas* (1933).

119 Robert Browning, 'Fra Filippo Lippi', *Men and Women* (1855).

119 Bernard Shaw, *Our Theatre in the*

Nineties (1932; reissued London: Constable, 1948), Vol. 1.

120 L. S. Lowry, in Noel Barber, *Conversations with Artists* (London: Collins, 1964).

121 Charles Demuth, *Creative Art 5*, no. 3 (September 1929), quoted in D. Ashton (ed.), *Twentieth-Century Artists on Art* (New York: Pantheon Books, 1985).

121 Joachim von Sandrart, *Teutsche Academie . . .* (1675), in W. Stechow, *Northern Renaissance Art, 1400–1600*, Sources and Documents in the History of Art (Englewood Cliffs, NJ: Prentice-Hall, 1966).

122 A. Palomino, Life of Velázquez, in *El Museo Pitórico . . .* , Vol. 3 (1724), quoted in E. Harris, *Velázquez* (Oxford: Phaidon, 1982). Reprinted by permission of Phaidon Press Ltd.

122 Ludwig Hevesy, 'The Klimt Exhibition', in *Acht Jahre Secession* (1906), trans. in P. Vergo, *Art in Vienna, 1898–1918* (Oxford: Phaidon, 1986). Reprinted by permission of Phaidon Press Ltd.

124 Ascanio Condivi, *Life of Michelangelo Buonarroti* (1553), in *Michelangelo: Life, Letters and Poetry*, ed. and trans. G. Bull, World's Classics (Oxford: Oxford University Press, 1987). Reprinted by permission of Oxford University Press.

124 William Shakespeare, *The Taming of the Shrew*, Induction, scene 2.

125 W. J. O'Driscoll, *A Memoir of Daniel Maclise, RA* (1871), quoted in R. Ormond, *Daniel Maclise, 1807–1870*, exhibition catalogue (London/ Dublin: National Portrait Gallery/ National Gallery of Ireland, 1972).

125 Gaspar Ofhuys, *Originale Cenobii Rubeevallis in Zonia prope Bruxellam in Brabancia*, *c.*1509–13, trans. in W. Stechow, *Northern Renaissance Art, 1400–1600*, Sources and Documents in the History of Art (Englewood Cliffs, NJ: Prentice-Hall, 1966).

127 Kenneth Rose, *King George V* (London: Weidenfeld & Nicolson, 1983). Reprinted by permission of Kenneth Rose, and Weidenfeld & Nicolson Ltd.

127 George Moore, *Modern Painting* (London: Walter Scott Publishing, 1893).

129 J. W. von Goethe, *Italian Journey* (1786), trans. W. H. Auden and E. Mayer (London: Collins, 1962).

129 Leopold Schefer, *The Artist's Married Life: Being That of Albert Dürer*, trans. J. R. Stodart (London, 1848).

130 Filippo Baldinucci, Life of Carlo Dolci, in *Notizie de' Professori del disegno da Cimabue in qua . . .* (Florence, 1773), Vol. 18.

130 A. Vollard, *Degas: An Intimate Portrait*, trans. R. T. Weaver (New York: Dover Publications, 1986). Reprinted by permission of Dover Publications.

130 Paula Modersohn-Becker, *Diary*, March 1902, quoted in G. Perry, *Paula Modersohn-Becker, Her Life and Work* (New York/London: Harper & Row, 1979).

131 J. B. Descamps, *La Vie des peintres flamands, allemands et hollandois* (Paris, 1754), Vol. 2.

132 Charles-Nicolas Cochin, *Essai sur la vie de M. Chardin* (1780), quoted in the original in P. Rosenberg, *Chardin*, exhibition catalogue (Paris, 1979).

132 Sir William Stirling-Maxwell, *Annals of the Artists of Spain* (1891), Vol. 4.

133 David Sylvester, *The Brutality of Fact: Interviews with Francis Bacon*, (London: Thames & Hudson, 1987). Reprinted by permission of Thames & Hudson.

133 Henri Matisse, in *Le Courier de l'Unesco* (October 1953), reprinted in H. Matisse, *Ecrits et propos sur l'art*, ed. D. Fourcade (Paris: Hermann, 1972).

134 Sylvia Plath, *Letters Home: Correspondence 1950–63*, selected and edited with a commentary by Aurelia Schober Plath (London: Faber & Faber, 1976). Reprinted by permission of Faber & Faber Ltd.

135 *The Letters of Michelangelo*, ed. and trans. E. H. Ramsden (London: Peter Owen, 1963), Vol. 1. Reprinted by permission of Peter Owen Publishers.

135 J. A. Symonds, *The Sonnets of Michel-*

angelo Buonarotti and Tommaso Campanella (London, 1878).
136 J. T. Smith, *Nollekens and His Times* (1828; reissued London: Century Hutchinson, 1986).
136 W. M. Rossetti, *The PRB Journal*, ed. W. E. Fredeman (Oxford: Clarendon Press, 1975).
137 Samuel Butler, 'Written Sketches', in *The Notebooks of Samuel Butler*, ed. H. Festing Jones (London: Hogarth Press, 1985).
137 Walter Pater, 'Lionardo da Vinci', in *Studies in the History of the Renaissance* (London: Macmillan, 1873; *The Renaissance*, revised, 1877, 1888, 1893).
138 René Gimpel, *Diary of an Art Dealer*, trans. J. Rosenberg (London: Hamish Hamilton, 1986). Reprinted by permission of Aitken & Stone Ltd, representing the estate of René Gimpel.
140 Sir Henry Raeburn, quoted in J. Greig, *Sir Henry Raeburn, RA* (London: The Connoisseur, 1911).
140 David Hockney, *My Early Years*, ed. N. Stangos (London: Thames & Hudson, 1988). Reprinted by permission of Thames & Hudson.
141 Sir William Sanderson, *Graphice* (1658), quoted in C. White, *Peter Paul Rubens* (New Haven, Conn./London: Yale University Press, 1987).
141 George Eliot, *Daniel Deronda* (1876), ch. 28.
142 The Hon. John Collier, *The Art of Portrait Painting* (London: Cassell, 1905).
142 Francesco Susinno, *Le vite de' pittori messinesi* (1724), original text (with translation, not utilized here) in H. Hibbard, *Caravaggio* (London: Thames & Hudson, 1988).
142 Wassily Kandinsky, *Reminiscences* (1913); *Kandinsky – Complete Writings on Art*, ed. K. C. Lindsay and P. Vergo (London: Faber, 1982).
143 Sir William Stirling-Maxwell, *Annals of the Artists of Spain* (1891), Vol. 3.
144 Paul Nash, statement in *Unit One: The Modern Movement in English Architecture, Painting and Sculpture* (1934), quoted in Herbert Read, *Paul Nash* (Harmondsworth: Penguin, 1944).
144 William Shakespeare, *Antony and Cleopatra*, Act II, scene 2.
144 G. P. Bellori, Life of Caravaggio, in *Le Vite de pittori, scultori et architetti moderni* (1672), trans. in H. Hibbard, *Caravaggio* (London: Thames & Hudson, 1988). Reprinted by permission of Thames & Hudson.
145 The Abbé de la Marre, *L' Art et la Nature réunis par Wateaux* (1736). The complete poem is printed in the original French in P. Rosenberg (ed.), *Vies anciennes de Watteau* (Paris: Hermann, 1984).
145 Pierre-Henri de Valenciennes, *Elémens de perspective pratique à l'usage des artistes . . .* (1820), trans. in J. C. Taylor (ed.), *Nineteenth-Century Theories of Art* (Berkeley and Los Angeles, Calif./London: University of California Press, 1989).
147 J. A. M. Whistler, *The Gentle Art of Making Enemies* (1892; reissued New York: Dover Publications, 1967).
148 Madame Tocqué, *Abrégé de la vie de M. Nattier* (1767; quoted in the original in P. de Nolhac, *Nattier, peintre de la cour de Louis XV* (Paris, 1925).
149 J. H. Benton, *The Scot Abroad* (1864), cited in D. Macmillan, *Painting in Scotland: The Golden Age*, exhibition catalogue (Oxford: Phaidon, 1986).
149 B. R. Haydon, *Diary*, 19 May 1846: *Autobiography and Memoirs*, ed. T. Taylor (London: Peter Davies, 1926), Vol. II.
149 Sir John Rothenstein, foreword to N. Carrington, *Carrington* (London: Thames & Hudson, 1980). Reprinted by permission of Thames & Hudson.
150 Max J. Friedländer, *From Van Eyck to Breughel*, trans. M. Kay (London: Phaidon, 1956). Reprinted by permission of Phaidon Press Ltd.
151 Leonardo da Vinci, *Notebooks*, in *Leonardo on Painting*, ed. M. Kemp, trans. M. Kemp and M. Walker (New Haven, Conn./London: Yale University Press, 1989).
151 John Webster, *The White Devil* (1612), Act V, scene 6.

152 Charles Baudelaire, 'The Painter of Modern Life', in *Le Figaro*, 1863, reprinted in *The Painter of Modern Life and Other Essays by Charles Baudelaire*, ed. and trans. J. Mayne (London: Phaidon, 1964). Reprinted by permission of Phaidon Press Ltd.

152 André Michel, in *Journal des débats*, 27 August 1889, cited in *Dreams of a Summer Night: Scandinavian Painting at the Turn of the Century*, exhibition catalogue, Hayward Gallery (London: Arts Council, 1988).

152 Emil Nolde, quoted in Werner Haftmann, *Emil Nolde*, exhibition catalogue (London: Marlborough Fine Art, 1964). Reprinted by permission of Nolde-Stiftung Seebüll.

153 A. Félibien, *Entretiens sur les vies et sur les ouvrages des plus excellens peintres . . .* (1725), cited in S. Madocks, '"Trop de beautez decouvertes" – new light on Guido Reni's late "Bacchus and Ariadne"', *Burlington Magazine*, September 1984.

153 Father Thorpe, quoted in A. M. Clark, *Pompeo Batoni*, ed. E. P. Bowron (Oxford: Phaidon, 1985).

153 The Bishop of Carlisle (1877), cited in Vern G. Swanson, *Sir Lawrence Alma-Tadema* (London: Ash & Grant, 1977).

154 Kenneth Clark, *The Nude* (Harmondsworth: Penguin, 1964 edn.). Reprinted by permission of John Murray (Publishers) Ltd.

155 Walter Crane, *An Artist's Reminiscences* (London: Methuen, 1907).

155 Paul Cézanne, quoted in H. B. Chipp *et al.*, *Theories of Modern Art: A Source Book by Artists and Critics* (Berkeley and Los Angeles, Calif.: University of California Press, 1968).

156 W. H. Auden, 'Musée des Beaux Arts', *Selected Poems*, ed. Edward Mendelson (London: Faber & Faber, 1979). Reprinted by permission of Faber & Faber Ltd.

156 Max J. Friedländer, *Reminiscences and Reflections*, ed. R. M. Heilbrunn, trans. R. S. Magurn (London: Evelyn, Adams & Mackay, 1969).

157 Edouard Roditi, *Dialogues on Art* (London: Secker & Warburg, 1960).

157 Clement Greenberg, 'Modernist Painting', Voice of America, 1960, reprinted in F. Frascina and C. Harrison (eds), *Modern Art and Modernism: A Critical Anthology* (London: Paul Chapman, 1988). Reprinted by kind permission of the author.

158 Stéphane Mallarmé, 'The Impressionists and Edouard Manet', in *Art Monthly Review*, 30 September 1876, reprinted in ibid.

159 Vern G. Swanson, *Sir Lawrence Alma-Tadema* (London: Ash & Grant, 1977).

160 Champfleury, *Grandes Figures d'hier et d'aujourd'hui* (1861), trans. in J. C. Taylor, *Nineteenth-Century Theories of Art* (Berkeley and Los Angeles, Calif./London: University of California Press, 1989).

162 L. B. Alberti, *On Painting*, ed. and trans. J. R. Spencer (New Haven, Conn./London: Yale University Press, 1966).

162 Albrecht Dürer, quoted in Erwin Panofsky, *The Life and Art of Albrecht Dürer* (Princeton, NJ: Princeton University Press, 1971). Reprinted by permission of Princeton University Press.

162 Ambrose Bierce, *The Devil's Dictionary* (1911), in *The Enlarged Devil's Dictionary*, ed. E. J. Hopkins (Harmondsworth: Penguin, 1971).

163 Aldous Huxley, *Along the Road: Notes and Essays of a Tourist* (1925; reprinted London: Chatto & Windus, 1974). Reprinted by permission of Mrs Laura Huxley and Chatto & Windus.

163 Julia Cartwright, *Isabella d'Este, Marchioness of Mantua* (London: John Murray, 1903), Vol. 1.

165–166 Owen McSwiney and Joseph Smith; the texts in J. G. Links, *Canaletto* (Oxford: Phaidon, 1982).

166 Lodovico Dolce, *Dialogo della pittura . . .* (1557), quoted in original Italian in P. Rossi, *L'opera completa del Parmigianino* (Milan: Rizzoli, 1980).

166 Life of Uccello, in Giorgio Vasari, *Lives of the Artists*, trans. G. Bull

(Harmondsworth: Penguin, 1987), Vol. 1. Reprinted by permission of Penguin Books Ltd.

167 Life of Giovanni Antonio Bazzi, called Il Sodoma, in *Lives of the Most Eminent Painters, Sculptors and Architects by Giorgio Vasari*, trans. Gaston du C. de Vere and Philip Lee Warner (London: Medici Society, 1914), Vol. 7.

167 W. Wilkie Collins, *Memoirs of the Life of William Collins, Esq., RA* (1848); reprinted East Ardsley: EP Publishing, 1972), Vol. 1.

168 *Reminiscences of Rosa Bonheur*, ed. T. Stanton (London: Andrew Melrose, 1910).

168 Evelyn Waugh, *Rossetti, His Life and Works* (1928; reprinted London: Duckworth, 1975). Reprinted by permission of the Peters, Fraser & Dunlop Group Ltd.

169 David Hockney, *My Early Years*, ed. N. Stangos (London: Thames & Hudson, 1988). Reprinted by permission of Thames & Hudson.

169 Anonymous writer, Barcelona, 1900, manuscript in Museo Picasso, Barcelona, trans. M. Sobre, printed in M. McCully (ed.), *A Picasso Anthology: Documents, Criticism, Reminiscences* (London: Arts Council/Thames & Hudson, 1981). Reprinted by permission of Thames & Hudson.

170 Pablo Picasso, statement, 1923: 'Picasso Speaks', translation of an interview published in *The Arts* (New York, May 1923), reprinted in H. B. Chipp *et al.*, *Theories of Modern Art: A Source Book by Artists and Critics* (Berkeley and Los Angeles, Calif.: University of California Press, 1968).

171 John Addington Symonds, *Renaissance in Italy: The Fine Arts* (1877; reprinted London: Smith, Elder, 1911).

171 Aldous Huxley, *Along the Road: Notes and Essays of a Tourist* (1925; reprinted London: Chatto & Windus, 1974). Reprinted by permission of Mrs Laura Huxley and Chatto & Windus.

172 Camille Pissarro, *Letters to His Son Lucien*, ed. J. Rewald (London: Routledge & Kegan Paul, 1980).

173 *Aretino: Selected Letters*, trans. G. Bull (Harmondsworth: Penguin, 1976). Reprinted by permission of Penguin Books Ltd.

173 Leo Tolstoy, *War and Peace*, trans. L. and A. Maude (London: Oxford University Press, 1931), Vol. 2. Reprinted by permission of Oxford University Press.

174 Oscar Wilde, *The Picture of Dorian Gray* (1891), ch. seven.

175 John Sargent, quoted in E. Charteris, *John Sargent* (London: Heinemann, 1927).

175 Otto Dix, *c.*1965, quoted in D. Ashton (ed.), *Twentieth-Century Artists on Art* (New York: Pantheon Books, 1985).

176 Anonymous, *Mélanges d'histoire et de littérature . . .* (1699–1700), cited in the original French in the catalogue of the Poussin exhibition (Paris: Louvre, 1960).

176 P. Fréart de Chantelou, *Journal du voyage du Cavalier Bernin en France* (1665), cited in J. Thuillier, *L'opera completa di Poussin* (Milan: Rizzoli, 1974).

176 C. R. Leslie, *Memoirs of the Life of John Constable*, ed. J. Mayne (London: Phaidon, 1951).

176 Eugène Delacroix, *Selected Letters*, ed. and trans. J. Stewart (London: Eyre & Spottiswoode, 1971). Reprinted by permission of Eyre & Spottiswoode.

177 From the Registro di Suppliche e Carte Pubbliche Concernenti le Arte, Venice, 1751–9, printed in original Italian in A. Mariuz, *L'opera completa del Piazzetta* (Milan: Rizzoli, 1982).

177 B. R. Haydon, *Autobiography and Memoirs*, ed. T. Taylor (London: Peter Davies, 1926), Vol. 2.

178 Egon Schiele, *Diary*, 1912, quoted in A. Commini, *Schiele in Prison* (London: Thames & Hudson, 1974). Reproduced by permission of Thames & Hudson.

178 Eugène Delacroix, *Selected Letters*, ed. and trans. J. Stewart (London:

Eyre & Spottiswoode, 1971). Reprinted by permission of Eyre & Spottiswoode.

179 Francisco Pacheco, *Arte de Pintura* (1649), trans. in E. Harris, *Velázquez* (Oxford: Phaidon, 1982). Reprinted by permission of Phaidon Press Ltd.

179 Filippo Baldinucci, Life of Pietro Testa, in *Notizie de' professori del disegno da Cimabue in qua* (Florence, 1773), Vol. 18.

181 Max J. Friedländer, *On Art and Connoisseurship*, trans. T. Borenius (London: Cassirer, 1942).

183 Sir Henry Raeburn, in J. Greig, *Sir Henry Raeburn, RA* (London: The Connoisseur, 1911).

183 Sir Henry Raeburn, in ibid.

183 Saki, 'The Treasure-Ship', in *Beasts and Super-Beasts* (1914), reprinted in *The Complete Works of Saki* (London: The Bodley Head, 1980).

184 Allan Ramsay, in *The Scarborough Miscellany* (1732), quoted in I. Gordon Brown, *Poet and Painter: Allan Ramsay Father and Son, 1684–1784* (Edinburgh: National Library of Scotland, 1984).

184 William Hazlitt, in *The Champion* (1814), quoted in Sir Joshua Reynolds, *Discourses on Art*, ed. R. R. Wark (New Haven, Conn.: Yale University Press, 1981), app. 2.

185 J. A. D. Ingres, in 1814, quoted in *Ingres raconté par lui-même et par ses amis*, ed. P. Courthion (Vésenaz-Geneva: P. Cailler, 1947), Vol. 1.

185 George Eliot, *Journal*, July 1858, quoted in J. W. Cross, *George Eliot's Life as Related in Her Letters and Journals*, new edn (Edinburgh: Blackwood, [1887]).

185 *The Notebooks of Samuel Butler*, ed. H. Festing Jones (London: Hogarth Press, 1985).

186 Marcel Duchamp, talk at the Museum of Modern Art, New York, 19 October 1961, given in D. Ashton (ed.), *Twentieth-Century Artists on Art* (New York: Pantheon Books, 1985).

186 Charles Baudelaire, 'The Salon of 1859', in Charles Baudelaire, *Art in Paris, 1845–1862: Salons and Other Exhibitions*, ed. and trans. J. Mayne (London: Phaidon, 1965). Reprinted by permission of Phaidon Press Ltd.

187 Andries Pels, 'Gebruik en misbruik des tooneels' (1681), cited in translation by M. Defesche in the exhibition catalogue, *Rembrandt 1669/1969* (Amsterdam: Rijksmuseum, 1969). Reprinted by permission of Rijksmuseum.

188 Eugène Fromentin, *The Masters of Past Time*, ed. H. Gerson (Oxford: Phaidon, 1981), pp. 230–2. Reprinted by permission of Phaidon Press Ltd.

189 Michael Kitson, *Rembrandt* (London: Phaidon, 1969). Reprinted by permission of Phaidon Press Ltd.

190 Hortico Catalogue, Spalding, Autumn 1988. Reprinted by permission of Hortico Nurseries.

190 John Dryden, 'To Sir Godfrey Kneller' (1694), *Poetry, Prose and Plays*, ed. D. Grant (London: Hart-Davis, 1952).

191 Erwin Panofsky, *Renaissance and Renascences in Western Art* (1965; reissued London: Paladin, 1970).

193 Tobias Smollett, *Travels through France and Italy* (1766), World's Classics (London: Oxford University Press, 1935).

193 René Gimpel, *Diary of an Art Dealer*, trans. J. Rosenberg (London: Hamish Hamilton, 1986). Reprinted by permission of Aitken & Stone Ltd, representing the estate of René Gimpel.

194 Eugène Delacroix, *Selected Letters*, ed. and trans. J. Stewart (London: Eyre & Spottiswoode, 1971). Reprinted by permission of Eyre & Spottiswoode.

195 Daniel Halévy, *My Friend Degas*, trans. and ed. M. Curtiss (London: Hart-Davis, 1966).

195 Oliver Goldsmith, 'Retaliation' (1774), in *Selected Works*, ed. Richard Garnett (London: Hart-Davis, 1950).

196 William Blake, annotation to an account of Reynolds' death, in Sir Joshua Reynolds, *Discourses on Art*, ed. R. R. Wark (New Haven, Conn./London: Yale University Press, 1981).

196 Richard E. Spear, *Domenichino* (New Haven, Conn./London: Yale University Press, 1982).
197 Alfred Tennyson, 'Romney's Remorse', *Demeter and Other Poems* (London: Macmillan, 1889).
199 'The Castle Builder', a fragment, *The Poems of John Keats*, ed. E. de Sélincourt (London: Methuen, 1951).
199 Lady Morgan, *The Life and Times of Salvator Rosa* (London, 1824), Vol. 2.
200 Fernande Olivier, *Picasso et ses amis* (1923), trans. J. Miller as *Picasso and His Friends* (1964), and cited in M. McCully (ed.), *A Picasso Anthology* (London: Arts Council /Thames & Hudson, 1981). Reprinted by permission of Thames & Hudson.
200 Richard and Samuel Redgrave, *A Century of British Painters* (1866; reissued Oxford: Phaidon, 1981).
201 *Letters of Peter Paul Rubens*, ed. R. S. Magurn (Cambridge, Mass.: Harvard University Press, 1955).
202 John Ruskin, *Modern Painters*, Vol. 1 (London, 1843).
202 Christopher White, *Peter Paul Rubens* (New Haven, Conn./London: Yale University Press, 1987).
203 J. W. von Goethe, in *Morgenblatt für gebildete Stände* (1816), in *Goethe on Art*, ed. and trans. J. Gage (London: Scolar Press, 1980). Reprinted by permission of Scolar Press.
203 C. R. Leslie, *Memoirs of the Life of John Constable*, ed. J. Mayne (London: Phaidon, 1951).
205 R. B. Sheridan, *The School for Scandal* (1777), Act IV, scene I.
205 W. Collins, *Memoirs of a Picture* (1805), ch. 18.
206 *Beloved Mama: Private Correspondence of Queen Victoria and the German Crown Princess, 1878–1885*, ed. R. Fulford (London: Evans, 1981). We acknowledge the gracious permission of Her Majesty The Queen for the reproduction of material subject to copyright.
207 Philip Conisbee, *Claude-Joseph Vernet, 1714–1789*, exhibition catalogue, Kenwood, 1976, under no. 75.
207 Jane Austen, *Persuasion* (1817), Vol. 2, ch. 6.
208 M. Butlin and E. Joll, *The Paintings of J. M. W. Turner* (New Haven, Conn./London: Yale University Press, 1977), under no. 252.
209 C. R. Leslie, *Memoirs of the Life of John Constable*, ed. J. Mayne (London: Phaidon, 1951).
209 M. Curtiss, *Bizet and His World* (London: Secker & Warburg, 1959).
209 G. P. Bellori, Life of Poussin, in *Le Vite de' pittori, scultori et architetti moderni* (Rome, 1672).
209 Elizabeth Croft, 'Memoir of Lawrence's Last Days' in D. E. Williams, *The Life and Correspondence of Sir Thomas Lawrence, Kt* (London, 1831), Vol. 2.
209 A. Vollard, *Degas: An Intimate Portrait*, trans. R. T. Weaver (New York: Dover Publications, 1986). Reprinted by permission of Dover Publications.
210 Anonymous review, reprinted in K. Flint, *Impressionists in England: The Critical Reception* (London: Routledge & Kegan Paul, 1984).
210 Robert Leslie's recollections of Turner were printed by Ruskin in the 'Dilecta' section (1886) illustrating *Praeterita: The Autobiography of John Ruskin* (Oxford: Oxford University Press, 1978).
211 Edward Edwards, *Anecdotes of Painters . . .* (1808), cited in I. Pears, *The Discovery of Painting: The Growth of Interest in the Arts in England, 1680–1768* (New Haven, Conn./London: Yale University Press, 1988).
211 Life of Signorelli, in Giorgio Vasari, *The Lives of the Painters, Sculptors and Architects*, trans. A. B. Hinds, Everyman's Library (London: Dent, 1963), Vol. 2. Reprinted by permission of J. M. Dent.
212 Maud Cruttwell, *Luca Signorelli* (London: George Bell, 1899).
212 W. Graham Robertson, *Time Was* (1931; reissued London: Quartet, 1981).
214 Denis Diderot, 'Salon of 1767', in *Oeuvres complètes de Diderot*, ed. J. Assézat (Paris, 1876), Vol. 2.
214 J. W. von Goethe in *Propyläen* (1799),

reprinted in *Goethe on Art*, ed. and trans. J. Gage (London: Scolar Press, 1980). Reprinted by permission of Scolar Press.

215 Arnold Bennett, *Journals*, ed. Frank Swinnerton (Harmondsworth: Penguin, 1971), May 1910.

215 Thomas Mann, *Lotte in Weimar* (1939), trans. H. T. Lowe-Porter (Harmondsworth: Penguin, 1968).

216 *Aretino: Selected Letters*, trans. G. Bull (Harmondsworth: Penguin, 1976). Reprinted by permission of Penguin Books Ltd.

216 C. R. Leslie, *Memoirs of the Life of John Constable*, ed. J. Mayne (London: Phaidon, 1951).

216 John Ruskin, *Modern Painters*, Vol. 1 (London, 1867 edn.).

217 *The Letters of Vincent van Gogh*, ed. M. Roskill (London: Fontana, 1983).

217 Joan Miró, *Selected Writings and Interviews*, ed. M. Rowell, (London: Thames & Hudson, 1987). Reprinted by permission of Thames & Hudson.

217 Benjamin Tedesco, in *Reminiscences of Rosa Bonheur*, ed. T. Stanton (London: Andrew Melrose, 1910).

218 (Sir) Osbert Sitwell, in *A Free House!; or, The Artist as Craftsman: Being the Writings of Walter Richard Sickert*, ed. (Sir) Osbert Sitwell (London: Macmillan, 1947).

218 G. A. Wallis, in W. Buchanan, *Memoirs of Painting* (London, 1824), Vol. 2.

219 Sir Joshua Reynolds, Discourse VI, in *Discourses on Art*, ed. R. R. Wark (New Haven, Conn./London: Yale University Press, 1981).

219 Simon Schama, *The Embarrassment of Riches* (London: Collins, 1987).

220 Basil Taylor, *George Stubbs, 1724–1806*, exhibition catalogue (Whitechapel Art Gallery, London). © The Trustees of the Whitechapel Art Gallery, 1957.

221 George du Maurier, *Trilby* (1894).

222 K. Malevich, *Tenth State Exhibition Catalogue* (Moscow, 1919), reprinted in T. Anderson (ed.), *Essays on Art* (Copenhagen: Borgen, 1969), and in D. Ashton (ed.), *Twentieth-Century Artists on Art* (New York: Pantheon Books, 1985).

223 André Breton, *What Is Surrealism?*, trans. David Gascoyne (1936), reprinted in H. B. Chipp *et al.*, *Theories of Modern Art: A Source Book by Artists and Critics* (Berkeley and Los Angeles/London: University of California Press, 1968).

225 *The Memoirs of Elisabeth Vigée-Le Brun*, trans. Svian Evans (London: Camden Press, 1989). Reprinted by permission of Camden Press Ltd.

225 Edith Wharton, *The House of Mirth* (1905); reissued Harmondsworth: Penguin, 1979).

226 Life of Albertinelli, in Giorgio Vasari, *Lives of the Painters, Sculptors and Architects*, trans. A. B. Hinds, Everyman's Library (London: Dent, 1963), Vol. 2. Reprinted by permission of J. M. Dent.

227 *The Diary of Joseph Farington*, ed. K. Cave, Vol. 8 (New Haven, Conn./London: Yale University Press, 1982), 15 December 1807.

227 J. B. Descamps, *La Vie des peintres flamands, allemands et hollandois* (Paris, 1754), Vol. 2.

228 Kenneth Clark, *One Hundred Details from Pictures in the National Gallery* (London: National Gallery, 1938).

228 *The Notebooks of Samuel Butler*, ed. H. Festing Jones (London: Hogarth Press, 1985).

229 Quoted in *Degas by Himself*, ed. R. Kendall (London: Macdonald Orbis, 1987).

229 E. March Phillips, *The Venetian School of Painting* (London: Macmillan, 1912).

231 Carlo Ridolfi, *The Life of Tintoretto and His Children Domenico and Marietta* (1642), trans. C. Enggass and R. Enggass (Philadelphia, Pa/London: Pennsylvania State University Press, 1984). Reproduced by permission of Pennsylvania State University Press.

232 W. Wilkie Collins, *Memoirs of the Life of William Collins, Esq., RA* (1848; reissued East Ardsley: EP Publishing, 1972).

233 Sir Joshua Reynolds, Discourse XI, in *Discourses on Art*, ed. R. R. Wark

(New Haven, Conn./London: Yale University Press, 1981).

233 Charles Lamb, 'Barrenness of the Imaginative Faculty in the Productions of Modern Art', in *Last Essays of Elia* (1833), in *The Collected Essays of Charles Lamb* (London & Toronto: Dent, 1929), Vol. 1.

234 John Ruskin, *Modern Painters*, Vol. V (London, 1860); *Modern Painters*, ed. & abridged D. Barrie (London: André Deutsch, 1987).

234 Walter Pater, *Greek Studies* (London: Macmillan, 1895).

234 Charles Ricketts, *Titian* (London: Methuen, 1910).

235 Denys Sutton in *Financial Times*, 21 February 1961, reprinted in *Delights of a Dilettante* (Trowbridge: Westwood Press, 1980). Reprinted by kind permission of Denys Sutton.

236 B. Nicolson, *The Painters of Ferrara* (London: Paul Elek, 1950).

236 Thomas Green the Younger, *The Diary of a Lover of Literature* (1810), cited in M. Butlin and E. Joll, *The Paintings of J. M. W. Turner* (New Haven, Conn./London: Yale University Press, 1977).

237 *The Times*, 4 May 1841, cited in ibid.

237 John Ruskin, *Modern Painters*, Vol. I (London, 1843); *Modern Painters*, ed. & abridged D. Barrie (London: André Deutsch, 1987).

238 John Ruskin, *Praeterita: The Autobiography of John Ruskin* (Oxford: Oxford University Press, 1978 edn.).

239 C. A. Du Fresnoy, *The Art of Painting*, trans. John Dryden (1716), quoted in E. Gilmore Holt (ed.), *A Documentary History of Art*, Vol. II (Garden City, New York: Doubleday, 1958).

239 Stendhal, *Rome, Florence, Naples* (1817), cited in M. Kitson, *The Complete Paintings of Caravaggio* (Harmondsworth: Penguin, 1985).

239 C. R. Leslie, *Memoirs of the Life of John Constable*, ed. J. Mayne (London: Phaidon, 1951).

239 *Ingres, raconté par lui-même et par ses amis*, ed. P. Courthion (Vésenaz/Geneva: Cailler, 1947), Vol. 1.

239 Asger Jorn, in D. Ashton (ed.), *Twentieth-Century Artists on Art* (New York: Pantheon Books, 1985). Reprinted by permission of Methuen & Co.

240 Richard and Samuel Redgrave, *A Century of British Painters* (1866; reissued Oxford: Phaidon, 1981).

241 A. Palomino, *Life of Velázquez* (1724), trans. in E. Harris, *Velázquez* (Oxford: Phaidon, 1982). Reprinted by permission of Phaidon Press.

241 Edouard Manet, cited in J. Brown, *Velázquez: Painter and Courtier* (New Haven, Conn./London: Yale University Press, 1986).

241 R. A. M. Stevenson, *Velasquez* (London: George Bell, enlarged edn., 1899); edn. revised T. Crombie, biographical study of the author by D. Sutton (London: G. Bell & Sons, 1962).

242 Maurice Baring, 'Velasquez and the "Venus"', *Diminutive Dramas* (1910; reissued London: Heinemann, 1925). Reprinted by permission of A. P. Watt Ltd, on behalf of the Trustees of the Maurice Baring Will Trust.

243 D. Sylvester, *The Brutality of Fact: Interviews with Francis Bacon* (London: Thames & Hudson, 1987). Reprinted by permission of Thames & Hudson.

244 Balthasar de Monconys, *Journal de voyage* (1666), original French text printed in A. Blankert, *Vermeer of Delft* (Oxford: Phaidon, 1978).

244 Marcel Proust, *Remembrance of Things Past*, trans. C. K. Scott-Moncrieff, Vol. 9, *The Captive* (London: Chatto & Windus, 1941).

245 Heinrich Heine, 'The Salon of 1843', *The Works of Heinrich Heine*, trans. C. G. Leland, Vol. 4 (London: Heinemann, 1893).

246 The Carracci, *Postille to Vasari's Lives*; the relevant quotation cited in D. Mahon, 'Eclecticism and the Carracci: Further Reflections on the Validity of a Label', *Journal of the Warburg and Courtauld Institutes*, vol. 16, nos 3–4 (1953).

246 John Ruskin, *Modern Painters*, Vol. V, 1860; *Modern Painters*, ed. and

abridged D. Barrie (London: André Deutsch, 1987).

246 *Letters of Vincent van Gogh*, ed. M. Roskill (London: Fontana, 1982).

246 John Steer, *A Concise History of Venetian Painting* (London: Thames & Hudson, 1970). Reprinted by permission of Thames & Hudson.

247 J. D. Passavant, *Tour of a German Artist in England* (1836; reprinted East Ardsley: EP Publishing, 1978), Vol. 1.

248 Charles Dickens, *Bleak House* (1853), ch. 7.

250 Guillaume Apollinaire, in *Le Petit Messager des Arts . . .* , 1 March 1915, reprinted in *Apollinaire on Art: Essays and Reviews, 1902–1918*, ed. LeRoy C. Breunig, trans. S. Suleiman (New York: Viking Press, 1972; Da Capo Press paperback, 1988).

250 Sir William Orpen, *An Onlooker in France, 1917–1919* (London: Williams & Norgate, 1921).

251 W. T. Whitley, *Gilbert Stuart* (Cambridge, Mass.: Harvard University Press, 1932).

251 E.-F. Gersaint, *Abrégé de la vie d'Antoine Watteau* (1744), reprinted in P. Rosenberg (ed.), *Vies anciennes de Watteau* (Paris: Hermann, 1984).

252 Amaury-Duval, in *Ingres raconté par lui-même et par ses amis*, ed. P. Courthion (Vésenaz/Geneva: Cailler, 1947), Vol. 1.

252 Walter Pater, 'A Prince of Court Painters', in *Imaginary Portraits* (London: Macmillan, 1887).

253 Frank Rutter, *Art in My Time* (London: Rich & Cowan, 1933).

254 W. Landgraf, in *Daheim* (1908), cited by R. Ormond in *Franz Xaver Winterhalter and the Courts of Europe, 1830–70*, exhibition catalogue National Portrait Gallery, London 1987–8). Reprinted by permission of the National Portrait Gallery.

254 Quoted in *Christopher Wood*, exhibition catalogue (London: Arts Council, 1979).

254 Joachim von Sandrart, *Teutsche Academie* (1675), trans. in *Johann Liss*, exhibition catalogue (Cleveland, Ohio, 1975–6).

256 Max J. Friedländer, *Reminiscences and Reflections*, ed. R. M. Heilbrunn, trans. R. S. Magurn (London: Evelyn, Adams & Mackay, 1969).

257 Life of Andrea del Sarto, in Giorgio Vasari, *Lives of the Artists*, trans. G. Bull (Harmondsworth: Penguin, 1987), Vol. 2. Reprinted by permission of Penguin Books Ltd.

258 Frederick G. Stephens, *Memoirs of Sir Edwin Landseer* (1874), cited in R. Ormond, *Sir Edwin Landseer*, exhibition catalogue (London: Thames & Hudson, in association with the Philadelphia Museum of Art and the Tate Gallery, London, 1981).

259 P. A. Lemoisne, *Degas* (Paris: Plon, 1954), cited in F. Sevin, 'Degas à travers ses mots', in *Gazette des Beaux-Arts* (July–August 1975).

259 Walter Richard Sickert, in the *New Age*, 6 June 1910, reprinted in *A Free House!; or, The Artist as Craftsman: Being the Writings of Walter Richard Sickert*, ed. (Sir) Osbert Sitwell (London: Macmillan, 1947).

259 Sir William Stirling-Maxwell, *Annals of the Artists of Spain* (1891), Vol. 3.

INDEX

NOTE: Page numbers in *italic* refer to sources